HARVARD HISTORICAL STUDIES • 173

Published under the auspices
of the Department of History
from the income of the
Paul Revere Frothingham Bequest
Robert Louis Stroock Fund
Henry Warren Torrey Fund

WILLIAM JAY RISCH

The Ukrainian West

Culture and the
Fate of Empire in
Soviet Lviv

HARVARD UNIVERSITY PRESS

Cambridge, Massachusetts
London, England
2011

Library of Congress Cataloging-in-Publication Data

Risch, William Jay.
  The Ukrainian West : culture and the fate of empire in Soviet Lviv / William Jay Risch.
    p.   cm.—(Harvard historical studies ; 173)
  Includes bibliographical references and index.
  ISBN 978-0-674-05001-3 (alk. paper)
    1. L'viv (Ukraine)—History—20th century.   2. L'viv (Ukraine)—Politics and
  government—20th century.   3. L'viv (Ukraine)—Social conditions—20th century
  4. Nationalism—Ukraine—L'viv—History—20th century.   5. Ethnicity—Ukraine—L'viv—
  History—20th century.   6. Ukrainian language—Political aspects—L'viv—History—
  20th century.   7. L'viv (Ukraine)—Relations—Soviet Union.   8. L'viv (Ukraine)—
  Relations—Europe.   9. Soviet Union—Relations—Ukraine—L'viv.   10. Europe—
  Relations—Ukraine—L'viv.   I. Title.   II. Series.

  DK508.95.L86R57   2011
  947.7'9—dc22   2010046740

For my parents

Contents

Foreign Terms and Abbreviations

CPSU Communist Party of the Soviet Union

CPU Communist Party of Ukraine

estrada (n.), *estradnyi* (adj.) variety music (Ukrainian)

gorkom City Committee of the Communist Party of Ukraine

KGB Committee of State Security

Komsomol Communist Youth League

KPZU Communist Party of Western Ukraine

MGB Ministry of State Security

moskal' (sing.), *moskali* (pl.) ethnic Russians or Russian speakers (Ukrainian)

MVD Ministry of Internal Affairs

NKVD People's Commissariat of Internal Affairs

obkom Regional Committee of the Communist Party of Ukraine

OUN Organization of Ukrainian Nationalists

OUN-B Organization of Ukrainian Nationalists—Banderite Wing

OUN-M Organization of Ukrainian Nationalists—Melnykite Wing

PryKVO Subcarpathian Military District

rahul' (sing.), *rahuly* (pl.) hicks, bumpkins (Ukrainian)

Rukh People's Movement of Ukraine

samizdat underground literature (Russian)

samvydav underground literature (Ukrainian)

SB   Security Service, affiliated with the OUN and the UPA

seliukh (sing.), *seliukhy* (pl.)   hicks, bumpkins (Ukrainian)

sovdepiia   Sovietdom, Soviet civilization (Russian)

stiliag (sing.), *stiliagi* (pl.)   fashion hounds, style seekers (Russian)

tusovka   collective youth bonding (Russian)

UPA   Ukrainian Insurgent Army

VIA   Vocal-Instrumental Ensemble

zaida (sing.), *zaidy* (pl.)   carpetbaggers (Ukrainian)

ZUNR   Western Ukrainian People's Republic

Note on Transliteration

Regarding transliteration, I have followed the Library of Congress system, leaving out all character modifiers. For added clarity I have removed all diacritical marks from proper names and well-known terms (like *glasnost*) in the main text and authors' names in footnotes. Some names reflect the language of the historical period (Lwów instead of Lviv for the city's Polish period). Because of ambiguities in cultural and national identification, Lvivians' names (except for authors' names) have been transliterated according to their Ukrainian equivalents. Commonplace English spellings are used for well-known names (for example, Yeltsin) or places (for example, Gorky). Kyiv rather than Kiev and Dnipropetrovsk rather than Dniepropetrovsk are used to reflect Ukraine's status as an independent state. Belarus and Belarusians are used instead of Byelorussia and Byelorussians to reflect Belarus's status as an independent state.

THE UKRAINIAN WEST

Introduction

In Soviet times, Lviv was a picturesque yet sullen provincial city in Western Ukraine. In the mid-1970s, a former Polish resident visiting it called it "a noisy city and at the same time somber; full of people, yet monotone; grey, like its daily life."[1] Yet it made history in the Soviet Union. While CNN and other major television networks in 1991 featured the demolition of Lenin monuments in Moscow, Leningrad, and other major Soviet cities, Lvivians had brought down theirs much earlier, in the summer of 1990.[2] Earlier, in March 1990, non-Communist candidates swept city and regional council elections. All twenty-four of the Lviv Region's deputies to Ukraine's Supreme Council were non-Communists advocating Ukraine's independence.[3] A former political prisoner, Viacheslav Chornovil, became head of the Lviv Regional Council. He told council members that Lviv, an "island of freedom," was to "end the totalitarian system."[4] Lviv epitomized this "island of freedom" by electing the first non-Communist city government in the Soviet Union outside the Baltic republics.[5]

Lviv had been at odds with Moscow long before this seismic shift in public action. It was at the fault line of rival projects of nation building and imperial dominance. Its residents read Polish newspapers and magazines and tuned in to Polish radio and television stations, more liberal than their Soviet counterparts. The city's Renaissance and early modern architecture, narrow winding streets, and cultural and intellectual traditions tied Lvivians more to Prague, Warsaw, Paris, or Florence than to Moscow or Kyiv. Older generations of Ukrainians and younger ones knew of past national movements that Soviet power had repressed. They viewed Soviets as

1

outsiders—"occupiers" or "carpetbaggers" *(zaidy)*. Sometimes they called such outsiders *moskali,* a slur against Russians and Russian-speakers.

Such tensions did not preclude cooperation. Young writers who had flirted with nationalist underground groups against Soviet rule after World War II came to admire the ideals of Marx and Lenin. Moscow's cultural life inspired young Lvivians. The nation did not govern daily lives. Still, Soviet officials unintentionally made Lviv Ukraine's "nationalist" city. It was second to the republic's capital, Kyiv, in the number of people arrested for political reasons in the 1960s and 1970s.[6] Former political prisoners organized mass demonstrations in Lviv against Communist rule in 1988 and 1989, gathering up to 150,000 people.[7] Demonstration organizers and new deputies to Ukraine's Supreme Council had faced trial behind closed doors in 1966 or had protested these trials publicly.[8] Chornovil's publishing essays abroad condemning this trial led to his own imprisonment.[9] How Lviv managed so rapidly to become this island of freedom inspired this book.

Empires, Nations, and Borderlands

While Chornovil could proclaim Lviv an island of freedom in 1990, such an epithet looked silly before Gorbachev's era of openness (or *glasnost*). Patterns of governance in Lviv and other parts of the post-Soviet sphere suggest that freedom has yet to arrive to much of it.[10] Still, the Soviet Union's collapse in 1991 produced a "paradigm shift" in understanding the Soviet past.[11] Among others, Francine Hirsch, Terry Martin, Ronald Grigor Suny, and Yuri Slezkine have emphasized the Soviet Union's role as an empire promoting a sense of nationhood among non-Russians. Coping with the disintegration of the former Russian Empire after 1917, early Bolshevik leaders instituted policies fostering attributes of nationhood—a common language, a common culture, a common ethnicity, a sense of a common history, and in some cases common territory—to draw non-Russians into their world socialist revolution. In the late 1930s, Soviet leaders curtailed such "indigenization" *(korenizatsiia)* policies, emphasizing the Great Russians' language and culture. They portrayed Great Russians as more "progressive," unifying the Soviet family of nations. Indigenization policies nonetheless transformed people's mentalities, making both nationality and class matter in people's daily lives.[12]

Others have emphasized that the Soviet Union, like other modernizing states, co-opted the local. In Turkmenistan, local elites defined what it meant to be Turkmen and used the Soviet rhetoric of national equality to demand concessions from Moscow's policy makers.[13] Yet Central Asia's natives perceived Soviet power as an alien force imposing its will. Such perceived threats led to popular resistance against unveiling women in Uzbekistan.[14] Soviet Europeans' feelings of condescension toward Central Asian natives ran high. Such sentiments erupted in tensions between Europeans and Kazakhs during the construction of the Turksib Railroad, associated with the Soviets' interwar "civilizing mission" in Kazakhstan.[15]

The Soviet Union thus was an empire that both liberated and exploited non-Russians. Its interwar years were a formative experience. The nation became a category of thinking that national opposition groups later exploited on the eve of the Soviet Union's collapse. However, these scholars do not address the crucial role that the Soviet Union's western borderlands, acquired during World War II, played in the Soviet state's demise. Since the mid-1970s, Roman Szporluk has stressed these lands' transformation of Soviet domestic and foreign policies.[16] The annexation of territories under the Molotov-Ribbentrop Pact of 1939—the Baltic States, Western Belarus, Western Ukraine, and Bessarabia—introduced different concepts of nationhood other than those inspired by the Soviet Union's interwar nation-building projects.[17]

For Szporluk, nineteenth- and early twentieth-century nation-building projects of the Habsburg Empire and the Balkans have considerably affected perceptions of nationhood in places like Ukraine, one of the core republics of the Soviet Union. Thus late Soviet Lviv defied postwar trends taking place in other Soviet Ukrainian cities. It became increasingly Ukrainian-speaking, with Ukrainian-language newspapers dominating the public sphere. Overwhelming numbers of Lvivians supported opposition candidates to the Ukrainian Supreme Council in March 1990 elections. Ukraine's immediate secession from the Soviet Union garnered nearly unanimous support in the regions of Lviv, Ternopil, and Ivano-Frankivsk, in a special question added to the March 1991 referendum on the Soviet Union's future.[18] Such trends indicated Western Ukrainians' tenuous loyalty to Moscow. Habsburg and Polish rule had left profound effects. Their church, the Ukrainian Greek Catholic Church (or Uniate Church), owed allegiance to the Vatican. Their idea of civilization came from Vienna. They were unlike Ukrainians living in pre-1939 Soviet Ukraine, whose church tended to be the Orthodox Church based in Moscow and whose idea of civilization came from St. Petersburg and later Moscow. Connections with

Central Europe and its history thus put Lvivians, and Western Ukrainians, at odds with the Soviet Union's imperial core for some time.[19]

However, the Soviet state incorporated and integrated such border regions with flexibility. Jörg Baberowski has highlighted the impact exporting the revolution to the Caucasus had on Moscow's policies. The failure of locals and outsiders to foment a cultural revolution contributed to the Stalinist terror of the 1930s.[20] Tarik Amar has accredited to the Soviet state its ability in postwar Lviv to devise a sense of local identity—what Amar calls "a specific Western Ukrainian Soviet identity"—after failing to compel the local population to "adopt a generic Soviet Ukrainian identity."[21] Amar does not really explain what this "generic Soviet Ukrainian identity" was. Like others, he employs a working definition of Sovietization that has its problems.[22] Sovietization concerned learning to bribe officials or trade illegally.[23] It embodied "the more insidious half-century of training in the conformism, bureaucratism, dullness, double-think and crude historical monumentalism, on which Soviet socialism had no monopoly but which it did spread with unrivalled energy and bumbling mastery."[24] While Amar's working definition aptly describes Soviet realities, it overlooks people's acceptance, if not embrace, of Soviet socialism's ideals. Nonetheless he underscores both local and all-Soviet factors contributing to Lviv's Sovietization. Efforts to create credible historical myths about the interwar Communist Party of Western Ukraine (KPZU) failed to resonate with local collective memory.[25] Attempts at transforming so-called backward local Ukrainians into more progressive Soviet Ukrainians failed in the late Stalin era. Coercion produced the local as a permanent category, similar to a nation or ethnic group. The survival of the remaining pre-Soviet-era intelligentsia, as well as continued "Western Ukrainian difficulties" after 1956, led to the persistence of a local sense of being Soviet Ukrainian.[26]

Soviet power's ability to empower and coerce the local thus cannot be underestimated. Practices of coping with daily life, what Pierre Bourdieu has called a *habitus,* enabled Lvivians to accommodate the public sphere's rhetoric and retain ties to past Galician perceptions of being Ukrainian. In private they honored past national movements labeled "bourgeois nationalist." In public they struggled against so-called Ukrainian bourgeois nationalism and built a Communist future.[27] They committed "preference falsification," publicly suppressing their private opinions for opinions deemed ideologically sound.[28] These were small acts of resistance, what James C. Scott has called "weapons of the weak," that happened in the production and consumption of popular culture and high culture. Different choices in lifestyle, reading some things and not others, local humor about the Party and the state, and the erosion of public stereotypes about Ukrainians' history, art, and literature acquired significance in a public sphere subject to censorship.[29]

However, Lvivians were not exactly Scott's Malaysian peasant subalterns. Soviet rule offered opportunities in education and employment that Polish rule did not provide. The Soviet state was real, yet nebulous in its functions. Popular resistance to 1930s Stalinism did not involve a monolithic state against a homogeneous society. Wartime and early postwar Soviet representations of Ukraine's past involved tacit dialogues among intellectuals, republic and local Party functionaries, and Moscow.[30] Thus intellectuals, with local officials' cooperation, blunted the effects of Russification and rehabilitated the so-called progressive features of Galicia's past. However, changing policies in Moscow and Kyiv fomented charges that such acts were "bourgeois nationalist." While not the subalterns of voiceless peasants, intellectuals and students were unequal partners of state and Party actors. This contributed to tensions over issues like language and historical memory.

Wartime occupation and reoccupation of the Baltic States, Western Belarus, Western Ukraine, and Bessarabia thus did not preclude co-optation of, if not support from, the locals. In the Baltic States, despite deportations and violent retaliation against post–World War II nationalist guerrillas and their supporters, Soviet leaders approached Sovietization cautiously, and local elites took advantage of this.[31] Outsiders and native Baltic nationalities found common ground. Russian and Estonian academics in Tartu, Estonia, despite ethnic and linguistic differences, faced social divisions within their own ethnic groups. They dealt with common challenges the Soviet system of higher education posed.[32] Locals, too, acquired a *habitus* that accommodated as well as resisted the Soviet public sphere. In the 1960s and 1970s, Lithuanians, Latvians, and Estonians, while in tense relations with Russians and Russian speakers, also took advantage of consumerism and materialism that the Brezhnev era offered. They learned to conform.[33] Intellectuals who spoke for the nation made tacit negotiations with state actors. Thus Lithuanian intellectuals, like independent Lithuania's first president, Vytautas Landsbergis, rehabilitated a prominent Lithuanian artist and composer in the twenty years after Stalin's death, incorporating him into the canon of Soviet Lithuanian culture.[34]

It is tempting to see this western periphery shaping policies in Moscow, the imperial metropolis, as peripheries have shaped modern Western European colonial empires.[35] However, colonialism as a category of analysis risks simplifying relations between center and periphery. Frederick Cooper has stressed the need to focus on the multiple historical contexts behind colonialism and the specific interrelationships complicating simple binary oppositions between colonizer and colonized.[36] Lviv demonstrates the "family resemblance" the Soviet Union had to colonial empires.[37] Like nineteenth-century European empires, the Soviet state revolutionized local Ukrainians' daily lives. It differed from European imperial states by assuming racial and ethnic equality.[38] Nonetheless, Soviet expansion westward produced what Amar calls a "socialist imperialism" aimed at civilizing a new kind of "backward" native, one contaminated by the evils of the bourgeois capitalist world.[39] Outsiders were the bearers of civilization.

Galicia's history defined the local's backwardness. At the fault lines of rival national and imperial projects, Galician Ukrainians bedeviled Soviet rulers, much like western borderland nationalities had troubled nineteenth-century Russian officials.[40] Their region influenced early Soviet nationality policies. Ukrainianization in the early 1920s was to undermine neighboring capitalist states like Poland which had Ukrainian minorities.[41] However, Galician Ukrainians understood nationhood in terms of common ethnicity, language, and culture. Their understanding clashed with Soviet projects of nation building. These projects promoted elements of national identity as a transitional stage to an international proletarian order. By the late 1930s, the Great Russians played a leading role in this transition. World War II policies encouraged the creation of Lviv and Western Ukraine as ethnically homogeneous and Ukrainian.[42] However, such events intensified issues of ethnicity, language, and culture among Lviv's Ukrainians.

Like other contested borderland regions, Galicia became the site of more sharply defined national communities.[43] Issues like the return of nationalist guerrillas and their sympathizers from prison and exile after Stalin's death had an impact on Soviet policy making in Moscow.[44] Unresolved debates over historical memory, the use of Ukrainian in public life, and the role of the state in regulating high culture and popular culture made relations between Lviv, the republic's capital Kyiv, and the Soviet metropolis Moscow highly problematic and later open to questioning.

Cities, Urban Space, and Lviv's Western Otherness

Lviv's emergence as a Ukrainian island of freedom concerned not just changes in demographics or language use, or the production and consumption of culture. Its urban space transformed the worldview of city residents. Lviv escaped World War II relatively unscathed, yet state actors altered its urban spaces, changed the city's identity, and projected the political power of the Soviet state.[45] Soviet socialism, rather than the forces of capitalism affecting other modern cities, generated Lviv's postwar urban space and transformed lives.[46] Still, certain parallels emerged between postwar Lviv and such Central European cities as nineteenth-century Prague and Budapest, which fostered a sense of nationhood and encouraged national minorities' assimilation.[47] This sense of nationhood meant belonging to a historical construct that not only divided humanity into nations with their own unique characteristics but also became a source of political power and the freedom and self-realization of persons.[48]

Postwar Lviv's national transformation built on Polish attempts at resisting Habsburg domination in nineteenth-century Lemberg. In competition with rival projects of Ukrainian nation building and Zionism, Poles transformed Austrian Lemberg into a mostly Polish Lwów on the eve of World War I.[49] Their efforts came to further fruition as local politicians and intellectuals commemorated the struggle for Lwów between Poles and Ukrainians in late 1918.[50] Competition between Ukrainian and Polish national movements for Lwów's urban space reflected an important element of nationalism noted by Liah Greenfeld. For Greenfeld, the emergence of nations and their ideals reflects "resentment" *(ressentiment)* toward a more modern other. In the case of Russian nationalism, it emerged among the Russian intelligentsia by the late eighteenth century because of a sense of resentment toward the more "enlightened" West.[51] Postwar Lviv's Ukrainians' sense of national identity thus came to reflect years of opposition to a supposedly more modern Polish other in Galicia. This rivalry with a more modern other, rather than processes of industrialization associated with the age of nationalism, shaped Ukrainian nationalism in postwar Lviv.[52]

State actors from Moscow, Kyiv, and Lviv, in cooperation with the local intelligentsia, directed this postwar transformation. Lviv thus resembled Wrocław and Kaliningrad, two other postwar cities transformed by Soviet-style socialism. Former German cities known respectively as Breslau and Königsberg, they experienced vast devastation, and their German inhabitants were expelled. As Polish and Soviet officials rebuilt these cities, they erased their German presence, both physically and metaphorically. The new Polish socialist Wrocław not only rid itself of German monuments, cemetery markers, and architectural decorations, but became part of Poland's "Regained Territories" *(Ziemie Odzyskane)*, organically Polish, yet separated by centuries of German conquest.[53] Kaliningrad experienced the erasure of its German skyline and new histories emphasizing East Prussia's connections to the Slavic world.[54] However, there were unintended consequences. Kaliningrad residents who grew up after the war embraced the city's German past, abjured by Soviet officials and citizens. By the 1960s, they championed the preservation of such ruins as the Königsberg Palace. A local patriotism had emerged, one more sympathetic to the German past.[55] Space itself thus inspired multiple centers of meaning, highlighting what Edward Soja sees as urban space's ability to affect relationships between social structures and individuals' agency.[56]

Such interactions between space and people were responsible for more than the rise of Ukrainian nationalism in Lviv. As Rogers Brubaker has noted, nationhood has its limits as an analytical category.[57] The nation mattered little in daily life for Lvivians. Ukrainians, Russians, and Jews cooperated with one another. Russian speakers and Ukrainian speakers did the same. Lviv's postwar transformation produced a number of identities, some that were Soviet, but others that could be viewed as anti-Soviet. Lviv thus resembled the deceptive, shifting phantasmagoria connected with modern cities, ones that took on multiple, contradictory images open to individuals' interpretation, evading stable meaning.[58]

Despite being a provincial Soviet city, Lviv beguiled and disturbed its new residents and visitors. To be sure, it became part of one Soviet polity. As Amar rightly notes, by the close of the Khrushchev era, at least Lviv's public sphere had acquired a local Soviet Western Ukrainian identity linked to myths of a pro-Soviet, revolutionary past. This could be seen in histories of the prewar KPZU and the largely fictitious World War II Soviet partisan organization, the People's Guard *(Narodna Hvardiia)*.[59] At the same time, Lviv embodied a "bourgeois nationalist" other lurking beneath the surface. Another one of Lviv's shifting images was that of being more connected to the West than other parts of the Soviet Union. This perception of Lviv being more Western suggests the need to view it as part of Central Europe. "Central Europe" has become an ideologically charged geographical term, suggesting a region culturally superior to that of Russia. Yet it is a useful term to explain the persistence of the local.[60] Legacies of Austrian and Polish rule inspired cultural and political movements oriented more toward events in this region than toward events in the Russian Empire. This caused difficulties for finding a "usable past" for postwar Galician Ukrainians. Shadows of Lviv's Polish past, seen in the popularity of Polish media and the presence of Polish tourists in postwar Lviv, affected the search for an "imagined West."

Perceived connections with the West merit caution. As a provincial Soviet city, Lviv saw more heavy censorship and cultural conservatism than in Moscow. The role of the West in the Soviet Union's dissolution deserves qualification. While Sergei Zhuk highlights the anti-Soviet orientation of rock music and other Western cultural trends in Brezhnev-era Dnipropetrovsk, greater attraction to Western culture did not make one anti-Soviet. Vladislav Zubok indicates that fascination with Picasso and Hemingway did not diminish young Russians' faith in socialist ideals during Khrushchev's Thaw.[61] As noted by Alexei Yurchak, the Soviet "imagined West," a product of late Soviet socialism, helped sustain it.[62] Lviv thus represented a compromise with the capitalist West and Soviet socialism.

However, Lviv was more than that. As a Western Ukrainian city, it played a crucial role in the fate of postwar Soviet Ukraine. To be sure, Kyiv, the republic's capital, fomented alternative conceptions of the Ukrainian nation. It later became the nerve center of Ukraine's independence movement. Benjamin Tromley has demonstrated that the Kyiv Sixtiers Movement (*Shistdesiatnytstvo* in Ukrainian) emerged not because of ties with Western Ukraine or because of long-standing national grievances. Social spaces formed in institutions of higher education and policies of Khrushchev's Thaw encouraged national self-expression as a means of reviving and improving Soviet socialism.[63] The Sixtiers Movement originated in Kyiv and affected young people's concept of the nation in Lviv. Kyiv had major journals, newspapers, and book publishers Lvivians relied on to formulate their sense of being Ukrainian. Lvivians paid close attention to political events there. Kyiv had its pre-Soviet intelligentsia—including those who had fought Soviet power in Ukraine's wars for independence in 1917–20—who became heroes for younger generations.[64] Kyivans were among the most vociferous in Soviet Ukraine's dissident movement.

It would be unthinkable to deny Kyiv's role as Ukraine's "primate city," as Roman Szporluk has called it, articulating and mobilizing national opinion throughout the republic.[65] Nonetheless, as Tromley points out, Kyiv students who became a part of the Sixtiers Movement overwhelmingly had come from rural provincial environments. Here, Ukrainians considered Russian more prestigious. Their lower-class rural origins and the marginalization of Ukrainians' national identity in Kyiv drew them to a Ukrainian national identity as a way of dealing with unfulfilled social opportunities. Khrushchev's Thaw offered Kyiv students, still committed to the ideals of Soviet socialism, a chance to combat Russian chauvinism rather than seek the Soviet system's overthrow.[66] Lviv may not have been the magnet for political opposition throughout Ukraine. However, local memories of Soviet power fueled a different understanding of the Thaw and Gorbachev's Glasnost. The same could be said of memories (however fragmentary) of past national liberation movements. While very much influenced by the ideals of Soviet socialism, Ukrainians of Lviv's post-Stalin generations thus perceived Soviet power as an alien force. This sense of Soviet power being alien thus encouraged private discussions on Ukraine separating from the Soviet Union. During Glasnost, it inspired mass demonstrations for Ukrainian sovereignty.

Such turns toward independence were not inevitable. Young Lvivians during the Thaw talked about improving the existing system to benefit Ukrainians. As university and institute scholars and members of artistic unions, they adhered to their mission as spokespersons for the advancement of Soviet socialism. In this sense, postwar Soviet politics of empire were highly successful. However, these Lvivians were treated differently from other Ukrainians. Lvivians were not Soviet enough. They were still connected to postwar anti-Soviet armed resistance and the bourgeois world, despite being Soviet Western Ukrainians. Thus Lviv became an object of curiosity, if not admiration, by Ukrainians from outside the region. Lviv did not bring about Ukraine's independence, but its unique experience of Sovietization made it a source of alternative perceptions of what it meant to be Ukrainian. That experience of Sovietization made local compromises with Party and state institutions fragile, thus inspiring the rapid emergence of Lviv as an "island of freedom" by 1990. While other cities of Western Ukraine also became part of this more Western, nationalist other, Soviet policy makers as early as 1944 had settled on Lviv as the region's cultural, economic, and political capital.[67] Hence its evolution as a Soviet Ukrainian city, and its contribution to cultural and political developments in the capital Kyiv, merit particular attention.

Finally, Lviv was not necessarily more anti-Soviet, Western, or democratic than other Soviet cities. A seemingly endless series of ideological campaigns against "Ukrainian bourgeois nationalism," led by Party and state activists eager to show their political credentials before superiors, make any references to an island of freedom in pre-Gorbachev times sound preposterous. While Lviv's pre-Gorbachev-era residents created islands of freedom in alternative social spaces, they were not alone. Steven Bittner and Vladislav Zubok discuss theaters, research institutes, and creative unions in Moscow and Novosibirsk that created enduring islands of freethinking.[68] Douglas Weiner sees communities of mostly biologists creating archipelagos of such islands of freethinking as early as the 1930s.[69] Soviet citizens arguably saw cities in the Baltic republics as more of a "near abroad" than Lviv. However, fragile compromises over language, historical memory, artistic and literary expression, and mass culture made this island of freedom a potential time bomb for the Soviet experience. Forged asymmetrically, at the goodwill of Party and state leaders, these compromises easily fell apart in the Glasnost era.

✿   ✿   ✿

The first section of the book examines Lviv in the context of the postwar Soviet West. Changing postwar Soviet nationality policies offered opportunities for compromise and conflict. As World War II turned Galicia into a Soviet West, Party and state institutions transformed urban space and public institutions into Ukrainian ones while de-Polonizing the city. Policies of coercion and co-optation fostered perceptions that this region differed from the rest of the Soviet Union. As Polish Lwów became Soviet Ukrainian Lviv, the new Lvivians—made up of different ethnic groups and Eastern and Western Ukrainians—came to cooperate with one another over time. However, the local Western Ukrainian remained someone not entirely reliable. Western Ukrainians came to identify with one larger Soviet polity, but still remained very connected to a different sense of being Ukrainian. Gradually Lviv became a Ukrainian "Soviet Abroad," where Polish media and contacts with Poles, contacts with the Ukrainian diaspora, and an architectural setting connected with Central Europe made Lviv seem more like the real West. This near abroad emerged in the simultaneous presence and absence of Poles, where recent Polish-Ukrainian violence made the Poles objects of both emulation and resentment. It was a more provincial near abroad than Baltic republic capitals.

The second part of the book turns to national issues affecting intellectuals and young people. Lviv's Ukrainian intellectuals challenged the more marginal, provincial role given to Soviet Lviv by engaging in culture wars over language, literature, and history. Members of the Writers' Union championed greater public use of the Ukrainian language and greater literary self-expression in Khrushchev's Thaw and after. While causing problems with local Party and state functionaries, and while political repressions in Ukraine in the 1970s greatly limited chances for greater national self-expression, Lviv writers contained trends favoring greater use of Russian. Their literary journal, *October (Zhovten')*, mobilized readers interested in nationally oriented literature. These writers and other intellectuals contributed greatly to discussions of nationhood in the republic's cultural establishment. In the Gorbachev era, such figures took part in Kyiv's political opposition that helped bring the Soviet Union down. Representations of Galicia's recent past by scholars, writers, and artists helped sustain some Soviet historical myths. However, they also eroded stereotypes about "Ukrainian bourgeois nationalism" in place since the Stalin era. Repressions in the early 1970s fueled a campaign against such interpretations. Conflicts between critics and defenders of such histories reflected factions not just within academia, but between locals and outsiders. Collective memory of the recent past continued to challenge such official histories. While sharply contested and altered by censorship, such collective memories lingered in folk songs, cemetery pilgrimages, literary works, and artistic representations. They suggested unresolved contradictions over what the new Lvivians should be allowed to remember and commemorate.

Later chapters address young Lvivians, those who came of age or began their professional careers after Stalin's death. These young Lvivians' private spheres challenged the cultural establishment's definitions of what it meant to be Ukrainian and what it meant to be young. Informal networks of fellow thinkers, inspired by events in Moscow and Kyiv, yet also Galicia's past cultural and political movements, tested publicly defined boundaries of Ukrainian nationhood. While accommodating Soviet realties, their networks fostered different interpretations of Ukrainian nationhood that helped mobilize support for the Soviet Union's collapse. At the same time, such informal groups were not so much about the nation as they were about being young, about creating alternative spaces of identity where people could subvert identities and enjoy one another's company. Nationalism became a rite of passage as well as a weapon of resistance. Fellow thinkers' informal circles promoted individual as well as national forms of self-expression. They reflected an archipelago of islands of freedom divided by culture and ethnicity. At the same time, mass culture and countercultures encouraged values and forms of behavior at odds with mainstream society and national paradigms. Yet issues of national and regional identity often surfaced, as seen with the behavior of city soccer fans, the use of local Ukrainian jargon by city countercultures, and Ukrainian rock and pop music. The book then concludes by pointing out the Soviet Union's western borderlands as a region that reinforced Soviet rule while destabilizing it in the end.

PART I

Lviv and the Soviet West

CHAPTER 1

Lviv and Postwar Soviet Politics

The collapse of Communism and Soviet rule in Lviv was not inevitable. It was unexpected. One poet captured the shock and confusion the evening after Lenin's statue came down. Rushing into a Writers' Union party, a friend of his announced, "Lenin's bust is on the ground!" He was greeted with "dead silence."[1] As they momentarily held their alcohol and sandwiches, these writers and their guests must have thought they were dreaming. Their response suggests Soviet rule, far from being destined to collapse, had created a sense of power and legitimacy very difficult to dispel. Union-wide policies of coercion compelled compliance, but also provided opportunities for accommodation and social advancement. Nonetheless, domestic and foreign political crises and the continued specter of "bourgeois nationalism" perpetuated local grievances. Such grievances fueled forces for radical political change during Glasnost.

✧   ✧   ✧

World War II transformed Lviv from a mostly Polish, multicultural city to one dominated by ethnic Ukrainians. Sustaining myths about the Soviet Union also had undergone metamorphoses. Amir Weiner has offered a compelling argument that the war renewed the revolutionary state's drive to create a Communist future. As the "Armageddon of the Revolution," the war challenged Soviet socialism's existence for the first generation of citizens to live under it. New tests of loyalty to the state and its revolutionary mission, based on people's wartime activities, emerged. Until the Soviet Union's collapse, personnel files contained information on whether or not people or their relatives had been on German-occupied territory. Victory renewed the revolutionary state's transformative powers, inspiring Soviet leaders to purify society of internal enemies, remove remnants of capitalism in the Soviet economy (as highlighted in Stalin's *Economic Problems of Socialism in the USSR* in 1952), and transform nature itself (as seen with Khrushchev's Virgin Lands campaign of 1954–56).[2] Until the mid-1950s, this drive for ideological purification took on biological and hygienic features, though Soviet officials sought to avoid degenerating into the racism of Nazi Germany or the capitalist world. Myths about the war assumed an ethnic hierarchy that marginalized the Holocaust and incorporated anti-Semitism into the October Revolution's sustaining myths. In reuniting Ukrainians under one Soviet state, the war led to myths about Ukrainians' reunification that affirmed ethno-national ties as part of the new Soviet polity advancing toward the Communist future.[3]

Others suggest limits to the postwar shift Weiner proposes. In German-occupied Ukraine, the war traumatized the local population, but it inspired neither nationalism nor revolutionary fervor.[4] After the war, Stalin concentrated more on restoring his ruling circle's prewar equilibrium than on revolutionary transformation. Despite shakeups of Party and state structures, elements of predictable, committee-based forms of governance prevailed. Stalin's ruling circle contemplated ways to scale back methods of repression, measures taken in the months following Stalin's death.[5] Nonetheless, the war had profound implications for Soviet nationalities policies in the late Stalin era. Ethnic or national categories determined political loyalty. Great Russians became the most progressive.[6] Soviet Jews disappeared from the war's list of victims and victors. Entire nations in the Caucasus region were identified with wartime collaboration and deported to Siberia and Central Asia.[7] Such actions affected the western borderlands. Fierce nationalist resistance broke out not just in Galicia, but in other parts of Western Ukraine and the Baltic republics. A rural guerrilla insurgency, fueled by Soviet efforts to collectivize agriculture, turned natives into targets for arrest and deportation. This violence became a civil war on the western borderlands from 1944 to 1948, producing divided communities long after organized armed resistance had ended.[8] Soviet police organs did not seek to repress entire nationalities on the western borderlands. They were selective, though extremely brutal, in their repression of insurgents and their supporters. In Western Ukraine, they fomented class warfare that contributed to victory over the insurgency.[9] However, this insurgency further validated official assumptions that the western borderlands were contaminated by foreign elements, collectively hostile, and politically unreliable. Much of the initial violence directed at insurgents and their supporters during this civil war came from perceptions that the western borderlands' local inhabitants had all collaborated with Nazi Germany in one way or another.[10]

The Cold War intensified the drive to purify the Soviet Union of enemies. This could be seen with the Zhdanov era, a mass campaign against foreign influences and dissent. Associated with ideological advisor Andrei Zhdanov, it began in 1946 and endured past Zhdanov's death in 1948. Recent scholarship suggests Zhdanov's actual role was marginal.[11] Several factors provoked this campaign, including the need to counter postwar Soviet society's growing assertiveness and restlessness, to put members of Stalin's inner circle on guard, and to purify the revolutionary state of "hostile" elements.[12] The Zhdanov era lauded the achievements of Great Russians and attacked people for "subservience to the West," "formalism," and "cosmopolitanism." Opposing "cosmopolitanism," it indirectly gave official support to postwar anti-Semitism. Such anti-Semitism received further sanction through persecuting members of the disbanded Jewish Anti-Fascist Committee and the so-called Doctor's Plot of 1953, where doctors of Jewish origin allegedly had killed Zhdanov and threatened the country's security. In Ukraine, the Doctor's Plot greatly resonated among the local population, encouraging all kinds of denunciations from below.[13] The Zhdanov era took on added features of a campaign against non-Russians' "bourgeois nationalism." Historians, writers, artists, and composers who had praised the "Great Ukrainian People" during the war were criticized for exaggerating Ukrainians' role in history and neglecting their "eternal friendship" with Great Russians.[14]

The Cold War fortified suspicions that the western borderlands were more foreign and susceptible to outside manipulation. Western Ukraine became one of the Cold War's first fronts. American military and intelligence services expressed interest in exchanging information with nationalist guerrillas fighting Soviet rule. Such contacts with the West, while superficial at best, became justifications for Soviet mass repression against nationalist guerrillas.[15] The Soviet state dissolved the Ukrainian Greek Catholic Church in 1946. The leading church for Galician Ukrainians, its ties with the Vatican became grounds for identifying it as the hireling of the Soviet Union's Cold War Western enemies.[16] Late Stalinism thus solidified ethnic and national categories, in ways that suppressed and liberated the western borderlands.

Succession Struggles and the Thaw

Stalin's death in 1953 gradually shifted Soviet politics of empire. Already aware of the need to reform an exhausted system, members of Stalin's inner circle retired the "cult of personality" and assumed "collective leadership."[17] Mass repressions ended. The Doctors' Plot was officially discredited. Partial amnesties of prisoners in labor camps and special settlements began. Soviet nationality policies underwent review, largely at the initiative of Lavrenty Beria, Stalin's former secret police chief who was jockeying for power.[18] Beginning with policy reversals in his old power base, Georgia, he launched a larger campaign against "Great Russian chauvinism."[19] Under Beria's influence, the Communist Party of the Soviet Union (CPSU) Central Committee passed a resolution on 12 June 1953 that called on Party and state organs to do more to promote local nationals to positions of leadership, replace functionaries who did not speak the indigenous languages of their republics, and have locals rather than ethnic Russians sent from Moscow become first Party secretaries of national republics.[20]

These reforms particularly affected the western borderlands, including the Party and state leadership in the Baltic republics and Belarus.[21] Beria concentrated on Western Ukraine, possibly to undermine Kremlin rival Nikita Khrushchev, whose power base had been Ukraine.[22] Due to Beria's efforts, a 26 May CPSU Central Committee resolution criticized Party and state officials for illegally repressing the local population, preferring Ukrainians from outside the region for appointment to leadership positions, and imposing the Russian language on the higher education system. This resolution, and a subsequent resolution by the Communist Party of Ukraine (CPU) Central Committee on 4 June, highlighted the need to promote local Ukrainians to positions of power and encourage Ukrainian language use in public life. First Party secretary for Ukraine L. G. Melnikov, an ethnic Russian, had to step down, replaced by A. I. Kirichenko, an ethnic Ukrainian and the republic's former second Party secretary.[23] Before his sudden arrest on 26 June, Beria had even bolder plans, including co-opting the "alien," outlawed Ukrainian Greek Catholic Church.[24]

Regardless of motive, Beria's reforms encouraged the integration of the western borderlands into the Soviet body politic. The indigenization of

Party and state structures continued after Beria's arrest and execution.[25] Underground nationalists and their supporters—including members of Western Ukraine's Greek Catholic clergy—returned from labor camps and places of exile. By 10 October 1956, as many as 45,000 former nationalist guerrillas and their allies had returned to Western Ukraine, nearly all of them (almost 41,000) to the countryside, their former base of support.[26] Nationalist activists experienced great disappointment when they returned from exile, noting how much the countryside, and younger generations, had become Sovietized.[27]

The Thaw, commonly associated with Khrushchev and his "Secret Speech" to the Twentieth Party Congress in 1956, accelerated such integration. It was a very contradictory period, where hopes for a renewal of Soviet socialism and more liberal cultural policies met opposition from Khrushchev himself.[28] Recent social history emphasizes continuities in Stalin-era values and practices and contradictory responses to Thaw-era policies.[29] Thaw policies favored collective forms of leadership, the end of mass repression, greater focus on individual forms of self-expression, criticism of materialist values, and greater rights for non-Russians.[30] Young intellectuals, emboldened by the war, had anticipated the Thaw, speaking in Stalin's last years of the need to restore Leninist norms of democracy and establish better relations between officials and society.[31] In his Secret Speech Khrushchev revealed crimes committed by Stalin's cult of personality, including the illegal repression of Party and state leaders in the late 1930s and the deportations of entire nationalities in World War II's closing months. Later, at the Twenty-Second Party Congress in 1962, he implicated political opponents with such crimes.[32] In the fall of 1962, Khrushchev encouraged further attempts at discrediting Stalinists by allowing poet Yevgeny Yevtushenko to publish his poem "Stalin's Heirs." With his blessing, the literary journal *New World (Novy mir)* published Alexander Solzhenitsyn's *One Day in the Life of Ivan Denisovych*, which for the first time publicly spoke about Stalin-era labor camps.[33]

Khrushchev's Thaw nonetheless was inconsistent, because of rivals' threats, perceived setbacks in the Cold War, and Khrushchev's own ambiguous attitudes toward Stalin, his former patron. Khrushchev and his allies passed over in silence the Ukrainian famine of 1932–33 and the repression of Party leaders like Trotsky, Kamenev, and Zinoviev. Khrushchev launched campaigns against "abstractionism" and "formalism" in art, first from 1957 to 1959, in the wake of the Hungarian Uprising and challenges from

Stalinists, and then in December 1962, after a visit to an exhibit of abstract art at a major Moscow art gallery.[34] While mass repression disappeared, Khrushchev turned to a more subtle form of coercion, mutual surveillance, to instill obedience. Institutions like collectives (*kolektivy* in Russian) at places of employment and study, "people's courts," "people's patrols," and the Committee of Party-State Control took on greater significance. In Oleg Kharkhordin's view, such institutions enforced individual conformity more systematically and methodically than the Stalin era's more random (and more violent) terror.[35] Forces from below undermined reform, as seen in opposition by conservative leaders of Leningrad's writers' union in 1962–63 to the new wave of poetry official institutions had initially sponsored.[36] The mass release of Gulag prisoners after Stalin's death created tensions that contributed to new practices of social exclusion by the Thaw's end.[37]

Khrushchev's nationalities policy was inconsistent. From 1954 to 1958, Khrushchev gave greater authority to republic agencies in economic and judicial matters. The Twentieth Party Congress emphasized the need to encourage the development of non-Russians' cultures. Khrushchev encouraged the rehabilitation of nationalities deported from their homelands during the war (except for ethnic Germans and Crimean Tatars), continuing a process already begun in the summer of 1954.[38] However, from 1958 until his removal from office, he turned toward policies perceived as favoring Russification of non-Russian republics and a recentralization of political power.[39] In the non-Russian republics and autonomous regions, non-Russian language courses became optional in Russian-language schools. While the new school law was never fully implemented in practice, and practically all permanent citizens of Ukraine studied Ukrainian in Russian-language schools, it sparked immediate opposition in non-Russian republics for allegedly encouraging the school system's Russification.[40] A number of non-Russian republics (Ukraine being an exception) experienced Party purges in 1958–61 over suspicions of disloyalty to Moscow. Beginning in late 1962, republics lost the autonomy they had gained in economic planning. Already during discussion of school reforms in late 1958, and in especially pronounced form during the Twenty-Second Party Congress in 1961, Khrushchev and his allies spoke of non-Russian nations' eventual assimilation into one larger community, that of the "Soviet people." This legitimated the Russification of non-Russian nationalities.

Amid the inconsistencies, the Thaw inspired optimism and rising expectations. The Communist Party's June 1961 resolution to establish Communism by 1980 conjured diverse visions for a better future, especially among the young.[41] New spaces of identity privately fostered social and political change.[42] In Moscow, students and young intellectuals, witnessing greater openness to the West in such events as the 1957 International Youth Festival, viewed de-Stalinization as an opportunity to renew and advance Soviet socialism.[43] Ukrainians and Baltic nationalities used criticism of Stalin's cult of personality to legitimate claims for greater national self-expression.[44] As for Ukraine, Khrushchev elevated its prestige by promoting Ukrainian clients to important posts in Moscow. In 1954, he added special pomp and ceremony to celebrations of the anniversary of the signing of the Pereiaslavl Accords by Ukrainian Cossack leader Bohdan Khmelnytskyi and Muscovite tsar Alexis Mikhailovich in 1654, dubbed the "Reunification of the Ukraine and Russia."[45] Such policies favoring Ukraine indirectly encouraged Petro Shelest, Party chief in Ukraine from 1963 to 1972, to promote quietly his republic's national language, national cultural activities, and national personnel.[46] Khrushchev and his successors made Ukraine essentially Russia's "junior partner" in the Soviet Union.[47] In Kyiv, the Thaw in institutions of higher education led to the formation of the Sixtiers Movement *(Shistdesiatnytstvo)*, a group of freethinking, nationally conscious young Ukrainians who equated Khrushchev's renewal of Leninist ideals with greater national self-expression.[48]

The Thaw posed a great threat to the Soviet state. On the western borderlands, nationalist guerrillas and their supporters, recently returned from exile, were seen as being in sympathy with worker unrest in Poland in October 1956 and the Hungarian Uprising the next month.[49] In early 1964, a Committee of State Security (KGB) report to the CPSU Central Committee warned that returned members of the nationalist underground, such as in Western Ukraine, were changing their tactics, encouraging young people to enter the Communist Party and promote "nationalist" agendas within the system.[50] Foreign policies, too, encouraged the specter of "bourgeois nationalism." Support for decolonization movements by Khrushchev and later leaders influenced underground nationalist groups, who turned to the rhetoric of the worldwide struggle against colonialism to justify their claims for separation from the Soviet Union.[51]

The Thaw thus epitomized tensions within postwar Soviet politics of empire. While inspiring hope for greater democracy and national self-expression, Soviet policies suggested that the Ukrainian nation's days might be numbered. As for Soviet policy makers in Moscow, they were not convinced that "bourgeois nationalism" had disappeared in the western borderlands.

Stability and "Stagnation"

Khrushchev's removal from power in 1964 initially brought relief to Soviet society. While his reforms had considerably narrowed wage gaps and raised standards of living, growth rates declined, and consumer shortages grew. Leonid Brezhnev, Khrushchev's successor, promised "stability in cadres," winning the support of Party and state functionaries alienated by frequent administrative reshufflings. Despite the failure of economic reforms in the mid-1960s, rising oil prices in the 1970s helped supply the country with consumer goods and steady wages. For most of Soviet society, including baby boomers of the "Sputnik Generation," the Brezhnev era thus became an era of stability and relative prosperity, a "golden age" compared to life after the Soviet Union's collapse.[52]

With this new stability, the Thaw came to an end. Soviet leaders grew increasingly intolerant of dissent. The circulation of underground literature critical of national discrimination and human rights abuses, called *samvydav* in Ukrainian and *samizdat* in Russian, led to closed trials of intellectuals in 1965 and 1966 across the Soviet Union. These trials produced a Soviet dissident movement increasingly at odds with the state. While maintaining a conspiracy of silence over the Stalinist past, Soviet leaders came to view any call for reforming Communism as ideologically suspect. This was especially true after the Soviet-led invasion of Czechoslovakia in August 1968, which brought an end to attempts there to bring about "socialism with a human face." Increasing conflicts with China damaged Soviet claims to leadership over the world Communist movement. They raised doubts about Soviet annexation of its western borderlands.[53] Soviet leaders thus intensified the ideological struggle at home while seeking rapprochement with the United States in the policy of Détente.

Despite the rhetoric about an intensifying ideological struggle, the Brezhnev era only parodied the ideological vigilance that predated the Thaw. Plans to build Communism by 1980 were toned down. Public life became increasingly ritualized. Contacts with the West were encouraged at least in Moscow during Détente.[54] The authoritative discourse of Soviet socialism, with its claims of bringing humanity to its highest stage of development, increasingly became devoid of content. Such an emphasis on performance over substance provided people outlets for creativity and expression among friends and acquaintances, in an "imaginary West" generated by Soviet and foreign sources.[55] Soviet nationalities policies reflected this state of ideological improvisation. Despite claims that a new community of nations, a Soviet people, was being formed as a result of the merger of nations, by the end of Brezhnev's rule, this rhetoric tapered off, replaced by admissions that the "flowering" of nations would continue for some time.[56] Notwithstanding these creative improvisations, the Brezhnev era became known for its political apathy, government corruption, and ultimately economic stagnation. Recent case studies highlight the apathy young people had toward public life.[57]

Ukrainian politics reflected the republic's crucial role as Russia's junior partner in the Brezhnev era. Shelest, despite supporting Khrushchev's ouster and agitating for Soviet intervention in Czechoslovakia, lost his job as Ukraine's Party chief in 1972. His published diaries suggest that growing conflicts with Brezhnev, Brezhnev's ideological advisor Mikhail Suslov, and other Politburo members provoked a campaign against his alleged promotion of Ukrainian national interests at the expense of the all-Union government.[58] His replacement, Volodymyr Shcherbytskyi, expanded Russian-language schools and promoted Russian in official correspondence.[59] From 1972 to 1973, a republic-wide ideological campaign erupted against all kinds of national self-expression. Valentyn Malanchuk, a former Lviv Party functionary and a protégé of Suslov's, banned entire lists of writers from publication when he was the republic's first secretary for ideology from 1973 to 1979. While Malanchuk's dismissal encouraged better relations with Ukraine's intelligentsia, the Russification of public life continued.[60] A prominent Kyiv writer's diary entries from 1974 to 1982 observed Ukrainian's virtual disappearance from republic state and Party functions.[61]

Given these shifting political winds, the Brezhnev era only on the surface resembled so-called stagnation. Public rhetoric belied conflicts over ideology and creative adaptations to it. In Lviv, national self-expression was allowed in varying doses, despite Malanchuk's witch-hunt. However, perceptions of growing Russification and increasing discontent with corruption and deteriorating economic conditions made the stability of the Brezhnev era precarious.

Gorbachev and the Collapse

Following his appointment as leader of the Soviet Union in 1985, Gorbachev, in his call for restructuring *(perestroika)* in the economy, openness *(glasnost)* in the media, and democratization in political life, revolutionized politics throughout the Soviet Union. Late Soviet socialism's authoritative discourse collapsed.[62] While Ukrainian Party leaders initially distanced themselves from Gorbachev's reforms, the Chernobyl nuclear accident in 1986, along with calls by Gorbachev for *glasnost* in public life, touched off protest against Russification, the suppression of individual rights, and ultimately Ukraine's status in the Soviet Union. The Soviet Union's failed war in Afghanistan and ethnic conflicts breaking out in the Caucasus region signaled the system's breakdown. With the discourse of Soviet socialism largely dead, Party leaders such as Leonid Kravchuk, independent Ukraine's first president, turned to the rhetoric of nationalism for political support. They joined national intelligentsias in asserting greater national rights. The convergence of popular protest from below, political maneuvering from above, new rhetoric from the intelligentsia, and weakness at the imperial center ended the Soviet Union.[63] The Soviet Union's collapse nonetheless was sudden. It was no wonder that Lviv's writers, of all people, were caught speechless when the cranes pulled down one of Soviet power's greatest symbols.

CHAPTER 2

The Making of a Soviet Ukrainian City

By the end of the 1960s, Polish Lwów had become antiquity for at least one former resident. On his August 1968 return to this city, a Polish-Canadian tourist recalled a young female employee at the Hotel "Intourist" insisted on speaking in Ukrainian, which he barely understood. When she found out that this tourist had lived in Lviv before the war, she started speaking to him in Polish, though with mistakes. She said that Lviv before the war had been Ukrainian and always had been Ukrainian. When the tourist retorted that it had been Polish before the war, her eyes lit up. She snarled, "But Lviv now is Ukrainian and it always will be Ukrainian!" The bemused tourist later congratulated her for defending her language like a "true Ukrainian."[1]

This encounter underscored Lviv's dramatic transformation by World War II and Soviet rule. The hotel employee with no memories of the war could not imagine Lwów. There had always been Lviv. Even if it had not always been there, it was no matter, because the Poles were gone for good anyway. Soviet policies created a city that gave Galician Ukrainians a sense of belonging to one Soviet Ukrainian national community, as well as one multinational state. They fostered a sense of local identity that was different from other Soviet regions. This uneasy conjuncture of the local, the national, and the Soviet caused future tensions between the new residents and their wider world.

Galicians into Soviet Ukrainians

Soviet policies turned Polish Lwów into antiquity. Besides transforming Lwów's ethnic composition, they reconstructed its urban space and public institutions. The new Ukrainian Lviv thus symbolized a community united by a common language, a common culture, a common history, and a common territory. Ukrainian Lviv was to become part of a national community that had finally overcome centuries of class and national exploitation by the Poles, the masters of prewar Lviv. They were finally united with their "brothers in blood" across Soviet Ukraine's pre-1939 border.

However, this national community was to be a Soviet Ukrainian one. In the context of postwar Soviet politics of empire, this meant one that was to be bilingual, embracing not just Ukrainian, but the language cementing this multinational state, Russian. In both theory and in practice, this bilingual community was to give preference not just to the language but also to the culture of the Great Russians, viewed by the eve of World War II as the most "progressive" in the Soviet family of nations, leading the rest in establishing socialism and building Communism.[2] Ukrainians' history, literature, music, and other cultural goods had achieved wider ranges of self-expression during the war, only to be circumscribed and made more explicitly subordinate to those of the Great Russians upon the war's end.[3] This subordinate role to that of the Great Russians, as well as to one imperial capital, Moscow, took place not just in the realm of cultural politics but also in the postwar transformation of Polish Lwów's urban space.

Like the peasants who were to become nationally conscious Frenchmen during the Third Republic, Galician Ukrainians were to become Soviet Ukrainians by adopting a certain political orientation.[4] Galician Ukrainians had to overcome their own "backwardness." This was a different notion of backwardness from that to be overcome by the locals of provincial Russia and Central Asia between the world wars. For the latter, "backwardness" meant a lack of the West's modern urban civilization. The backwardness to be overcome by Galician Ukrainians was the behavior and values of the Western capitalist world, inherited from Austrian and Polish rule. This latter notion of backwardness marked a turning point in Soviet history. Challenged by perceptions of being behind the Western capitalist world before World War II, Soviet leaders perceived themselves as moving beyond the West, creating a civilization for the rest of the world, one they exported to Central and Eastern Europe at the war's end.[5]

Being part of a Soviet Ukrainian nation thus emphasized an important element of what it meant to be Soviet. State and Party institutions were to govern the economy, cultural life, and politics. They were creating a civilization superior to that of the capitalist West. If these ideals had not been achieved, they would be achieved eventually with Party and state leaders' help. Being Soviet in Lviv thus meant condemning the actions and values acquired in one's bourgeois past. For Soviet leaders, Western Ukrainians had overcome this backwardness only at the end of the 1950s, as seen with the Lviv Region receiving an Order of Lenin from the Presidium of the Soviet Union's Supreme Soviet in 1958.[6]

While Soviet leaders by the end of the 1950s acknowledged that Galicians and other Western Ukrainians were no longer backward, postwar politics of empire had left an uneasy compromise with locals. Galician Ukrainians still adhered to notions of nationhood inherited from Austrian and Polish times. Postwar national guerrilla resistance against Soviet rule exacerbated tensions between locals and outsiders. It made local Ukrainians suspicious to outsiders long after armed resistance had ended. The locals' sense of being Soviet—of belonging to a progressive multinational polity advancing the world's highest form of civilization—thus seemed less than genuine. Understanding such conflicts over being Ukrainian and Soviet in Lviv thus requires addressing Galician Ukrainians' past, the impact of both Nazi and Soviet occupation policies on Western Ukraine, and the outbreak of armed resistance to postwar Soviet reoccupation.

Galicia and the Making of the Soviet West

In confronting Galicia, Soviet policy makers confronted a region unlike most of the other western borderlands, largely outside imperial Russia's influence. Incorporated into the Habsburg Empire in 1772, during partitions of the Polish-Lithuanian Commonwealth, Galicia in the late nineteenth century became a battleground between Polish and Ukrainian projects of nation building. Recent scholarship reveals that issues of national identity remained sharply contested between peasants and intellectuals. Nonetheless, Ukrainian and Polish intellectuals, encouraged by Habsburg reforms, set up rival political parties, newspapers, schools, sports organizations, reading rooms, and other social and cultural institutions to win converts.[7] Unlike Russian Empire counterparts, Ukrainian national activists created more of a grassroots movement. Such grassroots support inspired a sense of common ethnicity, language, and culture that World War I further radicalized.[8] With the Austro-Hungarian Empire's collapse in 1918, Galician Ukrainian politicians, with the help of Galician Ukrainian soldiers from the imperial army, seized power in Lwów and set up the Western Ukrainian

People's Republic (ZUNR). An army of over 100,000 men from across Galicia defended the ZUNR government, proclaimed on 1 November of that year. It engaged in all-out war with ethnic Poles for control of the province.[9]

Defeated in what became known as the Ukrainian-Polish War of 1918–19, veterans of the ZUNR army, along with younger Ukrainians, formed the Organization of Ukrainian Nationalists (OUN) in 1929 to resist Polish rule, which the Council of Ambassadors in Paris in 1923 had legitimated. Members of the OUN, under the influence of World War I and the politics of Europe's extreme right, became followers of the ideology of integral nationalism. Integral nationalism stressed authority, solidarity, faith, and organization as compensation for the socialism, democracy, and perceived lack of will that allegedly had defeated Ukrainian independence movements. Young OUN activists turned to bombings, sabotage, "expropriations," and assassinations of major Polish and Ukrainian political figures, Polish policemen, undercover agents, informants, and suspected Ukrainian "collaborators" in Galicia and in the former Russian province of Volhynia.[10]

Ukrainian politics were fractious in what became known as Eastern Galicia. Ukrainian political parties and politicians sought accommodation with Polish counterparts. The OUN's integral nationalism had a scant following. Poles and Ukrainians largely lived together, undisturbed, until the outbreak of World War II.[11] However, almost two decades of economic exploitation, Polish colonization, Polonization in language and cultural life, restricted access to higher education and state careers, and gerrymandered underrepresentation in parliament fueled movements like the OUN. For the young, participation in the OUN offered a chance to participate in national revolutionary politics.[12] This legacy of struggle and cooperation produced a Ukrainian identity closely tied with common ethnicity, language, and culture. It involved a host of political parties, organizations, and institutions influenced by the bourgeois West in its Central European form. Galician Ukrainians' sense of nationhood thus conflicted with later Soviet projects of nation building among non-Russians.

The Soviet invasion and annexation of Eastern Galicia and Volhynia in late September 1939 came at the end of a decade in which Soviet leaders explicitly identified such regions as a security threat. Soviet policy makers had turned to Ukrainianization—promoting ethnic Ukrainians to positions of power, as well as promoting elements of Ukrainian nationhood in public life—to influence Ukrainians in these regions of eastern Poland. In the

1920s they encouraged Galician Ukrainians to emigrate to Soviet Ukraine to take part in Ukrainianization policies, and they gave financial support to Galician Ukrainian intellectuals in Poland. Fears about "bourgeois nationalist" propaganda crossing the border from Eastern Galicia and Volhynia, made worse during the collectivization of agriculture and the famine of 1932–33, led not only to scaling back Ukrainianization but also to breaking ties with Galician Ukrainians and targeting Galician Ukrainian émigrés in the Great Terror of the late 1930s.[13]

Soviet annexation of these territories thus was more complex than that of the Baltic States the next year. Elena Zubkova has suggested that initially these states were to be in the Soviet sphere of influence rather than incorporated into the Soviet Union. In the fall of 1939, Moscow's leaders forbade their diplomats and military personnel in Estonia, Latvia, and Lithuania from telling locals that their states were going to be Sovietized. Up until May–June 1940, Soviet leaders were content with maintaining a sphere of influence, rather than annexing these states.[14] When invading Poland in late 1939, Soviet leaders had no such hesitations about joining its eastern territories to Soviet Ukraine. However, incorporating so-called Western Ukraine into Soviet Ukraine presented them with both an opportunity and a threat. While they exploited this event as the "reunification" of the Ukrainian people, they faced the danger of "bourgeois nationalism" affecting Soviet Ukraine. Soviet leaders faced considerable opposition from Poles. They dealt with cities that were populated by Poles and Jews, with Ukrainians being very small minorities (only 16.3 percent of Lwów's 1931 population).[15]

Until the 1941 Nazi invasion, Lwów became the "eternally Ukrainian" city of Lviv. Soviet policies set ethnic groups and individuals against each other. The latter strategy was to bring about a sudden "revolution from above" to rid the locals of the "backwardness" of their "bourgeois nationalist" world and introduce them to Soviet civilization. They transformed the city's urban space. Jan Casimir University, named for a major seventeenth-century Polish king, became the Ivan Franko State University, thus acquiring the name of local Ukrainian literary classic Ivan Franko. State and Party institutions were to make Ukrainian the language of daily communication, and schools and universities were to convert to Ukrainian-language instruction. The city's historical museum was to remove its exhibits glorifying Polish nationalism and instead portray the city with ancient Ukrainian roots. Ukrainians were to take on important posts in educational and research institutions. Thus a partial, yet significant, replacement of Polish personnel took place at institutions of higher education. In 1940, primarily Galician Ukrainian historians were hired in the Lviv branch of the Institute of History of the republic's Academy of Sciences.[16]

Lviv's Ukrainianization, like indigenization policies in the interwar Soviet Union, was not an end in itself. It was to create legitimacy and mobilize the local population on the behalf of building a new Soviet civilization. Those Party and state officials from pre-1939 Ukraine, otherwise known as Eastern Ukrainians, in charge of Lviv, preferred speaking and communicating in Russian. Their transformation of Lviv's economy into a socialist one wound up enriching Eastern Ukrainians and others from the Soviet heartland, discrediting official ideology in the eyes of local Ukrainians. The poor state of Soviet soldiers and other occupation personnel made Soviet civilization look backward.[17] Soviet policies toward Lviv's ethnic groups were inconsistent. By 1940, they began favoring the city's Polish national community, encouraging developments like the growth of Polish-language publications and the commemoration of national literary great Adam Mickiewicz.[18] Occupation officials broke up cultural, educational, and political organizations of Ukrainians, Poles, and Jews, arresting their leaders. In such arrests, they encouraged denunciations among Lvivians. They were to neutralize opposition, but also to root out their perceived backwardness. Such arrests, as well as rigged elections to ratify Western Ukraine's unification with Soviet Ukraine, were to instruct Lvivians in the political rituals of Soviet life.[19] As they retreated during the German invasion of June 1941, Soviet secret police executed untold thousands, many of them political activists or veterans of the Polish-Ukrainian War of 1918–19, held in prisons in Lviv and other Western Ukrainian cities and towns. German military and civilians found these bodies mutilated and badly decomposed.[20] Soviet occupation thus alienated Galician Ukrainians. At least 150,000 Western Ukrainians, many of them well educated, fled to the West as displaced persons when Soviet rule returned.[21]

German occupation from 1941 to 1944 radicalized policies set by their Soviet predecessors. Like the Soviets, they favored Ukrainians over Poles. Ukrainians occupied Lviv's low-level administrative posts and were preferred over Poles in quasi-academic training in the form of Special Courses (Fachkurse). They developed their own cultural institutions, newspapers, and journals. Policies favoring Ukrainians were limited. Poles remained in local administration. German occupation officials arrested OUN activists who had attempted to declare an independent Ukrainian state in Lviv on

30 June 1941, though OUN activists largely continued to work in the city administration.[22] German occupation policies further worsened relations between the city's ethnic groups. In their very first days, occupation officials fomented pogroms against Jews. Forcing Jews, who allegedly collaborated with the People's Commissariat of Internal Affairs (NKVD), to recover decomposing bodies from NKVD prisons, the occupation officials provoked killing and plundering of up to 4,000 Jews by the city's Poles and Ukrainians. At the notorious Brygidka Prison alone, 1,000 Jews were killed. Later moves to isolate and exterminate Eastern Galicia's Jews (the latter accomplished by August 1943 in Lviv) did not involve mass violence, but the help of Ukrainian Auxiliary Police *(Hilfspolizei)* and city government agencies staffed mainly by Ukrainians.[23]

Anti-Semitism among Ukrainians and Poles considerably waned after the pogroms of late June and early July, 1941. Some Ukrainians and Poles managed to hide Jews. However, German occupation greatly oppressed both Ukrainians and Poles, limiting their resistance to the Holocaust. Poles faced arrests and executions, and Ukrainians ran the risk of being sent to forced labor in Germany. Most were apathetic about actions against Jews, while both Poles and Ukrainians took part in denouncing Jews to authorities. National underground resistance groups, themselves increasingly persecuted by the Germans from 1942 on, paid little attention to the Holocaust, either out of tactical reasons or because of continued anti-Semitic orientations. The Holocaust worsened relations between Poles and Ukrainians in Eastern Galicia, with Poles fearing that Ukrainians hoped German policies of isolation and extermination would be directed at them next.[24] In Lviv itself, tensions grew between the remaining Polish and Ukrainian communities as German occupation officials favored one over the other and as the city's living conditions deteriorated.[25]

The Soviets' retaking Lviv in late July 1944 marked the definitive end of Polish Lwów and the formative years of Ukrainian Lviv. In a September 1944 agreement between the Polish People's Republic and Soviet Ukraine, Poles and Jews living in what was then Western Ukraine were to be "evacuated" to Poland, while Ukrainians living in Poland were to be "evacuated" to Soviet Ukraine.[26] This agreement meant the mass expulsion of Poles from Lviv. After numerous delays, Soviet officials were to finish the expulsion of Lviv's Poles by 1 September 1946, but they completed expulsions only as of 6 March 1947.[27] Soviet mismanagement (including bribes demanded of departing Poles), continued need for Polish skilled laborers, and resistance by Poles themselves slowed the expulsions. However, international recognition of Poland's postwar borders, street violence provoked by Ukrainian nationalists and the NKVD, threats of arrest and exile, and confiscations of apartments and ration cards forced Poles to comply.[28] Lviv's Polish population declined dramatically. In December 1944, at the start of expulsions, they had constituted 62.8 percent of the city's population. By 1 January 1955, there were only 8,600 of them, a mere 2.3 percent of the city's total population and only 5 percent of what had been its Polish community in 1939.[29]

Tarik Amar identifies a turning point in the period from 1944 to 1946. Lviv's Poles had become "irredeemable," incapable of joining the new Soviet Ukrainian polity, and had to leave.[30] Amar demonstrates fundamental interconnections between the unmaking of Polish Lwów and the making of Soviet Ukrainian Lviv. Galician Ukrainians, natives of districts close to Lviv, made up most of the migration into Lviv in the 1940s and 1950s.[31] Local Party activists, mostly natives of pre-1939 Ukraine, identified local Ukrainians as perpetrators of political unreliability and deception, much like the Poles before them.[32] As they emptied the city of its Poles in 1944–47, local Party and state officials targeted the surviving local Ukrainian intelligentsia for reeducation. In rituals of public humiliation and self-abnegation, historians, writers, and scholars of the prewar Ukrainian intelligentsia were to renounce their "bourgeois" pasts and overcome their "backwardness." Local Party officials and activists repeatedly criticized such confessions as dissimulating, hypocritical, or insufficient, a central part of the ritual. Intelligentsia members of all ages were to attend lessons at the Evening University of Marxism-Leninism. Such rituals, which also affected university students, were about educating local Ukrainians.[33] These Ukrainians were to break with their pasts and adopt the values and behaviors of other Soviet Ukrainians.[34]

Armed resistance to Soviet rule influenced these purification campaigns. Such resistance had its origins in the German occupation and wartime violence between Poles and Ukrainians.[35] OUN leaders had counted on German support for an independent Ukrainian state. Cooperation between German and OUN leaders spanned both Weimar and Nazi periods. German aspirations to revise the Treaty of Versailles and its territorial arrangements and undermine Poland facilitated their cooperation.[36] With the German invasion, two rival factions of the OUN—OUN-M, headed by Andriy Melnyk, and OUN-B, headed by Stepan Bandera—helped the

Germans establish an occupation administration in Ukraine. Both factions assassinated and terrorized each other. The OUN-B's leadership was nearly decimated when Bandera and his ally, Iaroslav Stetsko, tried to set up an independent Ukrainian state in Lviv. Stetsko, Bandera, and other OUN-B members were immediately interned in the Saxenhausen concentration camp for the rest of the war. The Germans killed as many as four-fifths of the OUN-B's leadership in 1941 and 1942.[37] OUN-M leaders, despite being more cautious, later ran into conflict with them and also faced repression.

OUN-inspired guerrilla resistance to German occupation first broke out in Volhynia, where tensions between its Ukrainian majority and Polish minority had been building up since World War I's end. As German occupation alienated Volhynian Ukrainians, and as Soviet partisans started to make forays into the region, a guerrilla army, the Ukrainian Insurgent Army (UPA), emerged under the leadership of Taras Bulba-Borovets. This first version of the UPA under Bulba-Borovets refused to conduct guerrilla warfare against Poles, focusing on the Germans instead. Remnants of the OUN-B leadership—now made up of mostly young, inexperienced men who advocated conspiratorial organization and acts of terror—decided in the wake of the German defeat at Stalingrad to form their own army. OUN-B leaders Roman Shukhevych and Mykola Lebed raised this army to resist Germans and Soviets and cleanse all Poles from Ukraine. They crushed Bulba-Borovets's UPA and an OUN-M army and formed their own UPA, taking in guerrillas loyal to Bulba-Borovets and Melnyk.[38] In the spring of 1943, this enlarged and reconstituted UPA killed about 40,000–60,000 of Volhynia's 200,000 Poles. Their killings were bestial. UPA guerrillas displayed beheaded, disemboweled, or dismembered bodies to compel surviving Poles to flee. The violence spread to other parts of eastern Poland, including Eastern Galicia, even after the Red Army had "liberated" Western Ukraine.[39] Between 1941 and 1945, such nationalist groups had killed up to 20,000–25,000 of Eastern Galicia's Poles.[40]

Thus Ukrainian guerrilla resistance became all-out ethnic war against Poles. The UPA was separate from OUN-B, but Soviet sources conflated the two, making reference to the "OUN-UPA" in internal reports and treating the two synonymously in a book exposing the crimes of "Ukrainian bourgeois nationalism."[41] They emphasized guerrillas' connections with the OUN and thus German occupiers. UPA leaders' efforts to obtain weapons, equipment, and food from retreating Germans and last-minute attempts by the German government in January 1945 to set up a Ukrainian

National Committee consisting of Bandera and other freed OUN activists only further obscured distinctions between the UPA, the OUN, and German occupation.[42]

From 1944 to 1948, the UPA waged particularly fierce guerrilla warfare against the Soviet state and ordinary Poles. Jeffrey Burds has emphasized the strength of UPA resistance then. UPA guerrillas had prepared themselves and the local population for Soviet rule's return. During the war they had developed elaborate networks of rural hideouts, called *skhrony.* To combat sagging morale and enforce discipline, the UPA's Security Service (SB) intimidated defectors and spies with vigilante executions, even punishing victims' family members. SB informants infiltrated NKVD operations. The NKVD, followed by their successors, the Ministry of State Security (MGB) and the Ministry of Internal Affairs (MVD), tried to crush the UPA and its leadership with indiscriminate mass violence against the local population, but UPA leaders successfully found replacements and informants and turned to small clandestine operations. However, by the early 1950s, Soviet forces had crushed UPA resistance by ending mass retaliation, removing security agents who had abused their power, and waging class war through radical agrarian reforms. They had deported or "repatriated" hostile elements and staged show trials of guerrillas who had murdered local civilians. Soviet forces had offered guerrillas amnesties, recruited local peasants into militias known as destruction battalions, and developed an elaborate network of informants among natives. Terror by nationalist guerrillas against suspected guerrilla traitors and civilians, as well as growing perceptions that the guerrillas were doomed to defeat, had compelled natives of the western borderlands to side with the Soviets.[43]

The UPA's armed insurgency and the Soviet retaliation that followed exhausted Western Ukraine. Soviet retaliation was massive. From February 1944 to 25 May 1946, Soviet Party and state organs, along with MVD forces, killed a total of 110,825 "nationalist bandits" and arrested 250,676 people in Western Ukraine. UPA terror, though on a much smaller scale, was also significant. In the same period, such insurgent groups killed 11,725 people, injured 3,914 more, and presumably took 2,401 hostages. These victims were Soviet collaborators, officials, and officers.[44] However, most victims of guerrilla violence in Western Ukraine and other parts of the western borderlands were local civilians.[45] In the chaos that followed the German retreat, both the UPA and the Polish Home Army were hard to distinguish from a growing number of apolitical, marauding bands of criminals. Such bands attacked, robbed, and killed locals, rebels, and Soviets alike. Soviet propaganda organs exploited such similarities to undermine the UPA's reputation.[46] Such criminal connotations lingered long after organized resistance had ended. Henrykh Bandrovskyi, Lviv's former secretary of the City Committee of the Communist Party of Ukraine (gorkom), recalled that around 1965, police uncovered the decomposed, stabbed body of a man involved in the nationalist underground who had spent his last years on a nighttime killing spree. The man's life had ended literally underground, his body discovered in the Poltva River flowing underneath downtown Lviv.[47]

At the height of nationalist resistance, both UPA and Soviet security units terrorized the local population with executions and public vilification of victims' corpses (including lopping off their body parts, carving symbols into their bare flesh, and placing them in unflattering poses).[48] The UPA inflicted a disproportionate share of their terror upon local Ukrainians in order to get them to comply with the orders of the nationalist underground. Of 11,725 assassinations known to have been carried out by Ukrainian nationalists against Soviet agents between February 1944 and December 1946, over half (6,250) were local Ukrainians, a figure that increases to two thirds (6,980) when local recruits for the Soviet security forces' destruction battalions are included.[49] Such figures demonstrate that the UPA insurgency against Soviet rule had become a civil war between Western Ukrainians. This no doubt encouraged Galician Ukrainians to side with Soviet power. Perhaps this is why the parents of one historian, a native of Galicia, in the 1960s viewed Soviet power as a "lesser evil."[50]

This armed uprising, as well as mysterious assassinations and criminal activity in Lviv itself, contributed to local Party and state leaders' suspicions about local Ukrainians' political reliability.[51] Between 1949 and 1952, as Soviet leaders began collectivizing agriculture and finishing off guerrilla insurgencies across the western borderlands, Lviv's Party and state officials faced a major crisis rooting out locals' worldview and behavior. This crisis of Sovietization affected the city's institutions of higher education, where students and faculty faced purges and political mobilization campaigns. Instead of helping local Ukrainians overcome their backwardness, Soviet policies treated them as an immutable category different from Eastern Ukrainians. Despite making them compliant, these purges, intimidation campaigns, and political mobilization drives failed to change behaviors or worldviews. Soviet policies thus shifted, imposing a Soviet Western Ukrainian identity instead on local Ukrainians.[52]

Soviet policies contributed to the ethnic homogenization of not just Lviv but also other parts of the western borderlands. Soviet foreign policy indirectly brought about the end of ethnic German communities that had been prominent in the capital cities of Tallinn and Riga.[53] Population transfers of about 65,000 Germans from Latvia and Estonia to Germany had taken place in late 1939, a consequence of the Molotov-Ribbentrop Pact that placed Estonia and Latvia and later Lithuania under the Soviet sphere of influence.[54]

Soviet policy makers more directly affected Vilnius. Like Polish Lwów, it had been a predominantly Polish city known as Wilno before World War II. Rival nineteenth-century nationalist movements—Belarusian, Lithuanian, and Polish—claimed Wilno as their own. Wilno was home to a Zionist movement that flourished before Wilno's Jews perished in the Holocaust. In granting Wilno to Lithuania and removing its postwar Polish population, Soviet policies completed the ambitions of Lithuanian romantic nationalists. As Lithuania's postwar capital, Vilnius now had a population that was overwhelmingly Lithuanian, and like Ukrainian Lviv, it became an eternally Lithuanian city.[55]

This formation of a Soviet West came at great price to the natives of the western borderlands. Sovietization was not just about creating homogeneous ethnic communities. It was about compelling natives to identify with a multinational polity that accepted Great Russians as their "older brothers" and disavowed themselves of the cultural, political, and social environments that had shaped them. The scale of repression in the Baltic States was on a much lesser scale. Rough estimates of population losses for 1940–41—including those deported, mobilized for war, massacred, or disappeared under mysterious circumstances—amount to 60,000 for Estonia (4 percent of its prewar population), 35,000 for Latvia (1.5 percent of its prewar population), and 34,000 for Lithuania (2 percent of its prewar population). Still, the educated elites of the Baltic States, too, faced arrests and deportations. Some prison massacres also took place during the Soviet retreat of 1941.[56] Under German occupation, locals participated in the elimination of Baltic Jews. Like the OUN in Lviv, local nationalists became entangled in German politics of occupation, which greatly compromised them after the war.[57]

Somewhat in the Baltics, but much more so in Western Ukraine, the war produced a Hobbesian state of nature where nationalist guerrilla units, Soviet partisans and security organs, and ordinary criminal groups robbed, raped, tortured, killed, and vilified the corpses of ordinary civilians.[58] The indiscriminate violence was at its worst in Western Ukraine. A Soviet security forces report on Soviet pacification efforts in the western borderlands demonstrated this. In 1944 and 1945, Soviet security forces killed a total of 98,696 "nationalist bandits" in primarily Western Ukraine, while they killed only 290 such "bandits" in Estonia, 925 in Latvia, and 3,935 in Lithuania. Ukrainian nationalist guerrillas and "bandits" constituted over 90 percent of the 107,166 "bandits" killed on the western borderlands.[59]

Along with this violence, the local population suffered from deportations and exile to Siberia for alleged collaboration with "nationalist bandits." Western Ukrainians bore the brunt of such deportations. In the city of Lviv alone, a total of 287 families were deported the night of 20–21 October 1947, and in the Lviv Region a total of 5,231 families and 15,774 people met the same fate. A report by the secretary of the Regional Committee of the Communist Party of Ukraine (obkom) to superiors in Kyiv and Moscow noted the great resentment and fear these deportations provoked among Lviv's local Ukrainian intelligentsia.[60] From 1944 to 1952, a total of 203,662 people were deported from Western Ukraine, with most of these victims (182,543) connected with the nationalist underground. Considerably fewer from the Baltics faced such repression. A total of 172,362 such people from all three republics were in camps and special settlements as of 1 January 1953.[61]

As with Western Ukraine, Party and state leaders in Moscow and the Baltic republics turned these conflicts into a civil war. The Latvian Bureau (Latburo), directed by Moscow, helped shore up the Latvian Communist Party and Soviet rule from 1945 to 1947 by employing locally recruited destruction battalions in the fight against "nationalist bandits." Rather than leaving coordination and leadership over this struggle exclusively to Soviet security forces, whose leaders were Russian-speaking outsiders, the Latburo recruited district party secretaries, who were often Latvians.[62]

The effects of this civil war were long-lasting. The violence divided rural communities. Such divisions came to the surface when Soviet leaders after Stalin's death amnestied "nationalist bandits" and their supporters and allowed them to return to the western borderlands. Locals' integration into Soviet life did not relieve Soviet leaders of anxieties about the western borderlands. Crises like the workers' uprising in Poland in October 1956 and the Hungarian Uprising the next month fueled Soviet leaders' suspicions that the nationalist underground had gained new life. They curbed the influence of "bourgeois nationalists" by getting local communities involved in prosecuting and punishing former nationalist partisans, focusing on the class aspirations of workers and peasants, promoting more locals to power, and encouraging the emigration of remaining Poles and other national minorities.[63]

Fears about returned guerrillas' influence on locals, especially the young, lingered through the 1960s. A KGB report to the Ideological Department of the Central Committee of the CPSU, dated 8 May 1964, strongly suggested this. Analyzing nationalist manifestations across the Soviet Union, it linked the emergence of young nationalist underground groups in the Baltic republics and Ukraine to agitation conducted by returned national guerrillas and relatives with connections to the nationalist underground. It indicated that such former members of the nationalist underground had changed tactics, urging young people to join the Komsomol, the Party, and so on to undermine the Soviet Union from within. The report identified contacts with Roman Catholic priests and underground "Uniate" (Ukrainian Greek Catholic) clergy as sources of inspiration for these young nationalists, a clear reference to Lithuania and Western Ukraine, the respective Soviet heartlands of these churches. Prewar and wartime literature, as well as Western radio broadcasts, had become their sources of information.[64] Similar fears resurfaced again in 1968, when Prague Spring emboldened Ukrainians in Transcarpathia.[65] Nationalist guerrillas for a long time had used dissimulation and deception to influence the population. As early as the late 1940s, UPA activists were urging young people to join the Komsomol to acquire skills in organizing and influencing people.[66]

Lingering suspicions about returned "nationalist bandits" and their supporters underscored the locals' political significance. However, like other colonial enterprises, relations between Soviet policy makers and the incorporated natives, despite being asymmetrical, were not static.[67] Soviet policies allowed local national identities in the Baltic republics that differed from the rest of the Soviet polity. Estonian architects in the late Stalin period continued professional practices and projects from the independence period. They passed on their behaviors and values to younger generations.[68] Less traumatized by war and Sovietization than Western Ukrainians, the Baltic local not only survived, but greatly attracted outsiders. Russians and others in the Soviet Union came to identify the Baltic nations as "Soviet Europeans," examples of people's successful compromises with Soviet rule.[69] In Western Ukraine, Soviet policy makers accommodated locals by transforming Lviv's urban space and institutions.

Institutional Ukrainianization

Almost immediately after retaking Lviv, Kyiv and Moscow began this transformation. A republic Central Committee commission's report of 15 August 1944 devised ambitious plans for the "restoration of the Ukrainian character of the city of Lviv" after centuries of Polish domination. Besides recommending Poles' "voluntary" repatriation, this report envisioned monuments to heroes from Ukrainian history, establishing Ukrainian-language cultural and educational institutions, and robust use of the Ukrainian language in Party and state institutions. Streets with Polish names were to have their older names restored or receive new ones.[70] Unlike the nationalizing of nineteenth-century Central European cities, Party and state institutions led Lviv's Ukrainianization. Their vision of what it meant to be Ukrainian was premised on belonging to a multinational polity where Great Russians played a leading role. Their idea of being Ukrainian involved adhering to the practices and values of Soviet socialism. However, Party and state efforts to transform Lviv's urban space, public institutions, and population ultimately involved incorporating local nation-building practices.

While Lviv's buildings and infrastructure escaped the destruction seen in Kyiv, Stalingrad, or other wartime Soviet cities, its prewar population largely fled or perished. Lviv went from having 500,000 people in 1940, during the early days of Soviet occupation, to as low as 149,000 people or fewer in July 1944. The subsequent removal of Lviv's Poles, who had made up nearly 63 percent of the city's population at the end of 1944, reduced the prewar population even further.[71] Moscow and Kyiv revived Lviv by designating it a major industrial center in 1945. Over the postwar period, Lviv became a major center of producing motor vehicles, textiles, light bulbs, and radio and telegraph equipment. Lviv supplied the Soviet Union with television sets and buses, and factories like Elektron, Kineskop, and the Lviv Bus Factory became well known throughout the Soviet Union. Lviv contributed to Soviet defense industries, producing tanks, military electronics, and bombsights.[72] Ukrainians from surrounding towns and villages, Eastern Ukrainians, Russians, and other Soviet ethnic groups came to work in the city's new or revamped industries. By 1955, the city's population was on the way to recovering its prewar figures. In that year, the city's total population had reached 380,000.[73]

The removal of Poles in 1944–47 and subsequent employment and migration policies eventually caused ethnic Ukrainians to dominate Lviv, as seen in Table 2.1. As of October 1944, ethnic Ukrainians made up 26.4

Table 2.1 Ukrainians and Russians in Lviv, 1944–89

	Ukrainians (%)	Russians (%)	Others (%)
October 1944	26.4	5.5	68.1[a]
January 1951	42.8	30.8	26.4
January 1955	44.2	35.6	20.2
1959	60.16	27.06	12.78
1979	74.0	19.3	6.7
1989	79.13	16.07	4.8

Sources: Roman Lozynskyi, *Etnichnyi sklad naselennia L'vova (u konteksti suspil'noho rozvytku Halychyny)* (Lviv: Vydavnychyi Tsentr L'vivs'koho Natsional'noho Universytetu imeni Ivana Franka, 2005), 197; Viktor Susak, "Etnichni ta sotsial'ni zminy v naselenni L'vova v 1939–1999 rokakh" (MA thesis, Lviv National University, 2000), 21, 34–35; Roman Szporluk, "The Strange Politics of L'viv: An Essay in Search of an Explanation," in Zvi Gitelman, ed., *The Politics of Nationality and the Erosion of the USSR* (New York: St. Martin's Press, 1992), 222.

a. Includes Poles prior to forced repatriation.

percent and ethnic Russians 5.5 percent of Lviv's population. The number of ethnic Russians then grew rapidly, reaching 30.8 percent by January 1951, while ethnic Ukrainians increased significantly to 42.8 percent. At the beginning of 1955, a total of 44.2 percent of the city's population were Ukrainian by nationality, while 35.6 percent were Russian. In the Soviet Union's 1959 Census, ethnic Ukrainians for the first time achieved a solid majority in Lviv—60.16 percent—while Russians constituted 27.06 percent, Jews 6.29 percent, Poles 3.94 percent, and Belarusians 1.25 percent. Ukrainians' presence increased steadily thereafter. By the 1989 Census, Ukrainians numbered 76.13 percent of Lviv's population, while Russians were a mere 16.07 percent, Jews 1.63 percent, Poles 1.24 percent, and Belarusians 0.74 percent.[74]

As they organized museums, theaters, universities, and other institutions to give Lvivians a sense of belonging to a Ukrainian national community, Party and state leaders in opportunistic fashion drew from Galicia's past national movements, both Polish and Ukrainian. Already in 1939, they had renamed the city's Jan Casimir University (named for a prominent seventeenth-century Polish king) for Ivan Franko (Ivan Franko State University, also commonly known as Lviv State University), a famous Galician Ukrainian writer. Its language of instruction officially became Ukrainian. As early as 1939, republic government leaders created the Mykola Lysenko

State Conservatory, named for a classic nineteenth-century Ukrainian composer, out of the Polish Music Society's conservatory. This conservatory resumed its work after the war. A 1955 Regional Department of Culture report on the development of Lviv's theaters from 1944 to 1955 indicated a number of other Polish institutions replaced by Ukrainian ones. By 1955 the former Skarbek Theater housed the Mariia Zankovetska State Drama Theater from Kharkiv. The opera house, known in Polish times as the Civic Theater, became the State Academy Theater of Opera and Ballet and later also bore Ivan Franko's name.[75] Polish national activists had founded and financed the construction of the Skarbek Theater and the Civic Theater as part of their attempt to make the city more Polish in the nineteenth century.[76]

New Soviet institutions originated from ones Ukrainian national activists had already established. The Lviv Museum of Ukrainian Art owed its building, staff, and even leadership to the Ukrainian State National Museum, founded by Ukrainian Greek Catholic Metropolitan Andrei Sheptytskyi in 1908. The republic's Academy of Sciences in 1951 established an Institute of Social Sciences whose building, library, and personnel had once belonged to the Shevchenko Scientific Society, a research institute set up by Galician Ukrainians in Lviv in 1873 with the help of Ukrainians from the Russian Empire.[77]

Museums, theaters, and other such public institutions fundamentally connected Lvivians to a common culture linked with a wider world of nations. Lviv's postwar theaters acquainted audiences with not just works by Ukrainian composers and writers, but Russian and world classics in Ukrainian translation. Nearly all the city's theaters offered Ukrainian-language productions, as a 1975 city theater guide suggests. Press articles reveal that the Mariia Zankovetska State Drama Theater presented audiences not just plays inspired by nineteenth-century Ukrainian masters like Taras Shevchenko, turn-of-the-century Ukrainian masters like Lesia Ukrainka, early twentieth-century Ukrainian writers like Oleksandr Oles, or contemporary Lviv writers like Roman Ivanychuk, but some of the first Ukrainian-language performances of Shakespeare in Soviet Ukraine. The city's opera and ballet theater put on Russian classics like Tchaikovsky's *Queen of Spades* in Ukrainian, which greatly impressed one Western correspondent in the late 1960s.[78] In the late 1960s and early 1970s, the opera and ballet theater acquired notoriety throughout the Soviet Union not just for its dance and music but also for its highly original set designs.[79] For Mykola Riabchuk, a young writer in the 1970s, the Zankovetska Theater's Ukrainian-language productions of Shakespeare's *Richard III* were a welcome relief from state-censored performances elsewhere. Such censorship had grown considerably with the republic Party leadership's repressions against the Ukrainian intelligentsia.[80]

Ukrainian-language performances of world classics engaged Ukrainians with the wider world, an example of nationalist theorists' attempts at promoting freedom and self-realization through belonging to a national community.[81] Similarly, as memoir literature of musicians and scholarship on Lviv composers suggest, music performances by the city's philharmonic orchestra and conservatory ensembles gave Ukrainians a sense that their national composers belonged to the wider world's high culture. Such ensembles performed works by Lysenko, the father of Ukrainian classical music, as well as more recent works by Galician Ukrainian composers like Stanislav Liudkevych, Mykola Kolessa, Anatoliy Kos-Anatolskyi, and such postwar generation Lviv composers as Myroslav Skoryk. Such Galician Ukrainian composers belonged to the prewar intelligentsia or were from prewar intelligentsia families. As such, trends in romanticism and modernism, popular under Austrian and Polish rule, heavily influenced their works.[82] Such connections with Central Europe broke stereotypes that Ukrainian composers were provincial variants of Russian classics like Tchaikovsky or Glinka. Lviv thus functioned like world cities, introducing new residents to a wider universe than that of rural and small-town Western Ukraine.[83]

Lviv museums provided a sense of belonging to one Ukrainian national community that transcended time and space, joining Ukrainians formerly divided by Austrian and Russian empires. Creating such an "imagined community" involved creating and representing a historical narrative that excised or marginalized elements of Lviv's past deemed not Ukrainian.[84] The Lviv Historical Museum, which used to emphasize the city's connections to a Polish national narrative, began focusing on a Ukrainian one. Efforts to dismantle exhibits connected with "feudal" and "bourgeois" Poland began already at the end of 1939. Permanent changes followed the war's end.[85] The museum, located on the city's historic Market Square, emphasized what regional Party officials called the city's "eternal Ukrainian character" and "unbreakable link with the land of Ukraine." As its 1976 guide indicates, while the Lviv Historical Museum paid symbolic tribute to "progressive" Polish figures from Lviv's past, its exhibits focused on the history of Ukrainians as a whole and Western Ukraine's efforts to become part of one Ukrainian Soviet socialist state.[86]

Party and state policies ridded Lviv's urban space of Polish and Jewish attributes and connected it to a Ukrainian national narrative. As a city Party committee secretary put it in 1947, the city's remaining monuments to Polish and Austro-Hungarian figures reminded viewers of the "suffocating" of Ukrainians' national culture and national liberation movement. As with Wrocław and Kaliningrad, where wartime destruction greatly aided such erasures of the past, Lviv's Party and state functionaries, on approval from Kyiv and Moscow, destroyed monuments or abandoned them to neglect.[87] In 1947, city Party and state officials demolished the historic Jewish cemetery, over the protests of the city's Jewish community, to make way for today's Krakiv Bazaar.[88] In succeeding years, city Party and state functionaries transferred monuments to Polish national heroes like King Jan III ˙Sobieski and nineteenth-century playwright Aleksander Fredro to Polish cities (Gdansk and Wrocław, respectively, themselves only recently transformed from German to Polish cities).[89] Local officials allowed the memorial complex in Lychakiv Cemetery for Polish soldiers killed in the Polish-Ukrainian War of 1918–19 to lapse into ruin. In the mid-1970s, a Polish tourist visiting Lviv heard from another tourist that the gravestones were all gone, with only empty frames *(varstaty)* and pieces of metal left.[90]

Writers, scholars, and journalists, at the encouragement of state publishers, infused urban spaces with a Ukrainian national narrative. A 1962 city guidebook claimed that Lviv's dozens of former Roman Catholic churches and monasteries, converted to government buildings, had no architectural value and were designed to impose the worldview of "feudal Poland" on Lviv.[91] Lviv's central historic district, Market Square, became Ukrainianized. This district, with its Renaissance and Baroque architecture, calls to mind Lviv's role as a major trading and administrative center for the Polish-Lithuanian Commonwealth and the Habsburg Empire. One popular history of Lviv, published in 1969, referred to Lviv as the "Ukrainian Florence." It made these architectural styles Ukrainians' own, omitting reference to their German, Italian, and Polish origins.[92]

Such public narratives, however, conformed to postwar Soviet politics of empire. Lviv's Ukrainian historical figures stressed unity with the Great Russians. Rooms 8 and 9 of the Lviv Historical Museum highlighted joint efforts by Russians and Ukrainians, "brother" peoples, to overthrow Polish rule in the late seventeenth and early eighteenth centuries. Such themes related to popular resistance to Polish and Ukrainian Cossack feudal lords.[93] Local Party and state leaders removed materials from research and public libraries deemed "bourgeois nationalist," even if they were Soviet-era publications critiquing "Ukrainian bourgeois nationalism."[94] Local functionaries purged libraries to show superiors their devotion to combating "Ukrainian bourgeois nationalists." They did so to project a sense of authority in front of subordinates. Thus one former Lviv State University student recalled their new chancellor, appointed in 1981, removing all the library's pre-1939 publications from circulation for special review.[95]

Culling libraries and museums of "bourgeois nationalist" effects led to the destruction of valuable cultural artifacts. This happened in July 1952, right as Party and state officials in Lviv, Kyiv, and Moscow sought to rid locals of their backwardness connected with the bourgeois world. Regional Party committee personnel destroyed hundreds of paintings and dozens of sculptures from the Lviv State Museum of Ukrainian Art. The authors of these works had emigrated West during the war, had been arrested and killed as "enemies of the people" in Soviet Ukraine, or had been involved in Galicia's "bourgeois nationalist" movements. Obkom officials conducted the operation illegally, through documents forged later by the museum's assistant director, Vasyl Liubchyk, an ethnic Russian born in the Stavropol Region, educated in Kyiv, who came to Lviv after the war. This assistant director, who had stolen museum pieces for himself, later slipped out of a ten-year prison sentence because the obkom secretary present at these works' destruction had become the republic's Minister of Culture. Ironically, this Minister of Culture had been on the 1944 republic Central Committee commission outlining plans to make Lviv Ukrainian.[96]

As these cases suggest, Party and state leaders, like other premodern and modern urban planners, used urban space to project certain power relations.[97] For Moscow policy makers, Lviv was to project a Soviet concept of nationhood where Ukrainians and other non-Russians owed their freedom and self-realization to a multinational polity where the Great Russians played a leading role. The Hill of Glory, completed in 1952, conveyed this message. It was built on a prominent plateau overlooking Lviv's central axis. A grandiose memorial for Soviet soldiers killed in World War II, it included an obelisk honoring the memory of imperial Russian soldiers killed in the 1914–15 Galician campaign. Before World War II, it had been the site of a cemetery for Austrian and Russian war dead. Like the Jewish cemetery demolished for a bazaar, the graves of the Austrian dead were disposed of as waste. Their gravestones in 1998 were lying at the entrance to Lychakiv Cemetery, slated for restoration. The Hill of Glory, with its preeminent location and central role in annual Victory Day ceremonies by the Brezhnev era, legitimated Russians' dominance over other nationalities. As with other Soviet historical narratives after World War II, imperial Russian policies became viewed as a "lesser evil" in non-Russians' national histories than others' policies. In this case, imperial Russian efforts to conquer Galicia in World War I became a "lesser evil" for Ukrainians than imperial Austrian rule, notwithstanding the repressions that tsarist occupation authorities meted out to leaders of Galicia's Ukrainian national movement.[98] Given Soviet policy makers' lack of interest in promoting memories of World War I, a war that the Bolsheviks opposed, the Hill of Glory represented a very unusual manner of conveying this idea of the Great Russians being a "lesser evil."[99] Given its construction in 1952, during efforts to compel Galician Ukrainians to renounce their local "bourgeois nationalist" past, the Hill of Glory disregarded local sensitivities quite openly.

Like other Soviet cities that drew on models set by Moscow, the Soviet Union's metropole, Lviv acquired a park that closely resembled Moscow's Gorky Park. Erected in 1949–52, the Bohdan Khmelnytskyi Park of Culture and Recreation bore the name of a Ukrainian national hero, a seventeenth-century Cossack leader. Otherwise, it duplicated the format for city parks set by Moscow in the 1930s.[100]

Renaming Lviv's streets, local Party and state officials incorporated urban space into a Ukrainian space, but one largely connected with the Soviet Union and the wider Soviet bloc. Acting in approval with Kyiv and Moscow, they reduced the number of Polish streets to a minimum between 1944 and 1969 while they increased the number of streets with Ukrainian names to 20 percent. However, Lviv's new street names were for Ukrainian historical figures who allegedly advocated unity with Russians, such as Bohdan Khmelnytskyi, or those who contributed to Russian culture or had sympathies for socialism. The names of Ukrainians who had been hostile to Russian rule—such as Ivan Mazepa, an eighteenth-century Cossack leader who advocated Ukrainians' separation from the Russian Empire—disappeared. While Soviet leaders sought to promote local revolutionary heroes from Western Ukraine after Stalin's death, they avoided honoring streets or squares with the names of major figures from the KPZU, dissolved for alleged "nationalist" deviations in 1938 and rehabilitated in 1956. They instead named streets for low-level KPZU activists, workers who had suffered from Polish repressions, or fictitious wartime Soviet partisan organizations. A plurality of streets renamed between 1944 and 1969 were dedicated to figures from Soviet history (24 percent by 1969). A significant number (10 percent) of Lviv's streets received geographic place names, exclusively ones referring to the geography of the Soviet Union (including Soviet Ukraine) and Soviet bloc countries.[101]

Despite such standardization, Moscow's early postwar policies displayed flexibility toward the local architectural scene. Soviet leaders shelved plans to reorient the city along new axes, which would have destroyed much of Lviv's historic architecture. Lviv's Lenin monument, obligatory for any Soviet city, did not become a tall statue atop the High Castle overlooking the city. Instead, a bust of Lenin was unveiled in front of the city's opera and ballet theater. The possibility that the artist, Sergei Merkurov—Moscow's leading sculptor, known for his monumentalism—may have chosen a more modest monument because Lviv reminded him of his days at Munich's Academy of Fine Arts suggests Moscow was not entirely insensitive to the city's Central European architectural landscape.[102] By the 1970s, local Party and state officials championed Lviv's Central European architectural heritage and supported projects aimed at its preservation.[103] As Ukraine's Party leadership under Petro Shelest permitted greater forms of national self-expression, some tacit concessions to Lviv's "bourgeois nationalists" took place, sometimes in surprising forms. The cover of a 1969 popular history of Lviv featured the colors of blue and gold, colors of Ukrainians' "nationalist" flag made popular during wars for independence in 1917–20.[104] Policies by Moscow and Kyiv thus accommodated as well as transformed the local.

As a provincial Soviet city, Lviv was subordinate not just to Moscow, but to Kyiv. It thus became marginalized as a center of Ukrainian culture. With Kyiv taking the lion's share of resources for theaters, museums, and universities, Lviv's public institutions faced problems with inadequate financing and general neglect. Local Party reports, directors' appeals to local officials, remarks made at local Party conferences, and press articles in the 1950s and 1960s suggest a host of such problems facing Lviv theaters. Lviv theaters struggled with poor finances and poor working conditions. They often lost performers to such major Soviet cities as Leningrad and Kyiv.[105] This lack of resources slowed the erection of new monuments. Despite the republic Central Committee commission's 1944 recommendation to erect monuments to such national heroes as Ivan Franko, Bohdan Khmelnytskyi, and Ukrainian classic poet Taras Shevchenko, only one such monument was built in Soviet times, and only after twenty years: a monument to Ivan Franko in front of the Ivan Franko—Lviv State University in 1964.[106]

Funding aside, a monument to Shevchenko, regarded as the nineteenth-century father of the Ukrainian nation and a cult figure for Galician Ukrainians, was noticeably absent from Lviv.[107] There had been repeated public calls for such a monument after Stalin's death. Western Ukrainians, such as an anonymous writer to the regional Party newspaper, urged that such a monument be built. The newspaper editor, speaking before obkom members discussing Beria's report on Western Ukraine in 1953, suggested that such an act would help resolve problems the report had noted, namely, the neglect of local Ukrainians by local Party and state officials. With the Thaw allowing more forms of national self-expression, Lviv's regional and city officials made plans for a competition to design a Shevchenko monument. However, nothing came of them. Downtown Lviv, unlike Kyiv or Kharkiv, remained without a Shevchenko monument until after Ukraine's independence.[108] The biographer of Lviv sculptor Dmytro Krvavych, who was active in Artists' Union circles, suggests that local officials held up the project for political reasons. In the 1970s, gorkom and obkom officials allegedly swore that no such monument to Shevchenko would be erected in Lviv while they were in charge.[109]

The history of Shevchenko's nonappearance was not necessarily an attempt by Moscow at Russifying Lviv. More likely, local and republic officials were conveying a message to Lviv's Ukrainian intelligentsia. By the 1970s, the republic's Central Committee secretary for ideology, Valentyn Malanchuk, was conducting an ideological campaign against Ukraine's intelligentsia. Lviv's Party and state officials, seeking to prove their political vigilance, found signs of "bourgeois nationalism" everywhere. On Lviv's Market Square, even the statue of Neptune, undisturbed for decades, had to be altered because the trident in his hand now resembled the symbol of the Ukrainian "bourgeois nationalist" trident.[110] Under no such circumstances could a Shevchenko monument appear in downtown Lviv.

The appearance of the Russian language in public life reflected similar concerns about political power. Local officials' neglect of the Ukrainian language had long been a problem for not just local Ukrainians, but for leaders in Moscow. In 1950, the Central Committee in Moscow took to task Party organizations in Western Ukraine for not making greater use of the Ukrainian language in public life.[111] Real changes with Russian's status arrived during the Thaw. When historian Roman Szporluk was a graduate student in Lublin, Poland, he visited Lviv twice in 1956, in July and August and then in November. He recalled Russian-language signs disappearing from Lviv's streets and public buildings.[112] This Ukrainianization of Lviv's streets had long-lasting effects. It was only with the close of the Thaw that city and regional Party officials allowed Russian signs to reappear. A Polish tourist from the West noticed Russian-language political banners all over the city in 1968.[113] When Glasnost arrived, Russification of the public sphere had made enough progress to inspire public protest. In 1988, a Lviv resident wrote an article for a leading republic newspaper expressing his outrage at encountering the Russian language everywhere in Lviv, on maps, on signs for streets and government buildings, in advertisements, and in government paperwork.[114]

While Party and Komsomol documents from 1953 to 1984 suggest use of both Russian and Ukrainian languages by local officials, it seems that who was in charge determined what language was spoken at Party and government functions. This can be seen with records of city Komsomol meetings. While they were mostly conducted in Ukrainian in 1971, when V. O. Kondratiuk was city Komsomol first secretary, they were mostly in Russian in 1982–83, when N. N. Makarenko was its first secretary.[115] Such a shift in language use was especially encouraged when Shcherbytskyi was republic Party chief from 1972 to 1989, affecting Party and state meetings across the republic. It was this factor that most likely encouraged the Russian language to reappear and become firmly entrenched in Lviv's public sphere. Local Party and state functionaries, eager to please their bosses in Kyiv, did all they could to get the language right. A story told about one former obkom secretary, Volodymyr Chuhaiov, illustrates this trend. When attending a republic Academy of Sciences meeting in Kyiv in the late 1970s as an institute director, Chuhaiov brought two versions of his speech, one in Russian and one in Ukrainian, and he asked which version was needed.[116]

Chuhaiov's efforts to please his superiors indicate that the Russian language was an important vehicle for asserting political power. Depending on the institution, native Galician Ukrainians thus spoke Russian. According to one Lviv journalist, the head of the Lviv Farm Implements Factory (*L'vivsil'mash*), a native of Galicia, spoke Russian in public functions, despite doing it badly.[117] Historian Iaroslav Isaievych, a former Galician villager who came to Lviv to study at Lviv State University in 1951 and remained there as a historian, recalled that when he lectured for the local

Society for the Preservation of Monuments in the 1970s, he spoke in Ukrainian, but people in administrative positions—including children of the local Ukrainian intelligentsia, whose parents had studied in Ukrainian gymnasia during German occupation, who had relatives abroad, who spoke Ukrainian at home—spoke Russian at work. On the other hand, years earlier, when he worked for extra money as a second-year university student in the early 1950s translating English-language technical manuals, the people in the chemistry lab, run by a local Ukrainian, spoke entirely in Ukrainian.[118] The hotel clerk was right to say that Lviv was and would always be Ukrainian. However, that sense of being Ukrainian carried a certain political orientation not open to public questioning until the Gorbachev era.

Lviv's postwar transformation resembled processes in the Baltic republics. Vilnius lost its Polish-majority population to deportations and its Jews to the Holocaust. Its new inhabitants were overwhelmingly Lithuanian. Its streets retained names given by leaders of independent Lithuania in 1940, but Soviet and Russian names had appeared by the mid-1950s. Like Lviv, Vilnius did not witness significant transformation of its downtown architectural scenes despite plans to do so.[119] Local planners considered razing Riga's city center, Old Riga (Vecrīga), damaged in the war, because of its German heritage. While Moscow architects intervened in 1954, some of its historic buildings were torn down. Moscow's subsequent efforts to restore Riga's architectural monuments discredited the medieval German cultural heritage and emphasized Latvians' friendship with the Great Russians.[120] Old Riga took on Latvian, not German, features in literary representations, such as in the poem by Vizma Belševica, "A Motif of Latvian History: Old Riga." The poem, written between the late 1960s and early 1970s, compared the silent resoluteness of Old Riga's stone sculptures and buildings to the howling winds of history, including past occupations of the city. The eternal Old Riga in this poem was Latvian, not German.[121]

However, Lviv's postwar transformation radically differed from that of Baltic counterparts. While they created Lviv out of a mostly Polish Lwów, Soviet leaders co-opted past state building efforts to convey legitimacy in the Baltics. In Riga, independence-era monuments like the Freedom Monument (1935) and the Brethren Cemetery (1936) survived demolition. Riga's postwar-era guidebooks, like one for 1982, emphasized these monuments' connections to class themes or universal themes about war. They left out their ties to independent Latvia's "bourgeois nationalist" leaders.[122]

While such elements of continuity included the survival of national elites, Baltic capitals like Riga and Tallinn faced more serious threats of Russification. Lviv was the least ethnically Russian city in the European part of the Soviet Union, with ethnic Ukrainians making up over 60 percent of the population by 1959 and 74 percent by 1979. By contrast, in Tallinn, the share of Estonians declined during those years. A total of 60.2 percent of the city's population was ethnic Estonian in 1959, but by 1979, that figure had declined to 51.3 percent. In Riga, the share of Latvians declined from 44.7 percent in 1959 to 40.9 percent in 1970, while Russians in 1970 formed a larger share of the population (42.7 percent) and the remaining population consisted primarily of Russian rather than Latvian speakers. The population of Vilnius increasingly became Lithuanian in composition, but the concentration of ethnic Lithuanians never reached that of Ukrainians in Lviv. The Lithuanian share of Vilnius's population was only 33.6 percent in 1959. While it climbed to 42.8 percent in 1970 and 47.3 percent in 1980, it was not anything like the 74 percent of Ukrainians in Lviv in 1979.[123] As a result, issues of national identity and ethnicity—especially in Riga and Tallinn, affected by strong waves of Russian-speaking immigration in the 1950s and 1960s—became perhaps even more charged than in Lviv, though such Russian-speaking immigrants moved to other republics rather than staying.[124] Common ethnicity, however, did not guarantee harmony between the new Lvivians. They were divided not just by ethnicity, but by region and social class, and such differences complicated relations with the new Soviet order.

CHAPTER 3

The New Lvivians

Lviv entered the postwar era virtually unscathed by bombing or artillery, but echoes of the wartime slaughterhouse were everywhere. An ethnic Russian Ukrainian who came with his family to Lviv in May 1945 recalled that their apartment building on Theater Street, in the heart of Lviv, composed of around 100 apartments, was about 70 percent empty. Its apartments had been abandoned by residents who had fled or been killed during the war. Lviv was dangerous, not just because of the rising crime in the city, but also because of violence perpetrated by the Ukrainian nationalist underground. Among his childhood memories of Theater Street, this respondent remembered machine-gunfire erupting one night, sending one small bullet through their apartment window. Among the victims of the night shooting were Red Army officers, killed at the corner of Theater Street and Trade Square.[1]

Lvivians who grew up after the war, children of Soviet Army personnel, recalled stories about their parents being attacked by armed nationalists on the street.[2] Still others heard the strangest rumors afloat. An ethnic Russian woman from Siberia, who came to Lviv with her husband in 1944, recalled that she and other young women working for the railroad administration were warned not to take apartments vacated during the war because they might be mined with explosives.[3]

These stories came from people whose families had been moved to Lviv to establish the new Soviet order. As such, they were easy targets for nationalist guerrillas and ordinary criminals who assaulted, murdered, and robbed unsuspecting people. There were other stories of postwar Lviv, told by the city's few remaining prewar residents. They remembered the deportations of suspected Ukrainian "bourgeois nationalists" and their family members. One such Lvivian, the daughter of a simple Ukrainian locksmith, welled up with tears as she recalled scenes of deportees passing down the street in open trucks, catching bread thrown by sympathizing passersby. "And that could have happened to us," she said in a trembling voice. This woman described her family as hardly enthusiastic for the new Soviet order. She mentioned her father's bewilderment about the Cuban Revolution, asking how was it possible that the Americans would be stupid enough to allow the "commies" *(komuny)* to take power right next door instead of trying to liberate people from Communism. Despite her memories of Soviet deportations and her father's private hostility to Communism, this woman, born in 1944, learned to take on other Soviet citizens' external behavior. She worked at a summer Pioneer camp for the regional military base, a camp heavily populated by ethnic Russians, and told them stories about Nikolai Kuznetsov, a Soviet partisan killed by Ukrainian nationalists in the Lviv Region toward the war's end. Asked how she could tell young Pioneers about Kuznetsov, she said that she just treated it as a job. She also mentioned in passing that at the time, she did not know the true story behind Kuznetsov, namely, his involvement in killing Ukrainian nationalists.[4]

Such residents, old and new, complicated Lviv's transformation into a Soviet Ukrainian city. Local Ukrainians, including those arriving from villages in Western Ukraine, had been eyewitnesses to Stalin-era repressions of nationalist guerrillas and their supporters. They had relatives or friends who had taken part in guerrilla resistance to Soviet rule. As for ethnic Russians and Russian speakers who arrived from other parts of the Soviet Union, they took for granted the idea that the Soviet Union offered the best way of life in the world and that the Soviet Union was fighting forces of reaction like bourgeois nationalism. On the other hand, such political issues mattered little in people's daily lives. The sister of the Lviv National University Archives director said that their family included an Austrian who came to Lviv in Habsburg times and a Russian who had come to Lviv with the Red Army during the war. When asked if there had been tensions between locals and non-locals in Lviv, she said that for "normal" people none really existed.[5] While the archivist's sister's family story would suggest to some that fellow "occupiers" of Lviv—Germans and Russians— "naturally" got along well with each other, Lviv's postwar history had countless examples where nationality did not matter, though it did become a useful category in addressing personal grievances with the state and with other people.

The new Lvivians, as strangers to this city, came to cooperate with one another and influence one another's values and behavior. At the same time, local Ukrainians perceived that outsiders, particularly ethnic Russians and Russian-speaking Ukrainians, had more privileges. Some of these outsiders, though far from all, speculated on locals' political reliability, contributing to assumptions that local Ukrainians were "Banderites," that is, fellow thinkers of the OUN-B organization under Stepan Bandera that inspired postwar guerrilla resistance to Soviet rule. Like others on the western borderlands, Galician Ukrainians became integrated into one multinational state, but never completely. Unlike the Baltic nationalities, Galician Ukrainians had difficulties identifying with fellow nationals from the republic's other regions. They were almost like a different ethnic or national group. This was because of the persistence of a local sense of being Ukrainian inherited from Austrian and Polish times, as well as Soviet policies that fostered a separate Soviet Western Ukrainian identity.

Ethnic Russians and Other Soviets

The new Lvivians were divided not just by ethnicity, but by language, culture, and region. Russian Lvivian Aleksandra Matyukhina studied daily life in Lviv, mostly fellow ethnic Russians and Russian speakers who remained after 1991. She identifies three major groups that arrived in the city: ethnic Russians and Russian speakers from other Soviet republics, Ukrainians from pre-1939 Ukraine (Eastern Ukrainians), and Ukrainians who arrived from villages in postwar Western Ukraine (Western Ukrainians). These new groups overwhelmed the few prewar Lvivians—Poles, Ukrainians, and others—who remained.[6]

Ethnic Russians and Russian speakers from other republics tended to be skilled workers, managers, and Party and state administrators. It is difficult to classify such people as willing colonizers. The Soviet state assigned them to work in Lviv, and they could be prosecuted under the law for refusing to take their new jobs. Nonetheless, these new Lvivians tended to be highly mobile as Party and state functionaries, which enabled them to transfer their positions easily. Significant numbers of Russians, drawn to family ties, better working conditions, and more attractive lifestyles in such cities as

Moscow, migrated back to Soviet Russia when given the chance, contributing to ethnic Russians' decline in Lviv's postwar population. While not being willing colonizers, this group identified very strongly with the Soviet state. At least for Matyukhina, these people assumed that the Great Russians' language and culture were more progressive than others in the Soviet family of nations. While open to new cultural trends from the capitalist West, they seldom interacted with other groups, especially Western Ukrainians and native Lvivians.[7] This most likely caused me difficulty finding willing interview respondents years later.

Lviv's urban spaces and state institutions contributed to this isolation. Families of Soviet Army and NKVD personnel lived in the general neighborhood of Konotopskyi Street and Pushkin Street (today's General Chuprynka Street). This street housed a major NKVD soldiers' base and other facilities connected with defense and law enforcement. Like its wartime ethnic German community, it became an exclusive neighborhood for those who most embodied the new political order. Two residents of this neighborhood—family members of NKVD personnel and regular soldiers—recalled that few Ukrainians lived there in Soviet times and that residents almost entirely spoke to one another in Russian. One of them, the son of an NKVD employee, said that he grew up exclusively among Russians and Russian speakers. He got to know Ukrainian-speaking Ukrainians only when he went to work in an airplane repair shop in 1962. Space itself—the distribution of postwar living space—affected the development of relations between groups in Lviv.[8]

The city's military base, the Subcarpathian Military District (PryKVO), fostered a separate Russian-speaking community. One of Soviet Ukraine's key military installations on the western frontier, PryKVO had its own Russian-language newspaper, *Glory to the Motherland (Slava Rodiny)*, established in 1941. By 1953, its personnel had organized Lviv's only exclusively Russian-language theater, the Lviv Russian Drama Theater of the Soviet Army. Its Russian-language productions lasted until the collapse of the Soviet Union. PryKVO personnel had their own neighborhoods, where Russian-language children played among themselves. On Engels Street, a set of square apartment buildings built in the 1960s, nicknamed "the incubator," became a neighborhood where children of military staff played and socialized, creating their own "Russian speaking zone," as one of its former residents recalled.[9]

This group of Russians and Russian speakers escaped facile generalizations. They were often the victims of Soviet power rather than its advocates.

Soviet Jews who came to Lviv from other regions of Ukraine and other republics became victims of growing postwar anti-Semitism. For instance, Simon Lure, a professor at Lviv State University's Department of Classical Philology, had been a victim of the anti-cosmopolitanism campaign associated with the Zhdanov era. He had to leave Leningrad, winding up in Lviv by 1953.[10] Oral interviews with Lviv's "locals" (that is, Ukrainian natives of Western Ukraine) suggested ambiguous relations with Jews. Almost all narratives in referring to someone as a "Jew" did so in a negative context. On the other hand, someone speaking off the record noted that Lviv's Soviet Jewish community had become an integral part of the city's cultural life. This person said that after Jews emigrated en masse, a great number of seats at classical music concerts were empty. The loss of Lviv's Jews meant the decline of the local concert scene. By the early 1970s, festering anti-Semitism, as well as a desire to escape declining economic conditions, compelled Lviv's Jews to leave for Israel, as seen in Komsomol cases from 1972 and 1973 expelling university students for preparing to emigrate or planning to do so.[11]

Others who were victims of Stalin-era terror had come to Lviv right after the war, presumably for reasons like Lure's. An ethnic Pole from Belarus, Stanislav Hofman of Lviv State University's Law Faculty, had been such a victim. As post-Stalin-era Party hearings indicate, Hofman had been briefly arrested on 14 July 1938 for allegedly belonging to a "Polish Military Organization." He had received a Party sanction in 1939 for not being vigilant about one "enemy of the people revealed."[12] As the Party cracked down on incidents of "anti-Soviet" behavior in the wake of unrest in Poland and Hungary in late 1956, Hofman became one of those singled out for criticism. He was mentioned in a 5 January 1957 report by the obkom secretary to his counterpart in Kyiv. Hofman supposedly had made "anti-Soviet" remarks at a meeting of the Law Faculty's Academic Council by demanding that the portrait of Andrei Vyshinsky, the director of Stalin's show trials of the late 1930s, be removed "in the name of Leninism." He said that there was no real Prosecutor's Office in the Soviet Union after 1929 because such people as Vyshinsky failed to uphold Leninist principles of the law.[13]

While Russian speakers from other republics were much more cautious in what they said, they nonetheless shared fates like Hofman's. An anonymous respondent to a questionnaire circulated at Lviv's Russian Cultural Center, born in 1917 in Volgograd, said that his parents, Don Cossacks, were loyal to Soviet power, "despite the fact that Dad was arrested three times." Another such respondent to this questionnaire, born in 1919 in Bashkiriia, said that her parents were "completely loyal" to the Soviet system and regime, though their entire family had been exiled to Kazakhstan in 1933.[14] Liubov Mesniankina, born to an ethnic Russian father and a Galician Ukrainian mother after the war, recalled her father talking about how his family was repressed as kulaks in Soviet Russia.[15]

Despite living in almost exclusively Russian-speaking neighborhoods, ethnic Russians and Russian speakers interacted with Ukrainian speakers and spoke their language. Daily encounters on the street, as well as work situations, encouraged this trend. Historian Iaroslav Isaievych, who moved to Lviv to begin studies at Lviv State University in 1951, recalled that city markets were one notable area where Lviv's Russian speakers conversed in Ukrainian. They did so to buy goods from local villagers selling food.[16] The anonymous female respondent from Bashkiriia worked in one of Lviv's hospitals after arriving with her family in 1949. While she spoke with hospital colleagues mostly in Russian, she spoke to local Ukrainian patients only in Ukrainian.[17] One local Ukrainian writer, Petro Kozlaniuk, at an obkom meeting of 12 June 1953, during discussion of Beria's report about discrimination against Western Ukrainians, mentioned in passing that he knew many Russians who came to Lviv, learned Ukrainian well, and even made public speeches in Ukrainian.[18]

Sometimes these Russian speakers formed connections with other Ukrainians and came to identify with the region in which they lived. The anonymous female respondent from Bashkiriia said she and her family befriended Lviv Ukrainian writer Anatoliy Dimarov. The Carpathian Mountains of Western Ukraine became one of their most favorite vacation spots.[19] Valeriy Sultanov, born in 1958, of ethnic Tatar and Russian descent, said that he learned to speak Ukrainian when he started working at the Lviv Ceramics Factory after finishing school. At this factory, where many employees were former Western Ukrainian villagers, he not only learned to speak Ukrainian but also learned more about Soviet rule in Western Ukraine, more than what school textbooks had to say.[20] Matyukhina underscores the impact personal contact with Western Ukrainians had on the customs and behavior of Eastern Ukrainians, Russians, and others, and vice versa.[21]

Speaking Russian in public or sending children to Russian-language schools did not necessarily mean support for Russifying Lviv. One journalist, an ethnic Belarusian and a child of Russian speakers who came to Lviv after the war, said that he anchored a local television news program in

Lviv in Russian not because of ideological convictions. He explained that he spoke in Russian on this program, a live program which he aired until 1989, because he used to get very nervous performing live, and he feared stumbling in Ukrainian. In daily life, he spoke with local Ukrainians in Ukrainian. Around 1965 or 1966, when he and his wife took in local Ukrainian boarders, he spoke to them exclusively in Ukrainian, which surprised the latter, who knew that he and his wife were Russian speakers. While he and his wife sent their son to a Russian-language middle school, they did so not because they did not want him to study in a Ukrainian-language middle school, but because the Russian-language school was nearest to their home.[22]

On the other hand, numerous accounts suggest that ethnic Russians, or at least Russian speakers, had contempt for learning Ukrainian in school. This Lviv journalist, born in 1940, mentioned that there were students in his Russian-language school who regarded studying Ukrainian as "useless" (*nepotribno*).[23] Lvivians born after the war told similar stories. One Lvivian Jew born in 1952, "Vitaliy," recalled not only senior classmates in his Russian-language school scorning their Ukrainian classes but also ditties Russian speakers sang or spoke that made fun of the Ukrainian language. One such ditty, a mixture of Polish and Ukrainian expressions, suggests that Ukrainian was just a mix of mangled Polish phrases: "*V Bziuchovycach my sia zdybaly z tobov, i [v nashim sertsi si] zashportala liubov*" (I met you in Briukhovychi [a suburb of Lviv], and we fell in love).[24] Other Lvivians, Grigorii Komskii (born in 1950) and "Alex" (an Israeli e-mail respondent to my questionnaire on Russians and Russian speakers, born in 1972), had similar classmates. Komskii attributed this to parents' influence, while Alex stressed that his school's ethnic Russians were the ones most often trying to get exemptions from Ukrainian classes.[25]

Such stories confirm Matyukhina's view that ethnic Russians regarded their language and culture as superior to those of Ukrainians. However, we need to treat them with caution. The ditty told by Vitaliy may not have been directed at Ukrainians, as he had claimed in his interview.[26] Mykola Riabchuk suggests that educated Ukrainians in Lviv made up expressions with Polish words in them as a way of making fun of daily life and the public sphere. Playing around with such foreign words made them look stylish or clever. Russian speakers may have done the same.[27] This ditty may have been directed at local Galicians, but not necessarily at Ukrainians. As for these and other stories about schoolchildren trying to get out of Ukrainian classes, such classmates may not have wanted to take them because they were boring. An account by another postwar Lvivian (born in 1957, the daughter of Galician Ukrainians) suggests that at least some people perceived Ukrainian classes to be less well taught in their schools than Russian courses.[28] School administrators of Russian-language schools possibly treated Ukrainian lessons as an extra burden, as Vitaliy hinted in his interview.[29] Nonetheless, contemptuous remarks about Ukrainian classes and ditties playing with Ukrainian may well have offended local Ukrainians.

Russian speakers as a rule did not completely assimilate to Ukrainian language and culture. One respondent, born in 1962 in Brody and who moved to Lviv with his parents at the age of six, said his mother was a "Ukrainian-speaking Russian" who taught Ukrainian in local schools. He described her as the exception, not the rule.[30] However, Russians and Russian speakers at least communicated with others in Ukrainian and were influenced by local Ukrainians. Russians and Russian speakers were acquiring facility in Ukrainian and using it in daily life, not just thanks to inhabiting Lviv's urban space but also thanks to the role of cultural and educational institutions. Despite Vitaliy's classmates' laments, they did their Ukrainian lessons.

Ethnic Russians, Jews, and other Russian-speaking nationalities thus failed to be model colonizers. They failed despite the fact that they had been sent to Western Ukraine as part of Moscow and Kyiv's strategy to combat bourgeois nationalism and bourgeois influences in this allegedly "backward" western borderland.[31] These people had complicated relations with the Party-state. They did not entirely look down on Ukrainians' language and culture. Nonetheless, they also played successful roles as colonizers. They were obedient. They knew what the Soviet state could do to those who were not. Even Professor Hofman expressed his contempt for Andrei Vyshinsky seemingly at the right time, when Khrushchev's Thaw emphasized the need to restore Leninist principles to Soviet law.

Eastern Ukrainians and Western Ukrainians

The Eastern Ukrainians were somewhat like ethnic Russians and other Russian speakers. Having grown up in Soviet Ukrainian cities in the 1930s, they either considered Russian their native language or accustomed themselves to speaking Russian with strangers. The father of one of the young in the "Russian-speaking zone" on Engels Street was a native of Central

Ukraine, from the Cherkassy Region.[32] However, Eastern Ukrainians, as beneficiaries of Soviet interwar indigenization policies favoring Ukrainians' language and culture, took part in encouraging the public use of the Ukrainian language in Lviv. They helped local Ukrainians appreciate their own national history and culture, thus aiding in the city's transformation into a Ukrainian one. Ievhen Lazarenko, an ethnic Ukrainian born in Voronezh, Russia, and educated in Kharkiv, Ukraine, originally spoke in Russian when he first worked as chancellor of Lviv State University in 1951. According to a student who attended the university during Khrushchev's Thaw, Lazarenko came to speak Ukrainian fluently. During the Thaw, he actively promoted Ukrainians' language and culture at the university.[33]

Another Eastern Ukrainian, Stepan Markovych Polovyi, came to Lviv after the war to teach schoolchildren geography and psychology. As one of his pupils at School Number 36 recalled, he taught them proper literary Ukrainian, was very well educated, and tried to persuade them that all Ukrainians were part of one nation. Polovyi suffered persecution in the Stalin era. He was arrested in 1952 for allegedly cooperating with the Germans during wartime occupation, and he was released shortly after Stalin's death.[34] Such Eastern Ukrainians thus embodied the problematic relations between state and society in the Stalin era. As teachers and as ordinary residents, they represented those forces that helped turn Lviv into a community united by a common language and culture.

While Eastern Ukrainians like Lazarenko and Polovyi showed great sympathy for Western Ukrainians, relations between Eastern and Western Ukrainians were far from simple, especially in the early postwar years. At an obkom plenary session of 12 June 1953 addressing Beria's report on the Party's discrimination against Western Ukrainians, local writer Petro Kozlaniuk, while praising Russian officials who learned Ukrainian, complained of Eastern Ukrainian ones (whom he derisively called "Little Russians" for their lack of pride in being Ukrainian) who regarded Ukrainian as inferior to Russian, appropriate only for peasants.[35] Two former students of the Lviv State Pedagogical Institute, who studied Ukrainian philology together in the late 1940s and early 1950s, recalled being very careful about what they said among Easterners out of fear of being denounced for "Ukrainian bourgeois nationalism."[36] Differences lingered among later generations of students. One former history student, recalling dormitory visits to classmates in the late 1960s, said that she enjoyed such visits. Mostly former Western Ukrainian villagers, these classmates sang Ukrainian songs, spoke Ukrainian, and told them more about Ukraine's past. There were no confrontations, but there was a certain "distancing" *(dystantsiia)* between the two, where, Nataliia Chernysh supposed, Western Ukrainians pitied their "Eastern" counterparts for being Russified and not knowing Ukraine's true history.[37]

Western Ukrainians differed from Eastern Ukrainians because of conflicts with Poles and political, cultural, and social trends originating with Austrian rule. Nonetheless, they, too, were strangers to Lviv. Halyna Bodnar, who spoke with eighty-one former Ukrainian villagers who migrated to Lviv from the 1950s to the 1980s (sixty-one of them born in 1945 or later), highlights these Ukrainians' complicated relationship with Lviv. Lviv attracted young Western Ukrainians because it offered them an escape from oppressive collective farms and promised jobs in new factories, higher education, or a trade learned through vocational schools. They faced tremendous difficulties getting adequate housing. The city's twisting streets, noise, and other urban features were alienating. These new Lvivians faced awkward social situations because of speaking village dialects, wearing old-fashioned clothes, and having problems learning Russian. They considered their stay temporary. They still saw themselves not really as Lvivians, but as former villagers first, or as neither Lvivians nor villagers.[38] These accounts suggest such migrations did not produce a sense of solidarity among Ukrainian speakers or identification with Lviv as a Ukrainian city. Nonetheless, their numbers became something that intellectuals and Party and state functionaries could reckon with as they appealed to national myths and symbols.

Lvivians as Europeans: The Prewar Ukrainian Intelligentsia and the Remaining Poles

Considering the impact of the Holocaust, the expulsion of Poles, and the flight of educated Galician Ukrainians westward, Lviv's prewar population was a meager percentage of the city's new population. The new Lvivians thus faced greater discontinuity than their Baltic urban counterparts. Nonetheless, Galician Ukrainians and Poles did not stand aloof from other Lvivians as Matyukhina suggests. These Lvivians became an important part of the city's "European" image. They formed a bridge to the cultural capital of interwar Galicia. As such, they helped foster a particular sense of being Soviet in Lviv, one more connected with Central Europe and the West than with Moscow or Leningrad.

Not only were Lviv's remaining Poles a minuscule portion of the population, but they were also significantly less educated than the prewar Polish community. For Ukraine as a whole, a mere 1.4 percent of all Poles had a higher education in 1959. Four fifths were manual laborers in 1970. In the Lviv Region in 1979, less than 40 percent (395 per 1,000 inhabitants) of its Polish inhabitants had completed a middle school education.[39] Only isolated cases of the Polish intelligentsia remained, such as Professor Adam Kuryllo, who taught construction engineering at the Polytechnic Institute and remained in his prewar residence until his death in 1980.[40]

Nonetheless, even Lviv's less educated Poles became ingrained in other Lvivians' imagination as part of its "European" past. Lviv's cleaning women and nannies included Polish servants left behind by Poles who fled westward. These single women dedicated themselves to taking care of their old employers' homes. They had no prospects of families of their own. An ethnic Russian born after the war spent his childhood at his grandparents' home on Dzerzhinsky Street (today's Stepan Bandera Street), where such women worked. For him, these Polish janitors were keepers of "a museum of European material civilization from the twenties and thirties." They were far more attentive to cleanliness than new Lvivians who succeeded them over the years.[41] Others told of Lviv being a much cleaner city in the 1970s thanks to such elderly Polish women. After a taped interview with her husband, Kosmo-Demian Vozniak, his wife and her friend, an ethnic Russian, talked with great nostalgia about these prewar Poles who cleaned the streets, putting garbage in small street-side containers.[42]

These stories by younger Lvivians may be somewhat romanticized, contrasting the dirtiness of post-Soviet times with their more stable, orderly youth. They still convey the good relations that developed between local Poles and the new Lvivians. Poles too poor or too elderly to leave became like family to new residents who had to share apartments with them. The widow of a Polish railroad worker who lived on today's Turgenev Street was one such Pole. She shared her apartment with a nurse from Russia and her infant daughter. The widow came to take care of the daughter like a grandmother. The daughter's first language wound up being Polish, not Russian.[43]

Lviv's few remaining educated Poles still contributed to the new city's cultural life. This could be seen with the city's Polish People's Theater. Petro Hausfater, a former violinist and concert master before becoming a middle school Polish teacher, founded it in 1958. It began as a drama group affiliated with the Lviv Teachers' Building before becoming an official amateur theater in 1962. By the end of the 1960s, another local Pole, Zbigniev Khshanovskyi, a graduate of the Shchukinskii Directing School in Moscow and an employee of the Lviv Television Studio, directed its plays. Republic-wide press materials talked about its innovative performances of such modern world classics as French playwright Jean Anuil's *Antigone* and Shakespeare's *A Midsummer Night's Dream,* and such Polish classics as Stepan Wyspiansky's *The Wedding* and poems by Cyprian Norwid. The theater gained popularity with wider Soviet audiences, performing in Moscow and Vilnius.[44]

Performances of contemporary world classics and Polish classics contributed to sustaining myths about Lviv's "European" features. One of Lviv's young writers in the 1970s, Mykola Riabchuk, emphasized that this theater put on very daring productions (including Tadeusz Różewicz's 1969 existentialist play, *The Old Lady Sits Waiting*) despite increased censorship under republic Party chief Volodymyr Shcherbytskyi. Their plays drew audiences not just among the city's remaining Poles but also among its Russian, Jewish, and Ukrainian intelligentsias. Oksana Kompaniets Lane, who came to Lviv from Kharkiv at the beginning of the 1980s to study acting, also recalled this theater as highly progressive.[45] Lviv's Poles served as a bridge to the city's prewar customs. Other Lvivians adopted their practice of visiting graves of friends and loved ones on All Saints' Day, November 1.[46]

Lviv's Galician Ukrainian intelligentsia played a similar role for the new Lvivians. Writers and critics like Mykhailo Rudnytskyi and Iryna Vilde, literary scholars such as Mykhailo Vozniak, and historians such as Ivan Krypiakevych bore the brunt of ideological purification campaigns that began in 1946. Such campaigns came at the beginning of the Zhdanov era and during attempts to root out Western Ukraine's nationalist insurgency. Repeated self-criticisms of their ideological sins, often very humiliating, as well as frightening, nonetheless did not result in their arrests or deportations. As Tarik Amar rightly points out, these rituals were about educating younger generations in what parts of these intellectuals' past made them backward. After Stalin's death, they became notable members of Lviv's cultural establishment, showing others a positive version of a local Soviet Western Ukrainian identity.[47] One oral interview suggests that at least one of these intelligentsia families became part of a privileged elite, with access to apartments, goods, vacations, and other privileges rarely enjoyed by Lvivians.[48] The old Galician Ukrainian intelligentsia, now acceptable (if not privileged) members of the local Soviet intelligentsia, greatly influenced students, historians, artists, and writers who came of age or began their careers in the post-Stalin era.

Sometimes even the demeanor and behavior of such educated Galician Ukrainians left a great impression on other ethnic groups. Grigorii Komskii, an ethnic Russian whose family once lived in the "Russian-speaking zone," was one such case. In his brief memoir about Lviv, he admits that he never had great sympathy for Ukrainian literary classics like Shevchenko. Yet his middle school teacher in Ukrainian language and literature, the son of a Greek Catholic priest and educated in Cracow, had a great impression on him. This teacher, in his politeness and in his efforts to instill a love for literature and the theater, epitomized the "European Lviv" that for Komskii has since been lost.[49]

Rahuly, Banderites, and Lviv's Otherness

While Komskii has great admiration for older Galician Ukrainians like his teacher, his memoir makes the most scathing criticisms of Western Ukrainian villagers who came to Lviv in later decades. Over the 1960s, 1970s, and 1980s, these former villagers came to work at new industries emerging in and around Lviv. They settled in high-rise concrete apartment buildings of new suburbs in New Lviv, Maiorivka, and Sykhiv. These neighborhoods were considered more rustic and uncouth than downtown Lviv. By the 1970s, these new neighborhoods had led to what one postwar generation Lvivian called the city's "ruralization."[50] For Komskii, these new Lvivians ended Lviv's European spirit. They ushered in littering and neglect and rude, tasteless behavior. Sykhiv, a suburb whose construction began in 1981, is the "anti-Lviv."[51]

Komskii's antipathy to Western Ukrainian ex-villagers reflects tensions between locals and non-locals. Komskii refers to later waves of migrations to Lviv's suburbs, but others before had expressed such antipathies toward natives of Western Ukraine. This included Lvivian Poles. Describing her childhood and youth in Lviv in the late 1950s and 1960s, Stefaniia Hnatenko recalled local Poles making contemptuous remarks about her as a Ukrainian. When she and her mother worshipped at Lviv's Roman Catholic cathedral, a major center of social life for remaining Poles, someone noticed her crossing herself in the Greek Catholic way. This Pole, noticing a Ukrainian in their presence, said in Polish, "See that, the hogs are back in church again!"[52]

City natives looked down on these ex-villagers not because of their ethnicity, but because of their social background. They were called *seliukhy,* originally a derogatory Polish term *(seliuchy)* for "peasants." Lvivian interview respondents born after the war recalled the term *rahul'* (*rahuly* in the plural) also being used to refer to such Western Ukrainian villagers. According to Lviv historian Ihor Chornovol, the term was derived from the Polish word *rohul,* a bun shaped like the horns of a bull. *"Rahuly"* in Ukrainian (*"raguli"* in Russian) derided the "hickish" behavior of ex-villagers.[53] The *rahuly* became the butt of urban jokes. One riddle told by a respondent went like this: "What runs crazy, like it's got horns on?" "Tram Number Six!" *(Shto takoe mchitsia kak beshennoe, rahuliami obveshennoe? Tramvai nomer shest'!)* Tram Number Six was the main tram line running from the train station to downtown Lviv. It was a route villagers took when coming to the city to work, to study, or to sell goods in public bazaars.[54] After his taped interview ended, Iuriy Hryhorian recalled himself and his friend getting into a fight with ex-villagers from a dorm in the new working-class suburb of Levandivka when they were young, presumably at the beginning of the 1980s. He and his friend used to call this dorm "Under the *Rahuly* House" *(Pid Rahuliatkoiu),* referring to its hick residents. Historian Ihor Chornovol, present at the interview with Hryhorian, later explained that local city youth nicknamed derisively all dormitories of professional technical colleges (*profesiyno-tekhnichni uchylyshcha,* or *proftekhuchilishcha*) as *"rahuly* houses" *(rahuliatnyky).*[55]

Even former Western Ukrainian villagers used the term. Volodymyr Kryvdyk, born in 1957, grew up in the suburb of Holosko outside Lviv. He recalled hearing his friends get into fights with *rahuly,* who lived in a nearby vocational school dormitory, in the early 1970s. Considering themselves to be Lvivians, and thus more "civilized," Holosko's young men looked down on these neighboring vocational school students. They grew irritated watching these village upstarts speaking Russian and acting like they were from the city. Quite often neighborhood youths got together and beat up these *rahuly,* or *seliukhy,* to teach them a lesson.[56]

These accounts, told by people born long after the war, suggest that the slur *"rahuly"* was a phenomenon of the 1970s and 1980s, when large numbers of villagers migrated to new apartment neighborhoods like Sykhiv, Komskii's "anti-Lviv." At least one respondent, who came to Lviv in the 1950s, said that he never recalled hearing the word.[57] These later references to *rahuly* suggest it was addressed to people because of social origin, not ethnicity, nationality, or culture. Still, there are some hints that the term easily could be used to put down local Western Ukrainians. One interviewee said that envious urban youth called ex-villagers trying to educate themselves *ra-huly*.[58] While the slur may have been directed at people's social background or behavior, one wonders if local Ukrainians who had moved to the city would have made such distinctions. Like the former villagers interviewed by Bodnar, they may have been highly ashamed of who they were. Such feelings of shame easily could have turned into grounds for resentment of Russian speakers by the end of the 1980s, when calls for a national revival permeated Lviv's daily life.

Western Ukrainians were considered more than just uncouth hicks. Their connections with past anti-Soviet resistance, both real and imagined, marked them off from other Lvivians. Despite successes at Sovietization and defeating the nationalist underground, stereotypes about local Ukrainians' political reliability lingered. Daily life conflicts inspired exploitation of such stereotypes. In the mid-1960s, long after Stalin-era terror had abated, such political accusations flared up in the Lviv Artists' Union. This can be seen in union Party committee meetings, regular union meetings, and union correspondence. Union members upset over working conditions and the allocation of art shops, apartments, and union leadership posts accused their colleagues of "nationalism" and favoring natives of Western Ukraine. They claimed that the union had become a "gang of nationalists and fascists."[59]

Similar denunciations surfaced elsewhere. An anonymous letter to the obkom, dated 4 February 1971, claimed that the administration of the Lviv State Zoological-Veterinary Institute, made up of local Ukrainians, was harassing Russians, other nationalities, and Eastern Ukrainians, trying to replace them with natives of Western Ukraine. The letter insinuated that these local Ukrainians had taken part in the Banderite underground or had cooperated with the Germans during the war. The obkom's commission investigating the matter found nearly all such accusations groundless, though it did admit that some of the accused did "cooperate with or had relations with nationalists."[60] People in the Party and state apparatus regularly inflated incidents into ones that were "nationalist" and "anti-Soviet," as Henrykh Bandrovskyi, gorkom secretary from 1964 to 1980, emphasized in an interview. They did it to enhance their political image.[61] In that sense, the local bureaucracy encouraged such denunciations about Western Ukrainians.

Sometimes inappropriate humor by Russian-speaking institutions conveyed such stereotypes. Such an incident happened some years earlier, in late 1962, during a conference organized by the Lviv branch of the Ukrainian Theater Society. At the end of this conference, dedicated to the 100th anniversary of the birth of Russian playwright Konstantin Stanislavsky, Lviv theaters and actors put on a variety show *(kapusniak)*, where they insulted local Ukrainian actors and writers. In their supposedly comic sketches, they made fun of the Ukrainian language and actors of the Zankovetska Theater, Lviv's main Ukrainian-language drama theater.[62]

The sketch making fun of Lviv writers, however, was the most politically insensitive one. It featured Lviv writers in what looked like both a house of prostitution and a "hideout" *(skhron)*. This kind of hideout was known for its use by underground nationalist guerrillas. During the sketch, Lviv writers, playing cards on a grand piano, made fascist-like salutes with their right hands and called out "Glory!" *(Slava!)*. Both raising one's right hand and proclaiming "Glory!" were a variation of OUN activists' greeting one another, where one person would say, "Glory to Ukraine!" *(Slava Ukraini!)* and the other would respond with, "Glory to the heroes!" *(Heroiam slava!)*. The sketch blatantly identified Lviv writers with the UPA postwar insurgency. In their complaint to the Lviv obkom, dated 24 November 1962, writers Rostyslav Bratun, Mykola Romanchenko, and Taras Myhal demanded that those responsible for such sketches be removed from their jobs.[63]

The anonymous denunciation about the Veterinary Institute was personally motivated. It was by an employee afraid of losing his or her job.[64] He or she most likely wrote it to get even with superiors. The conflict in the Artists' Union some years earlier erupted for similar reasons. However, the episode at the theater conference was about making fun of the locals. This sense of humor (or lack thereof) revealed genuine perceptions by outsiders about Western Ukrainians. Even the most loyal of them, members of the Writers' Union, key fighters against "bourgeois nationalism," were mere prostitutes of the state, not having shed their "bourgeois nationalist" past at all. While Tarik Amar rightly notes the creation of a local Western Ukrainian Soviet identity in Lviv by the early 1960s, this identity overlapped with an unofficial, amorphous stereotype of politically unreliable Soviet Western Ukrainians. Despite Sovietization, they were still some other to the rest of Soviet Ukraine, what I would call a "Banderite other," one connected to

Stepan Bandera, his OUN-B, and the UPA guerrilla insurgency that drew inspiration from OUN-B.

These connections to a Banderite other, not encouraged officially by Moscow, Kyiv, or Lviv, were an unintended consequence of Soviet publications unmasking the foul deeds of the Banderites during and after World War II. This attention to alleged Banderite crimes greatly intrigued, as well as frightened, citizens throughout the Soviet Union. As the guerrilla insurgency neared its end in 1950, Eastern Ukrainians were interested in what really happened. A housewife, hosting Lviv students on an internship in Nikopol, asked one of them in secret about these Banderites, evidently wanting to know firsthand what official sources did not say.[65] As Western Ukraine's guerrilla insurgency became a distant memory, legends about it fascinated, or at least mildly amused, outsiders. A Kyiv Central Committee Party functionary in the late 1960s recalled in his diary that in 1961, on his first visit to Lviv, not only did the city's "Europeanness" strike him, but also its recent "bourgeois nationalist" past. On that very first visit, he tried to imagine where this or that conspiratorial hideout had been some ten or fifteen years before.[66] While walking the streets of Lviv, this functionary had imagined an underground that did not even exist, as UPA resistance was based in the countryside.

Talk about Banderites surfaced in the late 1970s as Lviv students visited other parts of Ukraine and Russia. Some of these conversations became jokes. Lviv State University students, entertaining locals in the Kuban during summer collective farm work, claimed they even had automatic weapons at home.[67] However, students from the Poltava Pedagogical Institute on an archeological expedition with Lviv State University counterparts asked detailed questions about the OUN and the UPA.[68] Besides genuine curiosity, assumptions that Western Ukrainians were not fully loyal to Soviet power remained. Thus the Soviet media in late 1990 played on such perceptions. As Lviv's Ukrainians installed a non-Communist local government, toppled Lenin's statue, and began campaigning for Ukrainian independence, Soviet media—namely, the Moscow newspaper *Labor (Trud)* and central Soviet television stations—spread unfounded rumors that Ukrainian paramilitary bands were training in the Lviv Region, planning to seize power in Galicia.[69] Until the very collapse of the Soviet Union, Lvivians, despite being Western Ukrainian Soviets, were never completely Soviet.

Western Ukrainians' Ambivalent Integration

Lviv's Western Ukrainians faced difficulties integrating into one Soviet polity, not just because of compromised political pasts. They perceived Russians and Russian speakers dominating the city's economic and political life. Halyna Bodnar indicates that such impressions were strong even among oral interview respondents who emphasized the absence of national tensions. When asked who had had privileged positions in Lviv society, they readily identified ethnic Russians and Russian speakers.[70] Local Ukrainian administrators who spoke Russian at work presumably reinforced such perceptions.

When it comes to positions of power in the Party and state apparatuses, available data have been fragmentary, confined to occasional remarks made at obkom plenary sessions or in reports from the republic's Central Committee, and interviews with Lvivians during Perestroika and after the Soviet Union's collapse. Nonetheless, such evidence suggests Western Ukrainians were at a disadvantage throughout the Soviet period. As of May 1953, natives of Western Ukraine had only minuscule representation in Lviv's city Party apparatus. Not a single native of Western Ukraine was among the thirty-eight heads of the city's administrative organs.[71] Over a decade later, the situation had improved, but only slightly. A republic Central Committee report on political work in the Lviv Region, dated 31 August 1965, indicates that the region's Party functionaries in overwhelming numbers tended to be those from outside Western Ukraine (see Table 3.1). Anecdotal evidence from Bohdan Iakymovych, a district Komsomol secretary from 1979 to 1983, and Rostyslav Bratun, a former Lviv Writers' Union chief—people well acquainted with local Party functionaries—suggests such trends changed only slightly by the end of the 1980s. Western Ukrainians remained underrepresented in district, city, and regional Party apparatuses in Lviv, as well as in positions of leadership in factories and other enterprises.[72] The issue of who was "local" or "non-local" became a constant issue for local Party functionaries. Henrykh Bandrovskyi, gorkom secretary from 1964 to 1980, recalled that people raised this question when discussing who should be appointed personnel in the local Party apparatus.[73] For their part, non-locals resented when locals won promotions over them. One journalist, born in 1940, recalled his parents, Russian speakers who arrived in Lviv after the war, voicing their irritation about locals being promoted at the time of Beria's 1953 report on Western Ukraine.[74] As for

Table 3.1 Western Ukrainians' employment in the Lviv regional CPSU
apparatus, 31 August 1965

	Western Ukrainians	Others
Regional Party committee apparatus	13.6%	86.4%
City Party committees	17.7%	82.3%
District Party committees	25%	75%

Source: Tsentral'nyi Derzhavnyi Arkhiv Hromads'kykh Ob'iednan' Ukrainy
(TsDAHOU), 1/6/3859/40.

Note: "Western Ukrainians" refers to those born and raised in Western Ukraine, that
is, the Soviet Ukrainian regions of Lviv, Ivano-Frankivsk, Volhynia, Rivne, Ternopil,
Chernivtsi, and Transcarpathia.

the KGB and the military, ethnic Russians dominated both throughout the
Soviet period.[75]

Statistics on places of residence by neighborhood remain inaccessible to
scholars. However, recent publications suggest ethnic Russians and Russian speakers usually lived in Lviv's more prestigious neighborhoods. Officials at various levels of the Soviet Party-state lured Russians and Russian
speakers to positions in Lviv by offering them better living conditions. In
Ivan Terliuk's study on Russians in Western Ukraine, about 74 percent of
his ethnic Russian respondents interviewed said that they had received
housing within a year of their arrival in Western Ukraine.[76] Such recruiting
policies led to Lviv's two central districts (the Lenin and Soviet Districts)
being more often than not inhabited by Russians in 1989, while Ukrainians
and Poles were much less likely to live there (see Table 3.2).

Soviet power represented more than just favoring outsiders in employment and housing. It symbolized terror. That terror was deeply seared into
young eyewitnesses' memories. Writer Roman Ivanychuk, who attended
school in the Lviv Region during the war, spoke at length in his memoirs
about NKVD terror against nationalist guerrillas. Like others in oral history interviews, he described the NKVD displaying dead bodies, some
badly mutilated, of UPA fighters and their sympathizers. They stood on
display in front of public buildings to terrorize the population. During several conversations since 1998, one of the respondents, Teodoziy Havryshkevych, showed me the scar he received between the eyes when one NKVD
man, disgruntled that the young Havryshkevych would not identify the

Table 3.2 Residence in Lenin and Soviet
districts, Lviv, 1989

Nationality	Percentage of Lvivians in Lenin and Soviet districts
Russians	50.9%
Jews	51.7%
Belarusians	49.9%
Ukrainians	42.1%
Poles	41.2%

Source: Viktor Susak, "Etnichni ta sotsial'ni zminy
v naselenni L'vova v 1939–1999 rokakh" (MA thesis,
Lviv National University, 2000), 46.

dead bodies displayed, struck him.[77] A former student of the Lviv State
Pedagogical Institute, recalling her childhood in a small town in the Ternopil Region, could not hold back tears when she talked about last seeing
her father in 1941. An Orthodox priest, he was arrested that year and later
brutally murdered in a local NKVD prison. She recalled her father greeting his children with the first day of spring (1 March 1941) and leaving
home for work, never to return. She said that every year, when spring be-
gins, she movingly remembers that moment of her childhood.[78]

This aspect of Soviet power crucially influenced Western Ukrainians,
particularly those born between the mid-1920s and the mid-1930s. These
people did not resist Soviet power, because they feared it. The priest's
daughter emphasized that she avoided politics and kept a low profile
throughout the Soviet period. When a Pedagogical Institute faculty member and a student agitated her to join the Communist Party around 1953
(the time when Beria's report on Western Ukraine urged Party leaders to
co-opt more locals into Party and state structures), she refused.[79] An ethnic
Russian born in 1959, recalling her years growing up in the working-class
neighborhood of Levandivka in the 1970s, remembered that the neighbors
in their apartment block, Western Ukrainian families recently returned
from exile, were utterly silent about politics. They kept their distance from
her father, who repeated what he heard on Voice of America, voiced his
disgust for the Communists, and even took a swing at the Party organizer
at his factory shop.[80]

Memories of such terror or stories about them nonetheless influenced later political actions. Ivanychuk drew inspiration from Khrushchev's Thaw and wrote historical fiction with political subtexts. He became one of the Lviv Region's non-Communist deputies elected to parliament in 1990. Volodymyr Kryvdyk, one of the members of Lviv's first non-Communist regional council, recalled stories told by family members about armed resistance in Western Ukraine.[81]

Those familiar with such Stalin-era repression viewed Soviet power as an outside colonial force imposing its will. Such sentiments were especially strong during the late 1940s, during mass violence against the nationalist insurgency. M. D. Drahan, assistant director of the Museum of Ukrainian Art, allegedly drew comparisons between Soviet power and Russian colonizers in the wake of deportations of Ukrainian Lvivians in 1947. He said, "Soviet power is just like the tsarist power of Peter I. Russian Communists conduct themselves in Western Ukraine like harsh imperialists, only they hide under the flag of brotherhood of the same blood."[82] This perception of Soviet power was shared not just by Western Ukrainians, but by Eastern Ukrainians. When Beria's 1953 report on Western Ukraine criticized Party and state organs for discriminating against natives, Lviv State University chancellor Ievhen Lazarenko took advantage of the occasion to compare local officials' actions with the sins of colonial powers. He said, "Sometimes policy conducted in the Lviv Region was similar to policy colonizers conduct."[83] The idea of Soviet power being analogous to that of a colonial power resonated in later decades. From 1964 to 1967, an underground nationalist organization functioning in the Lviv Region and in the Ivano-Frankivsk Region, the Ukrainian National Front, produced an underground newspaper, *Freedom and Fatherland (Volia i bat'kivshchyna),* that called the Soviet Union an imperialist project.[84]

However, there had been not just Soviet terror, but terror by the UPA and the OUN in Western Ukraine. Such terror was conspicuously absent in all of the childhood memories of Lvivians I had interviewed. Recent scholarship in the West has clearly demonstrated that it took place.[85] Exploiting this legacy of terror by putting captured insurgents on trial helped build support for the Soviet state in rural Western Ukraine.[86] Western Ukrainians who were victims of such terror could identify Soviet power not necessarily as an alien force but as the lesser of two evils. Frustration with outsiders did not always mean national resentment against a colonial power. It took on class grievances that the state could manage more easily. As a female janitor told a Canadian tourist in 1969, "There used to be 'lords,' and now we have bureaucrats. But we didn't give in to the Poles, and we won't give in to the *moskali*," a slur directed at Russians and Russian speakers. In early 1965, a history professor at Lviv State University told fellow Communists that a drunk swaggered up to him at the city bus station and called him a "crook" and an "occupier" who "stole our land."[87] One oral interview conducted by Halyna Bodnar suggests that some local Ukrainians compared the privileged position of Russian speakers to that of the Poles before the war.[88] However, such grievances were by those who were not among Soviet Lviv's upwardly mobile. They were janitors, dispossessed small farmers, and rank-and-file factory workers. They were not attending university and planning to become members of the intelligentsia. They directed their resentment at bureaucrats, managers, and collective farm chairmen, not at the Soviet state. Still, a sense of irony about the *moskali* lingered among students and some intellectuals, even during the optimism of Khrushchev's Thaw. Scholar Ievhen Nakonechnyi, a Lviv native repressed at the end of the 1940s, related a joke about two Galician peasants in the Carpathian Mountains reacting to Yuri Gagarin's 1961 space flight, a great achievement for most Soviet citizens. The one peasant called out to his good friend that the *moskali* were in space. The friend, though, was disappointed to find out that only one *moskal'* had left Earth.[89] In the mid-1960s Lviv State University students still called such outsiders *moskali*, which one university Communist complained of at a university Party meeting in June 1966 addressing problems with ideological work and dissent.[90]

Western Ukrainians, even those most committed to Soviet power and its ideals, were frustrated with the results. Writer Petro Kozlaniuk, a member of the Party and a veteran of the KPZU, was head of the Writers' Union until his death in 1965. He also had been chair of the Lviv Regional Council's executive committee. In his diary entry of 17 September 1959, twenty years after the Soviet Army arrived and "liberated" Western Ukraine, he voiced his agreement with an old acquaintance who reportedly asked, "I don't know who liberated whom: we them or they us? Maybe we liberated them, our eastern brothers of the same blood. It was they who took the best positions and apartments, and all the places of leadership." Locals like him had dedicated their lives to establishing Communism in Western Ukraine. They occupied minor political roles, while Eastern Ukrainians had become their leaders.[91]

Kozlaniuk's disappointment with Soviet power twenty years after its arrival did not mean he considered the Soviet Union a colonial empire. Other KPZU veterans who lived to see the Gorbachev era were among its fiercest critics. KPZU veteran I. F. Syvokhip, appealing to Gorbachev in 1987, was highly critical of the Soviet state's reluctance to pay KPZU veterans the respect they deserved. Dissolved in 1938 for "hostile" activities, then rehabilitated in 1956, the KPZU received negligible attention from historians. The material support its veterans received was meager. As for Lviv, the Russian language had come to supplant Ukrainian at public events, on propaganda and street signs, and in official communications. Yet in 1989, when *glasnost* started to shake the Soviet system's foundations, Syvokhip denounced it. Writing to the local Party newspaper, *Free Ukraine (Vil'na Ukraina)*, he saw *glasnost* revelations about the Soviet past as highly dangerous, playing into the hands of the Soviet Union's enemies.[92]

Western Ukrainians' experiences with Soviet rule were somewhere between the musings of an aging, trenchant idealist Kozlaniuk and the tears of a little girl who had lost her father to the NKVD, tears that returned every spring to a still-grieving elderly woman. In a society where institutions required denunciations, censorship, varying degrees of terror, mobilized enthusiasm, and deception, it is difficult to assert things like the Soviet state engendering "social support" or "opposition." On the other hand, being Soviet for Lviv's Western Ukrainians did not mean terror alone. Some still saw it as a noble experiment whose implementation was in dire need of correction. Others may have located the system's evils with the Stalin era rather than with the Soviet system itself.

Rather than focus on a binary opposition between "society" and "state," it would be more useful to talk about the varying degrees to which Western Ukrainians over the generations came to cope with the wider world around them. They developed a general set of strategies from the society in which they lived, a *habitus*, as Pierre Bourdieu calls it, to cope with that society.[93] Such strategies included "dissimulation," a feature of Soviet society from Stalinist times onward. In such acts of dissimulation, noted by Sheila Fitzpatrick and Oleh Kharkhordin, people masked their true beliefs and identities for the sake of preservation or better living or working conditions.[94] Other strategies involved individuals defining themselves in relation to a wider Soviet community and the ideals it stood for. Still other strategies were more complex, with their practitioners adhering to very conflicting beliefs at the same time.

For Lviv's local Ukrainians, especially members of the prewar intelligentsia, dissimulation saved lives and furthered careers. Iryna Huzar, a German instructor at Lviv State University, had compromised herself during the war. She had fled with her husband, an SS Galicia Division soldier, to Silesia. After her husband had abandoned her and her child for another woman, she returned to Lviv to be with her mother. To her great fortune, Huzar's Silesian odyssey did not harm her career. She regained employment at Lviv State University. Years later, Huzar recalled that there was a meeting where she was accused of hiding facts about her former husband, but she defended herself by noting all her male colleagues in the room who were no longer responsible for their third and fourth wives. With the laughter in the audience, no one bothered her again about her former husband and his SS service. Still, in 1943, she had published a German textbook for the occupation government's Ukrainian gymnasiums. In the late 1940s, colleagues, eager to get rid of Huzar, claimed this meant she had collaborated with the Germans. While denunciations surfaced, university officials protected her. When she lost that protection in 1973, during mass firings at the university, this textbook became one of the reasons for her dismissal that year.[95]

A complicated family history, accusations of collaboration with the Germans, and career ambitions most likely drove Huzar to become one of the university's ideological watchdogs. As early as 1946 she took part in a purification campaign against Lviv's prewar intelligentsia, denouncing colleagues at Party meetings.[96] While narrating her life story, she not only left this out, but later denied even being a member of the Communist Party, which she had joined in 1954. One colleague recalled her writing denunciations and making their lives miserable in the German Philology Department of the Foreign Languages Faculty. He politely claimed that she was "not completely normal psychologically speaking" (ne zovsim psykhichno normal'na). Protocols of university Party committee meetings over the late 1950s and early 1970s, as well as documents related to Huzar's 1973 firing, confirm that she took great pride in being a Party activist, and they suggest that denunciations had poisoned relations with colleagues.[97]

Huzar's role as a Party activist reveals her career ambitions, her damage to others' careers, and perhaps her own loss of reason brought about by subconscious fears about what she had done during World War II. However, it tells us little about this Galician Ukrainian's actual political beliefs. They do not suggest that she had come to believe that Soviet civilization was superior to all others. The same could be said for an employee of Lviv's Museum of Religion and Atheism decades later, during greater censorship of the Ukrainian intelligentsia in the 1970s. The daughter of a Greek Catholic priest, of both Polish and Ukrainian ancestry, she became a very active member of the Communist Party, and colleagues remembered her constantly informing on them.[98] However, younger Galician Ukrainians learned more than the art of dissimulation. As university students and emerging writers, artists, and scholars, they came to identify with some of the ideals of Soviet socialism. They saw the chance to develop a more just future than that in the Western capitalist world.

Jochen Hellbeck has seen such attempts at defining one's own self, often in relation to a wider community, in diaries written in the Stalin era.[99] Analogous diaries from post-Stalin Lviv have not been made so accessible. However, interviews and memoirs suggest similar trends. Interview subjects who contrasted past views with the present, rather than adhering to standard accounts of the past produced by collective memory, revealed such attempts at identifying with the ideals of Soviet socialism.

Poet Dmytro Pavlychko, born in 1928 in the Ivano-Frankivsk Region of Galicia, offered such self-reflection in an interview published with the Lviv literary journal *The Bell (Dzvin)*. Pavlychko became a prominent member of the Writers' Union first in Lviv, then in Kyiv. At the end of the 1980s he became an outspoken critic of Russification in Ukraine and a member of the political opposition party, the People's Movement of Ukraine (Rukh). By the time of the Soviet Union's collapse, he had no problems admitting that he had been arrested and briefly jailed in 1945 for belonging to a pro-UPA youth group. However, in this interview, he admitted that in his youth, he came to embrace Lenin's ideals of national and social justice and saw the Soviet Union as advancing freedom and justice in the world. For many years he saw the problem of Russification as the fault of indifferent regional and republic bureaucrats rather than Moscow. Pavlychko represented one of those senior members of the post-Stalin generations who had turned from his young flirtation with Ukrainian nationalist guerrillas to official Soviet ideology. For him, this ideology benefited Ukrainians.[100]

Pavlychko's conversion story, however, was deeply conflicted. Historian Roman Szporluk, who met him in Lviv in September 1957, recalled that Pavlychko in private was "very anti-Soviet" and even told him that Lviv poet Iaroslav Halan, allegedly killed by "bourgeois nationalists" in October 1949 (leading to a purge of Lviv's institutions of higher education) in fact had been killed in a secret police operation because of his anti-Soviet views. Szporluk saw young Lvivians of Pavlychko's cohort, those born in the late 1920s and early 1930s, as compelled to dissimulate enthusiasm for the system. They did not confront it critically like more experienced, reflective members of the older generation born in the 1890s, namely, Moscow writer Ilya Ehrenburg or Kyiv scholar Oleksandr Biletskyi, the latter who became the subject of an article Szporluk published under the pseudonym "Pavlo Chernov" some years after Biletskyi's death.[101] Therefore Pavlychko's embracing the ideals of Marx and Lenin did not necessarily imply the degree of revolutionary enthusiasm of Pavlychko's Russian peers in Moscow during the Thaw.[102] The same could be said of Teodoziy Havryshkevych, the one who had gotten a scar from an NKVD man for not identifying bodies of dead nationalist guerrillas. While he had never even joined the Komsomol, let alone the Party, he told me that among the many books he had read was Marx's *Das Kapital* from beginning to end. While reading such books did not indicate conversion to Soviet socialism's ideals, such an act at least suggests an interest in what they were about.[103]

A later cohort of the post-Stalin generation born after World War II experienced a less conflicted conversion to the ideals of Soviet socialism. Unlike Pavlychko, they had no memories of Stalin-era repressions of the UPA and their supporters. They knew little or nothing about armed resistance to Soviet rule. Still, they had to deal with tensions between public and private spheres. One such oral interview subject, Oresta, born in 1957 to Galician Ukrainians, knew nothing about such events, including ones involving her family that caused her problems getting a higher education later. She enjoyed being in the Pioneers, the youth organization for early school-age students. She was an enthusiastic member of the Komsomol, becoming an activist already in school. In her early childhood and school years, she saw Communism as a noble idea. Her doubts about the Soviet system's adherence to such ideals came about only later, at her first job. Working at a Lviv store, she saw her boss, a veteran Party member, use her husband's KGB connections to protect herself and her staff as they stole store goods. Despite her admiration for the Pioneers and the Komsomol, she found out that she was different from other Ukrainians. While on summer vacation in Kyiv with other children at the age of ten, she acquired the nickname "Banderivka," as she was the only child at camp who spoke Ukrainian and was from Lviv.[104]

Oresta's emerging conflicts with Soviet socialism were part of a narrative that later placed her, at the end of the 1970s, with friends talking openly about the problems Soviet rule had brought to Western Ukraine. Her life story revealed the ambiguous relations Western Ukrainians—even those born long after the war—had with mainstream Soviet values and institutions. These ambiguities surfaced even more prominently in the life story of Lviv poet and journalist Bohdan Zalizniak. Born in 1946 in Galicia, he said that he knew from family members, former clergy members of the abolished Ukrainian Greek Catholic Church, that Soviet power was "the Antichrist." He personally sensed that the state was "Bolshevik" and "imposed [*nakynutyi*] on us." Nonetheless, he was interested in what life under Communism would be like in 1980.[105] Zalizniak's life story indicated the dual worlds that Western Ukrainians inhabited. Their *habitus* involved a syncretism of different values and behaviors, where Soviet power was alien yet still fascinating and full of possibilities. It was the failure of such possibilities that mobilized their support for radical political change at the end of the 1980s.

The Soviet educational system influenced young Western Ukrainians' *habitus,* instilling admiration for Russian culture. Russian lyrical songs and Soviet patriotic songs became a part of the daily lives of those who had grown up with Soviet power. Iaroslav Isaievych mentioned that during his school years in a small town in the Lviv Region, young Ukrainians became interested in the classics of Russian literature.[106] Roksolana Zorivchak, born in 1934, a local Ukrainian who attended Lviv schools in the late 1940s, mentioned that a style of writing love letters in Russian, first spread by children from Russian-language schools, became popular among Ukrainian-speaking schoolchildren.[107] Young Lvivians born long after the war, whose parents were Galician Ukrainians, became consumers of Russian-language texts, both Russian translations of Western literature and Russian writers "forgotten" or repressed during the Stalin era. Kosmo-Demian Vozniak, born in 1956, recalled such texts being important for him when he went to school in the late 1960s and early 1970s, since his school's Ukrainian literature program offered little other than what he saw as outdated nineteenth-century classics.[108] Listening to or reading such Russian texts did not mean an endorsement of Soviet power or admiration of Soviet culture. In Vozniak's case, censorship in the 1970s had marginalized Ukrainian-language publications that might have appealed to him. However, such accounts point to locals' extensive integration into Soviet life, almost on a subconscious level.

Throughout the new western borderlands, Soviet policies transformed cities, uprooted populations, and replaced them with new ones. They

incorporated indigenous nationalities into a multinational polity with varying degrees of success. Lviv and Vilnius had been transformed the most
and acquired the most political significance. Emptied of Jews and Poles,
they became showcases for Soviet policy makers. The making of Soviet
Vilnius accomplished romantic nationalists' dream of making Polish Wilno
into the capital of a Lithuanian nation-state.[109] The making of Soviet Lviv
represented the triumph of Western Ukrainians' centuries-long quest to
become part of one Ukrainian nation-state. Their transformation had further political implications. Concessions to Lithuanian national sentiments
led to discussions about Lithuania's "bourgeois" past that eventually undermined Soviet rule.[110] Ex-villagers who roughly became a majority of
Lviv's population by the end of the 1970s, despite Sovietization, represented a politically unreliable, Banderite other, an image Party activists,
disgruntled citizens, and obtuse theater troupes exploited.

While Lviv and Vilnius had much in common, Lviv was not the Western
other that Baltic cities represented, notwithstanding its anti-Soviet reputation. Some trends resembled those in Lviv. Top Party leadership positions
in Latvia and Estonia remained disproportionately in the hands of outsiders who arrived after the war.[111] Other scholars suggest Baltic nationalities'
grudging acceptance of, if not attraction to, Soviet institutions and Soviet
promises of upward mobility.[112] An English-language translation of ordinary
Estonians' life stories suggests the irrelevance of national issues in daily
life.[113] A collection of mostly memoirs on informal cultural life in 1960s and
1970s Latvia reveals only isolated cases where young people expressed demands for Latvia's independence (usually by flying the illegal independence-
era flag) or voiced anger over Russians' treatment of Latvians.[114] Relations
between Baltic locals and non-locals were not immutable. Outsiders, like
Russian-speaking Estonians (nicknamed "Yestonians"), Estonianized their
last names and learned to master Estonian. Russian speakers and Baltic
nationalities forged common alliances in such cities as Tartu and Riga.[115]

However, in the Baltics, local opposition to Soviet rule manifested itself
in more than just spontaneous outbursts about "occupiers" and *moskali*.
In Estonia and Lithuania, it became organized resistance. As Amir Weiner
has shown, unrest in the Soviet bloc mobilized such opposition during
the Thaw and shortly thereafter. Uprisings in Poland and Hungary by late
October 1956 produced a series of collective protests in one day alone
(27 October) in Tallinn among former students of prewar colleges, while
Tallinn university students talked of forming an independent student union.

In Lithuania, cemetery processions on All Saints' Day (2 November) in Kaunas and Vilnius turned into street demonstrations where people chanted slogans expressing solidarity with Poles and Hungarians. By contrast, protest at Lviv State University was limited to private remarks by some students and professors.[116] While the 1968 Warsaw Pact invasion of Czechoslovakia failed to produce the virulent opposition that erupted in 1956, organized political protest erupted in Estonia. In Tartu, during festivities for their fourth annual Student's Day on 19–20 October 1968, students in a mock parade carried sarcastic banners critical of Soviet foreign policy and Russification.[117] Lviv was not the Soviet West of Vilnius or Tallinn, but historical connections to lands farther west still made it different from other parts of the Soviet Union.

CHAPTER 4

The Ukrainian "Soviet Abroad"

Of all the newly incorporated western borderlands, the Baltic republics were the most foreign and the most interesting. Their capital cities' Western architectural styles (Gothic, Baroque, and *Jugendstil*) as well as their restaurants, coffee shops, music, and more fashionably dressed women made Russians and other Soviet nationalities feel like they were closer to the West. Baltic cities became the European backdrop to Soviet films. Baltic consumer products like radios, perfumes, and alcohol were deemed of high "European" quality. Speaking Russian with a Baltic accent became chic. Russians and other Soviets called these republics the "Russian Abroad," the "Soviet Abroad," or simply "Our Abroad." Baltic nationalities became "Soviet Europeans."[1]

The unofficial capital of Western Ukraine, Lviv, lacked the resources, elites, and institutions that real capitals like Vilnius or Riga had. However, it became a more provincial version of the Soviet Abroad. In May 1974, a fifteen-year-old high school student from the Eastern Ukrainian city of Dnipropetrovsk, Andrei Vadimov, could hardly contain his excitement from his class trip to Lviv. Vadimov came from a city closed to foreigners because of its military and space industries. In a diary entry for 20 May 1974, Vadimov conveyed the thrill he and his classmates had encountering their own Ukrainian Soviet Abroad. He wrote, "We enjoyed our trip to this city very much! For us, it was like traveling to a real West." Unlike Dnipropetrovsk, Lviv was open to foreign tourists. For this first time in his life, Vadimov met actual Westerners—American and Canadian tourists—and spoke with them in English. The best part of their trip was to Lviv's black market.

Here, seven from their group, including Vadimov and their Komsomol organizer, bought new albums of the British rock opera, Andrew Lloyd Webber's *Jesus Christ Superstar,* from Polish tourists. These tourists noticed their interest in rock musician Ian Gillan. Gillan, these teens pointed out, was their favorite singer in the hard rock group Deep Purple, and he sang in *Jesus Christ Superstar.* The Poles recommended that they buy not just the album but also crosses, since Gillan after all was their idol, and Gillan played the part of Jesus Christ.[2]

Vadimov's diary entry dramatized the role even this provincial Soviet Ukrainian town played as a part of the Soviet Abroad. Polish tourists, as well as "real" Western tourists, brought these Ukrainians closer to Andrew Lloyd Webber and the voice of Ian Gillan. They were a metaphor for Polish influences that made Lviv more like the West: tourists selling Western black market goods; newspapers, journals, magazines, and radio and television stations that allowed more information about the West; and Lvivians' own Western encounters via Poland. While the Canadian and American tourists spoke English, they most likely belonged to the Ukrainian diaspora that had gone West after the war and earlier. These diaspora Ukrainians, too, provided cultural goods and information that Soviet media and institutions did not always readily supply. For the new Lvivians and for other Soviet citizens, Lviv's architectural landscape, closely connected with its Central European heritage, drew them closer to Europe, just as the skylines of Riga, Tallinn, and Vilnius did.

However, Lviv's Soviet Abroad reflected major historical differences along the Soviet western borderlands. Lviv was connected with a long history of conflict and cooperation between Ukrainians and Poles. Like Vilnius, Lviv's Soviet Abroad was thus fundamentally linked to a Polish other whose presence and absence made the new Lviv much more connected to lands farther west than Moscow or even Kyiv. The more violent imposition of Sovietization, as well as the lack of Ukrainian state-building traditions in Lviv, made Lviv a much more marginal, though no less significant, part of the Soviet West.

The Polish Factor in Postwar Lviv

As Roman Szporluk has observed, Ukraine's emergence as a modern nation-state was fundamentally tied not just to the unmaking of the Russian Empire but also to the unmaking of the Polish-Lithuanian Commonwealth.

On the eve of World War I, a common Ukrainian national history, culture, language, and sense of territorial belonging made possible the idea of a sovereign nation-state that could provide direct engagement with the wider world, or the "West." Such a nation-state made irrelevant capitals like Vienna, St. Petersburg, Warsaw, or Moscow, and the high cultures connected with them, which included Polish and Russian culture.[3] In Galicia, this meant that combating Polish dominance and nascent Polish nationalism crucially shaped its nineteenth-century Ukrainian national revival, from the Revolutions of 1848 to World War I and beyond. The idea of one Ukrainian nation, first advanced in the Russian Empire and exported to Galicia, became more exclusionary in the late nineteenth century because of this confrontation with an increasingly aggressive Polish nationalism.[4]

Galician Ukrainians' sense of national identity thus developed in increasingly violent opposition to Poles and their language and culture. This opposition between Ukrainians and Poles culminated in wartime and postwar ethnic cleansing in Galicia and Volhynia.[5] The postwar making of Soviet Lviv involved its radical de-Polonization, a project conducted by officials in Kyiv and Moscow but also supported by Galician Ukrainians.[6]

However, as Timothy Snyder has demonstrated, violence between Poles and Ukrainians was not inevitable. Ethnic cleansing resulted more from the intervention of outside powers decapitating and radicalizing societies and schooling them to hate. An exclusionist Ukrainian nationalism did not have a monopoly on interwar Galician politics.[7] Henryk Józewski, one of Polish leader Józef Piłsudski's trusted advisors, co-opted Ukrainians in the Polish state's propaganda and espionage war against the Soviet Communist threat. In a project dubbed Prometheanism, Polish government officials from 1926 until Piłsudski's death in 1935 tried to win over Volhynia's Ukrainians through more liberal cultural policies. Such policies were to undermine Soviet Ukraine's Ukrainianization and thus encourage the Soviet Union's breakup.[8] Karol Grünberg and Bolesław Sprengel suggest a long history of Polish and Ukrainian cooperation, as well as conflict, through the nineteenth and twentieth centuries. This could be seen in the Polish uprisings of 1831 and 1863 in the Russian Empire, as well as in cultural and political developments in late nineteenth-century Galicia. Despite the Polish-Ukrainian War in Eastern Galicia in 1918–19, Poles under Piłsudski and Ukrainians under Simon Petliura formed an alliance to fight Bolshevik Russia in 1920. As violence broke out between Poles and Ukrainians in Volhynia in 1943, there were attempts by the Polish Home Army, however futile they were, to appeal to Ukrainians' aspirations for cultural and political autonomy.[9]

These complex relationships between Ukrainians and Poles affected Lviv's Soviet Abroad. Poland, once perceived as a dominating outside power for Galician Ukrainians, became an alternative source of information on the rest of the world. Lviv's Ukrainians, similar to postcolonial subjects, used the language of a past power of domination and assimilation to resist a new such power's practices of domination.[10] Postwar Polish political upheavals, while provoking sympathy among Lvivians and alarm among Soviet officials, failed to stir up much solidarity precisely because of past experiences with Polish domination.

In Lviv, Polish newspapers, journals, magazines, and books could be found in kiosks, in the downtown bookstore Friendship, and in the Library of Foreign Literature. Lvivians could subscribe to Polish periodicals through the local post office.[11] Their popularity was great among educated Lvivians. Lviv's writers and journalists' reading of Polish literary journals and newspapers impressed their Polish guest, journalist A. Ziemilski from the Warsaw newspaper *The People's Tribune (Trybuna Ludu)*, when he visited Lviv in November 1956.[12] This enthusiasm resulted from the significant easing of censorship by Władisław Gomułka's new regime when it came to power in October of that year. However, long after Gomułka's thaw passed, nearly every educated Lvivian had some Polish-language books on his or her shelves in the 1970s and early 1980s, as one writer from the time recalled.[13]

Polish media, which included radio and later television, provided a window on the rest of the world, something not so readily available in other Soviet provincial cities. The bookstore Friendship offered readers Polish-language translations of existentialist philosophers such as Heidegger and Camus and contemporary writers such as Sylvia Plath. Such writers epitomized the "decadent" capitalist West and its preoccupation with art for its own sake, focusing on the individual's introspection and inaccessible to broader masses. While Moscow published some of these works during the Thaw and after, it printed them in very limited quantities because of such objections. This could be seen with the Moscow publisher Progress's recommendation to all-Union Central Committee functionaries on 8 February 1964 to limit the press run for the selected works of existentialist writer Franz Kafka.[14] Because there were so few of them, no one in the provinces could find or afford them.[15] Polish military history journals and propaganda works on UPA violence against Polish civilians gave far more information than official Soviet sources on this movement, providing further insight into the Soviet state's nationalist opponents.[16]

Popular magazines, radio stations, and (by the 1970s) television stations from Poland illuminated major developments in mass culture abroad. Polish sports magazines told more about teams and athletes from around the world. Women's fashion magazines enjoyed popularity for similar reasons.[17] Polish radio stations broadcast world news less encumbered by state ideology than their Soviet counterparts.[18] Such periodicals as *Panorama, Youth Banner (Sztandar Młodych),* and *Cross-Country (Na Przełaj)* provided young people with far more news about Black Sabbath and Deep Purple, while *Panorama* acquired popularity among men partly because of its erotic photo on the next-to-last page of each issue. Polish radio stations helped a former rock musician hear the legendary live concert of the Rolling Stones in Warsaw in 1967.[19] By the early 1980s, when the Solidarity movement compelled Poland's regime to ease censorship, television programs drew considerable Lviv audiences. These programs, besides featuring major political events, drew audiences because of what they told about life in the capitalist West. Around 1981 or 1982, Polish television featured a propaganda movie on American life, called *This Is America,* which, according to one interview, intrigued many because of its exotic scenes of biker gangs, group sex, women mud wrestlers, and drug addicts. While resembling the "yellow press" in its stereotypes, it suggested to one of the interviewees all kinds of freedoms available to Americans that they did not have.[20]

Polish media thus helped form values and behavior challenging the public sphere. Artists' Union members had become so interested in avant-garde trends in the Polish art journal *Art Review (Przegląd Artystyczny)* that their own works had taken on "undesirable" influences for one republic Artists' Union leader visiting them in 1959.[21] In the early 1960s, Polish translations of contemporary Western works on philosophy and psychology inspired Lviv State University graduate student Ihor Sandurskyi to investigate the impact of the subconscious on Ukrainian literary works, a theme considered taboo prior to Khrushchev's Thaw, even more so in provincial cities like Lviv.[22] At the beginning of the 1970s, when Khrushchev's Thaw had long since ended and Ukrainian publications faced increased censorship, Polish publications became a vital connection to new literary trends for young writers. Poet Hryhoriy Chubai and his friends looked for artistic inspiration in Polish-language translations of avant-garde literature from the West, popular jazz music from Poland, and Polish reproductions of surrealist and other Western art masters, writing works largely for the desk drawer.[23] Polish media, like the humorous magazine *The Pin (Szpilka)*, attracted young Russian speakers.[24] Its jokes and caricatures inspired Polytechnic Institute students nicknamed the "Sybarites" to create their own underground Russian-language album. Making fun of official slogans, it got them into trouble with the KGB in 1970.[25] Women followed Polish women's magazines as they designed their own clothes at home.[26]

Other Soviet bloc countries provided such media and personal contacts. Like Poland, they tacitly adopted their own roads to socialism. After the failure of Hungary's 1956 revolution, Czechoslovakia's Prague Spring of 1968 promised "socialism with a human face" and provoked an invasion by Warsaw Pact countries. However, in comparison with the Soviet Union, all of these states (except for Albania) had a more liberal cultural policy. In March 1999, while interviewing a senior Lviv artist, I noticed the copy of a Czechoslovak art journal from the late 1960s in his shop. Even after Prague Spring had silenced more daring forms of self-expression, Czech journals helped inspire the Sybarites to poke fun at daily life.[27] According to rock musician Oleksandr Balaban, East German students formed Lviv rock and pop music bands.[28] Socialist states not aligned with the Soviet bloc, like Yugoslavia, provided alternative channels of information by the early 1980s. The Yugoslav rock journal *Jukebox (Dzuboks)* was so popular in Lviv that one rock musician's nickname became the journal's title.[29]

However, proximity to Poland and prewar Lwów's residents made Poland much more relevant. Lvivians born as late as 1930 in what is now Western Ukraine had attended Polish schools and thus knew the language. Younger Lvivians from this region did not know Polish so well, but they did hear Polish on Lviv's streets as children.[30] Mykola Riabchuk identified such bantering in Polish with a conscious manner of style meant to parody the dominant discourse or to look clever. Riabchuk associated such use of Polish more with relatives, family, and childhood impressions of what was "old" (pre-Soviet) Lwów rather than with a clearly identified Polish language.[31] The irony with which local Ukrainians used Polish thus did not indicate fluency in the language, but at least enough familiarity with it to facilitate the development of a Polish-language readership among Lvivians.

Besides Polish media, Polish tourists, like the ones selling high school students record albums, became channels for cultural goods and information on the wider world. A growing number of tourists came to Lviv from

Poland in the decades after Stalin's death. They were Poles forced to leave the city in 1944–46, as a 1968 account of a tour group's tearful, anguished reunion with former Lwów indicates.[32] Tourists and private visitors, besides paying respects to their former homes, engaged in black market trade. Such trade had caught the attention of Party functionaries in 1956, as they became disturbed by the impact of the Thaw on the western borderlands. A CPSU Central Committee report claimed that a lot of the approximately 700 Poles visiting the Lviv Region in the past several months speculated in Polish consumer goods.[33] A gorkom report to obkom superiors from early November 1956, dealing with students' political moods in the wake of unrest in Poland and Hungary, noted student complaints about such trade.[34] This black market was alive and well by the late 1960s and 1970s. Black market connections between Poles and Ukrainians supplied rock music records, jeans, t-shirts, tennis shoes, and sunglasses from abroad.[35] Such contacts became risky. Lviv State University students were expelled in 1978 for hosting Polish traders in their dormitory rooms. Another student expelled had managed to steal from Polish tourists by claiming to be a police officer, using his student identity card as a badge.[36]

Such contacts became a crucial substitute for actual travel to Poland. Oral interviews and memoirs indicate that it was difficult to obtain permission to travel even there, a "brother socialist" country, until at least the mid-1980s.[37] However, significant numbers of Lvivians did travel to Poland, either as members of delegations or as private tourists visiting relatives. Beginning in 1958, extensive contacts between border regions of Poland and Soviet Ukraine took place under the Society of Polish-Soviet Friendship and the Ukrainian Association of Foreign Cultural Ties. These involved delegations of soccer teams; theater, music, and dance ensembles; delegations of factory workers; and writers, artists, and scholars from the Lviv Region and other border regions. They visited such Polish regions as Lublin and Rzeszów.[38] Between the Rzeszów Region and the Lviv Region alone, as many as 100 delegations and groups had visited each side between 1959 and 1966.[39]

Participants went through rigorous background checks. A list of cultural figures from the Lviv Region recommended for a trip to Rzeszów Region for 19–23 April 1958 had the signature of regional KGB chief Shevchenko in the margins. Shevchenko had to approve the delegation. He most likely was the one crossing out names on the list and suggesting alternates for at least one person. Such visits thus had political importance, limiting who could go.[40]

Besides delegation visits, private visits to Poland were possible. An obkom report to the CPU Central Committee, dated 24 October 1973, suggests at least the scale of such private visits by the early 1970s. This report concerned Ukrainians' contacts with relatives abroad, part of an attempt to control the growing flow of political protest literature across the Soviet border. At the time of the report, there was a noticeable contingent of people going abroad for private purposes. In 1972, as many as 20,452 Soviet citizens from the region went abroad privately. By contrast, those going abroad in tourist groups amounted to only 3,690 people that year.[41] Since the report emphasized family ties with Poland among Lviv Region residents, these figures mostly concerned private visits to Poland.[42] Official institutions had to support citizens' applications. The Lviv State Conservatory's Party committee in June 1971 issued recommendations to students who needed permission to visit relatives in Poland.[43] These figures nonetheless indicate that some Lvivians could visit Poland on their own.

Delegation and private visits to Poland were revealing, as 1958 delegation reports to Lviv obkom leaders suggest. Party activists and officials reporting on a visit to the Rzeszów Region on 15–22 April claimed that foreign films playing there corrupted young people with "bourgeois ideology." Some theaters promoted plays that lacked a Party spirit. Paintings and musical works were "pessimistic" and "isolated from life," works "with an orientation toward the capitalist West." Delegation participants, though, consumed these attributes of bourgeois ideology they had reported on.[44] In June, a group of fifteen Pioneer youth from the Lviv Region encountered numerous "harmful" influences. At a camp in the Lublin Region, "Girls perm their hair, paint their toenails, sing adult songs, and dance to rock-n-roll." In Warsaw, Polish schoolchildren told them that Poles, owning cars and other American goods, lived much better than they did. Residents made unkind remarks about them, and Polish counterparts had the audacity to say that the Poles, not the Soviet Union, had funded the city's Palace of Culture.[45]

It is difficult to say how much these visits abroad actually changed Lvivians' minds. The sight of Poles experiencing higher standards of living most likely undermined the belief that the Soviet Union was the most progressive in the Soviet bloc. Discussions with Poles could challenge Soviet myths. Professor Mykola Krykun, born in Central Ukraine in 1932, in his oral interview presented a narrative where he gradually lost attachment to Stalin and the Soviet system he had established, losing faith in both by the late 1980s. He described his 1962 research trip to Cracow when he and a Polish colleague, Wacław Urban, watched a French movie critical of fascism, *We Are All Murderers*. Later, Urban said he had grown tired of such films. Krykun, brought up on hatred of Nazism, convinced of the Soviet Union's role in defeating it, was shocked and could not understand his indifference.[46] This encounter most likely played a role in the evolution of Krykun's views from loyalty to distaste for the Stalin era.

Natives of Western Ukraine, unlike the "Easterner" Krykun, came from families with vivid memories of Polish-Ukrainian violence. They probably had a very negative opinion of Poles in the late 1950s, when these direct encounters with Poles began. Besides complaining about Poles' being engaged in black market speculation, students in early November 1956 voiced outrage over Poles who "spread slanderous discussions about Lviv."[47] These "slanderous discussions" could have been about whether or not Lviv belonged to Ukrainians, a very sensitive issue for the new Lvivians. Polish and Soviet leaders had begun delegation exchanges to encourage proletarian solidarity across the border. This reflected Soviet attempts to stress class loyalties in the western borderlands in the aftermath of Polish and Hungarian unrest in the fall of 1956.[48] However, memories of violence between Poles and Ukrainians in Volhynia and Eastern Galicia were just over a decade old. While former Party archives do not reveal how Poles were received in the Lviv Region, reports by Western Ukrainian delegations to Poland suggest that such hostilities were very much alive. A Lviv Komsomol newspaper editor reporting to the obkom on his delegation's 1957 visit to Lublin noted overhearing a local Polish Workers' Party official making references to the 1943 massacre of Poles in Volhynia. This official said that the delegates from Lutsk in Volhynia wearing embroidered shirts were "bandits who used to burn and cut them up and now had come as guests."[49] In other incidents that year and next, someone called a group of Soviet and Polish youth singing Soviet songs on the street "cattle." An official privately referred to a delegation as "lice" *(voshyvtsi)*. A local Pole warned a delegate not to go out on the streets at night for risk of being killed. Two drunken men awarded a Lviv theater troupe wilted flowers. Lublin artists told delegates that Lviv should be a Polish city, not a Ukrainian one.[50]

In later years, Western Ukrainians of the older generations did not give up their misgivings about Poland. This is suggested in an interview with Roman Petruk, an artist influenced by Polish media in his youth in the 1960s. He recalled that his father, who had lived in Galicia in Polish times, took offense to his interest in Polish books, journals, and magazines. Poland had very negative connotations for his father, who had been imprisoned for political reasons under Polish rule and thus knew Poland firsthand as an occupying power. His son, by contrast, regarded such Polish texts as a window to "Europeanness."[51] Later generations with no memories of Polish rule or the violence between Ukrainians and Poles shared this different perception. Mykola Riabchuk, who with Hryhoriy Chubai and other young writers turned to reading Polish texts in the early 1970s, viewed their actions as a protest against Soviet life, what Riabchuk disparagingly referred to as "Sovietdom" (*sovdepiia*), centered primarily on Moscow. Such texts provided alternative definitions of what it meant to be young. Members of this circle avidly read a novel by Polish postwar novelist Julia Hartwig, *Apollinaire* (1961), based on the life of avant-garde French poet Guillaume Apollinaire (1880–1918). This novel about bohemian artists convinced them that they, too, were part of a carefree avant-garde yet to be discovered, marginalized by increased Soviet censorship of literature in early 1970s Ukraine.[52]

While such later Western Ukrainians turned to Polish texts as an alternative to Soviet socialism, other groups of Lvivians from families outside the region saw Poland as a successful compromise with Soviet socialism.[53] Such a compromise meant that these people saw the system as viable, in need of improvement but not radical change. They included wives and widows of Party functionaries at the obkom's special hospital, people overwhelmingly from outside Western Ukraine. Larysa Krushelnytska, recalling a hospital visit to her friend there in 1980, mentions these people avidly viewing Poland's more daring television programs on air in the era of the Solidarity movement.[54] An ethnic Russian who worked for a district Party committee office in Lviv in 1980 was among those watching Polish television's coverage of the Solidarity movement and the political crisis that came with it. As he noted prior to his oral interview, he saw the Soviet Union's collapse as a great catastrophe.[55] Another ethnic Russian admitted his attraction to Polish radio broadcasts of jazz music in his youth. An activist in Lviv's Russian Cultural Center who recalled Ukrainian nationalists' violence in his postwar Lviv neighborhood, he said that he regretted the Soviet Union's collapse.[56]

Ethnic Russians and Russian speakers were no different from counterparts in Moscow and other Soviet cities, where reading Polish-language texts from the Thaw period onward became a window to the West but not necessarily a sign of breaking with the ideals of Soviet socialism.[57] One Lvivian who was friends with Russians and Russian speakers, Ilya Lemko, speculates that Russian speakers and Poles shared a certain affinity for one another as dominant powers in Lviv. He thus explains why restaurants in the late 1940s played Russian-language translations of the Polish interwar song "Only in Lwów" and why Lviv's Russian intelligentsia in the 1960s became so infatuated with the jazz-rock music of Czesław Nieman and the romantic poetry of nineteenth-century Polish master Cyprian Norwid.[58] Lemko's generalization that Russians and Poles saw each other as superior to Ukrainians sounds too facile. This is especially so since one of the original performers of the Russian version of "Only in Lwów," a Swiss Pole, was arrested by the NKVD in Lwów in the spring of 1941 and died in the gulags in 1943.[59] Yet it suggests that Lviv's Russians and Russian speakers saw nothing incompatible between consumption of Polish cultural goods and adherence to Soviet socialism.

These mixed responses to Polish media and Poles affected Lvivians' responses to Poland's political crises. The "Polish October" of 1956 was one such example. News of it and the Hungarian Uprising the next month greatly alarmed Soviet leaders, especially since Polish newspapers covering these events were readily accessible in Lviv.[60] Some years later, the Polish October inspired Lvivians, including those with memories of Polish times. By 1959, a group of Lviv State University students of Ukrainian and Polish philology had emerged, nicknaming itself "The Cabinet" (*Gabinet*), using the Polish term for Gomułka's government.[61] According to one oral interview, it was an informal company of friends who drank beer, vacationed together in the Carpathian Mountains, and wrote poems making fun of themselves.[62] The Cabinet had its own ministers who took on the aliases of Gomułka's real ministers. One of them as "Minister of Foreign Affairs" was in charge of finding Ukrainian high school girls in Poland to correspond with. Aside from the joking, the Cabinet took a serious interest in literature that at the time could have led to their expulsion from the university. They read works by Ukrainian writers banned or "forgotten" in Stalinist times. Cabinet members studied the works of Dmytro Dontsov, a literary critic regarded as the intellectual spokesperson for Ukrainian integral nationalism. Ukrainian integral nationalism emphasized excluding ethnic minorities like Poles from the national community and obedience to charismatic authoritarian leaders. Members of the Cabinet included older students exiled in the late Stalin period for supporting Western Ukraine's

Ukrainian nationalist insurgency. These older students had clear memories of recent violence between Poles and Ukrainians. The Cabinet thus represented Western Ukrainians who clearly saw the "Polish road to socialism" as a role model for Ukrainians, who could one day have their own independent road to socialism. In that sense, the Poles had become people they could admire. However, in reading nationalists like Dontsov, they assumed the idea that Galicia and Lviv were theirs, not the Poles'. The Cabinet thus represented the love-hate relations between Poles and Ukrainians that had developed in modern Galicia.[63]

There is no evidence suggesting later events, namely, political crises in 1968 and 1980, inspired local Lvivian role models. Poland's political crisis in 1968, known as the March Events, erupted over a government ban on Adam Mickiewicz's nineteenth-century play *Forefathers Eve (Dziady)* at a Warsaw theater for its negative portrayal of imperial Russia. Protests by Poland's Writers' Union and Actors' Union inspired student strikes and seizures of buildings at Warsaw University and other Polish universities. Within a month the Polish government had crushed the strikes and arrested thousands of students. It launched a campaign against alleged Zionism among Poland's remaining Jews to neutralize social discontent.[64]

Poland's March Events did become of concern to Moscow, Kyiv, and Lviv. An obkom report to Central Committee superiors in Kyiv and Moscow, dated 27 March, reflected anxieties about both the March Events and Czechoslovakia's Prague Spring. It reported that a "significant portion" of the Lviv Region's population found out about the March Events through foreign radio broadcasts and newspapers, presumably Polish ones, ahead of Soviet media sources. Obkom leaders had Party organizations spend the month countering such "hostile" propaganda through meetings with the intelligentsia, Party propaganda workers, and leaders of institutions of higher education.[65]

As with other reports to Party superiors, this obkom report gave a selection of comments, suggesting both negative and positive responses to these events. A fourth-year student, claiming that Polish students had violated the law, said, "What freedom do they still need? How can't they understand that they are on shaky ground, that if it weren't for the Russians, no state like Poland would exist?" Other selected comments, though, revealed that people had very negative opinions of what the Polish government had done. It said Jews found Gomułka's speech in *Pravda* reeking of anti-Semitism. The report selected "hostile" comments by a former Greek

Catholic priest who once directed the church's seminary in Lviv, who said laconically that "the socialist system is starting to crack."[66] Such elect voices of sympathy came from Jews worried about a resurgent anti-Semitism and Greek Catholics (presumably working underground) hostile to socialism, but not from students. Besides the fourth-year student's negative comment about Poles, another one suggested student apathy was the norm. A fourth-year student at Lviv State University with a Russian-sounding last name, Natalia Zabolotnaia, privately said that "something can happen here, too, with us, because things can't go on like this." However, she emphasized that Moscow students were more politically active than Lviv students.[67] This student and the priest were very likely cautious in saying much about the March Events or about the Prague Spring. However, they imply that unrest among Polish students never went beyond private conversations.

There was similar passivity, mixed with muted sympathy, at the beginning of the 1980s. The emergence of the Soviet bloc's first independent trade union, Solidarity, in Poland in 1980 became an event Lvivians closely followed. The same could be said of the imposition of martial law in Poland late in 1981. Iaroslav Kendzior, a future leader in Ukraine's opposition movement at the end of the 1980s and later a People's Deputy in independent Ukraine's parliament, stressed years later that he diligently followed television coverage of the rise and fall of the Solidarity movement. Padraic Kenney met late 1980s Lviv activists who traced their interest in opposition politics to watching and listening to foreign broadcasts dealing with Solidarity.[68] However, at the time of this unrest, no unusual cases of dissent surfaced in Party reports. A 14 November 1980 obkom report to CPU Central Committee superiors suggests ambivalence. It hints that the "usual suspects," namely, former UPA participants or their sympathizers and the underground Ukrainian Greek Catholic Church, had been inspired to activate "bourgeois nationalist" work. No other groups—workers, students, or professionals—became sources of alarm.[69]

However, what was striking were the remarks from Lvivians highly resentful of Polish black market traders and Soviet subsidies being wasted on the Poles. On one occasion, in the fall of 1980, a group of Polish tourists approached Lviv's main downtown grocery store with long lines and urged the shoppers to rise up and protest, as they had just done in Poland. They were greeted with an outburst of rude comments that, according to an obkom report to Kyiv superiors, basically said that "the disruptions with groceries happened because they had to feed such loafers and speculators as the Poles."[70] Aleksandra Matyukhina also notes such resentment by Lvivians, though she adds that Lvivians often benefited from black market trades with Poles during the crisis.[71]

Despite some sympathy and admiration for Poles during these crises, indifference tended to be the norm. As Lvivians and other Soviets became passive consumers in the Brezhnev era, deteriorating economic conditions provoked resentment toward Poles. Such muted responses to events in Poland demonstrated the strengths and the weaknesses of Poland's contribution to Lvivians' Soviet Abroad. In opposing their Communist regime, the Poles won sympathy, including among Ukrainians who well remembered wartime violence. Their media and cultural goods gave them a window to the West. However, the legacy of animosity between Poles and Ukrainians did not disappear with postwar ethnic cleansings. Interviews with one former Lvivian, born after the war, illustrated this poignantly. While she greatly enjoyed watching the films of Polish director Andrzej Wajda in the late 1960s and while she saw Poland as a window to the West, she recalled with bitter irony when Poles at the local Roman Catholic cathedral called her, a Ukrainian, a "hog" (kaban).[72]

Soviet Party and state leaders, too, were ambiguous in their dealings with Poland. The Soviet Union had a postwar alliance with Communist Poland as a "brother socialist" state. Such an alliance legitimated exchanging delegations and media across the border. However, suspicions of Poles and Poland were quite strong, especially in the wake of workers' unrest in October 1956. For example, the Lviv obkom in a secret telegram to republic superiors on 30 November 1956 asked that the sale of Polish-language newspapers in the city be curbed. A number of the newspapers contained controversial items about the Soviet invasion of Hungary and articles compromising Soviet literature and the world Communist movement.[73] In the wake of such unrest, republic and all-Union leaders decided in 1957 to encourage the further emigration of Poles, as well as Hungarians, from the western borderlands.[74]

Despite these attempts at greater ethnic homogenization of the western borderlands, a Polish minority, although small, remained in Lviv, and their activities following the Polish October fostered suspicions about their loyalty to the Soviet state. For instance, on 12 May 1960, the Lviv KGB chief reported to the Lviv gorkom that the Society for Supporting Poles Abroad had a very negative impact on young Polish Lvivians at Middle School Number 10, one of Lviv's few remaining Polish-language schools. This society had planned a poetry and art contest for the upcoming millennium of Polish statehood that, in the local KGB's view, idealized Polish history. An exhibit of Polish city seals sent by this society, as well as speeches by Polish visitors, encouraged feelings that Poland, not the Soviet Union, was their homeland.[75] A year later, the Lviv gorkom found out that local Catholics, presumably Poles, had illegally organized summer camps for Lviv children each year, not only preparing them for things like their first Communion but also teaching them "nationalist songs."[76]

Lviv's low-level functionaries and Party activists remained suspicious of Poland long after 1956. In the wake of the March Events in Poland, Polish literature was singled out by local Party activists for encouraging pernicious values. One literary scholar at a 1968 Lviv State University Party meeting claimed that the "sexual licentiousness" promoted by a recently published Polish novel by Irena Krzywicka, *Love*, corrupted students and other young people. Krzywicka (1899–1994), known for her scandalous lifestyle in interwar Warsaw, wrote a number of works in fiction before she emigrated to Paris in 1965. Such books, either new or republished in Poland after the war, were a direct affront to official Soviet assumptions about sexuality and love.[77] When obkom leaders faced demands from Moscow to improve ideological work, one obkom report noted in 1973 that, among other things, foreign radio station broadcasts in Polish disoriented local residents.[78] Such suspicions of Polish media surfaced the year before when the KGB investigated Riabchuk, Chubai, and other young poets who had become fascinated with Polish texts at the beginning of the decade. These young poets were under investigation for compiling an underground journal, *The Chest (Skrynia)*, under the inspiration of Chubai, himself suspected of spreading "anti-Soviet" literature with other Ukrainian dissidents arrested in 1972. Riabchuk defended himself, noting that the Polish journals he and his friends read were perfectly legal. The KGB investigator replied curtly, "We know well what Poland is!"[79]

The secret police agent seemed to anticipate later events. As the Solidarity movement swept Poland in 1980–81, Party and state officials in Lviv closed the amateur Polish theater Riabchuk had come to admire and fired its director from the local television studio. With the imposition of martial law and the breakup of Solidarity at the end of 1981, Soviet leaders momentarily banned the importation of publications from Poland.[80]

The KGB investigator's sly remark to Riabchuk about a brother socialist country, Poland, epitomized how different this Soviet Abroad was from that in the Baltic republics. The Ukrainian Soviet Abroad involved a Polish other that was both admired and distrusted. Galicia's historical legacy fostered this ambiguous relationship. As for the Soviet state, this distrust of a Polish other reflected deeper issues in both Russian and Soviet history, namely, Poles' pernicious reputation on Russians' western frontier. The specter of Polish nationalism in the nineteenth century, for instance, affected the growth of Russian nationalism, anti-Semitism, and imperial fear of nationalist movements all along the western frontier.[81] In the Soviet period, trying to defeat the bourgeois Polish state inspired affirmative action policies for non-Russian nationalities, including those perceived to be Poles along the pre-1939 western border. Piłsudski's 1926 coup and Soviet problems collectivizing agriculture and waging cultural revolution turned Poles into a menacing fifth column. In waves of repressions that followed, culminating in Stalin's Great Terror, Poles more than any other nationality suffered arrests, executions, or deportations.[82] The age of mass terror had subsided by 1972, when a frightened young poet faced his KGB interrogator about an "anti-Soviet" notebook. However, the perception that the Poles could cause trouble did not.

The Ukrainian Diaspora and the Wider World

Ukrainians' family ties with lands farther west contributed to this Ukrainian Soviet Abroad. The Ukrainian diaspora—both in neighboring socialist camp countries as well as in the United States, Canada, and other capitalist countries—became a vital alternative channel of information. As with other diaspora communities, Ukrainians from abroad, as they interacted with their national homeland, offered a different sense of national identity to their Lviv counterparts.[83] As such, they subverted assumptions of what it meant to be Ukrainian, posing a significant danger to the Soviet state. Soviet officials in Lviv and Kyiv thus tried, with only mixed results, to co-opt their more "progressive" elements. Diaspora involvement in Ukraine's growing dissident movement only further highlighted the danger of outside forces colluding with so-called Banderite Lviv. Even in cases where their actions were apolitical—like sending parcels and letters or visiting family and friends—Ukrainians abroad challenged stereotypes of the West in Soviet propaganda, putting local Party and state functionaries on the defensive.

Galician Ukrainians had been immigrating to these countries since the end of the nineteenth century. A particularly large contingent—roughly two thirds of approximately 210,000—had done so after World War II.[84] Incomplete evidence suggests that a significant number of Ukrainians migrated to socialist camp countries, mostly Poland, after the war. One interview respondent, born in Lviv in 1948, said that her father, an ethnic Ukrainian, left her mother and joined relatives in Poland to inherit family property there. It is possible that he may have declared his nationality to be Polish in order to get permission to leave the Soviet Union.[85] A 1973 Lviv obkom report to superiors in Kyiv, identifying locals' ties with relatives abroad, hinted that many local Ukrainians had relatives in Poland, a result of Soviet population transfer policies in 1957–59 that were to remove Poles, not Ukrainians, from the region.[86]

Soviet leaders perceived the dangers posed by Ukrainians living abroad. In the early days of the Cold War, Western intelligence agents recruited Ukrainian nationalist refugees in the West, and the U.S. government sent some supplies to at least 30,000 nationalist insurgents in Western Ukraine.[87] With the Thaw promoting peaceful coexistence between East and West, republic institutions encouraged diaspora Ukrainians to visit Lviv, either as members of official delegations or as tourists. At Lviv State University, Chancellor Ievhen Lazarenko in the late 1950s arranged visits by Petro Kravchuk of the "progressive" Association of United Ukrainian Canadians. He extended invitations to academic conferences to some progressive Ukrainians in the early 1960s.[88] At the initiative of Ukrainian intellectuals, republic state and Party leaders organized the Society of Cultural Ties with Ukrainians Abroad in 1960. Its rationale was to point out Soviet Ukraine's successes to Ukrainians desiring greater ties with their native land.[89]

During the Thaw, as Lviv lost its status as a city closed to foreigners, Ukrainians in the capitalist West took advantage of visiting Lviv and the Lviv Region. By late May 1961, the number of foreign visitors from capitalist countries served by Intourist in Lviv had gone up twenty-one times from 1958.[90] A total of 3,841 foreign tourists from capitalist countries visited Lviv in 1965.[91] By 1971, there were 8,175 foreigners from capitalist countries visiting the Lviv Region as tourists.[92] As these figures grew, foreigners began visiting on private visas. A total of 25,150 had done so in 1972 in the Lviv Region.[93] Many of these visitors presumably were relatives from Poland, yet foreigners from the capitalist West also traveled privately, such as a Philadelphia architect and his wife in 1967.[94]

Such foreign tourists participated in political activities connected with Ukrainians abroad. Activists in western nationalist organizations, posing as tourists, distributed illegal literature in Western Ukraine. They attempted to set up networks of communication. A 1962 KGB report to the Lviv obkom indicated such attempts made by western tourists and outlined KGB propaganda efforts to win these tourists over.[95] A 31 August 1965 report by the republic Central Committee on ideological work in the Lviv Region acknowledged that foreign tourists contributed to the growth of "bourgeois nationalism" there.[96]

Kyiv and Moscow grew more alarmed at diaspora Ukrainians' propaganda influence as they dealt with the growing spread of underground protest literature by dissidents. This could be seen in a republic Central Committee resolution of 27 July 1971 on restricting *samvydav* literature. It identified "anti-Soviet émigré organizations" among those responsible for its circulation. This resolution ordered that the Administration of Foreign Tourism of the Council of Ministers enforce stricter oversight of foreign tourists' visits to prevent them from meeting with "politically wavering [*nestikyi*] people." The republic's KGB was to intensify its search of *samvydav* and other "ideologically harmful" literature at the republic's western border.[97]

Lviv's regional KGB chief, Mykola Poluden, highlighted the troubling influence Western diaspora organizations had. In remarks to an obkom plenary session of 20 November 1971, dealing with Moscow's criticisms about political work in the Lviv Region, he said that the Foreign Section of the Organization of Ukrainian Nationalists and the Foreign Office of the Ukrainian Supreme Liberation Council had tried to establish "direct organizational links in the Lviv Region" in 1970–71. They did so as foreign tourists, influencing younger intellectuals not affiliated with the old nationalist underground. He quoted the leader of a group of Canadian tourists who said that their goal was to discuss national issues with Ukrainians and thus persuade them to struggle for an independent Ukraine. Such tourists, highly educated, not only spread their own "nationalist literature" but also collected *samvydav* and "tendentious, anti-Soviet information." In 1971 alone, KGB personnel discovered about 150 foreigners trying to use tourism as a way of conducting such propaganda work, including eleven who were deported. He gave examples of such tourists from Britain, Sweden, and Canada gathering facts and spreading subversive literature.[98]

The KGB's fears were justified. Already in the early 1960s, networks spreading *samvydav* in Lviv obtained illegal literature through one historian's relatives abroad.[99] Diaspora journals and books were reaching Lvivians and undermining Soviet propaganda's effects. They caused one future dissident to scold a senior writer in the early 1960s for lying about the West's Ukrainian diaspora in a public speech she gave about her recent trip to America.[100] By the early 1970s, connections between the Western diaspora and poets Ihor and Iryna Kalynets had become the talk of Party and KGB organs. Ihor Kalynets by then could no longer publish his poems because of increased censorship after the Thaw. As one CPU Central Committee report indicated, his poems were satiated with religious themes, mysticism, and "excessive archaization of language." Kalynets thus circulated them underground. According to a CPU Central Committee report, circulating these poems among friends led to them winding up in the West. His family's biographer indicates that a British OUN-B-affiliated publication produced a book of his poems, hiding the name and place of publication (Belgium) to throw off KGB agents.[101] This book became evidence during the same obkom plenary session where KGB chief Poluden revealed the Western diaspora's subversive activities. After criticizing the local literary journal's editor for being too tolerant of Kalynets's ideological deviations (as if he had published his poems!), obkom secretary Vasyl Kutsevol read aloud some of the poems published abroad. In his literary performance, Kutsevol warned the audience that circulating such poems "by way of others' boots" (po inshykh khaliavakh) posed a danger to the Soviet people.[102]

Discussions between Kalynets's wife Iryna and Western diaspora Ukrainians suggested at least a cautious exchange of ideas taking place between Lviv's Ukrainians and their fellow nationals abroad. Records from her 1972 criminal trial for spreading "anti-Soviet propaganda" indicate that she had heated political discussions with Marko Horbach, a West German university student and Western diaspora activist. Kalynets testified that she told Horbach that the Soviet Union was closer to establishing "absolute democracy" than West Germany and that the Union of Ukrainian Youth, a Western diaspora organization, would fail in Western Ukraine as miserably as OUN-B had. Still, Lvivians like her were learning about Western disapora organizations. Other witness testimony indicates that she and her friends, speaking with Horbach, criticized the Soviet nationalities policy and the status of Ukraine and Ukrainian culture in the Soviet Union. Comparing their lot with that of Ukrainians in Poland, Czechoslovakia, and the capitalist West, they claimed that more often than not, Ukrainians living abroad fared better than Ukrainians living in the Soviet Union.[103] While younger intellectuals like Kalynets had moved away from the tactics of OUN-B and were critical of Western organizations, the West had become a standard of measurement against which they could criticize Soviet policies in Ukraine.

Such interactions with the Western diaspora, however infrequent, greatly alarmed Moscow ideologists by 1972. Mikhail Suslov and others had lost patience with the problem of "bourgeois nationalism" in non-Russian republics. The spread of *samvydav* from abroad continued. Under pressure from Moscow, the Ukrainian KGB in January of that year began arresting members of the intelligentsia spreading such literature, including Iryna Kalynets. Within months her husband Ihor was under arrest. The bait for these arrests was a young man from Belgium's Ukrainian diaspora, Iaroslav Dobosh. His early January visits to Ukrainian intelligentsia members' homes served as grounds for investigations, arrests, and criminal trials, as well as firings and expulsions from school. It began a series of repressions against Ukrainian intellectuals and students for the next two years.[104]

This wave of repressions against dissidents and their supporters did not stop the Western diaspora's political activity. Ukrainian diaspora organizations continued to reach out to Soviet Ukrainians. This could be seen in a Lviv city Komsomol committee report on law enforcement. The report, dated 31 March 1975, criticized the leaders of the Shevchenko District's Komsomol law enforcement patrol for allowing patrol members, while on duty, to confiscate "We Love Ukraine" *(My liubymo Ukrainu)* pins and give them to friends in 1974. Judging by the pins' wording ("Ukraine" instead of "Soviet Ukraine"), they had not been made in Soviet Ukraine. Ukrainian tourists must have been passing them around. Komsomol activists had no problem sharing them with friends, suggesting that they, too, were attracted to such alternative patriotic symbols.[105]

Countering the influence of the Ukrainian diaspora was no easy task, especially since the diaspora was not restricted to the capitalist West. Ukrainians in neighboring socialist countries, especially Poland and Czechoslovakia, threatened Ukraine's Party and state leaders with the specter of "bourgeois nationalism." The Polish Ukrainian newspaper *Our Word (Nashe slovo)* and its cultural supplement, *Our Culture (Nasha kul'tura)*, faced less harsh conditions of censorship. The same could be said of the Warsaw journal *Ukrainian Calendar (Ukrains'kyi kalendar)*. These publications, available in Lviv and other cities, introduced Western Ukrainians to figures in Ukrainian culture banned from publication in Soviet Ukraine. Lviv literary critic Mykola Ilnytskyi thus learned about interwar Lviv poet Bohdan-Ihor Antonych around 1963, through memoirs published by Antonych's lover either in Warsaw's *Ukrainian Calendar* or in the Czechoslovak journal *Duklia*. Until the end of Prague Spring, *Duklia,* the literary journal of the Ukrainian community in Prešov, was another such alternative channel of information. Diaspora publishers in Poland and Czechoslovakia provided Soviet Ukrainians with an alternative venue for publications, particularly as censorship made such publications difficult after Khrushchev's Thaw. Ihor Kalynets, before causing a scandal with his publication in the West, had published poems in *Duklia* in the 1960s, as well as in a Czechoslovak literary anthology in 1965. Literary critics, including Soviet Ukrainians, appeared in Polish and Czechoslovak diaspora periodicals with very positive reviews of Kalynets's 1966 book of poems, the only one he was able to publish in Soviet Ukraine before his arrest. Such publishers became crucial conduits for *samvydav* literature headed farther westward.[106]

Ukrainian publications in Prešov alarmed Ukraine's Party leaders during Prague Spring. Accessible to Ukrainians across the border, the publications did more than speak out about Soviet repression of Ukrainians. Immediately after the Warsaw Pact invasion, the newspaper *New Life (Nove zhyttia)* and the journal *Duklia* delivered strong protests against it.[107] The backlash against Prague Spring ended Prešov's vocal support of Ukrainian dissent. However, even disregarding Prešov, Soviet bloc diaspora publications were relatively more liberal channels of information about Ukrainians' history, literature, and culture. This could be seen with Polish Ukrainian publications long after the Polish October of 1956 had subsided and Polish dissent was reined in. In late 1960, Levko Lukianenko and other activists of an underground national separatist organization considered circulating *Our Word* as part of their propaganda tactics. Such tactics—not fulfilled because of their arrest the next year—included using the newspaper's information about Ukrainians' history and culture to promote greater national self-awareness and pride among Ukrainians. Iryna Kalynets recalled that her strong friendship with Viacheslav Chornovil, future leader of the Lviv Region's first non-Communist assembly, emerged later that decade after Kalynets and Chornovil talked about what they had read in *Our Word.*[108] With Poland loyal to the Soviet bloc, Soviet leaders in Moscow and Kyiv not only tolerated these publications, but encouraged cooperation with their Soviet Ukrainian counterparts. For example, the assistant editor of Lviv's literary journal, *October,* visited the offices of *Our Word* in Warsaw and gave an interview on cooperation between Polish and Ukrainian writers for its May 1972 edition.[109] The Ukrainian diaspora was therefore a factor that Soviet policy makers had to engage with constructively. Thus these policy makers permitted such alternative channels of information to continue.

Connections with the Ukrainian diaspora significantly influenced the emergence of alternative views on the Soviet system and its nationality policy. For others, Ukrainians abroad supplied important goods and general information on the outside world. A 24 October 1973 report by the Lviv obkom informed republic superiors measures they had taken to curb the influence of letters, packages, and financial gifts that the local population received from relatives living abroad. Republic Party leaders had initiated such moves to crack down on *samvydav* networks and dissent in 1972–73. This report suggested that packages and gifts provoked tensions locally. Locals with compromised pasts, including involvement with underground nationalists, were among the recipients. Recipients made money selling gifts on the black market, or they allegedly showed them off to neighbors, coworkers, and friends.[110] If these gifts failed to raise questions about life in the capitalist West, simple letters from abroad did. A Ukrainian Jew from Lviv who immigrated to Israel in 1974 talked about an elderly Galician Ukrainian peasant expressing bewilderment about what his neighbors' relatives from Canada had written. Their stories about Canada, related through this neighbor, made this peasant wonder aloud if Soviet newspapers were right describing poverty in the West.[111] News about Western prosperity sometimes provoked negative responses to the West among Soviet citizens.[112] However, these early 1970s Party reports in Ukraine suggest that such news did pose a potential threat to work on the ideological front.

This part of Lviv's Soviet Abroad thus shaped local Ukrainians' opinions about the actual West. However, it was still an incomplete, idealized picture of the West, much like other versions of Soviet citizens' "imaginary West."[113] An oral interview respondent who had relatives in the United States said that she used to have great sympathy for them, as they were Ukrainians "torn away from the native land." Her attitudes, however, changed when she met actual Ukrainians from the Western diaspora, first on a trip to London in 1991. Here, she saw that "they were not the people that we were thinking about." They were completely different.[114]

The Ukrainian West

Like Riga, Tallinn, and Vilnius, Lviv offered Lvivians and other Soviet citizens a sense of being more in Europe. Its downtown districts became known for their variety of architectural styles, not found in most Ukrainian cities, like Gothic, Renaissance, neo-Renaissance, Baroque, Secessionist, and *Jugendstil* trends, all featured in guidebooks for foreign and domestic tourists.[115] Despite initial alterations, policy makers in Moscow and Kyiv canceled early plans to transform Lviv's central districts radically. Local state and Party leaders instead promoted its diverse architectural heritage. Press materials and guidebooks highlighted local efforts to preserve Lviv's central historic districts in the 1970s. With the republic's Society for the Preservation of Monuments, they registered at least 130 historic buildings under state protection. Besides regulating the size and type of new construction permissible, city and regional agencies, in coordination with Kyiv, made the city's central districts a state architectural preserve in 1975.[116] Tourist guidebooks, published locally and in Moscow, highlighted Lviv's European architectural features.[117] In the words of one Kyiv newspaper, Lviv had become a "city museum."[118]

Lviv's historic district thus mostly remained as it was before the war, marked by small squares, narrow streets, and twisting lanes. It was among such compact and intimate urban spaces that Lvivians spent much of their leisure time. Going out with friends and acquaintances to such cafés as "Under the Lion" and taking walks through Lviv's central streets became a part of the new Lvivians' daily life, taking on the habits of their prewar predecessors.[119] For writers like poet Mykola Petrenko and his friends, downtown coffee houses, cafés, and bars lent themselves to what he called a "bohemian" atmosphere. Here poets, prose writers, and critics, as they drank alcohol and sipped coffee, read poems to each other, discussed books, gossiped, and joked about themselves, sometimes penning various ditties and poems at the table.[120]

Three such places became prominent gathering spots for young intellectuals in Lviv in the 1970s and 1980s: the bar "Nectar" on Saksahanskyi Street; the "Chocolate Bar," in the basement of the Svitoch Candy Store on Shevchenko Avenue, and by the end of the 1970s, the Armenian Street Café on Armenian Street near the Market Square. Bikers, hippies, and aspiring artists, writers, and rock musicians frequented the Armenian Street Café, reading poems by Esenin, Pushkin, or Russia's Silver Age masters or reading their own, singing prewar Polish songs about Lwów or Ukrainian folk songs, forming new rock bands, and enjoying intellectual conversation.[121] The Chocolate Bar became noted not just for its cakes and cognac, but also for its bard poets and its burlesque shows where young musicians parodied Italian pop songs in Ukrainian or sang jokes about Lviv in English. Friends of Russian graphic artist Oleksandr Aksinin mention Nectar as a popular gathering spot for young artists before the Armenian Street Café opened.[122]

These bars, coffee houses, and cafés were places where, free of the constraints of official institutions, people could more or less be themselves. While not allowing for open political opposition, they gave Lvivians a more authentic existence, not one dictated by appearances they had to keep up in the press, at university lectures and seminars, or at Party and Komsomol meetings. These spaces resembled "Café Saigon" in Leningrad, where young people from the late 1960s onward participated in the public sphere, yet distanced themselves from it through networks of friends.[123] This relative sense of intimacy and honesty, shared over coffee, alcohol, and food, allowed people to express universal human values amidst the vacuum created by modern cities like Lviv.[124]

Intimate gathering spots outside, such as the viewing deck of the High Castle overlooking the city skyline, the grounds around the Dominican Cathedral near the Market Square, the abandoned graveyard for Polish military dead in the Lychakiv Cemetery, and the garden of a former Barefoot Carmelite monastery became favorite gathering spots for hippies, bikers, university students, and other young people. Besides the "mysticism" connected with these centuries-old buildings and sculptures, such compact places offered an escape from false distinctions between people that the public sphere had made.[125]

Downtown Lviv thus greatly enchanted visitors. Tourist guidebooks cited Ukrainian and other Soviet intellectuals who claimed Lviv was one of Europe's best cities.[126] While it is not clear if Lvivians saw their city as resembling Baltic republic cities, they did make comparisons to them. This could be seen in suggestions by writers in the early 1960s to establish young people's cafés or coffee houses similar to those in Riga, Tallinn, or Vilnius, as well as Moscow. While these Lviv intellectuals used examples from the Baltic republics to justify new cultural policies, it could be that they made these comparisons out of conviction that their city was much like that of Riga or Tallinn and thus deserved such places of leisure for its young people.[127] This sense of belonging to the Soviet Abroad attracted people to Lviv. The city's architecture became at least one reason why young people from villages and small towns in the Lviv Region and other parts of Western Ukraine came there to study and then stayed.[128]

Architecture inspired poems, novels, paintings, and graphic art. This can be seen in graphic works of the Market Square environs by local artists

Figure 4.1. Bohdan Soroka, *Lviv City Center* (1981), from R. M. Iatsiv, *L'vivs'ka hrafika 1945–1990: Tradytsii ta novatorstvo* (Kyiv: Naukova Dumka, 1992). Used with permission of the artist.

Bohdan Soroka, Iryna Soboleva, and Petro Hrehoriychuk. Soroka's line engraving, *Lviv City Center* (1981) (Figure 4.1), composed from atop the High Castle, is a closely packed collage of the different buildings of the Market Square neighborhood and nearby Lenin Avenue (now Freedom Avenue). The center's serpentine streets and clusters of buildings draw the viewer into the picture and treat the city center as one organic museum piece of different styles of architecture. Soboleva's *Black House* (1972) (Figure 4.2) is a sample of her series of line engravings and lithography on historic Lviv made in the 1970s.[129] Her black-and-white depiction of this late sixteenth-century house on Market Square (part of the Lviv His-

Figure 4.2. Iryna Soboleva, *Black House* (1972), from Ie. P. Mysko, *Izobrazitel'noe iskusstvo L'vova: Zhivopis', skul'ptura, grafika* (Moscow: Sovetskii khudozhnik, 1978). Andrei Sheptytskyi National Museum, Lviv.

torical Museum), designed by an Italian master, accentuates the play between shadows and sunlight on this dark sandstone building. Hrehoriychuk's *Lviv: Armenian Alley* (1970) (Figure 4.3), an oil painting showing one of the passageways near the ancient Armenian Cathedral on Armenian Street, highlights its barrel arches and a young woman and an artist enjoying each other's company in the cool shade.

Such an assembly of Renaissance, Baroque, and other architectural styles drew Lvivians and others to a different urban space, a "Ukrainian Florence," as one popular history put it. This was the West, what scholars would call today Central Europe.[130] This was the West, but it was one where its multicultural past was erased or marginalized. While preserving the Market Square neighborhood, restoration specialists and artists gave it a Ukrainian flavor. The interior of a café called Under the Lion, when it opened on 19 Market Square at the end of 1965, epitomized this transformation of urban space. Students from the Institute of Applied and Decorative Art gave it a ceramic mural that portrayed not just the skyline of old Lviv but also Prince Danylo Halytskyi, the city's thirteenth-century Galician Ukrainian founder, and some members of his retinue. The design of the interior contained folk motifs highly compatible with Soviet socialist realism. The ceramic mural's central figure was not Prince Danylo Halytskyi, but a blacksmith brandishing his tool. The wall decorations resembled the ceramic art of the Hutsuls in the Carpathian Mountains, with a modern flair. The iron door to the employees' rooms had as its central figure a rooster found in village folklore. In emphasizing the life of simple Ukrainian workers and peasants, this café's interior had turned to a major Soviet art theme. It helped nationalize a landscape built mostly by Italian and other non-Ukrainian masters.[131]

Such transformations of the Market Square neighborhood broke from the city's Polish past. Writers' representations of its neighborhood did the same. Ukrainian highwaymen from the Carpathian Mountains became heroes of poems whose early modern dramas were set at Market Square.[132] In 1982, near Market Square, city Party and state officials erected a statue to Ukrainian Cossack leader Ivan Pidkova, at the site where he was executed by the Poles in 1578 (Figure 4.4). Poetry and popular histories portrayed Pidkova's brave defiance of death here.[133] Popular histories of the Market Square neighborhood accentuated Ukrainian craftsmen's contributions and Ukrainian village motifs to the designs of its buildings while depicting their Polish patrons with irony. One such history claimed that the beauty of a sixteenth-century chapel near Market Square was Ukrainian craftsmen's vengeance

Figure 4.3. Petro Hrehoriychuk, *Lviv: Armenian Alley* (1970), from Ie. P. Mysko, *Izobrazitel'noe iskusstvo L'vova: Zhivopis', skul'ptura, grafika* (Moscow: Sovetskii khudozhnik, 1978). Andrei Sheptytskyi National Museum, Lviv.

Figure 4.4. Petro Kulyk, *Ivan Pidkova* (1982). Photo by the author.

on the wealthy Polish merchant who had "stolen stone from the Ukrainian public" by financing this chapel's construction.[134]

In de-Polonizing such urban spaces, writers varied in how Ukrainian they were. A poem by an ethnic Russian published in the local Komsomol newspaper in early 1971 glorified the "incorruptible Slavic wisdom" of Lviv's first inhabitants. He suggested that Lviv belonged to Eastern Slavs, which included not just Ukrainians, but Great Russians and Belarusians. Ihor Kalynets, writing from exile in 1977, saw a Lviv always occupied by outsiders, with Ukrainians seemingly forever secluded in their medieval ghetto, Ruthenian Street near Market Square.[135] Lviv was for some an Eastern Slavic city, while for others it was Ukrainian. Regardless of these differences, the Poles and the legacy of the Polish-Lithuanian Commonwealth mattered little. They disappeared from such narratives.

Ola Hnatiuk discusses the difficulties contemporary writers like Iuriy Andrukhovych have had placing Lviv and Galicia into a Central European narrative. Central Europe's modernity is connected to Galicia's Austrian past, but not its Polish past. Hnatiuk suggests tensions between Poles and Ukrainians during interwar Poland as the possible reason why today's Galician Ukrainians have no real nostalgia for the Polish-Lithuanian Commonwealth.[136] The transformation of Lviv's urban spaces into a Soviet Abroad thus involved the emptying of its Poles. This happened not just physically, as in the deportations of 1944–47, but also metaphorically. In this "Ukrainian Florence," Ukrainian folk craftsmen had the last laugh over their Polish masters, while Ukrainians still wondered if they had left their ghetto.

Lviv became a Soviet Abroad for both locals and non-locals. Ethnic Russians and Russian speakers thus came to identify Lviv as their own. In his memoir essay of Lviv, writer and translator Grigorii Komskii, an ethnic Russian born in 1950, stresses the "European" Lviv that his family and other ethnic Russians came to adore. Spacious, ornate, and well-built apartment buildings quickly became home, and private services at home (like haircuts and shaves), left over from the old bourgeois world, made their lives more comfortable. Komskii was one of those students nicknamed the "Sybarites," inspired by Polish and Czech journals to create their own humorous texts.[137] A Russian speaker from Kharkiv, who aspired to become a Russian actress, became enthralled with Lviv when she came there to study acting in 1980–82. One of their theater school's instructors, local art scholar Volodymyr Osviychuk, inspired a great love for Lviv as he guided them on tours of its museums and architecture.[138]

For residents of provincial Russian cities, Lviv was more progressive than their own home towns. It became a more immediate version of the imaginary West that Soviet leaders engaged in and which Soviet citizens consumed eagerly, thus helping sustain late Soviet socialism.[139] This could be seen in the perceived abundance of Western music and Western fashions in Lviv. Iuriy Sharifov credited to Lviv his success as one of its early rock musicians, noting the crucial role Polish radio played in his life.[140] Another early rock musician, Aleksandr Balaban, said close contacts with Poland made Lviv much better connected to music developments abroad. He gave as an example his band's concert in the Russian provincial city of Gorky, where local rock music fans asked to copy the band's Western albums.[141] Moscow jazz artist and leader of the group Arsenal, Alexei Kozlov, recalling tours of such Western Ukrainian cities as Lviv and Chernivtsi in 1978, said that these western provincial cities were even ahead of Moscow in terms of new recordings and information on the latest in electronic instruments.[142] Because of such ties with Western jazz and later rock music, Lviv clubs became popular concert venues not just for young Lvivians but also for young people from Kharkiv, Leningrad, Kyiv, Moscow, and other Soviet cities interested in the light music and jazz of the 1950s and later the big beat rock of the 1960s.[143]

The Dnipropetrovsk teens admiring rock albums in Lviv in 1974 were not alone. Lviv became a mecca for Western fashions and Western record albums, not just for young people from other parts of Ukraine, but from other Soviet republics. Two Lvivians who used to stop by the "Holy Garden," a hangout for hippies, recalled people from as far away as Murmansk in the Far North and Magadan in the Far East coming to Lviv in search of Western rock albums.[144] Others have indicated that Lviv became the "jeans capital" of the Soviet Union because of its access to Western goods via Poland.[145]

To some degree, Lvivians had an impact on the cities they migrated to. Anna Brazhkina, a Russian translator of Ukrainian literature, recalled the tremendous impact Russian speakers from Lviv had on her native city, Rostov. In the mid-1980s, this "joyful and very free-willed [zapodiiats'kyi] Russian-language group from Lviv" acquired notoriety in Rostov for their love for marijuana and city life, as opposed to the locals' preference for wine and village life. Ten years of connections with these Lvivians changed Rostov's cultural scene and inspired her to become a translator of Ukrainian literature.[146]

Russians who became notable in Moscow's cultural and political life spent their childhood in Lviv. Iurii Bashmet, a leading concert violinist in

Moscow and other world cities, grew up in Lviv and attended its special music school for children. In his memoirs, he credits Lviv with making him the person he is today.[147] Grigory Yavlinsky, one of President Boris Yeltsin's liberal economic reformers and leader of the liberal party Yabloko in post-Communist Russia, was born in Lviv in 1952. He attended school there and later worked at the Raduga Glass Factory in 1968–69, before moving to Moscow.[148] In a film released for Lviv's 750th anniversary in 2006, he stressed the fond memories he had for Lviv, including the times he and friends exchanged Beatles recordings in one of the city's clubs known for its dances in the late 1960s.[149]

Lviv, like the Baltic republics, thus encouraged a more direct version of the imagined West, as well as a sense that there could be a compromise with Soviet socialism. The Baltic republic cities had their own extensive ties with diasporas in the capitalist West. Vilnius had access to more liberal Polish media. Tallinn had direct access to the real West, Finland, by way of Finnish television.[150] Young people in Riga created their imagined West with the help of Polish media, pirate radio broadcasts from Swedish ships on the Baltic Sea, and trips to nearby Estonia.[151] However, Lviv's Soviet Abroad and imaginary West were Ukrainian. They were provincialized, not just by Moscow, but by Kyiv. Lvivians regarded Moscow as having more liberal cultural policies than Lviv in the late 1970s and 1980s. Central Party officials were more attentive to the nationalities policy than were their counterparts in Lviv and Kyiv.[152] Notwithstanding accounts of Lviv's bustling black market in Western rock albums and its lively jazz and rock scene, others point to its provincial character. Jazz musician Volodymyr Kit, one of the members of the group Medykus, said that when their jazz band played at the first all-Union jazz festival in Tartu at the beginning of the 1960s, they were the only Ukrainian jazz band there, but the Moscow musicians playing had mastered jazz much better than they had.[153] His account suggests that the Soviet periphery indeed lagged behind the imperial center.

Lviv was not Tallinn. One of the frequenters of the freewheeling bohemian atmosphere of the Armenian Street Café, Russian writer Maryna Kursanova, said, perhaps not so ironically, that people gathered at the café in the 1980s "because there was nowhere else to go." Her recollections of her siblings' adventures in the 1970s featured trips to Tallinn, what Russians would regard as the real Soviet West.[154] Not only were there not as many interesting cafés as there were in places like Tallinn. In Tallinn, greater cultural expression was permitted. Thus hippie Oleh (Alik) Olisevych found

Tallinn to be the real imagined West for hippies and other countercultures in the 1970s and 1980s.[155] However, perhaps the most fitting contrast between Tallinn and Lviv could be seen in the autobiography of a district Party functionary in Lviv, Aleksandr Khokhulin ("Mankurt"). In a major exhibit for the Soviet Union's sixtieth anniversary in 1982, local officials banned nude sculptures by Estonian artists, causing the Estonian delegation to leave town in protest.[156]

Not all Baltic republic cities were alike. Young people growing up in Riga in the 1960s saw Tallinn as more Western than their city, since Tallinn had more bars and access to Finnish television.[157] Nonetheless, recent accounts of cultural life in Riga suggest literary, artistic, and music trends from the West affected young Rigans more than their counterparts in Lviv.[158] Several factors account for Lviv not measuring up to the kind of Soviet West found in Tallinn, Riga, or Vilnius. Romuald Misiunas and Rein Taagepera, as well as Amir Weiner, argue that significant linguistic differences, as well as the Baltic republics' proximity to the West, compelled Soviet policy makers to allow more liberal cultural policies in places like Tallinn, where these nudes banned by frightened Lviv bureaucrats were not a problem.[159]

Perhaps more importantly, wartime and postwar processes of Sovietization in the Baltics and Western Ukraine differed markedly. Tarik Amar describes a revolution from above aimed at overcoming the locals' "backwardness." The nearly complete emptying of Lwów's population through deportations, genocide, and flight to the West compelled the new Lvivians to spend years rebuilding cultural and educational institutions. They did so mainly with the help of Eastern Ukrainians and others from outside the region. Soviet cultural and educational institutions facilitated this postwar transformation.[160] The fact that Galician Ukrainians lacked the opportunity to develop state institutions like Latvians, Lithuanians, and Estonians between the world wars made this help from outside even more imperative. Weiner points out that the Baltics emerged from the war relatively unscathed, allowing greater survival of prewar elites and hence memories of the institutions and practices associated with them.[161] Elena Zubkova suggests that the new postwar elites in charge of all three republics faced a delicate balancing act between Moscow and the local population. Their policies led to significant violence and political repression, as well as Moscow's crackdown on "national Communists" in postwar Estonia, but by 1953 these policies had failed to produce more than outward conformity to the new order.[162] Because of this failure, Soviet leaders in the early years of

Khrushchev's Thaw began promoting the Baltic republics as something different from the rest of the Soviet Union, a so-called Soviet West and a showcase for the Soviet way of life.[163] Thus the Baltic republic capitals acquired the resources and institutional support for greater cultural experimentation and more extensive exchanges with the West.

Despite being twice provincialized, Lviv became a crucial battleground in Ukraine's cultural wars of the post-Stalin era. In the politics of language, literature, and history, Lviv's location at the fault line of imperial and nationalist projects, as well as Roman Catholic and Eastern Orthodox civilizations, placed it at the center of such cultural wars. Unlike the unfortunate Estonian sculptures, these were not problems local officials or their republic counterparts could throw drapes over.

PART II

Lviv and the Ukrainian Nation

CHAPTER 5

Language and Literary Politics

The battle for Ukrainians' language, literature, and history became vital for Lvivians, but it was closely connected with events in Soviet Ukraine's capital, Kyiv. With the discrediting of Stalin's cult of personality in 1956, it was here that Party and state functionaries, along with members of the Writers' Union, first reconsidered existing Soviet nationalities policies. It was here that the first public criticisms were raised about discrimination against Ukrainians' language and literature, as well as about their past. Republic-level institutions, as well as republic-level rehabilitations of cultural figures disgraced in the Stalin era, led to rising expectations for social and political change by Soviet Ukraine's educated elites.[1]

Though prompted by developments in Kyiv and Moscow, new members of Lviv's literary establishment pursued local agendas. The careers of two such writers illustrated the special dimension that language and literary politics took in Soviet Ukraine's western borderlands. Poet Dmytro Pavlychko, born in 1928 in the Ivano-Frankivsk Region of Galicia, briefly flirted with the nationalist underground at the close of the war. Along with a small group of teens, he was arrested and briefly detained in 1945 for belonging to a youth group affiliated with the UPA. Pavlychko came to embrace the ideals of the new Soviet order. He identified with themes of social and national justice championed by Lenin.[2] He wrote poems condemning the murderous deeds of the UPA and the OUN-B and the treacherous acts of the "Uniates," the Ukrainian Greek Catholic Church.[3] Pavlychko's colleague and friend, Rostyslav Bratun, was born in 1927 in Volhynia, which witnessed unspeakable violence against Jews and Poles in World War II.

Like Pavlychko, Bratun flirted with the nationalist underground. He belonged to an OUN-B-affiliated youth group around 1943.[4] He hid it from his biography until 1952, when he confessed it to a colleague at the Lviv newspaper he was working at. He lost his candidate status in the Party ranks, as noted when his personal case was discussed at the Party organization of the Lviv Writers' Union.[5] His personal appeal to Stalin, as well as the intervention of his aunt, a prominent actress in Soviet Ukraine, saved him from further trouble. Like Pavlychko, he went on to write a pamphlet condemning the nationalist underground and the Uniates.[6]

Both Pavlychko and Bratun acquired a general set of social strategies, a *habitus,* for coping with the new realities they faced. They embraced the ideals of social and national justice that the Soviet state stood for. This meant breaking with their past involvement with underground nationalists. As they went on to attend Lviv State University and pursue their early careers in the Lviv Writers' Union, they left behind what they presumably considered to have been the "foolishness" of their wartime youth. However, breaking with the past was not so simple. They, too, had experienced Soviet terror on the western borderlands. The Thaw allowed them the opportunity to address issues of national injustice that they had seen under Soviet rule. In 1957, in the early years of the Thaw, Pavlychko confided in a friend from Poland that the secret police had murdered a prominent Lviv writer, Iaroslav Halan, for anti-Soviet views.[7] Pavlychko began speaking out against what he saw as increased Russification in Soviet Ukrainian society. His poems, like "When the Bloody Torquemada Died," written the year before Khrushchev's "Secret Speech" condemned Stalin's cult of personality, suggested that many more changes were needed before the Soviet Union could overcome Stalin's legacy. Bratun, as editor of the city's literary journal, *October (Zhovten'),* in the mid-1960s, began broadening forms of individual and national self-expression in Ukrainian literature.

Despite the opposition they faced, these establishment writers and older colleagues stemmed the tide of Russification prevailing in postwar Soviet Ukrainian cities. While Bratun soon lost his job as editor, his successor made the journal a reliable, though more restricted, institution of Ukrainian national self-expression. With the onset of the Gorbachev era, both Pavlychko and Bratun pursued greater rights for Ukraine and soon demanded Ukraine's separation from the Soviet Union. The connections made between these writers and the republic's literary establishment underscored the crucial role Lviv intellectuals played in the Soviet Union's demise.

Language Debates in Post-Stalin Lviv

Even in the late Stalin era, Western Ukrainians in Lviv took Party and state organs to task for going too far in the campaign against "bourgeois nationalism." They complained about the lack of Ukrainian language use in public institutions.[8] When Soviet secret police chief Lavrenty Beria issued a report in May 1953 critical of similar policy mistakes, Lviv writers spoke out against Eastern Ukrainians who insinuated that Russian, not Ukrainian, was to be the language of city life.[9]

Political changes in Moscow and Kyiv inspired Lviv writers to renew their calls for greater respect for Ukrainians' language and culture. After Khrushchev's "Secret Speech" in early 1956, Ukrainian Party leaders initiated very cautious criticism of the Stalin era in the republic press that summer. Republic leaderships of artistic unions only joined in this cautious criticism in 1957. Despite this caution, the suggestion Khrushchev made in his speech, that the advancement of socialism was about the enrichment of nations, encouraged greater acts of national self-expression at the republic level. Composers and writers whose works in the late postwar period had been called "bourgeois nationalist" and "formalist" were rehabilitated over the next two years. New republic-wide journals on philosophy, history, the law, and economics—all in the Ukrainian language—appeared.[10]

In the second half of 1956, Lviv Writers' Union members at open and closed Party meetings drew on this thaw to demand greater respect for Ukrainians' language and culture. They revived concerns that the Ukrainian language and its defenders had been unjustly tarred as "nationalists" and that "Great Russian chauvinism" had overtaken local policy making. Obkom secretary Panas Iur further ignited writers' grievances when he allegedly told them in July that local intellectuals unfairly viewed the Russian language as an "eyesore" (*sil' v ochakh*), since in Polish times they had willingly sent their children to Polish-language schools. Iur further offended them by claiming ideological issues only interested the intelligentsia while everyone else was concerned about things like bread and shoes. At their closed Party meeting in early August, practically all the members speaking that day denounced Iur, and the first secretary of the obkom, Mykhailo Lazurenko, said that Iur did not speak for the obkom. By early December, when the Writers' Union held its annual year-end Party election meeting, unrest in Poland and Hungary revived the specter of "Ukrainian bourgeois nationalism." The union's Party activists eagerly demonstrated their ideological zeal. However, writers still vehemently defended themselves from such charges as being "nationalists" and used documents connected to early Soviet indigenization policies to justify their demands that state employees speak Ukrainian to Soviet Ukrainian citizens.[11]

It was in the midst of these debates, both in Lviv and in the capital, Kyiv, that Pavlychko criticized what he saw as Russification affecting Ukraine. In late September 1956, at a meeting in Lviv with teachers and writers discussing the problem of teaching Ukrainian literature at school (a problem raised by the republic's newspaper, *The Literary Newspaper* [*Literaturna hazeta*], that month), he castigated Ukrainian's secondary status. In schools, on movie screens, onstage, and on the radio, Russian was the preferred language, not just in Lviv but also in Ukrainian communities in Soviet Russia. Visitors from Soviet bloc countries observed Ukrainian's gradual disappearance in Lviv and other Ukrainian cities. Far more copies of *Lvov Pravda (L'vovskaia pravda)*, the region's Russian-language newspaper, were selling in Lviv than copies of the local Ukrainian-language equivalent, *Free Ukraine (Vil'na Ukraina)*. Schoolchildren, especially in Russian-language schools, thus considered only Russian literature worth reading. Calling for more open discussion, Pavlychko defended himself from Iur's charges in July of being an "apostle of nationalism." He said, "We need to stop calling people who wear embroidered shirts nationalists," referring to Ukrainians' national costume.[12]

At the end of 1958, Pavlychko published *The Truth Calls!* (a collection of poems) at a time where Russification was perceived to be threatening Ukraine's school system. A fierce debate erupted over Moscow's plans to reform republics' school systems so that students and their parents could choose whether or not to attend schools taught in the language of their respective republic. This proposed reform, along with other reforms of the Soviet school system, was announced in the central press on 16 November 1958. It produced objections from two prominent Kyiv writers, Maksym Rylskyi and Mykola Bazhan, who wrote in *Pravda* (11 December 1958) of the need to have Ukrainian and Russian classes made obligatory in all schools of the republic, regardless of their main language of instruction.[13]

Pavlychko's book, officially released by Lviv's state book publishing agency in January 1959, produced a sensation. Pavlychko included poems praising the Party and Lenin. Other poems, however, criticized those who had forsaken their native language. Some denounced Great Russian chauvinism. One poem alluded to the deaths of thousands of Ukrainian Cossacks who built St. Petersburg under Peter the Great. Yet another poem, "When the Bloody Torquemada Died," set in the time of the Spanish Inquisition, contained veiled criticism of not just Stalin himself, but the entire system he had built. According to the poem, as monks spread news throughout Spain of the Grand Inquisitor Thomás de Torquemada's demise, people "sobbed," not even smiling in secret, because "they probably remembered very well / That the tyrant died, but the prison still stands."[14]

Afraid of these poems' political implications, the obkom by the end of January 1959 decided to suspend the book's sales in Lviv's bookstores. Despite a recommendation by Writers' Union member Iuriy Melnychuk, written 2 February, not to ban it, the obkom bureau in its 13 February decree justified its position, claiming some of the criticisms raised in Pavlychko's poems were highly exaggerated, creating a "certain social danger." It reprimanded the director of Lviv's state book publisher and the head of the Lviv regional censorship body, Obllit, and called on the local Writers' Union to learn serious lessons from the incident. At closed Party meetings of the Writers' Union held some days later (17 February), writers objected to the decision to ban the book, but they approved a resolution recognizing the obkom bureau's decision as correct.[15]

Pavlychko's spirited criticism of perceived Russification reflected his own integration into the ideals of Soviet socialism. His poems targeted not just the Roman Catholic clergy but also careerist, boorish, and hypocritical officials, as the obkom bureau decree suggests.[16] Regional Party leaders assumed *The Truth Calls!* to be a threat because its poems' metaphors could be read as an attack not on Peter the Great or on the Grand Inquisitor, but on Soviet leaders and their subordinates.

Banning the book turned it into a bestseller. As he objected to the ban, Melnychuk described its consequences. Hundreds of people suddenly stormed bookstores for copies and called the Writers' Union angrily demanding explanations for the book's disappearance. Melnychuk heard that when a group of young people besieged Store Number Twenty's clerks with questions about the book's absence, some figure came up and told them to hurry up and go to the movie theater Ukraine, where there were plenty of copies still available. Thus interested buyers rushed to the theater, buying tickets so that they could get in and find their copy of Pavlychko's collection of poems. Such incidents happened at all the city movie theaters and special kiosks *(zakryti kiosky)*. Selling underground at exaggerated prices, the book had become a boon to "boors and sensationalists" *(obyvateli i liubiteli sensatsiy*).[17] What Pavlychko had said truly resonated with people, espe-cially since it was now considered to be rebelling against the state.

Pavlychko's defense of the Ukrainian language provoked attacks from Writers' Union members who saw him and others exaggerating the impact of Russification on Lviv, and perhaps intentionally. A Russian (or Polish) writer from Eastern Ukraine, Volodymyr Bieliaiev, was most likely a KGB informant who came to Lviv in 1944 to keep watch over local political moods.[18] He was known for trying to gain media fame on a variety of topics from "Ukrainian bourgeois nationalism" to the Holocaust and for writing numerous denunciations to Party organs.[19] Bieliaiev at Writers' Union Party meetings insinuated that defenders of Ukrainian like Pavlychko could one day take up arms against the state, a clear reference to Pavlychko's flirta-tion with a UPA youth organization. Bieliaiev said that people preoccupied with the presence of Russian-language signs on Shevchenko Avenue, one of Lviv's main streets, needed to focus more on the struggle against "bourgeois nationalists."[20] Tymish Odudko, an Eastern Ukrainian poet and journalist, lost his patience with writers like Pavlychko, who claimed that his own children could not even speak Ukrainian. Pointing out his daughter's high grades in Ukrainian at the university, Odudko shot back, "I won't make my children nationalists. They really will be communists."[21]

While Bieliaiev was at his usual métier compromising people, his innu-endos were premised on major assumptions outsiders to Western Ukraine had about the language issue. Soviet policy makers since the late 1930s had moved in the direction of a territorial rather than a linguistic sense of na-tionality, where the use of Russian in public life was not considered a prob-lem. This was an idea of nationality shared by Ukrainians in such eastern regions as Vinnytsia.[22] City and regional Party leaders, who came from such milieus, agreed. Gorkom officials did not express their opinions as ineptly as their colleague Panas Iur had. However, when discussing *The Truth Calls!* gorkom officials claimed criticisms by Pavlychko and others were "bab-blings" *(balachky)* that needed to stop.[23]

Pavlychko and other Lviv writers did not stop. Encouraged by policies in Kyiv under Party leader Petro Shelest, senior novelist Iryna Vilde brought up the language issue at a republic-wide writers' congress in 1966, criticiz-ing regional and republic Party leaders for excessive censorship, a tendency that led to the best writers turning to Russian-language publishers in Mos-cow. Two years later, poet and journalist Mykola Petrenko, responding to the regional Party secretary's public claim that the nationalities policy had been "solved," asked in front of other journalists why there were vocational schools in Lviv teaching in Russian.[24] Shelest's successor, Volodymyr Shcherbytskyi, heavily neutralized such debate by aggressively promoting the use of Russian at Party and state functions. Such actions affected Lviv's public sphere, leading to vociferous protests against Lviv's Russification at the end of the 1980s. However, establishment writers like Pavlychko had accomplished much as a pressure group by slowing down rather than ending Russification.

Lviv's Limited Russification

While regional and city Party leaders scolded writers for exaggerating the language issue, they made tacit compromises with them. Such compromises could be seen with newspapers, schools, and higher education. Establishment writers contributed to the growth of Ukrainian-language newspapers in Lviv. Copies of such Ukrainian-language newspapers for the region as *Free Ukraine* and *Leninist Youth (Lenins'ka molod')* featured articles by Writers' Union members, including journalists. They contributed to the readership of such Ukrainian-language newspapers through speaking engagements with the wider public. For instance, members of the Lviv Writers' Union, including its chair, Iryna Vilde, spoke to over a thousand workers of the Lviv Bus Factory in March 1966, performing poems and other literary works. Their speaking engagement marked the beginning of city-wide activities dedicated to the Twenty-Third Party Congress, including discussions and visits at Lviv's factories, state enterprises, and schools.[25]

Circulation statistics of Ukrainian and Russian-language newspapers for the Lviv Region from 1950 to 1975 suggest the growing appeal Ukrainian-language periodicals had gained. The Lviv Region's Ukrainian-language daily, *Free Ukraine,* enjoyed a steady increase in circulation figures, from 45,000 copies in 1950 to 88,000 copies in 1960, followed by 190,000 copies in 1970 and 227,000 copies in 1975. By contrast, its Russian-language equivalent, *Lvov Pravda,* circulated in much smaller numbers: 23,000 copies in 1950, followed by 38,000 in 1960, approximately 91,000 in 1970, and then 104,000 in 1975.[26] While there are no systematic figures for the city itself, this trend in newspaper sales suggested greatly different trends than in Eastern Ukrainian cities like Donetsk, where the Russification, not the Ukrainianization, of newspapers prevailed. The Ukrainian-language newspaper, *Socialist Donetsk (Radians'ka Donechchyna),* published in the city of Donetsk, had a circulation of only 55,000 copies in the Donetsk Region in 1975. The Russian-language newspaper, *Socialist Donbass (Sotsialis-ticheskii Donbas),* also published in Donetsk, by contrast had a circulation over six times larger, 373,000 copies.[27]

Besides this higher circulation of Ukrainian-language newspapers, Lviv experienced a steady decline in Russian-language schools since the Thaw began. Reports from the Lviv City Department of People's Education (two comprehensive reports on city schools, filed in 1955, for the period 1940–50 and for the period from the 1950–51 school year to the beginning of the 1955–56 school year, and yearly reports for the 1965–66 and 1970–71 school years) confirm this trend (Table 5.1). The number of students in Polish-language Soviet schools, while at an all-time high in 1945–46 (66.39 percent of all students), plummeted as deportations took their effect. By the 1950–51 school year, only 5.69 percent of all city school students attended Polish-language schools, and this dropped to less than 1 percent by the mid-1960s. Students in Russian-language schools went from a mere 13.08 percent of the total student body in 1944–45 to as many as 58.65 percent of all students in the 1955–56 school year. After this year, however, the percentage of school students in Russian-language schools steadily dropped, to 39.85 percent in 1965–66 and to 28.71 percent by 1970–71. In the meantime, the share of students in Ukrainian-language schools gradually became the majority for Lviv. Whereas 37.59 percent of all school students were in Ukrainian-language schools in 1955–56, and only 38.75 percent in 1965–66, by the 1970–71 school year, as many as 56.52 percent of all students attended Ukrainian-language schools. Even if mixed-language schools are not included in the total number of Ukrainian-language schools (some of these schools taught courses mostly in Ukrainian), it is clear that Ukrainian-language schools were on the ascendancy in Lviv. Indeed, in 1970–71, the percentage of students in Ukrainian-language schools (56.52 percent) was still significantly below the percentage of ethnic Ukrainians in the city (68.21 percent in 1970). The share of students in Russian-language schools in that school year (28.71 percent) exceeded the proportion of ethnic Russians in Lviv (22.27 percent). However, when other non-Ukrainian ethnic groups from other parts of the Soviet Union—groups that most likely attended Russian-language schools in significant numbers—are included with ethnic Russians (namely, Jews who made up 4.39 percent of Lviv's population in 1970, followed by Belarusians, who constituted 1.17 percent of Lviv's total population that year), this difference seems minimal (with a total of

Table 5.1 Schools by language of instruction, Lviv, 1940–71

Type of school	No. of schools	No. of students	% of total student body
Russian-language schools			
1940–41	4	1,705	4.11%
1944–45	2	2,280	13.08%
1945–46	9	7,500	28.63%
1950–51	32	19,279	56.44%
1955–56	31	24,667	58.65%
1965–66	30	27,043	39.85%
1970–71	29	21,320	28.71%
Ukrainian-language schools			
1940–41	40	18,857	45.50%
1944–45	17	3,579	20.53%
1945–46	25	10,130	38.66%
1950–51	29	12,937	37.87%
1955–56	27	15,809	37.59%
1965–66	33	26,302	38.75%
1970–71	41	41,979	56.52%
Polish-language schools			
1940–41	70	20,687	49.92%
1944–45	39	11,572	66.39%
1945–46	24	8,570	32.71%
1950–51	4	1,944	5.69%
1955–56	3	1,585	3.77%
1965–66	2	470	0.69%
1970–71	2	399	0.54%
Mixed-language schools			
1965–66	12	14,053	20.71%
1970–71	8	10,571	14.23%

Sources: Derzhavnyi Arkhiv L'vivs'koi Oblasti (hereafter DALO), R-402/3/126/172–73; DALO, R-402/3/242/11; DALO, R-402/3/386/106.

Notes: Figures for 1940–50 are total for all middle, seven-year, and primary schools. Figures for 1965–66 concern eleven-year schools, while figures for 1970–71 concern ten-year schools.

Total figures for the 1940–41 school year include two Jewish schools with a total of 173 students.

Percentages are rounded to the nearest hundredth of a percent.

Mixed-language schools constitute either Russian-Ukrainian or Ukrainian-Russian schools. They only appear in reports for the 1965–66 and 1970–71 school years.

27.83 percent of the city's population composed of ethnic Russians, Jews, and Belarusians in 1970).[28]

Unfortunately, there are no such data for Lviv city schools after 1971. The State Archives of the Lviv Region did not preserve files for the City Department of People's Education beyond the 1970–71 school year. Surviving records at the Bureau of Statistics for the State Administration of the Lviv Region for 1970–86 did not differentiate Lviv schools by language of instruction. State archives for the city of Lviv failed to yield any surviving data on Soviet-era city schools.[29] However, one recent publication suggests that in the 1980s, the number of Russian-language schools in Lviv may have increased, but not enough to indicate significant Russification affecting Lviv schools. In 1987, there were 103 schools in Lviv. Of these, 26 schools were Russian-language schools, while 11 were mixed-language schools, where classes were taught mostly in Russian. While the number of Russian-language schools had increased, nearly 74 percent of Lviv's schoolchildren were in schools with Ukrainian as the language of instruction.[30] This figure roughly corresponded to the percentage of Ukrainians in Lviv by that time (74 percent by the 1979 Census).[31]

To be sure, in mixed-language schools, where classes were taught in both Ukrainian and Russian, the language of instruction could easily become mostly Russian. Ukrainian-language schools presumably relied on Russian-language textbooks and other materials. Taking these factors into account, the school system was still inadequate for those advocating Ukrainian-language instruction. However, such trends were radically different from those in Donetsk and Kyiv. In Donetsk, as early as the 1959–60 school year, up to 98 percent of its schoolchildren were attending Russian-language schools. In Kyiv in 1987, fewer than 70,000 schoolchildren out of a total of 301,000 (less than 23 percent of the total school population) were studying in Ukrainian.[32]

Figures for Lviv's institutions of higher education are highly impressionistic, with specific data reported only when institutional, city, or regional Party leaders reported progress in implementing the Party's nationality policy. According to one gorkom secretary, in the fall of 1956, over 60 percent of lectures and seminar lessons were being conducted in Ukrainian at such institutions in Lviv, in contrast to only isolated cases not so many years earlier. However, this Party secretary reported these figures to the Writers' Union's annual Party election meeting, trying to head off criticism that not enough was being done to promote the Ukrainian language.[33] A later report of a specific institution of higher education casts doubts on this general figure's validity. A 1957 obkom report on the work of the Party organization of the Lviv State Polytechnic Institute mentioned the institute's lack of Ukrainian-language classes. Of its 535 instructors, only 124 read lectures in Ukrainian (or 23.4 percent), and only an additional 76 read lectures in both Ukrainian and Russian (or 14.6 percent). There were as many as 102 instructors who mastered Ukrainian but still taught in Russian. In a number of faculties, all instructors were teaching courses exclusively in Russian.[34]

At Lviv State University, the only figures available were for 1969. Charlotte Saikowski, a *Christian Science Monitor* reporter, found out that 78 percent of all lectures and seminars at Lviv State University were in Ukrainian.[35] Like the gorkom secretary, this official speaking to Saikowski may have glossed over the truth to win over his or her listener. While these figures need to be taken with caution, they at least indicate that some kind of general progress toward having more Ukrainian-language classes was taking place. A complete lack of available statistics after 1969 makes it even more of a risk to generalize about the state of the Ukrainian language in Lviv's institutions of higher education. At best, oral interviews suggest that while some instructors felt pressured to switch to teaching in Ukrainian in the 1970s, when the republic Party leadership encouraged greater public use of Russian, fields and disciplines still offered both Ukrainian-language and Russian-language instruction. At the Lviv State Polytechnic Institute, there was a trend of instructors switching to Russian-language instruction, but there were still courses taught in both Russian and Ukrainian. At Lviv State University's history faculty at the end of the 1970s, virtually all the courses were in Ukrainian.[36] According to one former student, an absence of technical literature made instructors turn increasingly to teaching in Russian, even if they knew Ukrainian, at Lviv State Polytechnic Institute. This reflected a republic-wide trend where the share of Ukrainian-language books published in the republic steadily declined over the 1960s and 1970s.[37] Given the lack of precise, reliable data, it seems that Lviv's institutions of higher education were less able than middle schools to offer Ukrainian-language instruction. Nonetheless, they at least provided the opportunity for nearly half, if not a majority, of courses to be taught in Ukrainian.

Despite the lacunae of data on language use in higher education, Viktor Susak suggests that the presence of the Ukrainian language in schools was making Ukrainian the local language of communication (Table 5.2). Census results for 1970 and 1989 indicate that an increasing share of families of

Table 5.2 Non-Ukrainians' knowledge of Ukrainian as a second language, 1970–89

	1970	1979	1989
Russians	43.63%	51.20%	56.58%
Jews	50.98%	58.87%	64.18%
Poles	40.59%	39.59%	38.97%

Source: Viktor Susak, "Etnichni ta sotsial'ni zminy v naselenni L'vova v 1939–1999 rokakh" (MA thesis, Lviv National University, 2000), 40.

Russians and Jews who came to Lviv from other regions after the war were starting to consider Ukrainian their second language. In the 1970 Census, a majority of Lviv's Russians (55.03 percent) said they mastered no other language besides Russian. Despite declining to 41.22 percent by the 1989 Census, this figure was still much higher than among Jews or Poles. Despite this reputation for not learning other languages, a rising number of ethnic Russians claimed to master Ukrainian as a second language. Ethnic Russians knowing Ukrainian as a second language increased from 43.63 percent in 1970 to 56.58 percent in 1989. On the eve of Ukraine's independence, most Russians were becoming acclimated to using Ukrainian as a language of communication. An even greater share of ethnic Jews did the same. Jews knowing Ukrainian as a second language increased from a bare majority in 1970 (50.98 percent) to a solid majority in 1989 (64.18 percent).[38]

As for ethnic Ukrainians themselves, by the time of the 1970 Census, a total of 94.1 percent claimed Ukrainian as their native language. By 1989, this figure had increased to 97.0 percent.[39] Of Lviv's remaining Polish population, a total of 38.97 percent by 1989 had claimed Ukrainian to be their second language, but they were seven times more likely than Russians and other nationalities to acquire Ukrainian not as their second language but as their native language, making them increasingly identified with the city's Galician Ukrainians.[40]

The growth of Ukrainian as a city-wide language of communication was not caused solely by the influx of Western Ukrainian villagers. Among the new Lvivians there were former villagers who earned the nickname *"rahuly"* for clumsily trying to speak Russian and look urban. Speaking Russian was a sign of urban identity. By the mid-1980s, it was more fashionable for rock groups to perform in Russian, not Ukrainian. Therefore, cultural and educational institutions played a vital role encouraging Lviv's Ukrainians and non-Ukrainians to respect the Ukrainian language. Oral interviews indicate that middle school teachers of Ukrainian language and literature rid young Ukrainians of assumptions that Ukrainian was a "hick language" *(vuykivs'ka mova)* or inspired among non-Ukrainian students a love for the works of classic Ukrainian poet Taras Shevchenko.[41] Lviv's Ukrainian intelligentsia, which included these schoolteachers, made Ukrainians' history, language, and literature appeal to others. Pavlychko's poems, (including *The Truth Calls!*) awoke young intellectuals to the dangers of Ukrainians' losing their language and culture, as a conservatory instructor recalled in an interview.[42] Such educated Ukrainians closely followed literary developments not just in Moscow, but in Kyiv and Lviv, including Lviv's literary journal, *October.* This journal brought the Thaw to life in Lviv.

Lviv's Literary Thaw

Khrushchev's Thaw inspired establishment writers to resist the marginalization they had faced during Stalin's cult of personality. In July 1956, writers pointed out the disadvantages they faced in the provinces compared to such capitals as Kyiv and Moscow, particularly regarding access to new literary works from abroad.[43] Others called on greater support for Lviv as a regional cultural center, proposing a regional literary journal and other periodicals for Western Ukrainian artists and writers.[44] When Rostyslav Bratun edited the city's literary journal, *October,* from late 1963 to 1966, he too sought to overcome this marginalization. *October* exemplified the literary establishment's accommodating official discourse while asserting a different stance toward Ukrainian literature.

As editor of *October,* Bratun refrained from politically controversial works. When one editor showed him a manuscript emphasizing national motifs in the poetry of Shevchenko and a famous Hungarian writer, he said it would be an excellent article, but in Paris.[45] He thus played a guarded role in Lviv's literary thaw, trying to make Lviv somewhat more like Paris. Speaking before a Writers' Union meeting on 25 January 1962, after the Twenty-Second Congress in Moscow initiated further criticism of Stalinism, he stressed that Ukrainian writers needed to win back the trust of their readers with works that were more "sincere, bold, and truthful" than works fostered by Stalin's cult of personality.[46] He sponsored Sunday poetry readings by young writers in front of the opera theater which later involved young artists, actors, and musicians. Bratun thus was like other Soviet establishment writers encouraging the flourishing of young people's poetry during the Thaw. He was among those in official artistic unions advising and defending Lviv's Club of Artistic Youth. This club's students and young intellectuals promoted the ideals of the Ukrainian Sixtiers Movement.[47]

When he became editor of *October* in 1963, Bratun, with the help of such assistant editors as Roman Ivanychuk, Roman Kudlyk, and others, supported innovative young writers and artists throughout the republic and made Ukrainian literature more oriented toward the wider world. Analysis of issues for the years 1964 and 1965 indicates that poems and essays on the Party, Lenin, and Soviet patriotism highlighted the journal's first pages on political holidays like the October Revolution, the anniversary of Lviv's liberation by the Soviet Army, and the twenty-fifth anniversary of Western Ukraine's joining Soviet Ukraine. Yet within such editions, there were short stories and intimate lyrical poems with nothing political in them (by such writers as Dmytro Herasymchuk, Volodymyr Luchuk, Roman Kudlyk, Oleksandr Lizen, Iuriy Koval, and Arkadiy Pastushenko). Some were by modernist and science fiction writers from Kyiv (Oles Berdnyk, Valeriy Shevchuk) or writers later banned by republic Party leaders (Vasyl Holoborodko, Ihor Kalynets, and Sviatoslav Karavanskyi). The journal enriched the literary canon by featuring Ukrainian-language translations of writers from England (C. P. Snow), the United States (Walt Whitman), and Spain (Federico Garcia Lorca). It included translations of works from such socialist camp countries as Poland and Czechoslovakia and such Soviet republics as Latvia where policies in art and literature were relatively more liberal.

Essays in literary and art criticism, citing Party congresses in 1956 and 1961 as calls for true Soviet democracy, criticized stereotypes in scholarship and art promoted in the Stalin era.[48] One writer took to task a scholar who had dismissed the role national forms of self-expression played in works by such Ukrainian literary classics as Ivan Franko. Turning to Franko's own works, he affirmed that all art is national as well as international.[49] Editions dedicated to the 150th anniversary of the birth of poet Taras Shevchenko and the anniversary of his death (numbers 3 and 5 for 1964, respectively) contained materials affirming the values of Soviet patriotism, but also devotion to a Soviet Ukrainian homeland. *October* featured works by or about victims of Stalinist repressions or those who had compromised themselves in wartime Lviv. Such writers included poet Myroslav Irchan, Galician Ukrainian children's writer Iuriy Shkrumeliak, novelist Hnat Khotkevych, humorist Ostap Vyshnia, and artist and writer Ivan Krushelnytskyi. It ran in serial form the gulag experiences of writer Volodymyr Hzhytskyi, a Galician Ukrainian who had immigrated to Soviet Ukraine in the 1920s. Another suppressed writer, Borys Antonenko-Davydovych from Kyiv, published a series of articles on the proper use of the Ukrainian language. In a book review he stressed the need to treat all languages of the world equally, including Ukrainian.[50]

The journal paid striking attention to visual design. It had far greater numbers of black-and-white drawings compared to issues before 1964. Ievhen Beznisko and Sofiia Karaffa-Korbut, both young Lviv artists, contributed them. If anything, *October* under Bratun's leadership promoted a sense of Soviet Ukrainian patriotism that tried to shed itself of the more restricted public sphere of Stalinist times.

October oriented Ukrainian readers not only toward the wider world, but to Central Europe. Bratun republished the "forgotten" Ukrainian poet from interwar Lwów, Bohdan-Ihor Antonych (1909–37). Antonych, influenced by modernist literary trends in interwar Europe, used symbols from Slavic pagan and Christian traditions to express himself. In this way he was like T. S. Eliot or Ezra Pound. His works became increasingly mystic and brooding, turning to apocalyptic themes of war and the depersonalization of urban life.[51]

In interwar Lwów, Antonych's introspection provoked rebukes by local Communist writers who accused him of diverting readers from the revolutionary struggle against social and national domination by the Poles. He had received a prize from a Greek Catholic foundation in 1936, which later linked him to the "reactionary" circles of the "Uniate" Church. The collection of poems that had won him this prize included the poem "A Word about Alcazar," which supposedly glorified fascist leader Franco's victory over the Republicans in Spain in the Battle of Alcazar. The actual text suggests it was a poem much more about the shock and awe caused by civil war.[52] However, any hint that Alcazar's defenders were heroes represented a clear affront to Communists championing the Republican side in the civil war. Thus Antonych became labeled "bourgeois nationalist" and "anti-Soviet" by both regional and republic Party leaders, a fact that Antonych's defenders had to reckon with.[53]

As editor of *October,* Bratun sought to rehabilitate Antonych by having as many as forty-four of his poems and ballads published in the second issue of the journal for 1964, as well as an article on Antonych's art. The next year saw the publication of a text of an opera by Antonych, based on the life of eighteenth-century Hutsul folk hero Oleksa Dovbush (a Robin Hood of the Carpathian Mountains).[54] Three years later, Bratun's colleague Dmytro Pavlychko followed up on these efforts by publishing a collection of Antonych's selected poems. Already on 15 November 1956, in the aftermath of Khrushchev's "Secret Speech," Pavlychko had raised the issue of rehabilitating Antonych's art before a Lviv Writers' Union meeting.[55]

The writers and editors of *October*, and later Pavlychko, returned Antonych to the public sphere by refashioning him into a positive role model for the Communist future. They emphasized the difficulties caused by "bourgeois nationalist" and "reactionary" circles in Western Ukraine's cultural life. Antonych's refusal to engage in political subjects or join various nationalist camps of writers, they said, was a form of politics resisting Ukrainian bourgeois nationalism. While admitting Antonych's flights into mysticism and religious metaphor were shortcomings, these writers said that Antonych was a product of his time. They preferred to accentuate the social messages present in Antonych's poems, such as the poverty of Lemko Region villagers (the region in the Carpathians where Antonych grew up), sinister scenes of city life in capitalist Lwów, and the vague sense of a new era awaiting civilization.[56]

With Antonych now the popular masses' poet, these critics and editors incorporated into the Soviet Ukrainian literary canon a writer influenced not by Russia, but by Central Europe. They widened the horizons of Ukrainian literature, making it not an imperial province of Soviet literature, but closer to the West. It was no coincidence that Antonych, who had an underground cult following prior to his rehabilitation, inspired an aesthetic rebellion by poets like Ihor Kalynets and Hryhoriy Chubai and, by the mid-1980s, Iuriy Andrukhovych and the Bu-Ba-Bu school of poetry. His poetry thus helped inspire young Lvivians' aesthetic rebellion.[57]

This new approach to literature by *October* resonated with the intelligentsia in Western Ukraine and elsewhere. As a report by the republic's Writers' Union noted, the journal's subscribers had gone up significantly throughout Ukraine, from about 12,000 when Bratun took over to as many as 17,400 as of June 1965.[58] Local Party leaders worried that *October* was gaining popularity among "unsound" elements. One obkom report on 4 March 1964 noted with alarm that among some intellectuals, "there has spread the opinion that 'Lviv finally has received a free Ukrainian journal.'"[59] Regardless of following accepted literary practices, *October* had left readers signs of a definite thaw. When the obkom leadership campaigned to remove Bratun, it caused one leading underground publication, Ivan Dziuba's 1965 *Internationalism or Russification,* to note this incident as a clear example of discrimination against Ukrainians' language and culture. For Dziuba, the journal had gone from being quite feeble to becoming one of Ukraine's leading journals, causing obkom leaders to demand Bratun's removal.[60]

The obkom bureau first tried to remove Bratun in May 1965, citing a number of ideological "shortcomings" in the journal.[61] The republic Writers' Union tried to defend him and won his case some time.[62] However, on 6 May 1966, the Secretariat of the CPU Central Committee approved the decision to fire him.[63] This campaign against Bratun, already brewing beneath the surface before 1965, ostensibly was about ideas. One obkom report, for instance, claimed that the March 1964 edition dedicated to Shevchenko contained a number of poems by Kyiv poet Ivan Drach that equated national oppression under Tsarist Russia with present conditions in the Soviet Union.[64]

Obkom functionaries justified firing Bratun by saying that the journal's literary critics "impose subjective views" and "defend formalist exercises of some artists and writers" in their articles. Editors had devoted an "excessive" attention to writers of the past, "exaggerating their significance and place in Ukrainian literature" as well as trying to "tone down their ideological deviations."[65] Efforts to rehabilitate Antonych received the greatest emphasis. Besides noting Antonych's award from a Greek Catholic foundation, the obkom bureau resolution firing Bratun noted that a lot of his poems published were marked by "a lack of politics," "pessimism," and "mysticism."[66]

In fact, obkom functionaries and Writers' Union members exploited such charges to settle scores with Bratun. Petro Inhulskyi had expected to become editor in 1963, only to see Bratun, with the connivance of other union members, get himself appointed in Kyiv. Inhulskyi readily helped the head of the regional state censorship agency find the slightest errors. For 1964 alone, state censors intervened in *October* publications over forty times, with fifteen materials removed altogether and some issues completely revised.[67] Timofei Odudko, in charge of censorship, for years had disliked Bratun. In 1956, during a drinking bout with other writers in a hotel, he provoked Bratun into talking about his Banderite past and then informed on him at the Party bureau of the city Writers' Union, claiming Bratun had made "anti-Soviet" remarks. During the campaign against the journal, Odudko, despite his involvement on its editorial staff and his responsibilities for press materials in the Lviv Region, cast doubts on the journal's political line in a city newspaper and at a regional Party conference.[68]

A central figure in the campaign was Valentyn Malanchuk. Malanchuk, obkom secretary in charge of ideology, had been bitter rivals with Bratun since their student days at Lviv State University in the late 1940s, when they vied for the hand of the woman who became Malanchuk's wife.[69] Malanchuk, moreover, was trying to sell himself before superiors in Moscow and Kyiv as an expert on Ukrainian bourgeois nationalism. Such ambitions led to his becoming the republic's Party secretary in charge of ideology in 1972, bringing about nearly a decade of the most rigorous censorship of national self-expression.[70]

As Bratun indicates in an appeal to the republic's Central Committee, Malanchuk, instead of helping him, constantly called him an "abstraction-ist" and a "formalist." The "errors" he pointed out included using Ukrai-nian words other than those deemed closer to Russian, an insinuation that the editors were engaged in linguistic separatism. Speaking before the ob-kom bureau, Malanchuk made references to Bratun's OUN-UPA past and the "anti-Soviet" remarks Odudko had attributed to him in the 1956 hotel drinking bout. He added that CPU Central Committee secretary Andriy Skaba had warned Bratun that he would lose his job if he made the slight-est mistake.[71] Malanchuk got his way. Bratun had to leave *October,* replaced by Mykola Romanchenko. Known for his connections with the KGB, Romanchenko, according to a former subordinate, made life unbearable at the journal, even seeking political subtexts behind poems' arrangements of colors.[72]

Bratun's dismissal came after Khrushchev had been removed from of-fice and his successors cracked down on dissent. Editors' signing a petition for a dissident on trial in May 1966 only hastened the act, though Bratun was not involved. Malanchuk, speaking at a Writers' Union Party meeting that punished the signatories, supposedly added to the drama by repeating a line Russian writer Maxim Gorky had issued first to Soviet writers at the end of the 1920s, then to writers of the capitalist world, urging both to serve the working class. He called out, "Whom are you with, whom are you with, workers of culture?!"[73] Bratun and other Soviet journal editors became momentary victims as the Party and the KGB cracked down on networks of underground protest. A similar case occurred with Alexander Tvardovsky and the leading Soviet literary journal, *New World (Novy mir),* in Moscow.

Their connections with Alexander Solzhenitsyn and the publication of his memoirs, *One Day in the Life of Ivan Denisovych,* led to Tvardovsky's being forced to step down at the end of the 1960s.[74]

Bratun's disgrace did not mean a complete end of Lviv's literary thaw. Bratun went on to become head of the Lviv Writers' Union in 1968, serving in that capacity until 1980.[75] Despite Romanchenko's unbearable leadership tactics, literary and artistic innovation continued. Nearly all of Bratun's editorial staff worked under Romanchenko. Judging from issues for the year 1967, the journal was still rich in graphics illustrations. One issue featured poems by two young writers, Iaroslava Pavlychko and Hryhoriy Chubai, whose works by 1971 faced discrimination because of suspicions over their political reliability.[76] Issues for 1967 included works by a victim of the Stalin era (Vasyl Bobynskyi) and a writer repressed in Stalinist times and then rehabilitated (Ivan Hnatiuk). Translations of other writers' works, such as by Latvian and Lithuanian poets, continued. While these last two cases of translation did not necessarily connect Ukrainians with the wider world per se, they represented the translation of literature that was under less rigorous censorship.

Romanchenko's own tenure lasted only a year and a half. In late 1967 he had to resign after his girlfriend was convicted in a murder case. A prose writer from the Galician city of Ivano-Frankivsk, Roman Fedoriv, succeeded him at the beginning of 1968.[77] Fedoriv headed the journal as *October* until 1988, when it was renamed *The Bell (Dzvin),* and he continued as editor until his sudden death in early 2001.

Fedoriv, like other editors during 1970s-era political repressions in Ukraine, faced enormous pressure from censors and local Party bosses. An obkom official, Volodymyr Podolchak, regularly attended editorial staff meetings and searched galley proofs for any material compromising the staff. A member of the obkom bureau, a high-ranking military officer, even threatened to send troops to the journal to "establish order." The situation calmed down only with Podolchak's removal from the obkom in the late 1970s, allowing manuscripts held up for years to be published.[78]

By the end of the 1980s, *October* fell behind the capital when it came to new literary trends. It nonetheless remained a fairly stable channel for articles on Ukrainian subjects.[79] Well into the 1980s, it was very popular among schoolteachers and other "patriotically" minded Western Ukrainian intellectuals, as poet Oleksandr Irvanets indicated. Its editors encouraged new talents, like the literary premiere of Irvanets, one of the founders of

Lviv's avant-garde Bu-Ba-Bu school of poetry, in the early 1980s.[80] Less rigorous censorship by the late 1970s, as well as this focus on measured national self-expression, allowed the journal to survive a precipitous drop in readership, as noted by Roman Szporluk. Circulation had dropped from 19,000 copies in 1972 to 15,400 in 1973, during the height of repressions against Ukraine's national intelligentsia. Circulation remained stagnant at approximately 15,200 copies for 1974 and 1975.[81] With the modest subsiding of censorship and Podolchak's removal from the obkom, circulation by December 1980 reached 19,000 copies, as its December volume's publishing information indicates. When the political situation under Gorbachev allowed for much more freedom of expression, *October* as *The Bell* more than trebled its number of readers, to about 60,000 by 1989.[82] It was an example of the Lviv cultural establishment's ability to negotiate through increased censorship and still offer a forum for national self-expression.

Establishment Writers and the Disintegration of the Soviet Union

In being members of the cultural establishment—or "workers of culture," as Malanchuk put it—such writers as Bratun, Pavlychko, and others had to be clear about their political allegiances in a world of two competing systems, capitalism and socialism. They were limited in what they could say publicly. As Soviet writers, they contributed to campaigns against "bourgeois nationalism," and they took part in condemning dissidents. As head of the Writers' Union, Bratun at Party meetings during Prague Spring condemned "revisionism" in Czechoslovakia and Yugoslavia. He accused Ukrainian dissidents like Viacheslav Chornovil of slandering the Soviet Union.[83] As editor of *October,* Fedoriv wrote in a 13 May 1972 report for KGB organs that the poems of dissident Iryna Kalynets reflected her lack of "common sense" as well as political unreliability. These remarks might have been a reaction to the poems themselves, some of which mocked him and other editors of journals. Fedoriv's report nonetheless demonstrated a willingness to cooperate with the secret police. He faithfully countered Ukrainian diaspora "slander" as a member of Ukraine's 1974 delegation to the United Nations' General Assembly in New York.[84]

It would be a mistake to identify such people as dissidents, but these were not people with easy roles to play. Affable, passionate, and sometimes dramatic in his gestures in interviews, Fedoriv emphasized the constant pressure that the KGB and the censors put on him. His colleague's story about local Party functionaries and military officers literally peering over their shoulders and even threatening to bring in the troops only underscored the pressure he faced. Poet Mykola Petrenko illustrated the fine line that separated dissidents from establishment intellectuals. In various meetings, formal and informal, over Ukrainian *horilka* (Ukrainian vodka) or cognac, he mentioned his personal acquaintance with Ukrainians who went to prison in 1965 and 1972. While walking to an artist's shop one night, he emphasized that the dissidents were the "tip of a great iceberg" of people much like them. In an interview earlier that day, he saw dissidents as little different from other Ukrainian intellectuals. What made them different was that they got caught spreading *samvydav* literature.[55]

Given the role the dissident movement has played in Ukrainians' memories since independence, it has become fashionable to identify oneself with it, but Petrenko's analogy of the iceberg is worth considering. Lviv establishment writers were very closely connected with underground circles arrested for spreading *samvydav*. Kyiv poet and literary critic Ivan Svitlychnyi, one of those active in the Sixtiers Movement in the early 1960s and later involved in spreading political *samvydav*, was one of those who helped the editors of *October* incorporate Bohdan-Ihor Antonych into the Soviet Ukrainian canon. According to a friend, Lviv artist Ievhen Beznisko, Svitlychnyi had somehow discovered Antonych's libretto for an opera on Oleksa Dovbush, and he showed it to Beznisko and his wife, the sculptor Feodosiia Bryzh. On friends' advice, Svitlychnyi brought it to *October*, whose editors published it in September 1965. Svitlychnyi, whose KGB surveillance of his *samvydav* activities led to his not being able to find a job or prospective publishers, had to agree to publish his commentary to the piece anonymously. By the time the piece appeared, he had been arrested, under investigation for spreading "anti-Soviet" propaganda. In this sense the cultural establishment and the cultural underground collaborated with one another.[56]

A friend of Svitlychnyi's, Bohdan Horyn, spread *samvydav* literature while working at the Lviv Picture Gallery and contributing articles to newspapers and journals, including *October*. Arrested in late August 1965, Horyn was among those put on trial in 1966 for "anti-Soviet" activities. Members of the Writers' Union defended him by asking the court to release him under their supervision, promising to "re-educate" him. The signatories condemned the anti-Soviet acts committed by Horyn and others on trial. Some of them argued that the petition was to redeem not just

Horyn, but the reputation of the Writers' Union, as they were responsible for Horyn's character.[87] The Thaw at one point had encouraged this practice of collectively redeeming accused criminals.[88] However, by 1966, such gestures had become political. According to novelist Roman Ivanychuk, one of its signatories, the petition was considered the best protest they could mount at the time. Regional Party leaders like Malanchuk interpreted it exactly as a protest. Malanchuk played a key role in the May 1966 Party meeting of the Writers' Union at which members discussed the signatories' behavior and meted out official reprimands to nearly all of them.[89] Later, after Horyn left prison and returned to Lviv, Ivanychuk, Petrenko, and another writer, Roman Lubkivskyi, received Party sanctions for having attended Horyn's 1973 wedding.[90] While these reprimands were removed within the year, their act was a political move not to be repeated.[91] During these 1970s-era political repressions, Party leaders in Moscow, Kyiv, and Lviv used similar methods to frighten others away from friends who were dissidents.[92]

Besides these personal connections with future dissidents, scholars, writers and artists shared dissident literature in utmost secrecy. Literary scholar Mykola Matviychuk, whom historian Hryhoriy Kasianov identifies as an expert in the trial of Bohdan Horyn and others in 1966, in strict secrecy shared his copy of Ivan Dziuba's *Internationalism or Russification,* a major dissident text, with colleague Mariia Valio at Lviv's Institute of Social Sciences sometime in the 1960s.[93] Establishment intellectuals thus agreed with dissidents' concerns about Ukrainians' identity. In return, dissidents came to incorporate the agendas of establishment intellectuals to justify more radical change. In the 1960s and 1970s, people connected with the more radical political underground used Pavlychko's poems to legitimize claims for Ukrainian independence. Hryhoriy Demian was a rural schoolteacher in the village of Slavske in the Lviv Region who secretly collected and distributed folk songs about the OUN and the UPA guerrillas. He was "known for his nationalist views and anti-Soviet sentiments," as a 21 September 1966 obkom report to superiors in Kyiv once said.[94] In an interview years later, he said he used Pavlychko's poems in class so that he could make his students think about national issues. The underground political program of the Ukrainian National Front, active in Lviv and other parts of Western Ukraine in the mid-1960s, cited lines from Pavlychko's poem "When the Bloody Torquemada Died" to argue for the Soviet Union's dismantling.[95] Russification of the school system and talk of the merger of national languages into Russian, first discussed by Khrushchev and others at the end of the 1950s and resisted by establishment writers in Kyiv and Lviv, compelled such young intellectuals as Bohdan Horyn's brother, Mykhailo, to spread literature favoring Ukraine's independence. Such was Mykhailo Horyn's explanation in his 25 April 1966 appeal to the republic's Supreme Court following his conviction for anti-Soviet activity.[96]

Such common fears about Ukrainians' future cast suspicion not just on those caught spreading *samvydav,* but on establishment writers themselves. As early as May 1964, a KGB report to the Central Committee in Moscow warned that past members of the nationalist underground, such as in Western Ukraine, were changing their tactics, encouraging young people to enter the Communist Party and promote "nationalist" agendas from within the system.[97] The fact that Pavlychko and Bratun—both involved with the OUN and the UPA as teens—had become members of the Communist Party and were challenging restrictions on national self-expression legitimated more "vigilant" colleagues' accusations that they were not to be trusted.

Like the Russian-speaking theater players who depicted Lviv writers in a Banderite hideout and a house of prostitution, others, too, speculated on their pasts. Such speculation emerged after Romanchenko had been removed as editor of *October* in 1967, in a collective letter and one written in Russian under the bogus name of Grigorii Serokvasha (roughly translated as "Gregory Raw Acid"). These letters accused local writers of forming a "nationalist nest" at the Writers' Union. This "nationalist nest" had nominated as Romanchenko's successor an inexperienced young poet, Roman Lubkivskyi, also a Western Ukrainian native. They planned to use him as a shield and seize "a serious weapon—a publishing organ of the Writers' Union," to pursue their own foul deeds, bypassing the "Easterners," writers from Eastern Ukraine who came to Lviv after the war. The final decision to appoint Roman Fedoriv, an outsider from Ivano-Frankivsk, as editor settled this conflict. Such letters nonetheless indicated that writers loyal to Romanchenko, if not Romanchenko himself, in their struggle over the Writers' Union and *October* exploited fears of closet Banderites.[98]

Even after this conflict over *October* was long over, anonymous denunciations linking local establishment writers to their Banderite past surfaced on the desks of Party leaders. The obkom in February 1971 received one such letter regarding a photo of Bratun with a beaming collective farm worker, Ekaterina Tverdokhlebova, in the 20 November 1970 edition of

Literary Ukraine, the republic's literary newspaper. Musing over Bratun's "lowered eyelashes," the anonymous writer suggested that Bratun had a bad conscience over the fact that he, a member of the Banderite underground in his youth, had tried to kill such people as this collective farm worker, who had come to the Lviv Region after the war to help new collective farms raise sugar beets. It said that Tverdokhlebova would have asked why Bratun was head of the Writers' Union in Lviv.[99] This letter, clearly designed to discredit Bratun, epitomized the power Western Ukraine's Banderite past had in casting doubt over the most loyal members of Lviv's intelligentsia.

It would be a mistake, though, to view such writers as Bratun, Pavlychko, and others as having never changed from their teenage days. Bratun himself admitted at the close of the 1980s that he followed the Party line consistently, however much it zigzagged.[100] The anonymous letters directed at Bratun did not result in some kind of punishment by local Party bosses. He remained head of the Writers' Union until 1980. Nonetheless, in adapting to the realities of Soviet life after the war, such people as Bratun had developed a complex set of strategies for coping that allowed for an understanding of nationhood differently than in other regions of Ukraine. It was one where common language and culture, not just territory, mattered. It was one where Ukraine did not necessarily need to share a common fate with Russia. It was one that shared cultural ties with Central Europe.

Because of this different understanding of Ukrainian nationhood, establishment writers from Lviv took advantage of political changes under Gorbachev to pursue agendas that favored greater sovereignty and ultimately Ukraine's independence. Bratun became an advisor to the Lion Society in Lviv in 1987, named after Antonych's 1936 collection of poems, *The Book of the Lion,* the recipient of a Greek Catholic foundation prize. Taking advantage of the rhetoric of Glasnost, the Lion Society revived interest in Ukrainians' culture and set up one of the city's first non-Party newspapers, *Progress (Postup).* In 1989, the Lion Society successfully put forward Bratun as a candidate to the USSR Supreme Soviet on a platform that espoused greater economic and cultural rights for Ukrainians and sovereignty for Soviet Ukraine.[101]

Fedoriv, editor of *October* and later *The Bell,* also became a USSR Supreme Soviet deputy in 1989 over the heads of candidates favored by the Party in Lviv. His journal became a major forum for exposing the injustices Ukrainian culture faced in the Brezhnev era and publishing works that this era had suppressed.[102] In 1988, Ivanychuk joined the Taras Shevchenko Language Society (later known as "Enlightenment" [*Prosvita*] after its nineteenth-century Galician predecessor). Branches of it, organized throughout Ukraine, promoted Ukrainian as the republic's state language, which was realized the next year. Ivanychuk helped form the alternative political movement Rukh and became a deputy to the Ukrainian Supreme Council that voted for independence.[103] Ideas since Khrushchev's Thaw had now become transformed into much farther-reaching political agendas.

Ukraine's independence, however, and the subsequent disintegration of the Soviet Union came not from the western periphery. It originated in the republic's capital, Kyiv. It was in Kyiv where such writers as Andriy Malyshko and Maksym Rylskyi complained to *Pravda* in 1958 about the lack of Ukrainian-language lessons in the republic's schools. It was here that newspapers like *The Literary Newspaper*, later called *Literary Ukraine*, called upon writers, educators, and officials to do something about the declining state of Ukrainian literature education, what prompted Pavlychko's impassioned remarks about Russification at a September 1956 Lviv teachers' meeting.

Western Ukrainians turned not just to Pavlychko to legitimate their political agendas. By the late 1970s, novelist Pavlo Zahrebelnyi had become a key figure in the republic's literary establishment in Kyiv. His words, too, mattered in Lviv's cultural wars. In 1977, during public discussion of a new constitution for the Soviet Union, a Lviv Region resident, using a bogus name, proposed to the editors of Lviv's newspaper, *Free Ukraine,* that an article to the constitution mandating use of the republic nationality's language in all public institutions be added. Speaking at a September 1977 obkom plenary session, the newspaper's editor gave this as an example of individuals' misinterpreting not just the Soviet nationalities policy but also prominent republic novelist Pavlo Zahrebelnyi. The editor (ironically, speaking in Russian, despite being editor of a Ukrainian-language newspaper) claimed that the anonymous letter writer, justifying his constitutional amendment, cited what Zahrebelnyi apparently had said in the press about a native language being the most precious thing for people's spirit.[104]

Other republic-level literary figures became authority figures for Lvivians in the years after the Thaw. Oles Honchar, head of the republic Writers' Union until Shcherbytskyi and Malanchuk had him replaced, spoke passionately at the 1966 republic Writers' Union congress about the need for Party and state officials to treasure and respect Ukrainians' language and literature.[105] In the 1970s and early 1980s, Honchar in his diary observed with alarm public events being increasingly conducted in Russian.[106] When the Chernobyl nuclear power plant accident in 1986 compelled Gorbachev to permit greater freedom of speech, it was the republic leaders of the Writers' Union who first mobilized opposition forces, forces that led to the formation of the opposition political party Rukh.[107]

At the same time, Lviv's writers and other establishment intellectuals played a significant role in the Soviet Union's disintegration precisely because of the influence they had in the republic's cultural establishment. In the early years of the Thaw, Lviv composer Anatoliy Kos-Anatolskyi urged establishment intellectuals in Kyiv to promote the Ukrainian language more vigorously. At a republic composers' congress in Kyiv in late March 1956, weeks after Khrushchev's Secret Speech, he wrote a poem for his friend in attendance, Kharkiv composer Petro Haidamak, where "Mother Ukraine" wept, imploring him, a "Haidamak" (a reference to leaders of a violent peasant rebellion against Poles in the eighteenth century), to speak in his native Ukrainian language.[108] An article he submitted to the republic literary newspaper, *The Literary Newspaper,* claimed that the Ukrainian language was only used as a "decoration" *(butaforiia)* in public. The article, which the newspaper decided not to publish, circulated underground in Kyiv. A report by the Central Committee of the CPU's Department of Science and Culture, dated August 1961, which analyzed "unhealthy moods" among students of the Philology Faculty of Kyiv State University, mentioned that there were students who organized a discussion of Kos-Anatolskyi's unpublished article in their dormitory. This report, accompanied apparently by KGB materials that were returned after Central Committee discussion of them, suggests the contributory, though not determining, role Lviv establishment intellectuals played in Kyiv's emerging Sixties Movement.[109]

Pavlychko, who was transferred to Kyiv in the early 1960s, played a more direct role in the capital's intellectual life. In Kyiv, he gained the support of republic Party secretary Petro Shelest, who not only helped him get an apartment in the city but also protected him from political accusations. Pavlychko became a major screenwriter for the republic's movie studio and later secretary of the presidium of the republic's Writers' Union. Under impressions from their trip to New York in 1966 as members of Soviet Ukraine's delegation to the United Nations General Assembly, he and Kyiv poet Ivan Drach tried to get the republic's Party leadership to encourage better contacts with "progressive" circles in the Ukrainian diaspora.[110]

At the end of the 1960s, he upset Central Committee functionary Ivan Hrushetskyi, a former Lviv obkom secretary, over the publication of a collection of poems, *Word Honer (Hranoslov)* (1968) that called attention to the neglect of Ukrainian, the corruption and vanity of officials, poems that Hrushetskyi accused of having "anti-Soviet" subtexts.[111]

In 1971, Pavlychko became editor of the journal *Universe (Vsesvit)*, which published Ukrainian-language translations of foreign literature. Under his editorship, which lasted until 1978, the journal published translations of works from writers in the capitalist West, from *The Godfather* to Kobo Abe's "The Box Man," works that could have been seen as anti-Soviet in condoning criminal violence or, in the case of "The Box Man," a person's complete withdrawal from society. Pavlychko demonstrated the merits of translating both works at a republic-wide Writers' Union meeting in 1975.[112] Lviv's young writers and educated professionals read its translations avidly and recommended the journal to one another. For Mykola Riabchuk and Hryhoriy Chubai, it was one of the few Ukrainian-language journals escaping the heavy censorship of the 1970s.[113] The journal became an "island of freedom" and expanded Ukrainian literature's capacity to reflect on the wider world, not being confined to the traditional themes of folk life and so on that the Soviet Ukrainian literary canon mandated. Pavlychko's role in the republic's literary establishment upset fellow writers, who, one CPU Central Committee report suggests, were very much aware of his past involvement in the UPA. However, as he made his own compromises with the regime, including denouncing dissidents, Pavlychko remained influential in the Writers' Union's republic leadership.[114] When the Gorbachev era brought Glasnost to Ukraine, he was among the first to take advantage of it. At a republic Writers' Union congress in 1987, similar to 1956, he shocked his audience with figures showing Russification's impact on Ukraine's school system, mentioning regions in the east and south that did not have a single Ukrainian-language school. Professor George Grabowicz of Harvard University, who happened to be at this congress, recalls the great impression that Pavlychko left on the packed audience in the October Palace (now the Ukrainian House).[115] Shortly thereafter, Pavlychko became republic head of an organization allied with Rukh.[116]

Pavlychko's contributions to the republic's cultural establishment were but one example of Lvivians moving to Kyiv and affecting cultural developments there. Other Ukrainians from Lviv, too, came to Kyiv and contributed to different notions of nationhood in the cultural establishment. Pavlychko mentions names of former Lvivians who became important in the cultural life of Kyiv, such as conductor Stepan Turchak, who was in Kyiv by 1963. Turchak was a conservatory student of senior Galician composer and conductor Mykola Kolessa. Kolessa, calling republic Minister of Culture Rostyslav Babiychuk, had arranged Turchak's employment, suggesting extensive networks of support between Lviv intellectuals and republic officials in charge of culture.[117] Pavlychko mentions the names of Lviv writers who, as editors in Kyiv, helped him out in his career. Poet Mykola Riabchuk, from the younger generation associated with the underground journal *The Chest,* speaks of Galicians who came to work as editors in Kyiv in the early 1980s.[118] Other evidence suggests that Lviv's cultural capital—stories about Lviv and Lvivians—became a part of the capital's reserve of anecdotes and legends. Such evidence appears in Oles Honchar's diaries. Besides mentioning Western Ukrainian admirers (including local officials) who kissed him on the hand for his stance on national issues, he conveyed anecdotes told by prewar Lviv writers like Mykhailo Iatskiv (an anecdote also recalled by Lvivian Mykola Petrenko) and stories told about the destruction of works of art at the Museum of Ukrainian Art in Lviv in 1952, suggesting republic writers' profound interest in Galician Ukrainians and their culture.[119] The very fact that Galician slang influenced Ukrainian slang in Kyiv also indicates that Lviv's integration into the rest of Soviet Ukraine fostered professional and personal ties that not just Sovietized Lviv but also Ukrainianized the republic's capital, Kyiv.[120] Lviv's writers illustrated the profound interconnections that had developed between Kyiv and Lviv. Historians from both cities also mutually influenced one another. Their interactions, however, illustrated the difficulties trying to fit Lviv into a larger Soviet Ukrainian narrative.

CHAPTER 6

Lviv and the Ukrainian Past

Khrushchev's Thaw revolutionized opportunities for national self-expression not just in literature and language but also in history. For the western borderlands, this meant a partial rehabilitation of the "bourgeois nationalist" past. The politics of history were only partly liberalized. They reflected Khrushchev's attempt at reviving revolutionary enthusiasm and returning to the Party's Leninist ideals after Stalin's cult of personality had been discredited. This revival of revolutionary enthusiasm appeared most clearly by 1961, with the adoption of the Third Program of the CPSU promising the achievement of a Communist society by 1980.[1] The western borderlands' recent past could thus incorporate events and people connected with the people's "revolutionary" aspirations, that is, their desire to establish a Soviet socialist society. In Lithuania, literary and artistic figures previously deemed "formalist" or "bourgeois nationalist" thus became incorporated into the Soviet Lithuanian canon, enough so that by the mid-1970s, republic Party functionaries claimed such figures as their own.[2]

In Western Ukraine, this included reinterpretations of Galicia's interwar history. The history of the Communist Party of Western Ukraine (KPZU) was an early example. It had been dissolved in 1938 for its supposed collaboration with "bourgeois nationalist" forces. The partial, though incomplete, rehabilitation of the KPZU from 1956 to 1963 was to provide a positive history for Western Ukrainians and Lviv. Rather than being backward inhabitants of the bourgeois world who had to rid themselves of their recent past, Western Ukrainians thus had the opportunity to embrace a Soviet

Western Ukrainian identity, one with its own revolutionary traditions dedicated to Soviet socialism's ideals.[3]

Such a usable past was fraught with problems. KPZU leaders allegedly had pursued "nationalist deviations," and they were not rehabilitated. Official histories of the KPZU failed to resonate either as historical narrative or as a site of popular memory. It was a political party whose support had become insignificant on the eve of World War II.[4] Rehabilitation of the KPZU, however, inspired historians, political economists, and writers to emphasize the "progressive" role of individuals and political movements clearly at odds with Soviet historical myths. Shifting political fortunes in Kyiv and Moscow made these accounts controversial. Scholars, journalists, and writers suddenly were accused of propagandizing "bourgeois nationalism." On the stage, plays set in interwar Galicia allegedly made Aesopian references to Ukrainians' culture under Soviet rule. Conflicts over Ukrainians' past reflected factionalism within Soviet academia and the impact of Lviv on academics' intellectual development. Official representations of the past, however controversial, faced popular memories that highlighted the limits of national self-expression in Lviv's public sphere.

The Search for a Usable Galician Past

While ridding Western Ukrainians of their "backwardness," Kyiv and Moscow sought to impose a local history that would legitimate Soviet rule. A republic Central Committee brigade report in August 1946 vehemently condemned Galician Ukrainians' "bourgeois nationalist" past. Still, it advocated propagandizing a list of appropriate events where they struggled for social and national liberation.[5] By the time of Khrushchev's Thaw, the call to return to Lenin's revolution spurred on similar demands from below. At Lviv State University in April 1957, a Law Faculty Communist urged Communists assembled to publish major works on Western Ukraine's revolutionary events for the October Revolution's upcoming fortieth anniversary.[6] In subsequent years, Party officials, writers, and scholars tried to demonstrate the popularity of Marxist ideals in the region. Such works were to prove that Galician Ukrainians had for centuries aspired to unite in one Ukrainian Soviet socialist state.

Party and state leaders' attitudes toward local historians and other social scientists shifted as they promoted a more usable past for Western Ukraine. In 1946, during a vigorous campaign against Lviv scholars' "bourgeois nationalist" views, republic Party and state leaders dissolved Lviv's branches of the republic's Academy of Sciences. Locals saw this as an attempt to break up Lviv's academic traditions and move scholarly activities to Kyiv.[7] This campaign had ended by the time Kyiv created the Institute of Social Sciences in 1951. The Institute of Social Sciences exemplified Moscow, Kyiv, and Lviv officials' efforts to co-opt the local intelligentsia for the sake of a more usable past. Galician Ukrainian scholars, including those recently disgraced for their "bourgeois nationalist" views, began working there. This institute incorporated prewar Ukrainian academic traditions. Its building, library, and much of its senior personnel were from the Shevchenko Scientific Society. This society had been a private research institution set up in Lviv in 1873 by Galician Ukrainians with the help of Ukrainians from the Russian Empire. It had been dissolved under Soviet rule in 1940.[8]

In 1953, as a result of secret police chief Lavrenty Beria's report criticizing national discrimination in Western Ukraine, historian Ivan Krypiakevych became institute director.[9] Krypiakevych, who served until his retirement in 1962, had been one of the main victims of the postwar campaign against bourgeois nationalist views in Ukrainian history. He subsequently denounced all past publications and promised to adhere to Marxist-Leninist positions. This was an accommodation with existing realities rather than a transformation of views. As Iuriy Slyvka, one of his former graduate students, recalled, Krypiakevych cited politically appropriate works by Marx, Lenin, and Soviet Party leaders in the preface and conclusion of his new works. Otherwise, he drew his own conclusions in the main body. This was common practice among Soviet historians whose formative years preceded the Russian Revolution of 1917.[10]

The Institute of Social Sciences thus accommodated Soviet realities. Its prewar-era scholars like Krypiakevych viewed Soviet power as a necessary means to further the interests of a Soviet Ukrainian nation-state. Its scholars reflected the limits of Sovietization. As late as 1970, only 40 percent of all Institute of Social Sciences employees were Party members, while up to 90 percent of employees in comparable institutions in Kyiv were.[11] Because the social sciences were an important outpost in the Soviet state's ideological front, the lack of Party members suggests the institute's relative aloofness from explicitly ideological tasks. As many as two essay collections criticizing Ukrainian bourgeois nationalism, one planned in 1952 and the other at the end of the 1960s, never saw completion.[12] Institute publications contained phrases condemning specific people, movements, and governments associated with Ukrainian bourgeois nationalism. However, refusal to criticize them at length helped mitigate condemnation of Galicia's past.

Institute scholars incorporated as much of Galicians' past as possible into a Soviet Ukrainian national narrative. Attempts by Khrushchev to revive enthusiasm for revolutionary traditions legitimated their incorporation of this past into a local revolutionary framework. Here the KPZU's 1956 rehabilitation was critical. Rehabilitating the KPZU allowed the reevaluation of other interwar institutions. KPZU activists involved in them lent them a "progressive," "revolutionary" character. The republication of KPZU materials or the removal of them from archival and library special depositories encouraged historians to explore other historical themes.[13]

In this manner institute scholars partially reevaluated, and sometimes rehabilitated, events and figures formerly labeled "reactionary," "bourgeois nationalist," and "counterrevolutionary." One early example of this was an article by historian Oleksandr Karpenko. Published in 1957 as "On the Character of the Revolutionary Movement in Eastern Galicia in 1918," it addressed the Habsburg monarchy's collapse in Eastern Galicia and the establishment of the Western Ukrainian People's Republic (ZUNR) in November 1918. The article called these events a popular revolution inspired by Russia's October Revolution and national revolutions sweeping the former Austro-Hungarian Empire. Like Russia's February Revolution, the bourgeoisie led it, though reactionary forces eventually betrayed it.[14]

While Karpenko emphasized the ZUNR government's demagogy and its betrayal of the Ukrainian people, he cited Lenin and Communist leaders in Soviet Russia, Soviet Ukraine, and interwar Galicia to support his claim that the events of November 1918 were a workers' revolution. In treating these events as a workers' revolution, Karpenko saw events leading to the formation of the ZUNR as a progressive development. This was a considerable departure from Stalinist times, where everyone associated with ZUNR, including ordinary people who had fought for it, belonged to a "bourgeois nationalist" movement. The 1956 rehabilitation of the KPZU had played a major role in this new interpretation. Declassified documents on the KPZU and contacts with surviving KPZU veterans led Karpenko to see events behind the ZUNR government as progressive, since KPZU leaders had officially viewed these events as such.[15]

Another example of accommodation was the institute's collective monograph under the grandiose title *Triumph of Historic Justice: The Natural Logic of the Unification of the Western Ukrainian Lands into One Ukrainian*

Soviet State. This monograph was published in 1968, on the occasion of the fiftieth anniversary of the October Revolution. It followed Khrushchev's ouster (1964) and Krypiakevych's retirement (1962) and death (1967). From the perspective of today, this monograph was hardly revolutionary. A disproportionate amount of its material (about 240 out of 790 pages) was dedicated to Western Ukraine under Soviet rule, which had lasted less than thirty years. The fact that the Soviet Ukrainian government had nominated it for a state prize in 1970 demonstrates its ideological soundness.[16]

However, the Thaw, republic Communist Party chief Petro Shelest's relatively tolerant treatment of Ukrainian national self-expression, and Krypiakevych-era traditions of scholarship influenced the essays in the book. This book justified Western Ukraine's incorporation into Soviet Ukraine owing to Western Ukraine's organic ties to one national community. Critical of bourgeois nationalist social, political, and cultural movements, the monograph acknowledged the positive contributions of their more progressive figures and organizations (for instance, the progressive members of Lviv's Shevchenko Scientific Society and organizations associated with interwar Galicia). It offered guarded compliments to bourgeois nationalist historians whose works had valuable facts though wrong interpretations. While mentioning the Great Russian people's services to Ukrainians' history, articles criticized tsarist Russia's World War I aims and tsarist-era historians' dismissal of Ukrainians' national movement as a product of "German-Austrian intrigue."[17] While authors praised progressive Poles, *Triumph of Historic Justice* called these lands eternally Ukrainian, dismissing émigré Polish scholars' rival claims.[18]

This cautious, diplomatic reassessment of Galicia's historical record was highly significant. Essays refused to call Ukrainians' national movement a product of German-Austrian intrigue, a notion historians and publicists insinuated before the Thaw. By criticizing tsarist Russian army actions in Galicia during World War I, essays dismissed claims imperial Russian policies were the "lesser evil" in non-Russians' national histories. Honoring imperial Russian soldiers on Lviv's Hill of Glory alongside Soviet soldiers killed in World War II had tacitly endorsed such notions. It was this surreptitious eroding of past stereotypes, rather than a frontal assault against them, that made *Triumph of Historic Justice* ideologically safe yet also a vehicle for new interpretations. The monograph incorporated Galicians within a Ukrainian national narrative and a greater Soviet imperial narrative while mitigating stereotypes about Galician Ukrainians' past.

Other Thaw-era works created an explicitly revolutionary, pro-Soviet narrative. Before he savaged the editor of *October* and led ideological campaigns against Ukrainian intellectuals in the 1970s, Valentyn Malanchuk, a Lviv obkom functionary, wrote about the exploits of young Komsomol members in what he called interwar Western Ukraine.[19] The turn to such a narrative led to highly questionable works promoting the supposed popularity of Marxist and materialist ideals. Such occurred with Volodymyr Levynskyi (1880–1953), a Galician Ukrainian writer, editor, and political activist. A republic Central Committee report of 25 July 1972 on scholars' erroneous evaluations of Levynskyi indicates that in 1960, Malanchuk began advertising Levynskyi as one of Galicia's first propagandists of Marxism and Leninism. Over the next decade, university scholars and journalists, primarily from Lviv, followed Malanchuk's example.[20] They emphasized Levynskyi's friendship with Lenin, whom Levynskyi had met in Geneva, Switzerland, during World War I.[21]

As with other national projects shaping historical memory, these involved collective efforts at forgetting, as well as remembering, the past, as Ernst Renan so aptly put it.[22] Such reinterpretations thus provoked criticism in Lviv, Kyiv, and Moscow because they violated more ideologically correct acts of collective remembering and forgetting. This happened with Karpenko's article on ZUNR. As a 27 February 1959 obkom report put it, Karpenko, in portraying the ZUNR's emergence as a product of a workers' revolution, had tried to rehabilitate the ZUNR government and the "counter-revolutionary" circles supporting it. The report took to task institute historian Iuriy Slyvka for expressing, in a review of another of Karpenko's works, supposedly favorable comments about the ZUNR government's activities.[23] Malanchuk apparently spearheaded the obkom's attack. An anonymous respondent who worked at Lviv State University and served as secretary for a university meeting discussing Karpenko's article recalled submitting the report to Malanchuk, then an obkom junior functionary. Malanchuk wrote the report to the obkom critical of the Institute of Social Science's ideological work.[24] The attack led to Karpenko's transfer from the institute. Protocols of institute Party committee and Academic Council meetings in 1958–59 suggested such a campaign to remove Karpenko, one directed at the obkom's insistence.[25]

Sometimes careless Party functionaries, later exposed by rivals or aggrieved colleagues, omitted materials that compromised progressive Galicians. This happened to articles and books that had spoken highly of

Volodymyr Levynskyi. Later denunciations of wayward scholars, subsequent recantations by such wayward scholars, and émigré accounts pointed out Levynskyi's complicated biography. Despite early admiration of Marxist ideas, Levynskyi joined a political party that disagreed with Lenin and other Bolsheviks over the nationalities question. In the 1930s, he criticized Soviet policies toward Ukrainians. When war broke out in 1939, Levynskyi fled westward to German-occupied Poland. Returning to Lviv with the Germans, he published articles highly supportive of German occupation and agitated for local Ukrainians to join the SS Galicia Division. He then fled westward with the Germans in 1944 and spent his last years in Vienna.[26] Around October 1970, the CPU Central Committee first received signals about scholars distorting Levynskyi's record. This signal probably came from Lviv State University instructors in the Department of Political Economy who held a grudge with colleague Stepan Zlupko. That very month (October 1970) their department investigated alleged problems with Zlupko's article on Levynskyi and other publications, hardly a coincidence.[27] Malanchuk, who was at the time in the republic's Ministry of Higher and Middle Specialized Education, managed to avoid serious punishment before changes in the republic apparatus led to his becoming CPU Central Committee secretary for ideology in 1972.[28]

Clumsy attempts at making Galician Ukrainians into Marxists and friends of Lenin were an extreme form of collective forgetting, an inept art parodied by such post-Soviet Ukrainian writers as Oleksandr Irvanets.[29] More subtle attempts at collective forgetting became sources of tension. The public rehabilitation of the KPZU, for instance, involved forgetting allegations about its leadership's nationalist deviations of the late 1920s. Such allegations remained in place during the Thaw and after. Such close associations between the KPZU and Galician bourgeois nationalism privately sowed misgivings about the KPZU's role in Galician history. One KPZU veteran, speaking at an obkom meeting with other KPZU veterans in 1967, claimed that not a few people in the Party tried to pretend as if they, KPZU veterans, did not exist. This distanced relationship may have reflected the KPZU's checkered past.[30]

Such misgivings about progressive figures in Galicia's past further intensified in light of student unrest in Poland and the Warsaw Pact invasion of Czechoslovakia in 1968. Scholars who suggested that national movements brought Soviet power to Ukraine supposedly advocated a Ukrainian road to socialism that, like Polish, Czechoslovak, or Chinese roads to socialism, threatened Soviet hegemony of the world Communist movement. Ukrainian Party leaders thus passed a series of decrees at the beginning of the 1970s ordering social science scholars to combat Ukrainian bourgeois nationalism more aggressively.[31] The campaign against revisionism and dissent, which peaked in repressions of republic intellectuals and students in 1972–73, inspired Party activists to portray even cautious attempts to revise Galicians' past as subversive.

Such trends led to charges that *Triumph of Historic Justice* rehabilitated politically suspicious individuals, institutions, and historical movements. Its authors allegedly downplayed Russia's role in Western Ukraine's movement toward union with Soviet Ukraine. Already such charges had surfaced in 1968, when the obkom ordered a review of the book. This review, by Vasyl Osechynskyi of Lviv State University, made such charges. This review temporarily halted the book's publication and required an Academic Council meeting of the institute to refute Osechynskyi's claims.[32]

The book's nomination for a republic state prize in October 1970 sparked renewed accusations from Lviv State University instructors. As an appeal by the institute's Party leadership to the Lviv obkom indicates, such accusations surfaced both at university History Faculty Party meetings and in a written denunciation to regional and republic Party organs. Institute leaders vigorously defended the book. A petition by the institute's director and secretary of its Party committee, sent to the CPU Central Committee at the end of 1970, stresses that republic Academy of Sciences editors, numerous reviewers, and a republic state commission had spoken favorably of the book.[33]

For the moment, institute scholars were safe from further accusations. Instead, they were preoccupied with Myroslava Hurladi's charge that the institute was a "nest of nationalists," more of which will be said later. Ukraine's changing political situation soon endangered the reputation of *Triumph of Historic Justice.* With the help of Ukrainian Communists, Moscow's leaders turned on Shelest after the latter had produced a book, *Our Soviet Ukraine* (1971), which they portrayed as an attempt to favor Ukraine over other republics. In that year, the CPSU Central Committee began investigating the Lviv Region's political situation. According to former CPU Central Committee functionary Vitalii Vrublevskii and former Lviv obkom functionary Iuriy Ielchenko, Valentyn Malanchuk, trying to oust Shelest, instigated these investigations with the help of his mentor, CPSU chief ideologue Mikhail Suslov. The investigations led to a CPSU Central Committee decree of 7 October 1971 on political work in the Lviv Region, which was highly critical of scholars revising "bourgeois nationalist" figures from Western Ukraine's recent past.[34]

By the fall of 1971, this CPSU Central Committee resolution had transformed *Triumph of Historic Justice* into an ideologically harmful work. The Lviv obkom's first secretary, at an obkom plenary session discussing Moscow's resolution, took to task *Triumph of Historic Justice* for stressing national over class factors in history and for including politically questionable figures from the past.[35] In January 1972, Lviv State University instructor Fedir Trubitsyn claimed at a university Party meeting that the political profile of over 150 people in *Triumph of Historic Justice* required investigation.[36] It was a time that did not bode well for national self-expression. Trubitsyn's remarks came after the arrests of dissidents in Ukraine. They coincided with Moscow raising serious questions about Petro Shelest's CPU leadership. Republic Party leaders justified Shelest's ouster later that year by charging that Shelest had encouraged the "bragging up" of Ukraine's role in the Soviet Union in *Our Soviet Ukraine*.[37] Events over the next two years led to the institute's director, Myroslav Oleksiuk, losing his job, while a contributor to *Triumph of Historic Justice,* Mykola Kravets, had to leave Lviv State University. Speculating on this growing campaign against revisionism, national bragging, and dissent, Lviv's scholars and Party functionaries went after Karpenko, Slyvka, and other scholars, using their representations of Galicia's past as ammunition.

Academic Politics and "Ukrainian Bourgeois Nationalism"

Roughly between June of 1968, at the high point of Prague Spring, and May of 1973, the climax of republic-wide repressions against Ukrainian intellectuals and students, various ideological campaigns took aim at Lviv scholars. The campaigns involved mostly historians at Lviv State University, but they also affected the Department of Political Economy and the Institute of Social Sciences. Political charges against scholars at both Lviv State University and the Institute of Social Sciences became intertwined, because the Institute of Social Sciences had been under Lviv State University rather than the republic's Academy of Sciences from 1963 to 1969, and some institute historians accordingly had been transferred to the university during that time.[38] Those accusing such scholars of propagandizing bourgeois nationalism were from Lviv State University. Most of them were from outside the discipline of history. They reflected the special role that such subjects as Political Economy, the History of the CPSU, Scientific Communism, and Scientific Atheism played at Soviet universities. These disciplines were mandatory subjects for all students, what Americans would call part of the core curriculum. Instructors of such disciplines were the university's ideological watchdogs. They cooperated closely with the university Party organization in dealing with ideological problems in teaching and research work, as well as with students' character formation (*vykhovannia* in Ukrainian). Their role as guardians of students' character formation became especially relevant when a group of students mostly majoring in Ukrainian history and philology were arrested in late March 1973. This incident led to further actions against Lviv scholars and potentially could have toppled Lviv State University's administration.

Oleksandr Karpenko was the first victim of these ideological campaigns. In 1960, he had been transferred to the university's Department of the History of the USSR after the scandal involving his article on the ZUNR. In June 1968, he was removed from teaching lectures because of "slandering" Soviet rule. In these lectures, he had talked about Stalinist terror against Ukrainian Communists and intellectuals in the 1930s and the violence used in collectivizing agriculture in Soviet Ukraine.[39] At a university Party committee hearing, the History Faculty dean, Petro Chelak, stressed that these lectures were no coincidence. He noted Karpenko's article on the ZUNR and an incident at the Academy of Sciences library in 1953, when Karpenko told coworkers to speak Ukrainian to readers, which almost resulted in his expulsion from the Party.[40] While the History Faculty's Party organization tried to fire Karpenko, the chancellor's office and the university Party committee intervened and mitigated the punishment.[41] In the fall of 1970, the History Faculty succeeded in firing him for these ideological "deviations." Iuriy Slyvka, transferred from the Institute of Social Sciences and appointed chair of Karpenko's department in 1969, came under fire for protecting Karpenko. Soon after Karpenko's departure, Slyvka quit and returned to his old job.[42]

In the History Faculty's Department of the History of Ukraine, Mykola Kravets, another institute scholar, had become its chair in 1968. Karpenko and Slyvka's former colleague, he allegedly allied with them and further protected Karpenko's "harmful" activity.[43] As denunciations targeted the propagandists of Volodymyr Levynskyi in 1970 and 1971, Kravets, too, became ensnared in the controversy. According to denunciations, Kravets had written a positive review of a book that had praised Levynskyi for being an early Galician Marxist. Soon critics claimed his own works, including a monograph on Ivan Franko, committed political "deviations."[44] Kravets quit and began teaching at Chernivtsi State University in the fall of 1972. After the March 1973 arrest of Lviv State University history students, university Party activists implicated Kravets. Many of these students had studied in his department. The university chancellor's office and Party committee in May of that year sent a letter to their Chernivtsi counterparts, accusing Kravets of having been a direct cause of these recent anti-Soviet activities. Kravets was forced to find work at Vinnytsia State Pedagogical Institute in Central Ukraine.[45]

Around the same time, other problems flared up at the university's Department of Political Economy and at the Institute of Social Sciences. At the Department of Political Economy, economist and Party propagandist Stepan Zlupko already had become embroiled in conflicts with colleagues. The conflicts emerged over alleged plagiarism and other irregularities in his publications record, objections over his 1963 acceptance into the university's doctoral program, and a power struggle at the department made worse by the department chair's alleged favoritism toward Zlupko.[46] Zlupko was removed from teaching duties on 18 November 1971 and later expelled from the Party and fired in January 1972. He lost his job because of an article he had written on Levynskyi and other publications with alleged ideological mistakes.[47]

At the Institute of Social Sciences, literary critic Myroslava Hurladi launched a single-handed campaign against the institute after her doctoral dissertation was twice denied a defense date in late 1969 and early 1970.[48] An obkom report to Kyiv and remarks made at institute Party organization meetings suggest what accusations Hurladi had made to the Lviv obkom and the CPU's Central Committee Control Commission. She claimed that personnel had taken honoraria illegally and that its leadership suppressed criticism. Institute colleagues claimed she had called the Institute of Social Sciences a "nest of nationalists," listing compromising materials on colleagues' pasts and accusing them of "anti-Soviet" comments and actions.[49] Institute Party members unanimously accused her of slander and voted to give her a reprimand with remarks on her personal record. They tried in vain to fire her.[50] Fourteen commissions from Moscow, Kyiv, and Lviv investigated that year, involving months of work and thousands of inspectors, as one institute Communist alleged. Party leaders in Lviv and Kyiv forced the Institute of Social Sciences to fire at least eight of its workers.[51]

Hurladi's campaign, along with controversy over *Triumph of Historic Justice,* cast a long shadow over the Institute of Social Sciences in 1970. The obkom gave its director, Myroslav Oleksiuk, a reprimand in his personal record for opposing Hurladi. Soon he, too, faced charges of committing ideological "deviations" and refusing to come clean, as he had published articles that had praised the Marxist-turned-nationalist Levynskyi. The final straw came in late March 1973, when his son was accused of deliberately not informing authorities about the group of students arrested. This incident cost Oleksiuk his job.[52]

The students' arrests nearly brought down the leadership of Lviv State University. As university Communists in 1973 discussed their consequences, they dropped hints that university chancellor Mykola Makysmovych, along with past and present university Party committee secretaries, bore responsibility for these nationalist activities, since they had protected people like Kravets, Karpenko, Slyvka, and Zlupko. History Faculty members accused them of undermining their faculty and its Party bureau.[53] One memoir account indicates these critics dropped hints that Maksymovych should step down.[54] Maksymovych, however, did not fall. He enjoyed enough protection from the obkom and from his wife, a former Soviet partisan in Galicia. Maksymovych, university Party committee secretary Tamara Starchenko, and others, however, received reprimands in their Party records. Department chairs and faculty deans were demoted. The university had to fire or give early retirement to many of the twenty-nine professors, instructors, and office personnel on whom the KGB had produced compromising materials.[55] While Maksymovych went on to serve until his death in 1981, criticisms of his leadership apparently continued. In the fall of 1975, the obkom investigated a letter (its author not indicated in the obkom's response) sent to the CPU Central Committee making accusations about Maksymovych (accusations also unspecified in this response). The obkom found the anonymous letter's accusations groundless.[56]

Overwhelming evidence shows that the people making denunciations or criticisms were not competent in the fields of Ukrainian history the accused had studied. Fedir Trubitsyn only had an undergraduate degree at the Lviv Trade and Economics Institute and some additional training in Kyiv. One Lviv historian recalled Trubitsyn claiming, either out of jest or pride, that he had never published anything, and thus he had never made ideological mistakes.[57] Mykhailo Menshov of the Department of the History of the CPSU, who took part in exposing "deviations" in Karpenko's lectures in 1968, admitted to other Party members that he had read none of Karpenko's publications.[58] Other alleged perpetrators of these ideological campaigns, identified below, were not specialists in Ukrainian history.

Hurladi's attack on the Institute of Social Sciences was the most pathetic. Protocols of institute Party meetings reveal a laundry list of odious acts: shrieking at colleagues (until "the ceiling moved," as one person said), calling people names, lying about her work record, accusing others of "nationalist" behavior and then taking those remarks back, calling people at home to make them approve her dissertation for defense, mocking and taunting an ex-Soviet partisan who was in tears, keeping a secret notebook of people's remarks, sending an office worker to spy on an institute Academic Council meeting, haranguing the director for not obeying the obkom, and using her husband (an obkom worker) to threaten the director's office and get documents for her honoraria. Some things, like taunting the former Soviet partisan, happened during these very meetings, suggesting that Hurladi behaved as wretchedly as others claimed.[59]

While Hurladi's campaign against the Institute of Social Sciences was an isolated incident, others waged a collective attack against Lviv scholars. A late 1970 appeal by the Institute of Social Sciences Party organization, responding to ideological charges against *Triumph of Historic Justice,* referred to a "group of people" in Lviv "who consciously take part in slandering scholars."[60] Ideological campaigns against Ukrainian bourgeois nationalism legitimated such acts. However, it is not clear how organized these attacks were and what were their motives. Lviv historians have referred to a "mafia" of instructors at Lviv State University causing not just dismissals and resignations at the university but also campaigns against the Institute of Social Sciences and its scholarship. This mafia primarily targeted Ukrainian scholars and Ukrainians' history and culture. While Ukrainians were involved in it, Russians and Jews were its driving force.[61]

It is tempting to see a cabal of devious pseudo-academics driving off in someone's car to plot the downfall of Ukrainian scholarship over tea, spread rumors that university professors were "organizing" the students against Soviet power, and seek the overthrow of the regional and republic Party leaderships. Such scenes surfaced years later in oral interviews. Documentary evidence indicates these ideological campaigns were not so neatly organized. At one January 1972 university Party meeting, when Trubitsyn alleged that over 150 people mentioned in the monograph *Triumph of Historic Justice* merited a background check, Roman Brodskyi, one of the so-called mafia figures, urged Trubitsyn to think it over.[62] Two other mafia members, Hryhoriy Herbilskyi and Iuriy Hrosman, lectured in Ukrainian. Herbilskyi had changed his nationality from Jewish to Ukrainian.[63] Vasyl Inkin sided with History Faculty dean Chelak in discrediting Karpenko. He made favorable remarks to his department about Chelak's role exposing Karpenko and Kravets's "ideological deviations." An anonymous respondent said Inkin did take part in criticizing Karpenko, but he expressed regrets about it later.[64]

Involvement in Party and state organs compelled at least some of these people to make denunciations. Vasyl Osechynskyi presumably attacked Karpenko and later the Institute of Social Sciences because of his role aiding local Party and (possibly) secret police bosses in ideological campaigns against bourgeois nationalism. Osechynskyi had taken on this role in the late Stalin era because he had spent German occupation in Lviv, a serious political mistake that could have cost him his academic career. Zlupko, fired from the Department of Political Economy, said that two people who denounced him, Menshov and Mariia Bilchenko of the Department of Scientific Atheism, had been on very good terms with him up to that point. Menshov even tried, in vain, to make amends after Zlupko had found work elsewhere. Thus others, perhaps colleagues, may have compelled Menshov and Bilchenko to attack.[65]

Instead of a well-coordinated mafia bent on destroying Ukrainian culture, there were conflicting networks within Lviv State University, with connections to the obkom, other Party organs, and perhaps the KGB, fueling political denunciations. Biographies of victims and perpetrators suggest a number of such networks. While these networks were partly driven by compulsion from above, group loyalties also mobilized their fight against Ukrainian bourgeois nationalism. This could be seen with the History Faculty, whose dean was Petro Chelak. Chelak and others dealt with three outsiders from the Institute of Social Sciences (Karpenko, Slyvka, and Kravets) who enjoyed the university chancellor's protection and support. Animosity toward these new colleagues may explain the intrigue that quickly enveloped Karpenko's dissertation defense in the mid-1960s. His colleagues at the Department of the History of the USSR sat on the manuscript for a considerable time. One anonymous source saw Chelak, along with department chair Osechynskyi, producing a document suggesting that Karpenko had refused to submit the dissertation for their review. Karpenko managed to defend it at Kharkiv State University, behind the backs of the faculty, with the help of the chancellor and a Kyiv friend.[66] Around the time of the defense, Osechynskyi questioned Karpenko's political reliability. He did so on 15 June 1966, at a closed university Party meeting discussing the recent arrests and trials of dissidents. One of those tried and convicted, Mykhailo Osadchyi, was a university journalism instructor who supposedly had been politically reliable. Osechynskyi may have calculated his remarks so that Karpenko seemed like another Osadchyi worthy of dismissal.[67]

Since Slyvka and Kravets were Karpenko's friends, they compromised themselves before this group loyal to Chelak. These ex-institute scholars formed their own group, protected by the university chancellor and the Party committee secretary. Karpenko reputedly went to the chancellor and the Party committee secretary quite often, behind Chelak's back, and behind the faculty's Party organization. Going to the Party organization or the chancellor was nothing out of the ordinary for Soviet academia, but Chelak, perhaps interested in bringing down the university chancellor, claimed that they were plotting against the History Faculty. After the student arrests of 1973, when university Party members debated what had gone wrong, Chelak, who was to lose his position as dean over the scandal, derided past claims that he and others had abused scholars like Karpenko. He instead claimed that Karpenko, Kravets, and Slyvka had been "Trojan horses" set up against the History Faculty.[68]

Two other groupings contributed to these conflicts. Three prominent "mafia" figures were Fedir Trubitsyn of the Department of Political Economy, Mykhailo Menshov of the Department of the History of the CPSU, and Iosyp Tomenchuk of the Department of Political Economy. Their names showed up on numerous letters of denunciation to regional, republic, and all-Union Party organs.[69] They knew one another very well, as they had worked in the Lviv Regional Higher Party School, a school for training local Party functionaries, until its dissolution in 1963. After the Higher Party School's dissolution, the obkom transferred them to Lviv State University. References to past connections with the Higher Party School appeared at various points in their university personnel files. At the university, they continued their "old boy" network as they wrote denunciations.[70] Occasionally others from Trubitsyn and Tomenchuk's department, the Department of Political Economy (F. I. Nazarenko) or from the Department of Scientific Atheism (Mariia Bilchenko) joined them as signatories.[71]

The Higher Party School had been under the obkom, and it was a training ground for gorkom and obkom Party functionaries. Trubitsyn, Menshov, and Tomenchuk most likely used old connections with local functionaries to compel Party organs to take action. Their denunciations—which, claimed the obkom in 1975, had been sent to the Lviv obkom, the CPU Central Committee, and the CPSU Central Committee—did have results.[72] As early as the fall of 1970 the obkom set up a commission to investigate scholarly works about "ideologues of bourgeois nationalism." Set up under mysterious circumstances—hints about it come from various remarks at university Party meetings and from written denunciations—it apparently was led by Trubitsyn and seven other scholars (including Tomenchuk, as other sources suggest), and it functioned as late as 1972.[73]

Under this commission's influence, the obkom bureau passed a resolution on 26 March 1971 condemning "serious distortions" and "political mistakes" made by scholars of Levynskyi and other early twentieth-century Galician figures. Among other things, this resolution had Levynskyi's manuscripts and published works placed in closed depositories at local libraries and archives. It ordered a commission to look into the ideas and activities of a number of Galician figures, suggesting that members of this earlier commission planned on uncovering such sins among other scholars.[74] These denunciations to Moscow apparently found an audience. An abridged version of the CPSU Central Committee's 7 October 1971 resolution criticizing political work in the Lviv Region spent an entire paragraph on the problem of institute and university scholars having "whitewashed" and "brushed up" (*priukrashivaly*) "certain ideologists of Ukrainian bourgeois nationalism."[75]

Besides gaining an audience in Lviv and Moscow, these instructors found at least momentary support in Kyiv. Hrushetskyi as head of the CPU Central Committee's Control Commission received at least one petition from Bilchenko and Trubitsyn. Having been Lviv obkom secretary, Hrushetskyi probably knew these instructors personally. It is not clear how much he supported them.[76] However, their denunciations played into the hands of Malanchuk, who got the CPSU Central Committee to investigate the political situation in the Lviv Region and thus discredit his nemesis, republic Party chief Shelest.

Despite such clever manipulations, these instructors' power was limited and fleeting. Obkom personnel did not always take their side despite services for the Higher Party School. According to Iuriy Slyvka, Kazymyr Pyrozhak, then obkom secretary for ideological issues, was fair to himself, Karpenko, and Kravets and criticized university instructors who had launched this ideological campaign against them. In his oral interview, he mentioned that "guys from the obkom" shared denunciation materials with him at the time of these conflicts.[77] Kyiv also did not offer denunciations unanimous support. A CPU Central Committee functionary sent to review Karpenko's lectures in 1968 suggested over dinner at Slyvka's home that people in Party organs there were unsure of how to deal with all these denunciations and allegations.[78]

Most importantly, an influential group at the university countered these people making denunciations. Chancellor Maksymovych, together with the university Party committee secretary, exerted enough pressure to have Tomenchuk removed as head of the Department of Political Economy in 1972, transferring him to the city's Polytechnic Institute. Trubitsyn, denied further employment in 1974, had to find work in Kazakhstan.[79] History Faculty instructors at odds with Karpenko, Slyvka, and Kravets faced the ire of the chancellor's office. Ivan Biliakevych had to leave the university. He found work at the Institute of Social Sciences with the help of a friend from the obkom. While Roman Brodskyi could not be removed from the university due to his academic degrees and title of professor, Maksymovych and the university Party committee secretary tried to make his life less comfortable. In 1973, shortly after the student arrests, they prevented him from gaining access to closed archival materials on Galicia's Zionist movement, under the pretense that using such materials could propagandize Zionism, deemed as lethal as bourgeois nationalism in Soviet discourse. The chancellor's office snubbed Brodskyi's wish to honor his seventieth birthday in 1977 with a university-wide reception.[80]

Group dynamics within Party organs and the university thus brought down the alleged authors of denunciations. Personal ambitions, rather than perceptions of Galicia's history, drove these campaigns. Such ambitions were strong not just among those making denunciations but also among denunciation victims. Karpenko had a reputation for being blunt and undiplomatic with people, which only could have earned him enemies. Regardless of injustices dealt to him, Karpenko's tendency to portray himself as "a special bird" (*bila vorona*) offended such people.[81] Zlupko earned the wrath of Department of Political Economy colleagues because of incautious remarks at a 1964 Moscow conference, which caused him to be withdrawn from the university's graduate school. Speeding up his dissertation defense and quickly publishing articles and books led to the discrepancies university Party members discussed and people like Zlupko's department colleague Trubitsyn pounced on.[82]

Veteran instructors may not have had very influential connections with higher Party organs, but they took great pride in what connections they had. Veteran instructors like Biliakevych, Brodskyi, and Trubitsyn exploited past services to the university, the Party, or security organs. Biliakevych had been a department chair, a dean of the History Faculty, and even university chancellor.[83] He was in the Soviet secret police in his youth.[84] As a teenager Trubitsyn had served in Soviet punitive military detachments (called the ChON, or *Chasti Osobogo Naznacheniia* in Russian) that fought the White Armies and other enemy forces in the Russian civil war of 1918–20 and later pacification campaigns of the early 1920s. Brodskyi had been in the 1930s-era Soviet predecessor of the KGB, the United State Political Organization–People's Commissariat for Internal Affairs (OGPU-NKVD). These connections with security organs gave them a sense that they truly looked out for the well-being of the Soviet state. They reinforced convictions that their understanding of Ukrainian history was the right one.[85]

Trubitsyn was especially proud of his services to the young Soviet state. In his university job application, instead of giving the usual terse account of family background, education, career, and current family life, he dedicated over half of his autobiography to his role as a member of a punitive military expedition unit in the Orenburg Region of Russia during the Russian civil war.[86] Brodskyi often bragged to students about his services to the secret police, including his coining the phrase "ten years without the right of correspondence" for Soviet death sentences in the Great Terror of the 1930s. Jokes about Brodskyi's supposed accomplishments (like his ability to see in the dark) were still circulating in the History Faculty when I worked there in 2002–2004.[87] Such loyalties to Stalin-era policies and institutions contrasted greatly with loyalties of the scholars under attack. According to a dormitory neighbor, Zlupko as a graduate student talked avidly about the nationality question and other political issues in the Thaw's first years.[88] Slyvka and his graduate school friends also drew inspiration from the Thaw.[89]

With such colorful, and odious, personalities, and with the intrigues that went on among so many different cliques, this ideological campaign was a very muddled affair. Unlike in the Stalin era, no one was arrested. Everyone found jobs at other academic institutions, though Kravets and Karpenko had to leave Lviv.[90] After 1973, historians at the Institute of Social Sciences and Lviv State University were free from such attacks. When the obkom in 1975 responded to new denunciations against *Triumph of*

Historic Justice, it cast them aside. The Party had taken a new direction toward Lviv scholars.[91] The worst of republic-wide repressions against intellectuals like them had ended.

These academic conflicts, however, tell much about Lviv's evolution as a Ukrainian city. Academic life here encouraged among scholars a Galician Ukrainian view of what it meant to be Ukrainian. This meant viewing anti-Ukrainian forces in both ethnic and cultural terms. The manner in which historians recalled the past in oral interviews suggests the prevalence of these assumptions. Such "speech acts" reflect assumptions that academia, along with other aspects of the city's public life, were not Ukrainian enough.

The written record indicates that ethnic Ukrainians dominated the History Faculty at the time of this ideological campaign against Ukrainian bourgeois nationalism. One university Party committee commission report, dated 12 October 1972, said that out of a total of twenty-nine scholars there, nineteen (65 percent) were Ukrainians, while there were four Russians, five Jews, and one Hungarian. This figure more or less reflected Ukrainians' share of Lviv's population (roughly 68 percent in 1970).[92] When it came to positions of influence in the faculty, such as membership in the faculty's governing committee, the Academic Council, non-Ukrainians in the late 1960s had disproportionate influence, but this influence had disappeared by the early 1980s.

An attendance roster for 19 April 1968, in History Faculty dean Chelak's employment file, indicated that there were nine Ukrainians presumed to be on the council, while as many as seven were non-Ukrainians, clearly out of proportion with their share of the city's population. Only one Galician Ukrainian—M. O. Ratych—was on the Academic Council.[93] Ukrainians did not come to dominate the History Faculty's Academic Council until the early 1980s. A 1983 attendance roster for the Academic Council, also from Chelak's employment file, indicated that ethnic Ukrainians, about half of them natives of Western Ukraine, made up over 80 percent of the Academic Council. All but one (Brodskyi, a Russian speaker) presumably had become acculturated to the Ukrainian language.[94]

The oral record, as nebulous and subjective as it is, conveys very strong impressions that outsiders, including ethnic Russians and ethnic Jews who came to Western Ukraine after World War II, controlled events at the History Faculty. One historian who succeeded Chelak as dean of the History Faculty and knew such figures as Karpenko, Kravets, and Slyvka said he had the impression that Chancellor Maksymovych's appointment of Kravets and Slyvka to department chair positions represented a certain "Ukraini-anization" of the History Faculty.[95]

The Russian or Jewish origins of ideological campaign participants—or imaginations of such origins—surfaced in oral interviews. Oral interview respondents strove to avoid remarks that could be deemed anti-Semitic. This provoked one respondent to edit out of his oral interview transcript explicit references to people as Jews. Russians and Jews nonetheless fig-ured prominently in the "mafia," with Ukrainians playing a secondary role.[96] One respondent's written account accuses Roman Brodskyi, an eth-nic Jew, of being responsible for Kravets's leaving Chernivtsi. He suppos-edly went to the university and KGB organs there to convince university leaders of his political unreliability.[97] One respondent claimed that Liubov Andriivna Ivanenko, who had led criticism of *Triumph of Historic Justice* at the History Faculty in October 1970, was a "Jewish chauvinist," though her employment record indicates that she was Russian by nationality. This same respondent alleged that Vasyl Inkin was Jewish, though another ac-count states that Inkin was an ethnic Russian, the son of Old Believers.[98] A respondent involved in these events claimed Jews had a tendency to show off in front of other people, which, he said, "Jews themselves" admit. These prejudiced assumptions about Jews were not unusual for postwar Soviet society, where anti-Semitism had been encouraged since the Zhdanov era. In Lviv, they defined the "anti-Ukrainian" forces of this so-called histori-ans' mafia, particularly its leaders.

At the same time, the biographies of ideological campaign victims sug-gest the impact Lviv's academic institutions had on Lvivians. All three of the historians targeted in these ideological campaigns—Karpenko, Slyvka, and Kravets—were outsiders to Galicia. Only Zlupko and Oleksiuk were native Galician Ukrainians.[99] Karpenko was a Party activist from Eastern Ukraine (the Chernihiv Region), Slyvka was from the Transcarpathian Re-gion, and Kravets was from the Chełm Region in Poland cleansed of ethnic Ukrainians at the end of World War II. These were regions not connected with the national movements flourishing in Galicia since the nineteenth century. All three scholars had been graduate students or senior research workers under Ivan Krypiakevych at the Institute of Social Sciences. Kryp-iakevych influenced them in their research, turning them toward Galician history. He encouraged Karpenko to find out more about the ZUNR. Slyvka, who supported Karpenko's views on the ZUNR, had written a bach-elor's thesis at Uzhhorod State University that criticized Krypiakevych as a student of the "bourgeois nationalist" historian Mykhailo Hrushevskyi. He later pursued a doctoral dissertation on a theme related to the ZUNR, turning to Krypiakevych for advice. Kravets began his career looking at nineteenth-century Galician history at Krypiakevych's suggestion.[100]

As seen with Karpenko's article on the ZUNR, these scholars' works conflated Galicia with Western Ukraine, a geographical category that Tarik Amar rightly identifies as a Soviet construction.[101] Nonetheless, as such scholars came to view Galicia's past with more sympathy, they found themselves characterized as part of Lviv's Banderite other. Like the writers mimicked as closet Banderites by actors at a 1962 Lviv theater conference, Western Ukrainian scholars acquired reputations for being politically unreliable. This is suggested in Myroslava Hurladi's attack on the Institute of Social Sciences as a "nest of nationalists." At a 28 May 1970 institute open Party meeting where colleagues confronted her about her allegations, literary scholar Stepan Trofymuk started to cry. He was among those Writers' Union members who in 1966 signed a petition offering to take responsibility for Bohdan Horyn, on trial for spreading anti-Soviet literature. Besides this blot on his record, Hurladi's accusations against him and others in the Department of Ukrainian Literature suggested that he should lose his job over anti-Soviet behavior. Trofymuk could not bear the pressure anymore. He told the audience that in the first days of World War II, he fought the fascists on the Soviet side, later helping Soviet partisans behind enemy lines in his native Volhynia. Hurladi cut him off: "Cry. Let him cry. What kind of a partisan is he? I dragged people like him out of hideouts, I shot them." (*Sl'ozu. Pustit' sl'ozu. Iakyi vin partizan. Ia vytaskuvala zi skhronu takykh, striliala.*) Hurladi made reference to a Banderite hideout, called a *skhron* in Ukrainian. Besides betraying her own past—that of a Soviet security forces agent shooting nationalist guerrillas—she played to the idea that no Western Ukrainian could be trusted, even an aggrieved Soviet partisan.[102]

Historical Memory and the Politics of Identity

This exchange between Hurladi and Trofymuk illustrated popular memory's ability to resist official interpretations of the past. Outsiders to the region remembered locals' hostility to Soviet power. Locals, in this case Galician Ukrainians, varied greatly in how they remembered their region's recent past. Among such memories were ones more sympathetic toward the Sich Riflemen and the Ukrainian Galician Army that had fought for the ZUNR against Polish forces in 1918–19. The same could be said for OUN resistance and the UPA insurgency.

All national narratives involve selecting, and censoring, dissonant memories.[103] Memories of Galicians' past liberation movements were very conflicting. The Polish-Ukrainian War was a lost cause. As such, people remembered it negatively. This could be seen in a poem written by a former Sich Rifleman who fought in the ZUNR's Ukrainian Galician Army. This poet, Myroslav Irchan, had just defected to the Red Army as the ZUNR collapsed. His poem, published in the Communist literary journal *Galician Communist (Halyts'kyi komunist)* in Kyiv in 1921, called Ukrainian Galician Army officers traitors who only cared about their own well-being. They were people who had misled and manipulated simple folk by proclaiming their love for the Ukrainian people.[104] Irchan was among those shot in 1937, at the height of the Great Terror. His immediate memories of the Polish-Ukrainian War suggested it was a shameful episode in Ukrainians' history.

Memories of the nationalist insurgency against Soviet rule were more recent and even more divisive. Not only had the nationalist cause been lost, but nationalist insurgents as well as Soviet police organs had committed terror against Western Ukrainian civilians. As in other parts of the western borderlands, nationalist insurgents killed more local civilians than Soviet security forces or representatives of Soviet government.[105] While my oral interviews emphasized Soviet violence against civilians and did not mention insurgent violence, Soviet institutions exploited memories of the latter. For instance, in 1966, Lviv State University Communists took part in a propaganda event in a village in the Lviv Region where dozens of villagers talked about the harm brought by the OUN, and four former OUN members spoke. According to one of the university Communists in attendance, these former underground nationalists "talked about how they were dragged onto the wrong path, into this conspiracy, how they became honest workers and how they became convinced of their miserable deeds and subversive acts and that they will warn their children [about these deeds and acts], too."[106] Some Western Ukrainians privately were sympathetic to UPA soldiers, but nonetheless viewed them as "foolish guys." Such were the sentiments of the grandmother of one Lviv writer.[107] The nationalist insurgency was a lost, and therefore foolish, cause.

Lost causes, however, could also produce local heroes who had taken the moral high ground. This happened in the American South after the Civil

War.[108] The residents of the Soviet Union's western borderlands underwent a similar experience. In Baltic republics like Estonia, postwar nationalist guerrillas created myths of themselves as heroes fighting for national independence in poems, folk songs, and oral legends. Many Estonians before the Gorbachev era knew little else of such guerrillas. Such legends had erased the civil war that had torn communities apart, a conflict captured in a 1965 film about Lithuanian national guerrillas by Vytautas Žalakevičius, *Nobody Wanted to Die,* shown throughout the Soviet Union.[109] Galician Ukrainians, too, created myths about UPA fighters cleansed of memories of interethnic violence and violence between Ukrainians. These myths and myths of earlier heroes gave them a sense of local pride. While they could not change the Soviet multinational empire, Western Ukrainians could take comfort in narratives of national and social liberation associated with their "small homeland."[110]

Amid stories about UPA terror, others circulated that forgot this terror. A young man from the Transcarpathian Region, neighbor to a UPA fighter returned from prison and exile, came to see such guerrillas as genuine Ukrainian patriots. As a student at the Lviv State Printing Institute in the late 1960s, he told fellow dormitory students very positive things about the UPA. In a Lviv Region village in January 1974, seventh and eighth graders sang Christmas carols and reenacted the manger scene with Ukrainian insurgents among the main characters. As Lviv's obkom secretary reported to superiors in Kyiv, their performance in villagers' homes included reciting "an anti-Soviet nationalist text, which was about mourning for Ukraine [*oplakuvannia Ukrainy*], a hostile attitude toward Soviet soldiers, and liberation by 'Ukrainian Insurgents,'" a clear reference to the UPA.[111]

In their performance, these schoolchildren presumably sang carols making positive references to the UPA, which were spread among families in Western Ukraine. Folk songs became key vehicles for paying homage to Sich Riflemen and Ukrainian Galician Army soldiers from the Polish-Ukrainian War of 1918–19 as well as the UPA. Such songs circulated among close family and friends. People sang them quietly at home or more boisterously after several rounds of alcohol, usually on such family occasions as weddings.[112]

Sich Riflemen's own ambiguous pasts made it possible to cast them as Soviet heroes. Sich Riflemen like Irchan had gone over to the Red Army during the Polish-Ukrainian War, and Soviet power had rehabilitated him in 1956. Thus some altered these songs, inserting "Red Riflemen" in place of "Sich Riflemen." However, even this strategy was risky, particularly in the late Stalin era. As an obkom report indicates, in late 1952, a young couple celebrating their wedding in a Lviv State Pedagogical Institute dormitory faced expulsion from the Komsomol and the institute because of singing such songs. While they and other students sang songs praising "Red Riflemen," the father and uncle of the bride used the words "Sich Riflemen" instead. Other classmates received reprimands from the Komsomol, while another student was also recommended for academic expulsion.[113] Some UPA songs popular in Lviv today suggest that they, too, were similarly transformed. One song refers to a "partisan" who lay buried behind an oak tree. This "partisan" could have been Soviet or UPA to a listener.

Such songs nonetheless were about true Ukrainian heroes who had died for their country, not evil men who terrorized Ukrainians and other ethnic groups. One respondent, born in 1940 in the Lviv Region, repeated lines from a song where the UPA soldier, dying after a shootout, asks that someone tell his family and loved ones that the three bullets he took in the chest were for his dear Ukraine. He had learned this song when he was about 6 or 7 years old, and over time, though not right away, he came to appreciate what it meant. This respondent later went on to become a non-Communist deputy elected to Lviv's Regional Council in 1990. For him, such songs gave him an alternative set of heroes, heroes who may have lost in the field of battle yet whose cause lived on among Ukrainians, including those who removed the Communist Party from power in Lviv. His recollections of mass demonstrations sweeping Lviv at the end of the 1980s included crowds of people of all ages singing songs connected with the Sich Riflemen, the Ukrainian Galician Army, and the UPA. Such a scene suggests that these local heroes existed for others, too, in private, coming to the surface en masse when censorship and political denunciations had died down.[114]

While these songs had been confined to people's homes, there were other ways of honoring such heroes in Lviv, as seen in annual pilgrimages to the graves of Sich Riflemen and Ukrainian Galician Army soldiers in Ianiv Cemetery. These pilgrimages had been common practice in Lviv before the war, usually during Green Holidays (Greek Catholic observances of Pentecost) and 1 November, All Saints' Day. People laid flowers and lit candles at the gravesites of soldiers and visited the graves of their own loved ones. In postwar Lviv, this tradition carried on among native Lvivians. Beginning in the late 1960s, as Khrushchev's Thaw came to an end and the ideological climate grew more hostile, local police organs cracked down on such visitors. Plainclothes KGB agents patrolled Ianiv Cemetery during such holidays, and people lost their jobs or were kicked out of the university if they were caught decorating graves. A Lviv State University graduate student was expelled for such reasons in 1971, as remarks made at a city Komsomol conference indicate. Pilgrimages nonetheless continued, even after arrests and other forms of repression affected the Ukrainian intelligentsia in 1972–73. As one Western tourist noted in 1975, people still sang Sich Riflemen songs near the cemetery during Green Holidays, with some stealing their way to the gravesite through back paths. Others, such as Tetiana Vorobkevych, came a day in advance of such holidays to avoid attention.[115]

Intellectuals in the public sphere articulated ideas that people like the Sich Riflemen, and even OUN activists, were true Ukrainian heroes, regardless of having been swindled, betrayed, or defeated. They emphasized their devotion to ideals that constituted Soviet socialism. Artists created works that in camouflaged form portrayed as noble heroes those who had been involved with the Sich Riflemen and organizations later connected with the OUN. *Unvanquished Galician Woman* (1960) (Figure 6.1), by Lviv sculptor Bohdan Popovych, was dedicated to Olha Basarab, a female Sich Rifleman who, as a member of an underground organization resisting Polish rule, died at the hands of Polish military police in 1924. Popovych had gotten the idea for such a sculpture while working on a monument to Soviet prisoners of war in Ianiv Cemetery. A stranger there pointed out Basarab's grave. He said that Basarab, killed by the Poles, deserved a more fitting monument than the simple marker standing there.[116]

Popovych's statue never became a monument for her grave, and it certainly had no chance of becoming so in Soviet times. Basarab's organization, the forerunner of the OUN, was soundly condemned in Soviet historiography. However, Popovych's friend, sculptor Petro Kulyk, produced a monument for another former Sich Rifleman, Stepan Melnychuk (1968), erected in the city of Ivano-Frankivsk (Figure 6.2).[117] Melnychuk fit the bill for Soviet heroism. Like Irchan, he left the Ukrainian Galician Army upon the ZUNR's collapse and joined the Reds. Unlike Irchan, who faced a Soviet firing squad in 1937, Melnychuk achieved early martyrdom at the hands of the Poles. He died while on a 1922 guerrilla expedition against Polish forces in Galicia's Ternopil Region. A Polish punitive expedition caught him and two other guerrilla leaders and executed them. Just before Polish soldiers shot him, Melnychuk allegedly was singing the lines to the international Communist anthem, *The Internationale*.[118] There was no better way for a Soviet patriot to die.

Figure 6.1. Bohdan Popovych, *Unvanquished Galician Woman* (1960). Used with permission of the artist.

Both *Unvanquished Galician Woman* and *Stepan Melnychuk* fit the Soviet canon of sculpture. They are untrammeled workers standing up for justice, with the woman modeled after Basarab bearing a grimace that makes her appear male. Melnychuk's stare of defiance—with large hollow eyes and a calm, sharply chiseled face, prepared to face his executioners without fear—is particularly striking. In these works of art, the struggle between Poles and Ukrainians for control of Eastern Galicia in the early 1920s, after the defeat of the ZUNR government, finds former Sich Riflemen (and Riflewomen) as popular heroes refusing to give in to the chains literally binding them at the hands and feet. However, they reflect memories reshaped into regional narratives compatible in Soviet Ukraine's official histories. Melnychuk epitomized the impact of Communist ideals on interwar Galicia better than Volodymyr Levynskyi, the subject of inept propagandist works. While

Figure 6.2. Petro Kulyk, *Stepan Melnychuk* (1968). Used with permission of the artist.

panegyrics to Levynskyi were being investigated by Party organs in 1970 for distorting facts, that same year, Kulyk's statue received honors by the Union of Journalists in a republic competition, "Art to the People," sponsored by the republic newspaper, *Ukraine Pravda (Pravda Ukrainy)* and the republic Artists' Union.[119]

A novel by senior Galician Ukrainian writer Iryna Vilde, *The Richynskyi Sisters,* portrayed an entire period of Galician history with greater sympathy than official histories. Vilde completed the novel's first edition in 1958, and she and theater producer Bohdan Antkiv arranged it as a play for Lviv's Mariia Zankovetska Theater ten years later. The novel, set in a Galician small town on the eve of World War II, concerns a family coping with the sudden death of its husband and father, a Greek Catholic priest. Besides portraying the Richynskyi sisters' different reactions to their father's death and the catastrophic financial situation that follows from it, Vilde views former Sich Riflemen, and even members of the OUN underground, as true Ukrainian patriots misled by their leaders. One of the Richynskyi sisters, Nelia, falls in love with Markiian Ivashkiv, in prison for his OUN activities, and marries him. While Ivashkiv comes to find common language with fellow Communist prisoners, his motives for joining the OUN are portrayed as pure, a reaction to discrimination and violence against Ukrainians by Poles in Galicia.

The dramatization of *The Richynskyi Sisters* produced a scandal at the republic level. An instructor at the republic Central Committee's Department of Culture, reporting on the rehearsals and the premiere he had attended in Lviv in October 1968, said Ivashkiv had become the ideological heart of the play. He raised objections to Vilde's own attitudes toward Galicia's past. She allegedly said that too many accounts of this period in Galicia's history were treated in black-and-white fashion. Only 25 percent of the population, she added, had been Communist or "nationalist," while "all the rest were patriots."[120] Because of this scandal with Party leaders, the theater's directors had to make some changes to the play after its premiere. According to actress Larysa Kadyrova, who played the role of Nelia, who fell in love with Ivashkiv, the monologue where she professed her love for Ivashkiv was removed. Later producers excised the entire scene where she and Ivashkiv met in prison.[121]

Other changes, though, were minor. Iulian Turchyn, then a member of the theater's Art Council, recalled Vilde vehemently defending the play during discussions of its premiere with Party and state functionaries.[122] Her defense of the play, and her reputation as a Soviet Ukrainian writer, probably saved it from significant censorship. Roman Ivanychuk, who was close to Vilde and who wrote the preface to one of her collected works, noted that one song with a melody of a nationalist song from the 1930s was removed, along with some controversial words, but the play remained largely unchanged.[123] Thus a dialogue between young Communist Bronko Zavadka and attorney Orest Bilynskyi, which also raised the Kyiv functionary's ire, remained in place. Fedir Stryhun, who played Zavadka, said that the initial controversy over Bilynskyi's lines soon died town, and the scene remained as it was for the rest of the theater's performances of the play.[124]

This grudging toleration of *The Richynskyi Sisters* embodied the reckoning Party and state officials had to make, both in Lviv and in Kyiv, with popular memories of Galicia's past. They tried to Sovietize such memories, not just in mythology about the KPZU, but in myths about political movements with even more problematic relationships with the Soviet state. The cover of a popular book on Lviv, published in 1969, had the blue-and-yellow colors of the Ukrainian nationalist flag connected with the ZUNR government. Song books produced by republic-level publishers rearranged Sich Riflemen songs, adapting them to more neutral themes. A Red Army songbook, published in Kyiv and Kharkiv in 1946, has "A Cossack Went to War," which is absolutely identical to the Sich Riflemen song "A Rifleman Went to War" except that "Cossack" has replaced "Rifleman." The 1946 version is called an anonymous "Ukrainian folk song," while the 1992 version, today's Sich Riflemen version of the song, has the names of the composers (R. Kupchynskyi and M. Haivoronskyi), names associated with the song's bourgeois nationalist past.[125] Regional and city officials fostered new rituals to replace interwar Galician ones. In the month of May, for instance, they commemorated the death of Vasyl Kozak and others killed in worker demonstrations in Lviv in 1936, and the demonstrators were given a prominent memorial in Ianiv Cemetery. Kozak's death and burial site became prominent in popular histories and guidebooks. Mariana Dolynska, describing events leading up to her 1973 arrest, recalled attending one annual memorial service for Kozak at the cemetery. These new rituals and symbols in Ianiv Cemetery thus had become a Soviet alternative to rituals in November that used to commemorate Sich Riflemen buried there.[126]

The Soviet state accommodated other aspects of Galicia's past, including the preservation of its oldest monuments. The Museum of Folk Architecture and Life in Lviv, an outdoor museum for eighteenth-century churches, homes, and other monuments of village architecture from Galicia and other parts of Western Ukraine, was one such example. Conceived in the last days of World War II, its plans at first were dismissed as "bourgeois nationalist" in 1946 and put off for some time. Members of Lviv's intelligentsia, inspired by such open air museums in the Baltic republics, brought the project back to life with a petition to Moscow's Central Committee in 1964. It opened as a museum in 1972.[127]

Such preservation projects reflected Soviet leaders' attempts to deal with growing criticism across the Soviet Union about people being deprived of their past and hence their identity. In Soviet Russia, intellectuals and young people became alarmed at the destruction of historic monuments and the decline of village life. Beginning in the mid-1960s, Russian intellectuals and young people thus expressed a growing interest in historical preservation. In the 1960s village prose movement, Russian writers expressed their concerns about the loss of rural Russia's traditional values. Both movements were conservative, seeing Western influences encouraged by the Thaw as responsible for the perceived decline of Russian culture. They increasingly enjoyed support from Party and state functionaries, though their more critical remarks about the Soviet state sometimes led to repression.[128] For non-Russian intellectuals, these fears reflected different concerns, namely post-Thaw official rhetoric legitimating the merger of nations and the formation of one Soviet people. Ukrainian writers like Oles Honchar (1968) and Kazakh writers like Chingiz Aitmatov (1980) raised fears about their nationalities losing their sense of dignity through the loss of historical memory.[129]

In Lviv, Roman Fedoriv and Roman Ivanychuk, beginning in the 1960s, turned to writing historical fiction precisely because of their fear that Ukrainians were losing contact with their past.[130] Fedoriv, shocked that schoolchildren near the famed medieval town of Halych knew nothing about Halych's history, wrote novels about the medieval Rus' principality of Galicia and Volhynia so that young Ukrainians would not forget their past. Among these works were *The Father's Lamp (Otchyi svityl'nyk)* (1976).[131] Ivanychuk, incensed at the 1964 destruction of priceless documents in Ukrainian history at the Academy of Sciences library in Kyiv, a fire seen as set by the KGB, wrote the novel *Hollyhock (Mal'vy)* (1968), which strongly condemns, through historical allegory, those who forget and betray their own people. After Shelest was removed from the republic's Party leadership for national "bragging," Ivanychuk's novel attracted the attention of Party organs and was confiscated from libraries and bookstores.[132]

In Lviv, the politics of historical preservation collided with Soviet politics of empire. As Soviet Ukrainian leaders in the 1970s embarked on an ideological campaign against Ukrainian intellectuals, their counterparts in

Lviv proceeded to dismantle Sich Riflemen gravestones in Ianiv Cemetery. According to a local KGB report, dated 24 April 1972, city officials had these gravestones demolished in 1971, over the protests of such people as Iryna Kalynets, at the time on trial for anti-Soviet activities. Such an act drove home this suspicion that Ukrainians' past—here Galician Ukrainians' past—was ultimately disposable.[133]

Critics attacked the 1968 dramatization of *The Richynskyi Sisters* for "unhealthy" analogies to the present. The CPU Central Committee functionary reviewing the play was dumbfounded by what he heard and saw. As he sat in the audience of Lviv's Zankovetska Theater, attending the play's October premiere, the Galician lawyer Orest Bilynskyi responded to the wry observation by a young Communist, Bronko Zavadka, that Bilynskyi had given up caring about Galician Ukrainians' social and national oppression. He responded with a monologue that outraged the Kyivan functionary, for "he [Bilynskyi] tells them [the audience], even angrily and indignantly, that today, so to speak, history is being falsified, 'heroism is called treason,' 'memorials of the ancient past are being plundered,' and so on." With dismay, the Kyiv official noted that "a certain portion of the viewers perceives this incorrectly and responds to this with applause."[134]

These lines remained in the play for the duration of its performances, which lasted until 1984.[135] They resonated with the audience for several reasons. Popular memory was ambivalent about this period of Galicia's history. Some saw the Polish-Ukrainian War as led by swindlers and opportunists, while others viewed it as a time of Ukrainian heroism. Local Communists and nationalists alike were committed patriots. However, the audience most likely knew from popular memories that the official record was not the complete story. They knew that official histories had distorted Ukrainians' past to utter absurdity. True, a cheering crowd did not mean support for a political message. Art scholar Volodymyr Osviychuk, when asked about the play, could only recall that the superior acting greatly impressed him. He remembered no particular political message.[136] Bilynskyi's monologue in the play, preserved in the theater's archive, differs significantly from what he says in the actual novel. While in the novel Bilynskyi makes general references to nations dominating and distorting past achievements of other nations, in the play, he focuses his anger explicitly at Polish occupation of Galicia.[137] Some people admired the play because it portrayed elements of Galician life that they as locals could readily identify with, like attending the Greek Catholic Church, dissolved since 1946. Kyiv film producer and critic Roman Korohodskyi, who was friends with Lviv actors and actresses and who watched the play a number of times, stressed that this play was popular because it made Galician Ukrainians feel like they were "at home."[138]

Notwithstanding these other appealing features of the play, Bilynskyi's monologue remained very much open to "anti-Soviet" readings, not just in the novel itself (where stronger allusions to the Soviet present could be made), but in the actual onstage performances by Oleksandr Hrynko. Hrynko's own life fueled these lines with explosive power. A native of Galicia who took part in the People's Assembly that ratified Western Ukraine's incorporation into Soviet Ukraine in 1939, in 1941 he was arrested for "bourgeois nationalist" activities (displaying the Ukrainian national colors in an arc set up to welcome Soviet troops in his home village in 1939). He spent the next decade and a half in Soviet gulags, returning home only in 1956. Recalling years later his past roles in the Mariia Zankovetska Theater, he turned to his role as Bilynskyi in *The Richynski Sisters*. Hrynko emphasized that the theater was the only place where he could say the things that Bilynskyi said. He spoke Bilynskyi's monologue with such passion and with such conviction that he realized that his decision to become an actor was not a mistake after all.[139]

The people protesting the hammering apart of Sich Riflemen's gravestones three years later may have been in that audience drowning Bilynskyi with applause in October 1968. However, the story about Ianiv Cemetery was not so simple. Officials stopped the destruction. Writing about his 1975 Lviv trip for a Western diaspora newspaper, a Western diaspora Ukrainian said that while the Sich Riflemen graves at Lychakiv Cemetery had vanished without a trace, those at Ianiv Cemetery remained. One story he had heard attributed these gravestones' salvation to an ethnic Russian, a retired Soviet Army colonel. This colonel, who used to maintain cemetery plots for Soviet soldiers in Europe, successfully petitioned Moscow to preserve the graves. According to the tourist, the retired officer claimed that these soldiers deserved "the same respect as the graves of Soviet dead," as these were, said the tourist, "riflemen, peasant sons, who fought Polish oppression."[140] However apocryphal it might be, this story suggests that the Galician Ukrainian local had been accepted as a Western Soviet other in the Soviet historical imagination. Galician Ukrainians' struggle against Polish domination was a noble one. However, in private circles, Galician Ukrainians knew that their heroes were much more than that. Oleksandr Hrynko was not the only one who understood the significance of his lines.

CHAPTER 7

Youth and the Nation

Dissonances between official representations of the past and people's collective memory underscored the fragile compromises making Lviv both Ukrainian and Soviet. Outside the public sphere, in close family gatherings, student apartments and dormitories, cafés, and art shops, Lvivians read about and discussed people connected with the region's "anti-Soviet" past. These milieus fostered a *habitus* that incorporated a variety of conflicting values, like the young man who knew from family that Soviet power was the "anti-Christ" and imposed from outside, yet was intrigued about the future Communist society of 1980. Such conflicting values set young Lvivians apart from their Moscow counterparts.[1] For young people who remembered the war and the postwar nationalist insurgency, Khrushchev's Thaw unleashed a flurry of emotions suppressed by such conflicting values. As seen with Lviv writers and historians, the impetus for this thaw came from Kyiv, the republic's capital. However, the way it resonated in Ukraine's western borderlands amazed contemporaries.

One telling example of this was in the spring of 1962, when two Kyivan poets, Ivan Drach and Mykola Vinhranovskyi, and Kyivan literary critic Ivan Dziuba, spoke at Lviv State University's Assembly Hall. These young writers belonged to the Sixtiers Movement, Soviet intellectuals associated with radical intellectuals of 1860s Russia. Inspired by criticism of the Stalin era during the Thaw, they challenged conventions in art, literature, and other forms of expression constricting the rights of the individual and, in the case of Ukraine, the rights of the nation. At this literary evening, their speeches and poems decried the cowardice of the republic's literary

179

establishment and called for a renewal of their nation's language and culture. Students and other young people in the audience, including novelist Roman Ivanychuk, were spellbound. After years of experiencing repression and forced silence in Western Ukraine, someone was speaking for them. The crowd went wild. Ivanychuk writes, "The young public, which then still didn't have the courage to cry out 'shame' and 'glory' [as in street protests], applauded incessantly, applauded rhythmically—as if pounding nails into the lid of the coffins in which the spiritually dead had taken rest."[2]

This sensational literary evening inspired students and young professionals to challenge existing rules on national self-expression. Through personal contacts with these Kyiv Sixtiers, there soon emerged a Club of Artistic Youth, modeled on Kyiv's club. This club reexamined past figures in Ukrainian culture and restored to public memory those "forgotten." Forming personal networks with young Kyivans, young Lvivians shared the optimism that Soviet socialism could be improved. However, there were also voices among them calling for Ukraine's independence, and these influenced the republic's emerging dissident movement. Arrests sparked a 1966 petition from Lviv Writers' Union members that tried to free one of them, Bohdan Horyn, from prison. This act caused a senior union member to blame these Kyivans who had spoken at the university in 1962 for all this anti-Soviet trouble.[3] Later, influenced by Sixtiers' protest literature, Lviv State University history and Ukrainian philology students pasted up protest leaflets. Posting leaflets led to their arrests in late March 1973. As KGB investigations revealed, this group had talked about Ukraine's separation from the Soviet Union.

Such networks paved the way for Ukraine's dissident movement, but this was only part of the story. In the post-Stalin era, young Soviets brought up in the Thaw and later in Brezhnev's "Era of Stagnation" developed their own private spaces for enjoying one another's company.[4] The texts created in such private spheres did not always deal explicitly with politics. Some rebelled against the restrictions placed on art and literature in the public sphere, especially as censorship grew more severe in the 1970s. Others, reveling in the cynicism and irony of the Brezhnev era, took to making jokes out of daily life. Space itself—the space of the apartment, the dormitory room, or the art shop—along with censorship of the public sphere fragmented these underground networks along ethnic, regional, and cultural lines.[5] Nonetheless, such spaces challenged the discourse of the public sphere. At the end of the 1980s, intellectuals who were products of these spaces articulated and mobilized support for Ukraine's independence.

Young People and the State

While contemporary interpretations about Ukrainian dissent assume a binary opposition between state and society, the actions of both were profoundly intertwined.[6] Promoting the interests of non-Russians, while at times a formality, was an integral part of Soviet state policy. Because the Soviet state was not monolithic in its actions toward non-Russians, various institutions and officials tolerated, if not encouraged, questions about what it meant to be Ukrainian, particularly during Khrushchev's Thaw.

In Soviet society, as in imperial Russian society, the intelligentsia had a special role to play in serving the people and the state. The Stalin era had transformed the intelligentsia. It now represented all of those with an undergraduate education. Everyone attending institutions of higher learning was expected to take on the intelligentsia mission of serving the people and the state and acquiring the values and habits of "cultured" individuals. While distrusted, the Soviet intelligentsia was a critical ally in articulating ideological matters and resolving economic problems.[7] The Thaw witnessed a rebirth of the idea of the intelligentsia as spokespersons for the people.[8] As future members of the intelligentsia, Ukrainian students in higher education in Lviv acquired the notion that they were to serve not just the Soviet state and the Soviet people. As new national awakeners they were to serve Ukrainians.[9] At the same time, as seen with Lviv's libraries and museums, what kind of nation could be represented faced certain limits, limits that the Thaw only partially changed. Politics saturated all aspects of young people's daily lives, becoming increasingly ritualized and less brutal, yet having an extremely powerful influence over them. As in earlier periods of Soviet history, no one could escape the state, no matter how nebulous it was in practice.[10]

Educational institutions, cultural institutions, and the Komsomol facilitated the discussion of national issues during the Thaw. Lviv State University was one key example. It sponsored the literary evening that brought such thunderous applause in 1962. Its chancellor, Ievhen Lazarenko, stirred up a Ukrainian national revival there. Earlier that year, taking advantage of the 1961 Twenty-Second Party Congress's criticism of Stalin and Stalinists, he urged members of the Writers' Union to foster greater respect for

Ukrainians' language and literature, noting the problem of people's indifference to such issues caused by Stalin's cult of personality.[11] Former university instructor and scholar Bohdan Zadorozhnyi recalled that at some meeting where he was present, Lazarenko disagreed with an obkom representative regarding the Ukrainian language's role at the university. When Lazarenko in his speech demanded more courses taught in Ukrainian, the obkom representative immediately remarked that it would be impossible to build Communism without the Russian language. Lazarenko in reply said diplomatically that while it was true that one could not build Communism without Russian, one could not build Communism without Ukrainian. This exchange underscored Lazarenko's attempt to foster a national renaissance in the spirit of Khrushchev's Thaw, which promised to create a true Communist society by 1980.[12] In his memoirs, Ivanychuk emphasized that Lazarenko encouraged students like himself, repressed in the Stalin era, to study or renew their studies. Determined to instill greater love for Ukraine's literary heroes, he led pilgrimages of students and faculty to historic sites connected with leaders of Galicia's nineteenth-century Ukrainian national movement. This included visits to the birthplaces of Ivan Franko and early nineteenth-century national awakener Markiian Shashkevych. Lazarenko had a young Lviv sculptor design a bust of Shashkevych for the latter's birthplace, an indication of his great admiration for Shashkevych.[13]

University organizations became important for young people interested in Ukrainians' identity and culture, both during the Thaw and after. Franko's Blacksmith Shop *(Frankova kuznia)*, its literary studio, inspired new forms of Ukrainian literary expression during the Thaw.[14] Student research groups, namely, those connected with the History Faculty, drew young people curious about their nation's past. The student choir and dance ensemble, *Cheremosh,* brought together students from a variety of disciplines interested in Ukrainian culture.[15] Student organizations thus fostered informal contacts that later grew into private discussions about what it meant to be Ukrainian. Ivan Svarnyk in an oral interview suggested that his History Faculty research group and *Cheremosh* brought together the young people later arrested in 1973 for spreading anti-Soviet leaflets.[16]

Lviv's city schools, sometimes long after the Thaw, gave young people more respect for Ukrainians' literature, language, and history. Middle school teachers of Ukrainian language and literature made at least some schoolchildren realize that it was not a "hick language" *(vuykivs'ka mova).*[17] At least in the early 1960s, middle schools, including those with Russian-language instruction, had evenings honoring Shevchenko's birth and death.[18] By the late 1970s, there were some downtown schools that had no Shevchenko evenings, an effect of 1970s-era political repressions against Ukraine's national intelligentsia.[19] However, there were also schools that fostered an interest in Ukrainian history and language, sometimes reflecting their prewar heritage. According to one respondent born in 1965, his school, Middle School Number 34, originally was a Ukrainian gymnasium sponsored by Greek Catholic Metropolitan Andrei Sheptytskyi before the war. Besides the respect its Ukrainian language teachers gave to Ukrainian, its history lessons and field trips revealed more about Ukrainian history than what standard textbooks told.[20]

Oral interviews credited the Komsomol with contributing to the development of national cultural activities. They brought people with common interests together and established unofficial networks of fellow thinkers. Republic Komsomol activities, like republic student conferences, brought together Lvivians and Kyivans.[21] Kyiv city Komsomol leaders' sponsorship of a Club of Artistic Youth in 1960 later resonated in Lviv and other Soviet Ukrainian cities.[22] Young Lvivians in 1963 created a similar club under regional Komsomol leadership. This organization, uniting young writers, artists, musicians, and scholars from university age on up, noticeably widened the boundaries of Lviv's Ukrainian culture from 1963 to 1965. In literary evenings and seminars, it promoted "forgotten" writers and explored aspects of Ukrainian cultural history that had been ignored or censured during the Stalin era. This club brought together people who soon spread *samvydav* literature.[23] Its participants indicated that this club represented a chance, through legal means, to affirm their Ukrainian national identity, which the Party's ideology, in their view, undermined by interpreting the world through class categories.[24]

At the same time, Lviv's Club of Artistic Youth was influenced by attributes of the Thaw elsewhere, including Moscow. The club resembled other Thaw-era youth initiative clubs meant to revive enthusiasm for socialist ideals while giving young people a chance to enjoy leisure time together.[25] Like Sixtiers in Moscow who rediscovered and worshipped the poet Vladimir Mayakovsky, the Club of Artistic Youth in Lviv, according to its president, Mykhailo Kosiv, put on Ukrainian-language performances of Mayakovsky in one of its literary evenings.[26] Kosiv himself may have shared the Thaw's revolutionary idealism, at least for a time. A fellow literary critic recalled his shock hearing Kosiv, a Galician Ukrainian who had witnessed

Soviet terror, reject his private criticisms of Soviet power and insist in the 1960s Thaw era that he, Kosiv, was a Marxist.[27]

Later, at the end of the 1980s, when Gorbachev's policy of Glasnost considerably widened freedom of speech, Lviv's Komsomol again facilitated the development of such organizations for young people. Local Komsomol leaders sponsored an organization called the Lion Society, which dealt with exploring and promoting Ukrainians' culture and reexamined issues of national identity. Rostyslav Bratun, the former editor of *October*, helped sponsor it. The Lion Society differed from the earlier Club of Artistic Youth. It set up its own independent newspaper. It nominated Bratun, a reform-minded candidate, to the 1988 CPSU Party Congress in Moscow.[28] There is no evidence that its members shared Thaw-era hopes for a Communist future.

After completing higher education, young intellectuals found opportunities in state institutions to create social spaces more autonomous from the public sphere. In cities like Moscow and Novosibirsk, theaters and research institutions became oases of freedom after the Thaw had ended.[29] In Lviv, actors and actresses of the Mariia Zankovetska Theater recalled its being a haven of sorts, where people could express themselves freely not just during the Thaw but later. Actress Larysa Kadyrova, who began performing at this theater in the 1960s, remembered it as a "center of Lviv's spiritual life." The theater united actors, artists, art critics, musicians, and writers. Inspired by the Thaw, its actors encouraged a democratic working environment. Bohdan Kozak, who officially began performing at the theater in 1963, said that around this time, he and younger actors, speaking at an open Party meeting of the theater, demanded that all employees speak Ukrainian both offstage and onstage. This Ukrainian theater, set up in Lviv by Eastern Ukrainians in late 1944, had been known for its actors and directors speaking Russian offstage. Older colleagues, including Eastern Ukrainians, complied. Around 1967, when there was no chief director, they, younger actors, arranged a mock "court" in their theater club, Dialogue, to judge each other's strengths and weaknesses onstage and assign new roles. Critics, writers, and fellow actors took part. Kozak said the court attracted older participants interested in improving their own stage skills. The new director later discouraged this practice, but his successor, Serhiy Danchenko, encouraged it in the 1970s, as Danchenko, a much younger director, admired the club members' sense of initiative. Along with this relatively democratic atmosphere, the theater put on unofficial art exhibits in the foyer, giving local artists a chance to display works that might not normally make it to official exhibitions. Kozak recalled senior actors like Oleksandr Hrynko, Borys Mirus, and Bohdan Kokh telling them stories about their days as political prisoners in Soviet gulags.[30]

Lviv's Institute of Social Sciences did not have the kind of autonomy that academic institutions in Novosibirsk or Moscow had. They did not have great access to foreign literature, and they certainly did not have the opportunity to organize discussion clubs like Novosibirsk scholars. Yet its younger scholars, too, found it to be an oasis of freedom. Feodosiy Stebliy, who began working there as a historian of Ukraine in 1957, stressed that the institute was much more democratic than Lviv State University. One could speak more freely within the institute's walls. For instance, a colleague, Mykola Kravets, used to pass by his office and utter remarks that it would be better if Ukraine were one day independent. Such remarks could not have been said in a university office. Both Stebliy and Iuriy Slyvka, later one of the victims of the university's ideological campaigns, shared news about Prague Spring with institute colleagues. They kept up with these events through Czech and Slovak newspapers available then in Lviv's kiosks. Stebliy recalled that the Soviet intervention was a great blow to him and his colleagues.[31]

While state and Party institutions enabled young people to exchange ideas and reflect on what it meant to be Ukrainian, their practices also caused disaffection. Despite Lviv's Ukrainianization, educational institutions' use of Russian textbooks influenced ordinary speech and provoked discussions. One student at Lviv State University, explaining to university Komsomol members in early 1968 his reasons for distributing underground, "anti-Soviet" literature, said that he started reading literature on Russification in Ukraine after someone at a Lviv store noted the Rusisms in his speech and started talking with him about language use in higher education.[32] Here the habit of walking the city's streets, and encountering its residents, challenged the authority of state and Party institutions.[33]

State and Party institutions made students' lives both difficult and amusing. Lviv State University highlighted such situations. One oral interview respondent, Iaroslava Sereda, who studied at the Mathematics Faculty at the end of the 1950s, recalled with displeasure the constant copying of citations from Party documents and the classics of Marxism-Leninism at the university research library. Students had to use them during mandatory lessons in Scientific Communism, Dialectical Materialism, and the History of the Communist Party of the Soviet Union. The absence of such notes was regarded as inadequate preparation for lessons. She said that while the Komsomol often organized interesting events for students, for her and several others, Komsomol meetings themselves were boring.[34] In the Soviet system of education, students studied not individually but in academic groups, where at least one person in each academic group provided information for the secret police. Anyone exhibiting dissident behavior was suspected by others of being a secret police provocateur sniffing out politically unreliable students for expulsion.[35]

Oral interviews mention the arbitrary behavior of university authorities. Sereda, reflecting on her attitudes toward the Soviet system, noted that Party organs to a certain extent addressed ordinary citizens' grievances. At the same time, she noted injustices at Lviv State University when she was an office worker at the correspondence department of the Mathematics Faculty. One instructor publicly, at union meetings, criticized the faculty dean, a Party member, who favored athletes during entrance exams, which was illegal. The chancellor's office and the Party committee reacted, and the faculty dean was removed from his post. However, he did not receive further punishment.[36] Her husband, Volodymyr Sereda, mentioned that in the spring of 1957, he got into trouble in his last year studying at the Physics Faculty for protesting its unfair allocation of jobs to graduating students. University Party committee reports indicated that Sereda lost his fellowship as a result of this protest. According to Sereda, he also lost the letter of recommendation from the faculty's Academic Council needed to enter graduate school.[37]

Those with important Party connections behaved impudently, not just toward students, but toward faculty and administrators. At one 1957 university Party meeting, a university Communist complained about the gorkom secretary using the university's gymnasium exercise field to park his car. For him, local officials' promises to help the university with instructional and dormitory space rang hollow, because a riding hall for the local military commander stood empty while students had to exercise outside.[38] Despite the social mobility that a university education gave, students were aware of classmates being treated differently because of family connections. One student at a university open Party meeting on 22 November 1956 complained that children of major city Party and state workers who were skipping classes left a bad impression among students from Western Ukrainian villages.[39]

Ideological campaigns against "bourgeois nationalism," initiated by individual university instructors or officials—through convictions, fear, or personal gain—often were directed even at petty incidents of national self-expression. At Lviv State University, for instance, the university's vice chancellor at the end of the 1960s was rumored to have canceled an innocent-sounding literary evening or folk ensemble concert because it was a "nationalist" activity.[40] Actor Bohdan Kozak's 1966 performance of Ivan Franko's poem "Moses" (1905) was an example of such a "nationalist" event. Kozak recited this poem at the university, at a concert marking the end of a republic-wide conference dedicated to the anniversary of Franko's birth. Franko's poem belonged to the Soviet Ukrainian literary canon as an example of the Russian Revolution of 1905's influence on Galician Ukrainians. Kozak, looking for something different to present his audience, used this argument to convince the concert's director to let him perform it. However, the poem's references to Moses and the Israelites' forty years of waiting in the wilderness alluded to Ukrainians' long wait for national liberation. Its lines thus could provoke "bourgeois nationalist" readings. When Kozak recited "Moses" at this concert, he fell to his knees and cried out, "My people, tortured utterly and shattered, / Like a poor cripple at the cross-roads lying, / By man's contempt, as if with scabs, bespattered!"[41] The students and other guests, electrified, greeted him with thunderous applause. After that performance, Kozak's director complained of all the trouble he had caused. In subsequent years, neither Kozak nor his theater colleagues were invited to perform at Lviv State University.[42]

Such fears about "bourgeois nationalism" grew more intense during political repressions in the 1970s. History students arrested for putting up protest leaflets in late March 1973 explained to Komsomol hearings that one of their history instructors had accused a student of supporting "nationalism" because this student questioned why a wall newspaper had to be in both Russian and Ukrainian. This same instructor, as well as a History Faculty Komsomol bureau member, had told one of them that a school literary evening of Ukrainian poetry was a bad idea and that Russian works should be featured instead. Probably out of similar motives, this Komsomol bureau member opposed having a faculty arts club.[43]

The arbitrary behavior of university authorities, the excessive regimentation, and the political rituals did not necessarily lead to young people questioning the legitimacy of Soviet socialism or the state. Students could readily ascribe such phenomena to individuals' abuse of power or the continued influence of Stalin's cult of personality. Such was true for students' counterparts in Kyiv and Moscow during the Thaw.[44] Years later, in oral interviews, eyewitnesses could incorporate these incidents into narratives underscoring past disenchantment with the Soviet era. Other students shrugged off politics altogether. Interviews with Lviv State University students from the early 1950s and the late 1960s revealed students who knew nothing about secret police informers and who confessed that they and their classmates were overwhelmingly apolitical.[45] One former student of the Polytechnic Institute noted his failure in the late 1970s to get classmates together to talk about news from Western radio broadcasts. His classmates simply were not interested.[46] Political rituals such as October Revolution and May Day parades were days off from school, with the real fun (dances and parties) following the parades.[47]

State and Party surveillance over student discussions, while formidable, was incomplete. Komsomol and Party organizations reacted belatedly and superficially toward perceived ideological dangers. This happened in late 1956, after worker unrest in Poland and the Hungarian Uprising. Lviv State University philology students' anti-Soviet remarks, provoked by the Soviet Army's bloody crackdown on the Hungarian Uprising, became common knowledge to such organizations only in January 1957, after the university Party organization had been given orders from the CPSU Central Committee to root out "anti-Soviet" elements. Only then did the Philology Faculty's Komsomol activists speak out about such incidents.[48] A report filed by the CPSU Central Committee that same year pointed out that Lviv's institutions of higher learning took an interest in students' moods only during such crises as the Hungarian Uprising.[49]

A lack of available dormitory space made it very difficult for institutions of higher learning to keep track of students' behavior. This was especially true for Lviv State University in the late 1950s, when postwar reconstruction and defense spending made resources for higher education scarce. As of July 1957, only 1,200 students of a student body of 4,300 lived in dormitories. A vast majority of them had to live in private apartments. Many were not even that lucky, sometimes sleeping in the city's railroad station when it was warm.[50] The housing situation became so desperate that a group of students in 1961 literally took over three rooms in an empty building promised by the government to the university on September 17th Street, living in them as squatters.[51] An émigré's account suggests that it was only at the end of the 1960s that the university dealt with this housing situation significantly, building dormitories on what is today's Pasichnyi Street, far from the university campus, on Lviv's outskirts.[52] However, these new buildings hardly made private apartments a thing of the past, given the later expansion of the city and the university. As of 1977, there were over 12,500 students enrolled at Lviv State University, indicating that its student body had trebled in size in the course of twenty years.[53]

In the late 1950s and 1960s, university Communists knew well the outside ideological influences affecting students who did not live in dormitories. They noted, for example, elderly ladies who kept icons in their rooms.[54] Such places—apartments, as well as private art shops—became epicenters of alternative social spaces to that of the public sphere.

The Social Spaces of the Cultural Underground

The late 1960s apartment gathering shown in Figure 7.1 epitomizes the alternative spaces that troubled Lviv State University Communists a decade earlier. Here young Lviv writers, musicians, and artists attentively listen to Ihor Kalynets recite his poems. At the time, Kalynets was having difficulties publishing in Ukraine. Censorship had intensified with the Thaw's end. Such gatherings helped him share his new works with others. Friends at such gatherings helped spread Kalynets's poems abroad, an act that eventually got him into trouble with the Party and presumably the KGB by late 1971.[55] Such apartment gatherings could challenge state security organs in other ways. Two participants said that besides listening to Kalynets's poetry readings, they held lotteries to raise money for political prisoners' families. However, these gatherings were not just about activities that could be viewed as anti-Soviet. These young writers, artists, and musicians held New Year's costume parties and sang Christmas carols. They were gatherings about collective fun as well as mutual support and subversion.[56]

Turning private space into alternative forums for discussion and collective fun had a longer history, predating the Thaw. Despite the risks of punishment, even before the Thaw, students and young intellectuals could not stop talking the truth to each other, whether in outbursts, hushed tones, or parody. As portrayed in Ilya Ehrenburg's novel *The Thaw*, Soviet citizens in the Stalin era had learned to say one thing in public and act quite differently in private.[57] One respondent, recalling his years at the Lviv State Polytechnic Institute from 1945 to 1950, said students, rather than fearing Stalinist terror, were, just like other young people, amused by the absurd times they lived in. They especially found amusing all the grand achievements attributed to Stalin. They composed poems and ditties making fun of Stalin's

Figure 7.1. Scenes from the cultural underground: a private reading of poems by Ihor Kalynets, end of the 1960s. Used with permission from the collection of Tetiana Vorobkevych, Lviv.

various treatises and other classics of Marxism-Leninism, quietly repeating them for kicks in dormitory rooms and in institute hallways. Some students even came up with a game where, drawing randomly from some sheets of paper that had scientific topics on them, players had to devise academic "papers" spontaneously, making sure that they sounded as absurd as possible and had all the appropriate citations of classics by Stalin, Lenin, Marx, and Engels peppered in.[58] Another student from those years said he and close friends got together in apartments and quietly sang folk songs connected with the nationalist insurgency, songs that officially were regarded as showing solidarity with hostile bourgeois nationalist elements.[59]

These people went back to classes, attended public meetings, and kept their deeds out of public sight. Others, though, were not so cautious and paid a price. A student at Lviv State University's Philology Faculty, Iuriy Shymanskyi, was expelled from the Komsomol and the university in late February 1954 after eight of his dormitory roommates sent a furious letter to their Philology Faculty Komsomol bureau, claiming that the student had imposed "anti-Soviet and nationalist views" on them. Besides noting all sorts of perfidious acts, including selling stolen watches on the black market, picking fights with roommates, and hurling vile (and indecent) names at roommates' parents, they gave a list of fourteen political statements attributed to him.[60]

The statements may not have reflected what Shymanskyi said. Most of them were retold by either the petitioners or the school Komsomol bureau secretary conducting Shymanskyi's hearing. Shymanskyi himself challenged their accuracy. Other grievances probably caused his accusers to hype up what he had said. Such accusations still revealed what kinds of conversations went on in that dormitory room, which Shymanskyi had shared with them for three years. The *"moskali,"* he allegedly said, referring derisively to Russians and Russian speakers, "lord over my grandfather's land." The Komsomol bureau secretary claimed Shymanskyi said that Russians and Jews ate his ancestors' bread, and that most of them in Lviv "are scoundrels and bandits." He supposedly made disparaging remarks about Soviet writers and books on Ukrainian history, and he complained about deteriorating standards of living.[61]

Shymanskyi's outbursts and the lack of immediate denunciations against them suggest that there were lively conversations going on among Ukrainian students in Lviv even before the Thaw had affected Lviv. Shymanskyi and several of his roommates most likely were Galician Ukrainians who had just recently witnessed the bloody suppression of the nationalist insurgency, as well as collectivization, arrests, and deportations. Efforts by the state to promote myths about Ukrainians' and Russians' "eternal" friendship, as seen in official 1954 commemorations of the 300th anniversary of the signing of the Treaty of Pereiaslavl between Ukrainian Cossack leader Bohdan Khmelnytskyi and Muscovite Grand Prince Alexei Mikhailovich, were seen as a sham, as one of Shymanskyi's fourteen alleged remarks hinted.[62]

Outbursts of hostility toward the *moskali* and the Jews, cynicism about Russian and Ukrainian friendship, biting parodies of Stalin's cult of personality, and collective performances of folk songs honoring armed rebels suggest underground, or semiconcealed, social spaces of resistance. In the company of friends and fellow thinkers, they protested, either symbolically (as seen with the folk songs and the jokes) or directly (as seen with Shymanskyi's political remarks). Such company carved out social spaces that became alternatives to those of the public sphere, while not becoming completely separate from that sphere. After all, the students making bogus research papers knew which Soviet classics to cite.

The Thaw and subsequent political unrest in the Soviet bloc fomented similar discussions. Worker unrest in Poland and the Soviet Army's armed intervention in Hungary in November 1956 stirred up passionate, though concealed, discussions about the Soviet state. Obkom reports and a July 1957 obkom plenary session dedicated to improving ideological work with youth suggested this. At a public question-and-answer session on current political events, a number of Lviv State University students submitted anonymous questions that allegedly supported the Hungarian Uprising, spoke favorably of "Ukrainian bourgeois nationalists," and paraphrased "anti-Soviet remarks" made by foreign radio stations. Ukrainian students in the Philology Faculty privately questioned the collectivization of agriculture and the Soviet state's one-party system, as well as criticized public treatment of Ukrainian literature. Relations between Ukrainian philology students and Russian philology students had become strained over these and other issues. A physics student, the leader of his faculty's Komsomol organization, was expelled from the Komsomol and the university for making similar comments about Ukrainian literature and Soviet policies.[63]

In the late 1950s, the return of political prisoners connected with the nationalist insurgency sharpened private debates about the Soviet system. In a file of documents from around 1956, an undated Central Committee report filed in Moscow said that about 10,000 such people had returned to the Lviv Region after this amnesty. About 2,096 had returned to Lviv, and 1,270 of them remained in the city. Local organs of state security moreover knew little of what these people were doing in Lviv and in the Lviv Region, a source of great concern.[64] Soviet leaders' amnesties of nationalist guerrillas and their sympathizers after Stalin's death caused major tensions within society on the western borderlands, the heart of intense armed resistance. Local responses to unrest in Poland and Hungary in late 1956 convinced Soviet leaders to curtail the return of such people from prison and exile, as they were seen as potentially reinvigorating "bourgeois nationalism" on the western borderlands.[65] Nonetheless, those who had already returned and renewed their university studies enriched discussions about the Thaw. For instance, the informal group of Ukrainian and Polish philology majors that gathered at the end of the 1950s, nicknamed the "Cabinet," included such returnees. They confidentially told younger classmates, such as poet and future dissident Ihor Kalynets, about their experiences in concentration camps. One of them, Teodoziy Starak, in an interview said that he openly shared his skepticism about Khrushchev, whom Kalynets had viewed with great hope when he was a student. In expressing such doubts about the Soviet regime's ability to reform itself, and in sharing their own memories of the Stalin era, such people encouraged younger generations to consider more radical change, including perhaps Ukrainian independence, as necessary.[66]

Such discussions, particularly at times of political crisis, demonstrated the subversive power of these alternative social spaces. At the same time, these students in the 1950s were part of the emerging culture of *kompany*, circles of close friends and fellow thinkers who simply enjoyed being with one another as well as discussing ideas important to them.[67] Art shops like those of Feodosiia Bryzh and Emmanuil Mysko, writers' apartments, and the Academy of Sciences graduate school dormitory on Academy Street (now Shevchenko Avenue) became places for collective fun and serious discussions about cultural developments in the Soviet Union and abroad.[68]

Members of the Cabinet drank beer, penned hilarious poems about one another, and took vacations together in the Carpathian Mountains. The Lviv State Polytechnic students in the late 1940s were not exchanging angry outbursts about Stalin, but parodying attempts by scholars to curry favor with him. Similar gatherings in the Thaw's early years conveyed this atmosphere of collective fun. At Lviv State University's Physics Faculty, physics students and graduate students, amid their rounds of drinking *horilka*, playing cards, telling jokes, and talking politics, put together some humorous writings entitled *The Bachelor* to mark New Year's Day in 1958. While the collection of writings and political conversations led to political charges and investigations by the university Party committee, these young physicists relaxed and made fun of each other as young bachelors.[69] At the Academy of Sciences graduate school dormitory, graduate students, writers, artists, and other young intellectuals made fun of official ideological slogans by such stunts as greeting one another with the slogan, "Long live the armed forces and its leadership!" Over time, as he became the dormitory's most senior resident, Iuriy Slyvka, who later became involved in controversies at Lviv State University's History Faculty, acquired the epithet of "chief of headquarters."[70]

As with other such Soviet Thaw-era gatherings, these spontaneous meetings became forums for discussing political changes in Moscow and Kyiv, changes expressed in literature and the arts.[71] Thus cultural developments in Moscow acquired importance. Writers privately discussed and sometimes made public references to Vladimir Pomerantsev's 1953 article "On Sincerity in Literature," Ilya Ehrenburg's *The Thaw* (1954), and Vladimir Dudintsev's *Not by Bread Alone* (1956), literary works that first challenged restrictions placed on literature and criticized insincerity, selfishness, and corruption.[72] Vasily Aksyonov and Yevgeny Yevtushenko, known throughout the Soviet Union for their role in Moscow's Sixtiers Movement, were among the many guests at private gatherings in the art shop of sculptor Feodosiia Bryzh. Ievhen Beznisko, Bryzh's widower, mentioned these names in an oral interview that took place at Bryzh's shop.[73] Art critic and later dissident Bohdan Horyn indicated the great impact Sixtiers poets in both Moscow and Kyiv had on young Lvivians like himself in the early 1960s.[74] One former Lvivian who became involved in dissident activities in the late 1960s stressed that for herself, developments in Russian culture in those years were as important as developments in Ukrainian culture.[75] Students attending university in the late 1970s, both at Lviv State University and the Lviv State Polytechnic Institute, read copies of Alexander Solzhenitsyn's *One Day in the Life of Ivan Denisovich* (legally published in 1962 but removed by then from public circulation).[76]

However, when it came to the Thaw, literary events in the republic's capital became the most important for Lviv's young Ukrainians. In the early 1960s, students and young intellectuals simply devoured poems, essays, and books published in Kyiv by such Sixtiers as Drach, Vinhranovskyi, and Dziuba, as well as by poets Vasyl Symonenko (who died of cancer in 1963 at the age of 28), Lina Kostenko, Ivan Svitlychnyi, and many other Ukrainian writers close in age.[77] As shown by the enthusiastic reception some of them received at Lviv State University in 1962, such writers addressed vital issues of national identity for young Ukrainians in Lviv, namely, the marginalization and suppression of literary life in the republic and efforts to impose Russian on the public sphere. It was from Kyivans that young Lvivians learned to negotiate with the Komsomol and create their own Club of Artistic Youth.

Kyiv thus transformed Lvivians' understanding of what forms of national self-expression were possible, especially at the beginning of the 1960s. At the same time, Lvivians' Western Ukrainian backgrounds crucially shaped their perceptions of the Thaw. Not only did recent political repression make Lvivians so enthusiastic for this Ukrainian Thaw. The cultural capital of Galicia, including its prewar Ukrainian intelligentsia, drew them to a kind of thaw that eventually turned them away from Moscow.

Young Lvivians and Galicia

Galicia's cultural capital—its prewar Ukrainian intellectuals, publications, and institutions—significantly influenced Lviv's post-Stalin generations. Tarik Amar emphasizes that the local intelligentsia that had survived the war and Stalin-era terror became important in Western Ukraine's Sovietization. They provided a positive Soviet Western Ukrainian identity to younger generations.[78] However, these elder members of the new Soviet Western Ukrainian intelligentsia were not just adhering to the public role given them by Soviet officials. Intellectuals from Lviv's prewar Galician Ukrainian intelligentsia became role models in the Thaw and beyond, challenging assumptions that being Ukrainian meant alliance with the more "progressive" Great Russian people.

Composer Stanislav Liudkevych, who died in 1979 at the age of 100, was such a leading authority figure at Lviv State Conservatory and among wider intellectual circles.[79] Ukrainian pop music composer Volodymyr Ivasiuk came to Lviv's conservatory in 1972 with hopes to study under Liudkevych, a master of classical arrangements of Ukrainian folk songs.[80] Like other senior artists who had survived the war years, Roman and Margit Selskyi as late as the end of the 1970s drew younger artists to their home. Here the artists became acquainted with prewar Ukrainian art journals published in

Lviv and with the Selskyis' experiences studying and working in Paris and Cracow.[81] Novelist Iryna Vilde hosted at her home and at her Carpathian Mountains dacha numerous young writers, artists, musicians, and scholars, acquiring the Hutsul name "godmother" among the younger members of Lviv's intelligentsia.[82]

Liudkevych and other prewar Galician intellectuals were models of an "*intelihent*," a person with manners and bearing worthy of emulation.[83] Like the historian Ivan Krypiakevych, they stood in stark contrast to typical Soviet functionaries who tried to "pose as democratic types" *(pidrobliatysia pid demokratychni typazhi),* or those who were "careerists, charlatans [*prystosuvantsi*], and carpetbaggers [*zaidy*]," with "carpetbaggers" clearly referring to Russians and Russian-speaking Ukrainians who came to Lviv after the war.[84] For these younger Ukrainians, they represented an authentic elite, one with the aristocratic manners associated with the intelligentsia of pre-Soviet times. With notable exceptions, such as university chancellor Lazarenko, the intellectual elite raised under Soviet rule were assumed to be crass, unprincipled, and hostile to Ukrainians.

Young Lvivians were much like their Thaw-era counterparts in Moscow who turned to older intelligentsia figures like Boris Pasternak for inspiration. Young Muscovites revived the notion of the intelligentsia's being critical spokespersons for the people. Unlike them, however, young Lvivians' older mentors had even more problematic relations with Soviet power, particularly since Galicians did not become the same enthusiasts for Soviet utopian experiments of the 1920s and early 1930s.[85] Galician Ukrainians admired Soviet Ukrainianization policies in the 1920s, and the Soviet Ukrainian government even provided them financial support. However, Soviet Ukraine's 1932–33 famine and the Great Terror alienated them.[86] To be sure, such older intellectuals tried to conform to the new order and not make waves. Liudkevych, for instance, was known to be very diplomatic, as one Lviv conservatory instructor and music scholar born in 1930 recalled.[87] His works received public praise for encouraging the brotherhood of the Russian and Ukrainian peoples, as noted with his 1905 symphony *The Caucasus (Kavkaz),* written in honor of the 1905 Russian Revolution. The prewar intelligentsia thus encouraged younger Ukrainians to conform and adapt rather than advocate the Soviet system's overthrow.[88]

On the other hand, this spirit of conformity did not mean wholehearted consent to the new order. Liudkevych's symphony *The Caucasus* was inspired by a Taras Shevchenko poem that hardly spoke of friendship toward

Russians. Shevchenko's "The Caucasus" (1845) fiercely attacked Russian imperialists' ventures into the Caucasus region. Along with denouncing the blood spilled by the Tsar, it called on all his oppressed subjects to struggle for freedom. The 1905 Revolution inspired Liudkevych to compose the symphony. However, for Liudkevych, a subject of the Austro-Hungarian Empire, the revolution was about the liberation of nations—above all, fellow Ukrainians—from imperial Russian domination, not the Russian working class's struggle for freedom.[89]

Toward the end of his life, as ideological campaigns against the republic's intelligentsia in the 1970s stifled national expression, Liudkevych became quite bitter with Soviet policies. Soviet censors confiscated a 1973 edition of Liudkevych's collected essays on music because it mentioned names of Ukrainians who had emigrated to the West or had compromised themselves politically. Publishers then released a dramatically smaller collection of essays (about 150 pages, compared with about 500 pages in the original edition). The incident greatly upset Liudkevych, to the point where he made uncharacteristic outbursts about Soviet policies. In late 1974, when he was given a Friendship of Peoples award for his ninety-fifth birthday, such outbursts provoked a small political scandal. Upon receiving this award at a special meeting of the state conservatory's departments of composition and the history and theory of music, he said that he did not deserve the award because he did not uphold the ideals of the Party and Communism. He wondered aloud why so many past socialists were regarded negatively (that is, regarded as "bourgeois nationalists") and why "nationalist" music was so bad, since all music was nationalist in one form or another. The next day, the conservatory's Party committee bureau contained the scandal by having its secretary read a statement noting that Liudkevych was using an older definition of the term "nationalism" than what was used in current Soviet scholarship. One conservatory professor who heard Liudkevych's outbursts and was present at the Party committee bureau meeting dealing with them recalled that Liudkevych complained in his last years that "other forces" had come to dominate the conservatory that he and others had originally founded.[90]

Liudkevych thus embodied the uneasy coexistence between older Galician Ukrainians and Soviet power. Decades before this scandal, Liudkevych did not hide his ironic attitude toward Soviet power. An anecdote popular among young intellectuals and students, originating in the 1950s, mentioned that Liudkevych said that Soviet power came in 1939 and that "there's nothing we can do about it."[91] As the anecdote suggests, the Soviet regime was an alien force that had to be accommodated. The fact that it became a common anecdote suggests it resonated among students and intellectuals of the Thaw generation. Others, too, shared this distanced relationship with Soviet power. Iryna Vilde expressed such sentiments to literary critic and future dissident Bohdan Horyn in the early 1960s. Vilde was defending her decision to repeat what Soviet propaganda said about America and its Ukrainian diaspora. She did this while speaking to the Institute of Social Sciences about her recent trip there. Upset that Horyn accused her of lying, she told him that serving the state might bring something useful for literature, while fighting it would only bring on the state's swift vengeance.[92]

Literary critic Mykhailo Rudnytskyi, the victim of postwar ideological purification campaigns directed at the local intellectuals, also became an obedient member of the Soviet intelligentsia. However, he was known for making scathing criticisms at Lviv State University conferences about the state of Soviet Ukrainian literature and Ukrainian language use, especially during the Thaw.[93] Remarks at these conferences and at Writers' Union functions became objects of discussion at the university's annual Party organization meeting in 1961.[94] Sometimes his remarks exuded irony and cynicism. One young literary critic in those years remembered hearing him say, "There used to be revolutionary poetry, now there's Party poetry."[95] None of these people shared Boris Pasternak's admiration for Stalin's revolution from above as a noble experiment.[96]

Such elder intellectuals turned their young counterparts' attention from Moscow and Kyiv to Europe itself, suggesting other sources of inspiration for Ukrainian art and literature. The sources of artistic inspiration for Roman and Margit Selskyi came not from Moscow or Kyiv, but from Cracow and Paris. The same could be said of writer Mykhailo Iatskiv, whom young poets and scholars in the late 1950s used to take out for drinks and ask about his days in an early twentieth-century trend in modernist literature in Lviv known as the "Young Muse" movement, condemned in Soviet times as a "decadent" movement that preached "art for art's sake."[97] As seen in Lviv's politics of history, scholars from Lviv's prewar intelligentsia like Ivan Krypiakevych provoked new questions about Galicia's past. Lviv's prewar intelligentsia thus encouraged younger Ukrainians to become loyal to Soviet power and accommodate it but also identify themselves in ways different than what the public sphere defined as being "truly" Ukrainian.

Besides these living contacts with the recent past, Lviv became a source of books, newspapers, and journals that gave a different perspective not just on Ukrainian culture but on the Soviet Union. Artists visiting the Selskyi home, for instance, enjoyed the opportunity to read old issues of art journals that the city's prewar Ukrainian art association used to publish. Such journals differed from the city art institute's official curriculum, which stressed the merits of "progressive" nineteenth-century Russian itinerant painters and taught very little about European or Ukrainian masters.[98] Friends passed around old copies of the *Literary and Scholarly Herald (Literaturno-naukovyi visnyk)*, edited by Dmytro Dontsov, known for his openly anti-Soviet views in the 1930s. Such journals gave their young readers information about both Russian and Ukrainian literature and Ukrainian history left out of Soviet publications and school lessons.[99] Searching through the attics of Lvivians' homes for such publications thus helped address a curiosity that, in the words of one respondent, school simply did not satisfy.[100] Yet even at the university and at the city art institute, students gained access to such publications, put away in special closed depositories, with the help of librarians who trusted them.[101]

Such publications were perceived as a dangerous alternative channel of information. The problem of young people finding such materials from "grandpa's attic" and talking about what they had read among friends was so acute that one regional Komsomol secretary, speaking at a university Komsomol conference in October 1966, talked about the need for Komsomol members to be more vigilant.[102]

A turning away from Moscow could also be seen in the continued influence of the Ukrainian Greek Catholic Church. This church, which dominated religious life among Ukrainians in Galicia, combined the rituals of Orthodoxy with subordination to the Pope in Rome. It had been central to Ukrainian national movements in Galicia since the early nineteenth century. The Soviet state abolished this church in 1946 and had its clergy and infrastructure forcibly merged under the Russian Orthodox Church. An entire underground network of Greek Catholic congregations spread through Galicia after World War II. Some congregations operated in the city of Lviv, at times uncovered by the secret police and given high publicity for their supposedly "illicit" behavior, as seen in one 1964 republic newspaper article.[103] As 1970s-era repressions seriously affected national forms of self-expression, regional Party leaders in September 1973 targeted underground Greek Catholics—or Uniates, as they were referred to derogatively—for punishment at their places of work.[104] Still, the underground Greek Catholic Church continued. One oral interview respondent mentioned that she and her husband allowed church members to use their small Lviv apartment for services in the early 1980s.[105] This underground network, though, was very secretive. Historian Bohdan Iakymovych said that while he knew one of his uncles was a Greek Catholic priest and had his daughter baptized by him, he had no idea until 1988, the time of Gorbachev's Glasnost, that one of his friends was an underground bishop.[106]

In addition to these parallel church structures, Greek Catholicism still influenced the new church subordinate to Moscow. Greek Catholic priests, including those who had been exiled for criticizing the church's abolition in 1946, used their new positions as Russian Orthodox Church clergy to continue Greek Catholic practices. The Council for the Affairs of the Orthodox Church expressed its consternation with such practices in its 4 January 1957 report to Moscow's Central Committee. The report said that some of these priests agitated for the restoration of the Ukrainian Greek Catholic Church, citing its abolition as having taken place when Stalin's cult of personality had violated "socialist legality."[107]

Such clergy had an influence among young Lvivians, encouraging alternative channels of information about the wider world. For instance, in the mid-1960s, a former Greek Catholic priest who had returned from Siberian exile and preached in an Orthodox church in Lviv, Father Klius, discussed religion and philosophy privately with a group of schoolchildren. In these discussions, he introduced them to writings by Metropolitan Andrei Sheptytskyi which equated Stalinism with fascism.[108] In a city where such Greek Catholics, or Uniates, were publicly portrayed as agents of fascism and other "reactionaries," Father Klius became a source of information not just on Christianity, itself frowned upon in propaganda, but on ideas much more critical of the Soviet system.

Greek Catholicism's influence over what it meant to be Ukrainian surfaced in Lvivians' daily religious practices. In the late 1950s, despite being forced to work on Easter or Christmas Day, university students observed the holiday with special dinners in their dormitory rooms.[109] In later decades, people from all walks of life, including those from families not native to Galicia, observed these holidays with special meals. Even traditional greetings associated with Galicia, such as "Christ is risen!" or "Glory to Jesus Christ!" had become a noticeable part of Lviv's street life. One Central Committee report made in Moscow in 1957 expressed concern that such greetings, tolerated by the police, took place on streets and in trams, trains, buses, and trolleys throughout Western Ukraine.[110]

Other Greek Catholic practices continued, like Christmas caroling and the reenactment of the manger scene (*vertep* in Ukrainian). Such practices had been largely confined to Western Ukrainian villages before the mid-1960s. Then, in mid-1960s Lviv, a group of young writers, artists, musicians, and scholars got together and began caroling and reenacting the manger scene at homes of friends and acquaintances. Caroling sometimes took place in other people's homes. Local police organs, including Komsomol volunteer law enforcement, tried to discourage carolers by detaining people for allegedly disturbing the peace, or giving reprimands to or even expelling university students. Lvivians tried to avoid problems with the police by engaging in public caroling only on the outskirts of town. Others exercised greater caution. In Christmas processions and in Christmas caroling, revelers disguised such practices as New Year's Day celebrations on the streets. They altered carols so that, for example, "Bethlehem" was replaced by "the Kremlin" and "the New Year" for "the Son of God." Often they avoided trouble by singing New Year's carols, known in Ukrainian as *shchedrivky,* since the authorities permitted them.[111]

Still, some scandalous incidents happened in downtown Lviv, such as when crowds gathered and sang carols in front of the city's New Year's tree, which stood in front of the opera theater. For New Year's Day, 1968, law enforcement agencies cracked down on this caroling and apprehended suspicious carolers. University students were among those apprehended, and on 5 January 1968 they received reprimands from their Komsomol organization. More importantly, city authorities after this incident moved the New Year's tree far away from the center of town, to the Bohdan Khmelnytskyi Park of Culture and Recreation, so as not to attract unwanted attention. The tree returned to the opera house only with the Gorbachev era.[112]

While this may have sounded like an act of overly zealous caution, Western Ukrainian carolers were known for singing songs that had political subtexts. Examples of such carols were "Joy has come to the world . . ." *(Nova radist' stala . . .),* rearranged to glorify the coming of the UPA to free Ukraine, and "Sad Holy Night . . ." *(Sumnyi sviatyi vechir . . .),* dealing with arrests and deportations to Siberia that occurred in 1946.[113] An émigré recalled that in the late 1960s, during the New Year, young men snuck into large crowds in front of the New Year's tree while it still stood in front of the opera theater. After quickly passing out protest leaflets or making provocative speeches, they darted away from police agents.[114]

Local officials were aware of the political challenge posed by these elements of Galicia's cultural capital. To some degree, police informants kept private activities in check. One such place for informal gatherings, Bryzh's art shop mentioned earlier, was known for "stool pigeons," forcing people to watch what they said and did.[115] Individuals made sure that they disguised themselves as carefully as they could. A former student at Lviv State University during the Thaw recalled his shock at seeing his journalism professor, a Party functionary, at a private gathering. He feared the professor would catch him making "anti-Soviet" statements. His host reassured him, explaining that the professor was "our man" *(nash cholovik).*[116] It was in these trusted circles, inspired by events in Kyiv and Moscow but also nurtured by Galician cultural capital, that young Lvivians began circulating subversive texts.

Secret Texts, Dissent, and Youth Rebellion

In Lviv and other Soviet cities, the dissident movement that emerged from such circles possessed not the streets, but "self published literature" *(samvydav* in Ukrainian, or *samizdat* in Russian), and the private spaces in which they were generated, circulated, and consumed, as its main weapons. Such literature, secretly typed or printed for limited audiences, at first consisted of literary works denied publication. It later included essays, letters, and entire book manuscripts that aired political grievances, from warnings about Stalinist abuses of individual rights to complaints that the Stalin era had been unjustly besmirched.[117] In Ukraine, as in other non-Russian republics, these secret texts were highly critical of the Russification of public life and discrimination against non-Russians' language, culture, and constitutional rights. These texts emphasized improving the existing Soviet system. They reflected the optimism of young people during the Thaw. However, the Thaw developed differently in Lviv and other parts of Western Ukraine. Recent memories of Soviet occupation and repression conditioned locals' responses to the Thaw. Thus their underground texts portrayed the Soviet Union as an empire dominated by Russians and called for complete independence from Moscow, as seen with the underground newspapers of the Ukrainian National Front for 1964–66.[118] As people involved in the spread of *samvydav* materials were arrested and put on trial, petitions that protested these trials and other abuses of human rights circulated as secret texts.[119] Despite different characteristics of Western Ukraine's *samvydav* literature, the emergence of networks reproducing and circulating *samvydav* linked Lviv with important developments in the republic's capital. For instance, young Lvivians circulated an essay claiming that the Soviet state was responsible for the 1964 fire that devastated Ukrainian materials at Kyiv's Academy of Sciences library.[120]

The story of Soviet dissent's emergence in Lviv had high drama. The 1962 university literary evening for Kyiv's Sixtiers had inspired it. After overhearing an older Communist privately dismissing it as babble by "today's flies," Mykhailo Horyn, a psychologist working at the city's truck factory, spoke up during remarks after the performances. Horyn, born in 1930 in the Lviv Region, had vivid memories of Soviet repression, and the Sixtiers' call to resurrect Ukrainians' national culture deeply moved him. Speaking to those assembled, he said that despite what some people in the hall (pointing to them) said of these young writers, "A new force is entering literature, and they aren't today's flies—they're for forever!" The crowd greeted him with stormy applause. While somewhat acquainted with them through the press and through correspondence, it was at this literary evening that Horyn became friends with one of the Kyiv Sixtiers, literary critic Ivan Dziuba.[121]

Not long after this, Horyn, together with his brother Bohdan, personally met with Dziuba and other young Kyivan writers and began spreading *samvydav* literature, until both were arrested in 1965.[122] Their meetings with Kyivans resembled scenes from spy novels. In one interview, Dziuba recalled that rather than meeting in Lviv, the Horyn brothers in the summer of 1963 came to the secluded resort community of Briukhovychi, where he was staying with his wife and mother-in-law. Both brothers, dressed in black trench coats, talked the whole time about forming an underground political organization.[123] Another Kyivan writer, in a semifictional account based on a summer 1963 meeting with them, mentions the Horyn brothers promptly burning a note that recommended him as someone they could trust. They discussed politics in total silence, scribbling on pieces of paper that also were probably burned.[124]

In such secrecy, the Horyn brothers and their Kyivan counterparts around 1963–65 discussed ways to bring about an independent Ukrainian state. In this sense they instilled the Thaw with more radical meaning than Moscow or Kyiv counterparts, or even young Lvivians in the late 1950s.[125] They went beyond most Lvivians who, in the late 1950s and 1960s, talked about improving the existing Soviet system on Ukrainians' behalf.[126] Recalling his friendship with Kyivan poet and dissident Ivan Svitlychnyi in 1963, Mykhailo Horyn states that conversations with Svitlychnyi and other Kyivan Sixtiers gave him hopes to renew Ukraine's struggle for independence from Moscow. As Horyn's account suggests, independence was not to be achieved by armed struggle, as the OUN and UPA had attempted, but by influencing Ukrainians' consciousness.[127]

The Kyivans preferred working within legal means, through literary evenings and such public organizations as the Club of Artistic Youth. In contrast, the Horyn brothers, in connection with mostly Kyivans and Lvivians (including Ivan Svitlychnyi), started distributing underground protest literature, in conspiratorial ways reminiscent of the OUN and UPA's underground press. Such literature not only criticized shortcomings in Ukraine, such as the Russification of the school system, but also advocated Ukraine's separation from the Soviet Union (as seen in the *samvydav* text "Contemporary Imperialism"). In late August 1965, as Soviet leaders in Moscow and Kyiv began to crack down on dissent following Khrushchev's fall from power, the Horyn brothers were among those arrested and put in prison for spreading literature deemed hostile to Soviet rule.[128]

In succeeding decades, until his last release from prison in 1987, Mykhailo Horyn served a number of sentences in Soviet prison camps, with prison interrupted by periods of freedom during which, performing various menial jobs in Lviv, he resumed underground political work. His memories of the camps were quite gripping, particularly when he described finding one of his cell mates, Iuriy Lytvyn, another Ukrainian dissident, dead from a self-inflicted knife wound to the stomach.[129]

Mykhailo Horyn's involvement in spreading political *samvydav* texts were a turning point in Lviv's cultural underground, where young intellectuals chose to oppose the regime rather than seek its improvement. His childhood experiences suggest that Galician Ukrainians greatly resented Soviet rule and were eager to see its end. Both of his parents in Polish times took part in organizations later connected with the OUN. In 1939, his father was arrested for such involvement, freed only with the Nazi invasion of the Soviet Union. When Soviet rule was restored in 1944, he went on the run with the UPA insurgency. He returned to his family later, protected by an amnesty given to supposed Red Army deserters. In the late 1940s, Horyn and his brother barely escaped a convoy of people to be deported to Siberia. At school, the political situation was so tense that classmates left death threats for their director in the school toilet.[130]

Given the impact of the UPA insurgency and Soviet terror, it was no surprise that intellectuals like Horyn played a prominent role in Ukraine's dissident movement. According to one study, of 749 active participants in acts of political opposition to the regime in Soviet Ukraine in 1969–72, a total of 283, or 38 percent, were from the republic's capital, Kyiv, while 190, or 25 percent, were from Lviv, constituting a total of 63 percent of the dissident movement. Lviv had essentially become the second most important city in the republic for political dissent.[131] While Benjamin Tromley argues convincingly that Lvivians' connections with Kyivans did not become a sufficient cause for the emergence of the Ukrainian Sixtiers' national renaissance, these connections among young intellectuals helped radicalize the Sixtiers Movement in the mid-1960s. The arrest of the Horyn brothers and other Lvivians at the end of August 1965 provoked protests in the upper echelons of the cultural establishment. Dziuba, along with poet Lina Kostenko, disrupted a 3 September 1965 meeting of the presidium and Party committee of the republic Writers' Union in Kyiv, informing the Union of these illegal arrests.[132] The very next day, at Kyiv's newly built Ukraine Movie Theater, Dziuba and poet Vasyl Stus tried to protest the arrests publicly. After the premiere of the award-winning film *Shadows of Forgotten Ancestors* by Sergei Paradzhanov, they shouted out news of these arrests and called for a protest, their voices drowned out by the theater fire alarm.[133]

Such dissidents as Horyn and Viacheslav Chornovil played an instrumental role in the tumultuous events that shook Lviv and Ukraine at the end of the 1980s. Horyn was among former political prisoners speaking to assembled crowds, urging demonstrators to protest the Communist Party's monopoly on power and demand more rights for Ukrainians. He was one of the founders of Rukh and among twenty-four non-Communist deputies elected to Ukraine's Supreme Council from the Lviv Region in March 1990. Chornovil, Horyn's friend, became head of the Lviv Regional Council and led the effort to dismantle Communist rule in Lviv and the surrounding region.[134] However, dissidents' protest literature was a small part of a wider culture of secret texts young Lvivians circulated from the 1960s to the end of the 1980s. Some of these texts expressed interest in dissent, but reflected a search for identity rather than a clearly defined political program. Some texts merely flirted with the idea of separating from the

Soviet Union. Still others asserted the values of individual expression and introspection, often inspired by Lviv's role as a provincial Soviet West.

Years after the Horyn brothers' arrest and imprisonment, students, schoolchildren, and vocational school pupils had not yet decided to take these brothers' path. However, dissent was on their minds. One such example was a group of Lviv State University students apprehended in late March 1973 for putting up protest leaflets throughout the city. This incident, as retold by Ivan Svarnyk, also had elements of cloak-and-dagger intrigue. It started with some history students who since April 1971 had been independently researching forbidden topics in Ukraine's history and culture. They were outraged at a 1973 ban on local celebrations honoring the memory of national poet Taras Shevchenko. Since the fall of 1972, they had been reading *samvydav* literature highlighting injustices against Ukrainians under Soviet rule. In this climate of increasing persecution of national self-expression—which reached its peak in 1972–73—they wanted to act.

A friend of theirs from the Philology Faculty, Hryhoriy Khvostenko, told some of them that one Zorian Popadiuk, recently expelled from the university, and his mother had made leaflets protesting the ban and that they could spread them through Lviv. Some of them agreed to meet with Popadiuk. The meeting took place in absolute secrecy. They met in the Chocolate Bar, a noted gathering spot for young people in the 1970s, located in the basement of the Svitoch Candy Store in downtown Lviv. They were to recognize Popadiuk by the color of his jacket. Popadiuk greatly impressed these students and seemed to be from a different world. For Svarnyk, he displayed a sense of moral superiority, suggesting a willingness to spend years in prison for his convictions. As students, they seemed much more naïve. They also sensed that people from outside Lviv wanted to involve them in this protest, which was greatly flattering. They agreed to help Khvostenko and Popadiuk spread the leaflets. The night of 28 March, under the cover of darkness, they got together at a park bench in front of the Gunpowder Tower, a medieval landmark near Market Square. They divided up the leaflets, fanned out across the city's districts, and pasted them on the walls of buildings, on telephone booths, and even inside running trams. Within a few hours, the KGB had arrested all of them.[135]

These arrests shook both Lviv and Ukraine. At least fifteen students were expelled from Lviv State University. Popadiuk and one of his friends landed prison terms.[136] Party leaders in Moscow and Kyiv attacked university instructors for failing to head off influences of "bourgeois nationalism." As a result, security organs produced compromising materials on a total of twenty-nine instructors and office assistants. Considerable numbers of these personnel lost their jobs or faced early retirement.[137] The scandal almost toppled the university administration as Party members accused it of coddling "bourgeois nationalist" historians who had corrupted these students.

This group of students was engaged in politics. Their members read *samvydav* literature by Sixtiers Ivan Dziuba and Valentyn Moroz. At the same time they were students who (like other Lvivians and citizens of the Soviet Union) played with the symbols and heroes of Soviet historical myths. One group participant, historian Mariana Dolynska, recalled when they played revolution while drinking coffee at a Lviv coffee house. They created a Bolshevik government where the role of Nadezhda Krupskaya (the single female member of the Communist Party's Politburo in the 1930s) fell to her.[138] Thus, in their gatherings, there were elements of collective fun, where they could, in hidden form, mock Soviet reality and its "heroes."

Although Alexei Yurchak suggests that Soviet youth during the Brezhnev era found meaning in public organizations like the Komsomol, the experiences of these students illustrates a more complex situation. Though Dolynska prior to the arrests accepted the reality of the Komsomol and was a member of the regional council, in her interview with Taras Budzinskyi, she emphasized that she and her family did not accept the Soviet regime. She talked about repressions that her relatives, Galicians, faced in Stalinist times. Her public activities were generally a formality for her, obligations that she had to fulfill, though during her university years she became fascinated with Komsomol work as a means of doing something useful for people. Unlike Leningrad students that Yurchak focuses on, Dolynska in her life story shows how strained relations were between young Lvivians and the public sphere during late socialism.[139] Consequently, Dolynska and these other fellow-thinkers, inspired by Gorbachev's Glasnost, freed from restrictions placed on them, became an important force supporting Ukrainian independence. During her interview, Dolynska mentioned fellow thinkers who organized Rukh and other reform-minded groups in Lviv at the end of the 1980s. She talked about her own role starting a Rukh chapter at her place of work.[140]

Still, it would be a mistake to compare the actions of these students to those of dissidents like Mykhailo Horyn. These students agreed that Ukraine needed to separate from the Soviet Union, and they imagined how to accomplish it. Khvostenko, for instance, did this in some articles for the underground university newspaper *Progress (Postup)*. Students of the History Faculty wrote a political program in a similar revolutionary spirit. Several years later, there emerged suppositions that KGB organs found the program and seized it during a search at Dolynska's home, or Stepan Sluka destroyed it before a search of his dormitory room.[141] However, these students' conspiratorial activities cannot be compared to the activities of Horyn and others. On the one hand Dolynska talked about the fear that she felt on 25 October 1971, when she agreed to take part in the group's underground activities. She sensed that she would not finish her university studies.[142] On the other hand, these students did not have jobs to lose. They did not have families or children at risk like Horyn, Chornovil, or other dissidents. Their political discussions and spreading leaflets reflected a young, inarticulate rebellion against the status quo.

Taras Budzinskyi's interviews with Dolynska confirm this. During her interview, she completely disagreed with the interviewer's assumption that she and her History Faculty classmates had created a "group." She claimed that their so-called program did not foresee specific political actions. Instead, it concerned scholarly ones about Ukraine. Moreover, they wrote the program jokingly, over coffee "like it always is with Galician Ukrainians." When these young people spread leaflets, Dolynska was in Moscow at a student conference. She said that if she had been in Lviv, she might have been able to convince her friends not to make such an "ill-conceived and senseless" *(neprodumanyi i bezhluzdyi)* act.[143]

Thus these students, though not indifferent to national issues, still had not decided what to do or how to make changes in society. It is also worth adding that this was primarily a group of males, which the decision to appoint Dolynska "Krupskaya" during informal gatherings suggests. These young men together sought ways out of the situation Ukraine was in, but at the same time they played with revolutionary activity. Though at the end of the 1980s they supported civic organizations that stood for Ukraine's independence, one could assume that these students' underground activity reflected a certain maximalism characteristic of their young age. Besides that, underground activities gave them an alternative male role to that of builders of a Communist future. Their desired future was linked to an independent Ukraine.

Such youthful flirtations with overthrowing the Soviet system and establishing an independent Ukraine broke out all over Lviv in the 1970s. They emerged in surrounding small towns and villages. Ironically, these incidents happened right when Lviv dissidents like Ihor and Iryna Kalynets were going to jail.[144] University students, mostly male, privately gathered in apartments and other places and dedicated themselves to obtaining Ukraine's independence, with one group even reciting its own "confession" before Shevchenko on annual March holidays honoring Shevchenko.[145]

Others, including teens, provoked public scenes. Teens quickly passed around political leaflets and made outbursts in front of the New Year tree. Even pranks acquired a political context. Oleksandr Tsiovkh, who was an English philology student at Lviv State University at the end of the 1960s, recalled one such incident. One morning in 1969 or 1970, he saw that one of the rooms for History Faculty courses was sealed up with crime scene tape, and either police or KGB agents were milling around. He then heard that the room had become a crime scene because someone had drawn a Ukrainian Trident, regarded as a nationalist symbol, on the blackboard. A special investigation was launched, and rumors spread that some subversive organization had been responsible.[146]

Other acts show the influence of Soviet institutions as well as teenage daring. The regional police chief, reporting the results of KGB investigations to the Lviv obkom, conveyed such information about a secret society of small-town teens. Just outside Lviv, a group of vocational school teenagers, overheard by KGB agents and subsequently disciplined, had tried to do something akin to what Dolynska and her friends did in Lviv's cafés. However, they were even more radical. Meeting at a snack bar called Beef Stew (*Chanakhy*) in the rural district of Horodetskyi on 19 December 1972, these teens not only came up with a program to establish an independent Ukrainian state, but Ukraine was to be populated exclusively by ethnic Ukrainians. Besides planning to distribute propaganda and elect officers, they came up with an oath all its members had to swear to.[147] The oath was highly suggestive of its members' youthful romanticism: "I, a son of Ukraine, swear before my comrades, swear before my fellow thinkers, never to betray my ideas, to be faithful to the idea and struggle for it to the last drop of my blood. If I betray my oath, then may the stern hand of my comrades, my fellow thinkers, punish me."[148]

This oath suggested the subconscious influence of Soviet symbols. It bore an uncanny resemblance to that sworn by Soviet partisans in Lviv during German occupation, the text of which the Lviv Historical Museum included in its exhibits in the 1970s.[149] It is quite possible that these young men might have visited this exhibit when on tours of Lviv organized by the

Pioneers or the Komsomol. Soviet symbols inspired other spontaneous acts, like displaying the outlawed blue-and-yellow Ukrainian "nationalist" flag in Western Ukrainian villages and small towns, two cases of which were mentioned at a Lviv obkom plenary session in late 1971.[150] In the late 1970s, in the words of one participant, movies or adventure novels about Soviet partisans or young revolutionaries hoisting flags over enemy territory led them, teenage boys in Kryvchytsia, a neighborhood just outside Lviv, to try to send out balloons with the illegal Ukrainian flag on May Day. Their subversive act failed because of a shortage of helium.[151]

These young people's worldview thus borrowed from the heroism of Russian and Soviet revolutionaries of the public sphere. They were engaged in a rite of passage, daring each other to go over the line and make up nationalist political programs or fly nationalist flags. They may not have cared about politics at all. As one of those teens who had tried to fly nationalist balloons indicated, his fellow conspirators did not take part in mass political demonstrations that shook Lviv in the late 1980s.[152] Rather than conspiratorial action being a vocation, as it was for Horyn, Popadiuk, and other dissidents, it was purely an adventure. The atmosphere of the *kompany* could be both nationalist and great fun.

Besides this youthful desire to test accepted rules, young artists and writers challenged limits to individual self-expression. Influenced by past intellectual trends and by Polish media, they broke ranks not just with public censorship but also with the civic pathos of the Sixties that had so overwhelmed young people in the early 1960s. Instead of offering straightforward political slogans associated with love of Ukraine and its people, abstract painters and younger writers offered highly symbolic texts that, in their themes and in their complexity, spoke for the individual rather than for the larger community. Unlike the Sixties, who during the Thaw could publish their works or exhibit their art, these young artists and writers wrote and displayed their canvases almost exclusively for each other. In challenging the ability of a text to represent reality "objectively" (that is, through one perspective), these texts shared the postmodern worldview captured by such postwar abstract painters as Anselm Kieffer and Jackson Pollock or such surrealists as Salvador Dali.

An "underground academy" of art organized by painter and art instructor Karlo Zvirynskyi epitomized this trend. With eight or nine students from the Institute of Applied and Decorative Art whom he came to trust, Zvirynskyi in his apartment introduced these art students to subjects forbidden or highly marginalized. From the end of the 1950s to the mid-1960s, he led lessons in art, literature, philosophy, Ukrainian history, and music. A friend of Zvirynskyi's, a Greek Catholic priest named Father Borys, gave lectures on religion. Zvirynskyi became a "living link" with Lviv's pre-Soviet art traditions, having grown up in Galicia and collected prewar literature on Ukrainian art, having befriended older artists like Roman Selskyi, and having attended during German occupation an art academy led by Lviv artists who later went abroad.[153]

Zvirynskyi and his pupils looked over interwar-era reproductions of European masters and discussed interwar Galician Ukrainian artists. Polish media became a crucial part of their unofficial curriculum. Zvirynskyi discovered new trends in abstract art like the paintings of Jackson Pollock by listening to Polish-language broadcasts of the BBC. He shared such knowledge with his pupils, as well as copies of the Polish art journal called *Art Review (Przeglad Artystyczny)*. They read together, usually in Polish translation, such contemporary writers as Kafka, Joyce, and Proust, as well as such philosophers as Sartre and Nietzsche. Zvirynskyi and his pupils conducted private exhibits of each other's works for themselves and for close friends.[154]

Zvirynskyi's underground academy thus offered a variety of alternative channels of information to Institute of Applied and Decorative Art students. As this institute's title suggests, it had been organized to present Ukrainian art not as part of the fine arts, but as part of folk and craft arts. It abolished its departments of painting and sculpture in the early 1960s after a scandal involving a student's "formalist" works. Roman Petruk, one of Zvirynskyi's underground academy students, viewed this administrative move as an attempt to reduce the influence of such elder Galician art figures as Selskyi and others who taught in these departments. The biographer of sculptor Dmytro Krvavych, Valeriy Hrabovskyi, drew similar conclusions.[155] Zvirynskyi's underground academy thus offered an alternative orientation for Ukrainian art. The Greek Catholic priest's lessons underscored the underground Greek Catholic Church's impact on young intellectuals. Even more important was the different orientation the academy gave toward art and its representation of the world. Instead of depicting the world objectively and scientifically, art could capture reality in all its contradictions and complexities, offering multiple, highly symbolic perspectives that appealed to the viewer's subconscious.

Such examples of postmodernist art can be seen in such paintings as *Relief-VI* (1960), by Zvirynskyi himself, and *The Wound* (1968), by one of his academy pupils, painter Oleh Minko (Figures 7.2 and 7.3). Zvirynskyi's

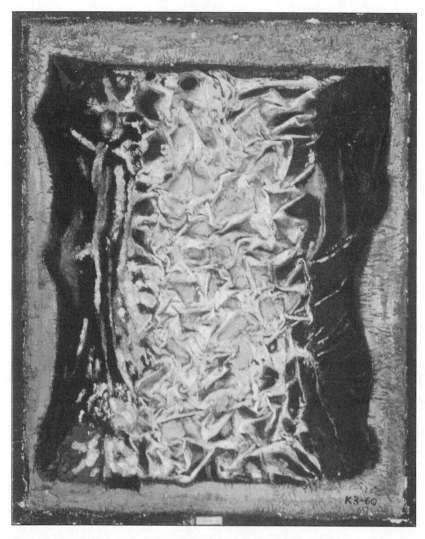

Figure 7.2. Karlo Zvirynskyi, *Relief-VI* (1960), from Tamila Pecheniuk and Khrystyna Zvirynska, *Karlo Zviryns'kyi* (Lviv: Malti-M, 2002). Used with permission of Khrystyna Zvirynska.

Figure 7.3. Oleh Minko, *The Wound* (1968), from Oleh Minko and Iryna Minko-Murashchyk, *Tainopys* (Lviv: Kompaniia Gerdan, 1998). Used with permission of the artist.

Relief-VI, made of cardboard, paper, glue, and paint, conveys various emotions in a raised, textured column in shades of black and white, set against a stark gray background. It may represent some kind of worn tombstone, yet in its use of relief figures and contrasting colors, it also suggests the trunk of a tree in the fall, at a time when trees lose their leaves and evoke feelings of death. It is in this use of relief figures and colors, though, that the viewer feels the stark realities of death and human suffering. One of Minko's later paintings, done after his years in the underground academy, represented reality through various symbols conveyed by shapes and combinations of colors. *The Wound* depicts simultaneously two facial expressions, one smiling at the viewer and the other, on the left side, exclaiming in pain at the sight of a nail pierced through the subject's hand. In depicting these two conflicting emotions in grotesque form on a disproportionately elongated head, Minko emphasizes the human psyche's ability to hide its wounds and contain conflicting emotions at the same time.

These paintings, kept from public view, suggest an aesthetic rebellion among young intellectuals, similar to abstract art trends in Moscow during the Thaw but drawing from Poland and Galicia for inspiration.[156] Young poets and prose writers likewise created secret texts for friends that drew heavily on symbols, metaphors, and in the case of poetry, free verse to appeal to individuals' subconscious. As with Zvirynskyi's underground academy, they looked to Lviv's pre-Soviet intellectual traditions and Polish media for inspiration. Friends who heard or read their works often included young artists influenced by abstract art, even some of Zvirynskyi's own underground pupils.

Poet Ihor Kalynets, whose poems' secret distribution abroad alarmed republic Party leaders in 1971, was born in 1939 in the Lviv Region. He was inspired by the free verse and religious symbolism of the Ukrainian poet Bohdan-Ihor Antonych, whose neo-romantic and modernist works circulated underground in the Thaw's early years, before Lviv's *October* began publishing them again. Kalynets's poems, read before friends (who included, among others, Zvirynskyi's pupils) and circulated in *samvydav* form, are built on complex arrangements of symbols connected with love, Ukrainians' past, and Christian and pagan beliefs. While Kalynets dedicated some of his poems to friends in prison, he avoided one clear political message, be it about the Soviet state or about the Ukrainian nation.[157]

Writers born after the war who had become friends with Kalynets and his wife, Iryna, created their own underground journal, *The Chest (Skrynia)* (1971). As seen earlier, these writers consciously modeled their art, literature, music, and philosophy on Polish media. Mykola Riabchuk, one of the journal's creators, and memoir materials by Riabchuk and others about poet Hryhoriy Chubai, suggested how this journal came about. Chubai and his friends first envisioned a journal after putting together humorous collages of newspaper stories, photos, and headlines on the Chubais' bathroom walls. It was a journal that was to have nothing to do with politics. However, it was an alternative to Soviet literary journals, which they saw offering no chances for publication, given their views on aesthetics.[158]

The Chest suggests the strong influence of both Ukrainian artistic trends and Polish media. The cover itself draws from Ukrainian art traditions, resembling the book cover designs by Kyiv graphic artist Heorhiy Narbut (1886–1920), who among other things designed stamps for the short-lived, "bourgeois nationalist" Ukrainian People's Republic (1917–20). *The Chest* includes a translation into Ukrainian by Chubai of a play by postwar Polish modernist playwright Tadeusz Różewicz, *The Hilarious Old Man*, as well as commentary on the significance of Różewicz's "Theater of Inconsistency," which is contrasted sharply with traditional realist plays. As with Zvirynskyi's underground academy, the journal's contributors share the view that art is not about depicting reality objectively, but about evoking symbols connected to that complex reality in ways that affect the audience's subconscious and force them to draw conclusions for themselves. Its poems and other texts rely on pagan and Christian symbols, as well as themes of love, childhood, and jazz music, to stir up the individual reader's emotions and inspire further reflection. As with the poems of Kalynets, who was an early mentor, literature is not about evoking civic pathos, but about entering into a dialogue with the individual.[159]

This aesthetic rebellion was not overtly political. However, in such societies under Communism, everything, including the personal, was political.[160] These young intellectuals chose not to participate in the public sphere and not to submit to its restrictions, but instead to create for the apartment room, the desk drawer, or the trusted friend. When such artists became involved in politics, their secret texts became a threat to the state. Protesting for political prisoners and spreading *samvydav* led to the arrest of Kalynets and his wife in 1972. When Kalynets was on trial for "anti-Soviet propaganda and agitation" in 1972–73, his poems served as evidence to convict him, though ultimately they were thrown out as evidence on appeal.[161] One review of his poetry, done for KGB investigators, stressed that Kalynets intentionally complicated his poems to mask their true message.[162]

Expressing oneself in complex symbols put the individual above the collective in the creative process. Underground paintings and poems thus asserted individual freedom. They became ways to identify with Central Europe and the West, given the strong influence of Polish media and prewar intellectual trends. Such acts of aesthetic rebellion continued in Lviv through the 1970s and 1980s, encouraged by friends of Chubai, who died in 1982. Some of Chubai's friends became friends with leaders of a new aesthetic rebellion, poets of the Bu-Ba-Bu school of poetry like Viktor Neborak and Iuriy Andrukhovych.[163] By the time of the Soviet Union's dissolution, such trends led to the Bu-Ba-Bu school of poetry and its playful mockery of Ukrainian and Soviet symbols, as seen in literary and musical "happenings" (vyvykhy) staged on Lviv's streets in the early 1990s.[164]

The Cultural Underground and the End of the Soviet Union

As writers, historians, and artists helped transform Lviv into a Soviet Ukrainian city, the compromises they made with Party and state institutions were fragile. Young Lvivians' private spheres, while heavily influenced by public institutions, challenged such compromises. Young Lvivians read books banned or "forgotten" by Soviet publishers. They heard stories about Galician cultural trends that university lectures, school lessons, or university textbooks ignored. They heard stories about past repression. Educational and cultural institutions helped them form such private networks of fellow thinkers. The optimism of the Thaw, combined with the defeat of the nationalist underground, compelled the vast majority of them to seek to improve Soviet socialism rather than tear it down.

This was not the renewal of revolutionary enthusiasm seen in Moscow's Thaw generation. While they had accepted the realities of being Soviet Western Ukrainians, young Lvivians drew inspiration from lands farther west, particularly Poland. Their heroes became fragments of a Galician Ukrainian intelligentsia who chose loyalty to the Soviet Union for survival. For many young Lvivians, the improvement of Soviet socialism was the means to an end. They hoped it would one day lead to greater autonomy, if not independence, for Ukraine. Thus students and young intellectuals utilized practices of daily life examined by Michel de Certeau, such as reading, writing, or socializing with friends, as ways of resisting social constraints thrust upon them. As already seen with one student, walking the street and interacting with its people, another practice discussed by Certeau, led to conversations about the Russification of higher education and later political dissent.[165]

Such acts did not produce the kind of political opposition witnessed on the streets of Tallinn in 1956 or on the streets of Tartu in 1968. Singing subversive Christmas carols on the street or discussing Ukraine's need to separate from the Soviet Union could end young Lvivian students' future membership in the intelligentsia. Habits of reading, writing, and socializing often were about enjoying the collective fun of the group. Sometimes they led to teenage acts of daring that had no real political purpose at all. However, such practices of daily life inspired ideas which some of these young Lvivians later articulated into discourses of political opposition. Thus Dolynska and her friends, while not knowing what to do for Ukraine in 1973, became active in its independence movement at the end of the 1980s.

Apartments, art shops, cafés, theaters, and sometimes government research centers produced these islands of freedom in a sea of censorship, empty ritual, and political witch hunts. However, these were islands in a larger archipelago of informal social spaces. Russians and Russian speakers had their own islands of freedom, often separate from, though sometimes interacting with, Ukrainian-speaking ones. In 1970, Lviv State Polytechnic Institute students, who acquired the nickname the Sybarites, created a notebook of poems, stories, photo montages, and caricatures that made fun of daily life. They faced punishment from their institute's Komsomol after someone turned in the notebook to the KGB. Among the materials compromising the group was a photo montage with the title "The Mind, Honor, and Conscience of Our Epoch" *(Um, chest' i sovest' nashei epokhi).* The montage was deemed anti-Soviet because the title, an official slogan extolling Soviet young people, was for a photo of young men in front of a pile of garbage.[166] Other such circles of young Lvivians avoided controversy and, though marginalized, offered alternative views on literature, art, philosophy, and politics. In the late 1970s ethnic Russians and Russian speakers born after the war gathered at a stained glass–making shop on Market Square where a friend, Ihor Klekh, worked, to read semilegal publications in Russian and enjoy one another's company.[167] From the mid-1970s until his death in a plane crash in 1985, Russian graphic artist Oleksandr Aksinin (1949–85) and other young artists, many of whom graduated from the Lviv State Printing Institute, gathered at the café Nectar on Saksahanskyi Street and in people's apartments to engage in similar pursuits.[168]

These circles of fellow thinkers somewhat resembled their Ukrainian-speaking counterparts. The Sybarites and the friends hanging out at Klekh's art shop consumed Polish texts like the humor magazine *Szpilka*.[169] These were people who distanced themselves from political themes popular at Artists' Union exhibits. In the words of Aksinin's friends, they represented an "internal emigration" whose members were turned off by the public rhetoric of Party and Komsomol organizations. Their company of friends represented for Ihor Diurych truly democratic values.[170] Some of them had friends among Ukrainian speakers. The circle of friends around Aksinin and his wife, Engelina Buriakovska (1944–82), included the Galician Ukrainian graphic artists Bohdan Pikulytskyi and (as one of Buriakovska's ex libris designs indicates) Ivan Ostafiychuk.[171]

However, these were consumers of Russian texts or Western texts in Russian translation. Texts by Dostoevsky, Russian Silver Age thinkers, or Western philosophers helped Aksinin explore philosophical issues of personalism, existentialism, and psychoanalysis.[172] The Sybarites made references to Chekhov in their notebook or compared themselves to Mayakovsky.[173] In these circles, Ukrainian texts were conspicuously absent. While Engelina Buriakovska wrote short stories for the cultural underground, they were Russian-language texts for Leningrad and Moscow *samizdat* journals.[174]

These alternative social spaces demonstrated that Lviv's post-Stalin generations were deeply fragmented along ethnic, cultural, and regional lines. The Russian-speaking circles just mentioned were almost exclusively children of Soviet Army officers and other personnel who came to Lviv after the war. A former Lviv State Polytechnic Institute student recalled the separate worlds such Russian-speaking and Ukrainian-speaking circles inhabited in the late 1970s.[175] Therefore, it was probably no accident that, years earlier, Galician Ukrainian dissidents like the Horyn brothers never knew Russian speakers like Evgeniia Ginzburg, author of *Journey into the Whirlwind,* who lived in Lviv in the 1950s and 1960s. In the early 1960s, Bohdan Horyn received a typed copy of this book about Stalin-era gulags through two Russian Lvivian friends, Alik and Ihor Vvedenskyi, but neither he nor his brother met Ginzburg personally.[176] Such fragmentation reflected the impact of censorship. Russian speakers most likely knew nothing of Ihor Kalynets because the latter could not publish. It also reflected the impact of space on these relationships.[177] These were circles of friends who met in apartments, art shops, and cafés. This, as well as distrust of informants, made for a very diverse, but scattered, cluster of islands of freedom.

The Sybarites reflected another dimension of young Lvivians' lives. They presumably received their nickname for leading a life devoted to pleasure and instant gratification. Their circle resembled the collective bonding of friends in a familiar gathering spot, what was called the *tusovka* in Russian in late Soviet times, and the collective fun it experienced. They were not so much about resistance or rebellion as getting together as a group in a certain space, deconstructing identities through acts of momentary pleasure, and therefore offering possibilities for both resistance and conformity.[178] This atmosphere of collective fun was not something the rebellious history students identified with. As Mariana Dolynska pointed out while reviewing my text, for her, the *tusovka* crowd was different from theirs. It represented children of the Party elite who had access to goods.[179] At any rate, the Sybarites hinted at another aspect of young people's lives, namely, the desire to escape politics and have fun. Young Lvivians of all backgrounds dropped out of politics, listened to the latest music, rooted for sports teams, or escaped onto the silver screen.

CHAPTER 8

Mass Culture and Counterculture

Despite living in a so-called Banderite town, young Lvivians acted on other categories besides the nation. They felt the vibrations of changes throughout the postwar world. Roman Ivanychuk identifies the ferment of the 1960s with the Ukrainian last names of Drach, Dziuba, and Vinhranovskyi. For others, the 1960s were associated with John, Paul, George, and Ringo. Amateur rock artist and later radio producer Ilya Lemko described, with tremendous enthusiasm, the influence the rock music of the Beatles had on him and his school classmates.[1] Global countercultures, including those of hippies, bikers, and by the early 1980s punks, appeared on Lviv's streets. Such young people shocked, and amused, others. In January 1970, poet Rostyslav Bratun, sharing news with his Moscow friend about some "home-grown" hippies, bragged that not even Moscow had such a "sensation." He joked that his colleague Ivanychuk now feared that the People's Volunteer Militia would clip off his beard.[2]

In the Soviet Union and in Eastern Europe, intellectuals were still very influential in articulating nationhood. However, modern industrial societies, including those in the Soviet bloc, were changing because of the growth of mass education, technology and bureaucracy, professionalism, and the communications industry. While intellectuals remained important, mass culture and the figures associated with it—stars in television, rock music, soccer, and films—made intellectuals less politically decisive than, say, their nineteenth-century counterparts.[3]

In Lviv, such figures increasingly attracted young people, despite the influence of high culture and village folk traditions. While somewhat no-

220

ticeable in the early 1950s, this was especially true for those born after World War II. Jazz, pop, and rock music from the West, as well as films and soccer, became an important part of daily life, especially for the young. Western films provided alternative models of behavior. Soccer games offered a sense of collective identity bridging language and ethnic barriers. They suggested a local identity at odds with a larger Soviet one. Rock music from the West inspired countercultures like hippies and punks. However, elements of a Lviv identity, if not a Ukrainian identity, surfaced in soccer games, the counterculture of the hippies, and rock and pop music. These elements did not lead to a political program that advocated greater rights for Ukrainians. However, they underscored how much Lviv had become a Ukrainian city by the Gorbachev era. A Ukrainian pop star's mysterious death unleashed regional and national grievances, ones articulated again with even greater force under Gorbachev.

Between the Village and the Big Beat

During the early years of the Thaw, more than bourgeois nationalism or the specter of Hungarian-style uprisings worried local Communist Party leaders. In 1957, Lviv obkom leaders, addressing ideological problems with young people, criticized the pernicious effects of jazz music, fox-trots, and boogie-woogies in city clubs. In the late 1950s, other city Party meetings raised alarms about the drunken brawls, the gambling over *horilka*, the smoking, the spitting on floors, and the tracking in dirt that soured such dances, designed to help young people become cultured.[4] From the mid-1950s to the mid-1960s, Lviv was somewhere between the rough-and-ready elements of the postwar village and the era of big beat music associated with the Beatles, between Ukrainian and all-Soviet light music and new Western music styles.

Since the Zhdanov era, Soviet leaders railed against the harmful effects of culture from the capitalist West. They castigated admirers of Western fashion as "fashion hounds," or *stiliagi* in Russian, though countercultures connected with different styles flourished in postwar Stalinist times. When it came to jazz, the Thaw somewhat lessened these tensions. In the summer of 1956, the Polish Blue Jazz Band toured the Soviet Union, one of the first instances where jazz music again enjoyed public performances.[5] In such provincial cities as Lviv, Party leaders were loath to change. When calls came to combat anti-Soviet phenomena after unrest in Poland and

Hungary, they readily included the struggle against the "rotten West" in their repertoire. At one obkom plenary meeting in 1957, an obkom secretary vented his disgust for local admirers of Polish "blue jazz," inspired, no doubt, by the Polish Blue Jazz Band's recent appearances. It was nothing more than "a cacophony, squeaking, screeching, a roaring of wild animals." "*Stiliagi* roared," he said. "Maybe out of fascination, maybe from the awakening of a truly animal instinct."[6]

This Party secretary went out of his way to hammer at jazz music and fashion hounds in the city, but he was making an elephant out of a fly. Young intellectuals greatly admired the high culture of classical music. The prewar Galician intelligentsia had become their role models. Traditional intelligentsia values thus influenced their identity. One respondent, an instructor at an institution of higher education, regarded Presley fans as less "conscious" elements of society. He insisted that the more conscious, thinking elements listened to music by Ukrainian composers. In daily life, there were cases where intelligentsia members sang Ukrainian and Polish "light hits" (*shliagery*) from Polish times, for instance, during family holidays (name days and birthdays).[7] One memoir account suggests that Lviv State University students from the village in the late 1950s who had friends from the local Galician Ukrainian families learned such prewar songs and came to like them. For poet and later dissident Ihor Kalynets, memories of his friendship with Teodoziy Starak, which began at the university in 1956, included being introduced not just to songs by the UPA but also to dance songs from interwar Lviv, songs not really present on student dance floors then, as such music was heavily Russified. Such songs, which Kalynets and Starak sang at parties with friends, included humorous Ukrainian songs as well as Polish "hooligan" (*batiarski*) songs. One of these hooligan songs was sung during drills for military lessons outside Lviv.[8] However, for future intelligentsia members, concerts at the opera theater and the Philharmonic became the preferred places to enjoy music, and this was classical music.[9] Lviv State University and other institutions of higher education viewed classical music as essential in the upbringing of the future intelligentsia, as one university Party committee report noted.[10]

Many Lvivians could not afford themselves jazz or rock albums or the flashy new dress of so-called fashion hounds in the late 1950s. Most young people were from Western Ukrainian villages, primarily Galician ones. For them, material circumstances were quite dire. Getting a watch, let alone a flashy new tie or an Elvis Presley record, was very difficult.[11] For ethnologist Aleksandra Matyukhina, the more privileged families in Lviv, such as Russians from the military and Party elites, had greater access to jazz music, rock music, and Western fashions.[12] While this generalization is debatable, Lviv's native urbanites not only listened to but also performed Elvis Presley songs. Musician Volodymyr Kit, a local Ukrainian born in Lviv in 1939, recalled two such young people. One of them was a young man named Richard at Middle School Number 44 who played Presley's songs on his acoustic guitar. Richard, who acquired the nickname "Elvis" among friends, could not really sing such songs at local dances because there were no amplifiers then in the second half of the 1950s. However, he played them for small parties.[13]

The absence of Presley's songs at late 1950s school dances suggests that Presley's influence was weak. Instead, Soviet patriotic songs and Russian lyrical romances from Soviet films and radio programs were much more common among young Lvivians in the 1950s. Roksolana Zorivchak, a native of Lviv who attended university from 1951 to 1956, regarded Soviet patriotic songs about World War II as obligatory and not really popular among Western Ukrainians, though Russian lyrical songs were.[14] Iaroslav Isaievych, who grew up in a small town in Galicia and attended university around the same time as Zorivchak, suggested a more complex situation. Recalling his early childhood in the Lviv Region around World War II, he said that Soviet patriotic songs about the war, heard so frequently on the radio, became part of local Ukrainians' music regardless of choice. He recalled a patriotic song devoted to Stalin, the lyrics written by Ukrainian poet Maksym Rylskyi, was also frequently sung in his early childhood. Later, by his university years, young people (at least those who were originally from the city) sang Russian lyrical songs from the movies. Isaievych said that young people were neither for nor against such songs, lyrical or patriotic. They simply became a part of people's everyday life.[15] Thus accounts by Andriy Sodomora, a student in classical philology attending university around the same time (1953 to 1958), as well as by Iryna Shabat, who began her studies toward the end of the 1950s, mention matter-of-factly the presence of Russian lyrical songs among young Lvivians who either were from Western Ukrainian villages or grew up in Lviv.[16]

Ukrainian folk songs and light music enjoyed great popularity. Isaievych remembered that in his student years, such young men like him, former villagers, sang Ukrainian folk songs often, including at camps for obligatory student military training.[17] Another interview indicates that young men singing or humming folk songs in the hallway during class breaks was a common scene.[18] In 1955–56, the main student auditorium of Lviv State University greeted with enthusiasm a Ukrainian song, "The Embroidered Towel (Dear Mother of Mine)," with words by Andriy Malyshko and lyrics by Anton Maiborod—with such great enthusiasm that the soloists performed three encores of it.[19] While she did not recall ever hearing Elvis Presley, one math student from this university fondly remembered when, at the beginning of the 1960s, she and a group of her classmates sang "Hutsul Girl Ksenia." This song was popular in Galicia prior to World War II, and amateur composer Roman Savytskyi wrote it in 1932. In the 1950s various Soviet ensembles performed it, and it became well known throughout the Soviet Union. Helping gather the harvest in a village, classmates collectively sang "Hutsul Girl Ksenia" at a village club dance and thus came to know locals their age.[20] Such songs helped break down barriers between city and countryside for Western Ukrainians. "The Embroidered Towel" contains themes of love for one's mother and one's home, while "Hutsul Girl Ksenia," an interwar romance, is set in the Carpathian Mountains, home of the Hutsuls.[21]

Unlike other Soviet provincial cities, which experienced rock-and-roll and other Western music trends as early as the mid-1950s, young Lvivians' connections with folk music were much stronger.[22] This may have been partly because Greek Catholicism still had considerable influence in Western Ukrainians' private lives, making them much more connected to national and village ideals. At any rate, as late as the 1970s, when rock music had definitely affected urban life in the Soviet Union, Ukrainian teenagers growing up in Lviv's outskirts knew very little of the world of rock music. This was true for Ihor Pidkova, born in 1960, who grew up in the satellite town of Kryvchytsia near Lviv. Another resident of Kryvchytsia, Mariia Kazimira, born in 1929, agreed, estimating that it was not until the eve of Ukrainian independence when young people in her community listened to rock music. As Pidkova recalled, teens his age sang Ukrainian folk songs, particularly Cossack songs. Pidkova found out about the world of rock-and-roll only when he started attending Middle School Number 8 in central Lviv.[23]

How representative was Pidkova's experience remains questionable, as another interview respondent, born in 1957, recalled villagers in his native Ternopil Region near Lviv dancing to 1970s Western disco hits. Other interviews suggest at least the perception that those originally from Western Ukrainian villages tended to "lag behind," so to speak, when it came to music and fashion.[24] While difficult to measure, rock music and jazz affected all young Lvivians in some manner. A former Ukrainian philology student at Lviv State University in the mid-1950s said that while few had listened to Elvis Presley records, his hairstyle, and even his light blue dress shirt, became widely popular among university students.[25] Rock stars like Elvis, while seldom heard, at least counted for style. It is very likely that with living standards improving in the village by the 1970s, village youth were not that immune to rock music.

While Lviv's local functionaries railed against jazz in the months following unrest in Poland and Hungary, they gradually came to tolerate, however grudgingly, the new tastes in music. Volodymyr Kit recalled that in the mid-1950s, while neither jazz nor the boogie-woogie was recognized at the official level, amateur orchestras playing a mixture of boogie-woogie, jazz, and light hits performed at club dances all over the city. Such musicians found opportunities to play music in city movie theaters, during the half hour or so before films were shown. Kit's own path to jazz music started at Middle School Number 8 in downtown Lviv, where he and other musicians, participants of their school's wind orchestra, set up their own small boogie-woogie group that played at dances.[26]

By the beginning of the 1960s, the Thaw compelled city Party and state leaders to encourage jazz groups through officially registered groups known as Vocal-Instrumental Ensembles (VIAs). VIAs were affiliated with the regional philharmonic orchestra, and city enterprises and educational institutions sponsored them.[27] Local intellectuals, inspired by the Thaw, supported such music. Composer Anatoliy Kos-Anatolskyi, himself an interwar Lviv composer of jazz, swing, and light music, chided provincial officials in 1962 for being too afraid to encourage such music. Moscow already was doing this, while people in Lviv, out of frustration with local Ukrainian stations, were tuning their radio sets to Warsaw. Both he and young poet Dmytro Pavlychko urged that more be done to incorporate such music.[28]

The jazz VIA Medykus, led by Ihor Khoma, illustrated the reemergence of professional jazz music in postwar Soviet Lviv. Kit was one of the group's first musicians. In interviews, he said that it began as the jazz quintet Rhythm *(Rytm)* at the end of the 1950s. Quintet members rehearsed at one of the city's few remaining Polish-language middle schools, where the cultural atmosphere was more liberal (thus even allowing women's variety show performances). At the beginning of the 1960s, the group performed at the first all-Soviet jazz festival held in Tartu, Estonia, playing a light orchestral hit by Kos-Anatolskyi, "At the Tram Stop" *(Na tramvainiy zupyntsi)*.[29]

Kit recalled that their group was the only one from Ukraine at this festival, yet their counterparts from Moscow played far better jazz.[30] At least one local functionary complained about this group's onstage performances in January 1962, but it nonetheless enjoyed support from others.[31] By the middle of the 1960s, as Medykus (a VIA affiliated with the Lviv State Medical Institute), this group had become a professional jazz orchestra. Khoma, an institute instructor, encouraged all the members to get a medical education, which they did, working at the Medical Institute, while Khoma's younger brother Oleh became a physics instructor there. In Kit's opinion, their connections with the Medical Institute, and probably Ihor Khoma's careful selection of good musicians, probably contributed to the band's stability. Nearly all of its members performed with the band up to the mid-1970s.[32]

By the end of the 1960s, Medykus had become prominent not only in Lviv's music scene but also in other parts of the Soviet Union. Its composers became renowned for combining jazz rhythms with Ukrainian folk motifs.[33] Medykus and other jazz and variety music (estradnyi) VIAs performed in city Komsomol-sponsored competitions. The most prominent competition was the annual Young Estradnyi Groups City Contest, first organized in 1968. It took place every spring at the Gagarin Palace of Culture, with a final concert in the outdoor "Green Theater" of the Bohdan Khmelnytskyi Park of Culture and Recreation. This competition promoted popular music with jazz elements. The Komsomol reporter covering the 1971 contest emphasized efforts by virtually all the participants to incorporate folk melodies. In that year, Khoma won a prize for best amateur song and for being the contest's best musician.[34] However, by then, younger generations were enthralled not with jazz, but with the Beatles, the Rolling Stones, and other legendary figures of rock-and-roll.

Rock, Pop, and the Postwar Generation

While Elvis Presley figured only vaguely in Lvivians' memories of the late 1950s, rock music had become part of young Lvivians' lives by the time of the Beatles' worldwide invasion. Popular histories by Lvivians born after 1945 stress the variety of groups that people their age and younger listened to in the 1960s and 1970s, from British and American blues rock, hard rock, and classic rock to American soul and finally disco.[35]

As in other Soviet cities, young people in Lviv discovered such music through foreign radio broadcasts, records smuggled in from abroad, or copies made first on X-ray plates and then on reel-to-reel tapes. Foreign students from Third World countries and socialist camp countries provided new recordings.[36] With over 100,000 students of higher education in Lviv, foreign students at the Lviv State Polytechnic Institute and the Lviv State Medical Institute became important sources of records. Arab and African students supplied records from abroad, while East German students set up early rock bands.[37] Lviv became a major concert venue for Soviet and Eastern European rock bands. Magnetic Band from Estonia and Pyramid *(Piramis)* from Hungary gave concerts at the Philharmonic, which caused a scandal for local Party and Komsomol organizations in the fall of 1982.[38]

Polish media, contacts with Poles, and family ties with Ukrainians in the capitalist West informed young Lvivians about new trends in rock. Polish rock artists performed and made a great impression on young audiences. Czesław Nieman, a jazz-rock artist from Poland who moved further into avant-garde rock compositions at the end of the 1960s, was one such example. According to one scholar, Nieman's 1977 Lviv concert was a major event in the history of Lviv's rock music. The same could be said of Tadeusz Nalepa, a blues rock artist and founder of the group Breakout, who came to Lviv in 1976.[39] Other socialist camp countries, as well as the nonaligned socialist Yugoslavia, played a significant role in Lviv's rock music scene. Besides East German student rock bands, radio stations from countries like Romania and the Yugoslav rock journal *Jukebox (Dzuboks)* attracted listeners and readers.[40]

As with jazz music earlier, rock music and the state had an uneasy coexistence. Party and state officials across the Soviet Union conflated jazz, rock, and the mysterious boogie-woogie with one another.[41] Local Party and state functionaries, similar to cultural conservatives in the 1950s West, easily exploited rock's loose, wild behavior to prove its harmful influence. Condemning the 1982 Lviv performance of the Soviet Estonian jazz rock band Magnetic Band, one city Komsomol leader said that the band disgraced itself with its "shrieking onstage, marching around with a guitar over the shoulder, imitating the shooting up of the audience, and egging on disorder in the hall."[42] A popular legend suggests that in 1981, the riot that broke out from the cancellation of one amateur rock band's school performance became interpreted by the district police as a demonstration against food shortages, when in fact the teenage boys making the commotion were chanting, "We don't need bread—we're full with 'The Uncles' [the name of the band], we don't need the sun—'The Uncles' shine on us!"[43] The older generations seldom accepted the new rock music, leading to generational conflict. One senior member of the Writers' Union, Taras Myhal, showed off to his son and his son's friends his own copy of the rock musical album *Jesus Christ Superstar* in the 1970s (the very album Dnipropetrovsk teens were so happy to find in Lviv). Others Myhal's age saw this music simply as "noise." Ilya Lemko recalled a friend's mother blaming "those guitarists" for corrupting her son and causing other social ills.[44]

Despite distrust of rock music, Lviv's Party and state institutions accommodated these new tastes. In the second half of the 1960s, the Lviv regional radio station, which was monitored by the obkom, featured a program called *The Music Shelf.* This program, which played for half an hour on Saturdays, featured such hits as "Satisfaction" by the Rolling Stones, as well as light music by French pop artists Joe Dassin and Charles Aznavour.[45] The state tolerated rock music by officially sponsored VIAs and amateur rock bands playing at clubs, cafés and restaurants, houses of culture, schools, and institutions of higher learning. Some amateur bands collided with local authorities, such as the Uncles. Formed in 1975 by Ilya Lemko and friends from his neighborhood, the Uncles played not just English-language rock hits, but some Ukrainian-language ones of their own, earning them the reputation of being "nationalist" in the late 1970s. Because of this reputation, the band had to outwit school authorities ingeniously, pretending to be a Chilean or a Ukrainian folk ensemble before suddenly bursting into rock hits that sent teachers and school directors into fits.[46]

Despite the Uncles' misadventures, there was nothing controversial about rock groups playing in clubs sponsored by institutes, factories, and schools by the early 1980s, as two such rock concert fans remembered.[47] VIAs and amateur groups performed in Lviv in the late 1960s and 1970s despite occasional harassment. Rock musician Oleksandr Balaban said that, except for following certain rules about hair length and changing some of their repertoire, VIAs oriented toward rock and jazz music had the chance to play in Lviv. They performed their own music and a variety of Western rock hits at city dances, from songs by Chicago to Deep Purple and Led Zeppelin. VIAs had to perform a certain number of songs by Soviet composers, but sometimes these composers merely signed off on what the VIA's own musicians had created. Such VIAs competed in the city Komsomol's annual spring music contests, the ones that earlier had hosted jazz bands.[48] By the early 1970s, according to Volodymyr Kit, nearly every factory or state enterprise had an amateur rock group, replacing the wind orchestras that had played jazz and light music.[49]

Two major VIAs, Oreol led by Oleksandr Balaban and Arnika, led by Viktor Morozov by the mid-1970s, epitomized not just rock music's entrance into the cultural mainstream but also its incorporation into Ukrainians' national culture. Oreol was affiliated with the regional philharmonic orchestra. Kit from Medykus began Arnika at the Lviv Regional Pharmacy Administration in the early 1970s when he started working there as a doctor. According to Kit, Morozov, along with Viktor Kanaiev, joined the group at the suggestion of the director of Moscow's Central Television Station, in charge of selecting groups for the all-Union talent show *Hello, We're Looking for Talent!* (*Allo, my ishchem talanty!*) At the height of their popularity in the 1970s, Oreol played at dances at the club Lvivhaz, and Arnika performed for dances at the Policemen's Club. Both were major dance clubs in central Lviv, and a rivalry of sorts developed between them and their respective clubs. While in Arnika, Morozov wrote songs for the group that combined rock and Ukrainian folk motifs. In its 1972 record, produced by the Soviet record firm Melodiia, Arnika included some electric guitar arrangements of folk songs by Ukrainians from the Lemko Region. The cover of its 1976 album, with band members posing in front of a thatched-roof village home in Lviv's outdoor historical museum, illustrates Arnika's Ukrainian folk attributes.[50]

Arnika acquired some notoriety in its early years for a supposedly controversial song it had won recognition for at the 1974 Moscow talent show broadcast on Central Television. Volodymyr Kit, one of Arnika's directors at the time, explained that the song "The Black Field" (*Chorna rillia*), a rock arrangement of a Ukrainian folk song, became a cause célèbre among local Party functionaries for trivial reasons. Lviv's obkom secretary, when asked by his personal secretary what he thought of Arnika's performance on television, commented that the song was "a little too sad." His secretary and others in the apparatus inflated his remarks into a political accusation, which at one point even alleged that the song was Banderite motivated. During a brief period when Arnika was not invited to perform at official concerts, obkom personnel debated among themselves if Arnika was appropriate for such venues. While some claimed that the folk song had a nationalist subtext, others, including the head of the Regional Administration of Culture, pointed out that official choirs sang it. After listening to the group perform, local Party and state officials allowed the band to perform at concerts again. The mother of one of the band's members, head of the Regional Pharmacy Administration, Vira Vasilieva, a high-ranking Party member with two Order of Lenin awards to her name, played a crucial role in defending Arnika from these political charges, and she told Kit what had happened to the group at the obkom.[51]

Arnika epitomized rock music's merging with folk themes, folk images, and mainstream Soviet record producers. It was part of the emerging Soviet variety music (or *estrada*) scene. Oreol was primarily a Russian-language band that produced its own songs—first in hard rock, then in fusion, disco, and then hard rock again—over the 1970s and 1980s. However, it, too, underwent a certain Ukrainianization. Its mandatory repertoire included popular Ukrainian songs by Bohdan Ianivskyi and Volodymyr Ivasiuk.[52] This tendency to adapt Ukrainian folk music to the rock rhythms of electric guitars and drums even surfaced in a VIA organized by African students at the Lviv State Medical Institute. Calling themselves the Lyons, the English approximation of Lviv, the "City of Lions," its members played rock adaptations of folk songs from the Carpathians, which greatly impressed one Komsomol newspaper correspondent in 1970. Its members wore Hutsul costumes, reinforcing the band's fusion of Western rock instruments, African voices, and Ukrainian folk music.[53]

As the 1970s music scene turned to disco, Komsomol organizations sponsored discos in Lviv and other cities. For Soviet leaders, disco encouraged more optimistic, politically neutral, and less sexually explicit music and dance.[54] Soviet discos played such Western hits as Boney M and ABBA alongside Soviet dance tunes, and some held cultural activities dealing with popular music and fashion. In 1980 Lviv was next to the republic's capital, Kyiv, in the number of discos functioning under Komsomol supervision (a total of thirty as opposed to thirty-three in Kyiv). Disco offered no room for live bands or for hard rock music. Thus one song by the Uncles referred to disco as "rotten" and strutting on "fashionable platform shoes." Local Komsomol leaders touted the Romantyk Palace of Youth, built in the Bohdan Khmelnytskyi Park of Culture and Recreation in 1978, as the flagship of such discos and as a "cultured" place for relaxation. Ironically, after 1991, it acquired the reputation of being one of Lviv's most crime-ridden nightclubs.[55]

Local composers for Lviv's *estrada* scene epitomized the impact of Western rock, pop, and disco music on mainstream Soviet music. Two Lviv composers, Volodymyr Ivasiuk in the 1970s and Ihor Bilozir in the 1980s, produced such music. Ivasiuk, originally from the Chernivtsi Region in Western Ukraine, came to Lviv in 1972 to study medicine and music. In the 1970s he produced popular hits known throughout the Soviet

Union, sometimes in collaboration with Lviv writers. Two of his songs, "The Red Rue" *(Chervona Ruta)* and "The Fountain" *(Vodohrai)*, written in Chernivtsi in 1970, earned him fame across the Soviet Union in television music shows, films, and all-Union song contests in 1970–72, performed by singers Nazariy Iaremchuk, Vasyl Zinkevych, and Sofiia Rotaru. Rotaru— Ukraine's equivalent of Cher or Diana Ross—went on to immortalize these and many more of Ivasiuk's songs on major record albums, the radio, and television in the Soviet Union, both in his lifetime and after.[56]

Ivasiuk's songs represented a synthesis of folk rhythms and legends from the Carpathian Mountains and elements of jazz, fusion, rock, and country music reminiscent of Richard Harris's "MacArthur Park" (1968) or the jazz-rock fusion of the early Chicago. Ivasiuk aspired to become a professional composer and not the producer of "light hits." However, Beatles and American country and rock music significantly influenced him. The jacket cover of Taras Unhurian's memoir of Ivasiuk shows Ivasiuk from the 1960s playing his guitar and singing, his hairstyle and dress resembling those of one of the Beatles in the mid-1960s. One oral history respondent, "S. P.," noted that he had lent Ivasiuk a reel-to-reel tape of Crosby, Stills, and Nash, on the eve of Ivasiuk's fatal disappearance in 1979.[57]

Ihor Bilozir founded a VIA called Rhythms of the Carpathians *(Rytmy Karpat)* (1977–79), under the Lviv Bus Factory, and later the Bonfire *(Vatra)* in 1979, under Lviv's philharmonic orchestra. Republic and local press materials from the time characterized Bilozir's music as that which drew upon folk themes and rhythms with the use of electric guitars and electric synthesizers. Bilozir's music did not become as legendary as Ivasiuk's. Press materials nonetheless indicate the group's success. His band gained notoriety across the Soviet Union in 1981 when it performed for Baikal-Amur Railway construction workers and for the city of Alma-Ata. Another sign of success was the support the band had from local Party officials. In 1983, Lviv's city Komsomol committee secretary contrasted Magnetic Band's scandalous behavior with the Bonfire's successful Soviet Peace Fund concert.[58] Aleksandra Matyukhina recalls that the Bonfire acquired such a solid reputation that it performed at "closed parties" for district and regional functionaries at the disco club Romantyk.[59]

Not all young people cared for Ivasiuk or Bilozir. Ilya Lemko of the Uncles said rock enthusiasts like him viewed Ivasiuk as a "Ukrainian Iosyp Kobzon," referring to the Russian Soviet pop artist of the 1960s and 1970s known for his Frank Sinatra–style romances and songs glorifying the Komsomol, heroes from World War II, and other schmaltzy themes.[60] However, such pop music attracted people who otherwise had no interest in rock. One oral interview respondent observed that Western Ukrainian villagers he visited in the 1970s were avid listeners of Ivasiuk.[61] Ivasiuk's "The Red Rue" had become greatly popular in Lviv as early as 1971. A local newspaper that year happened to mention one drunken vocational school student, trying to crash an elegant ball at the city's opera theater, belting out the song's first lines before being hauled away by volunteer security guards.[62] For generations born after 1945, Ivasiuk's music (as performed by Nazariy Iaremchuk and others) became their music, alongside the "legendary Beatles" and the French pop singer Joe Dassin.[63]

Music by Ivasiuk and Bilozir united Lvivians born after World War II. Their music became popular dance music not just for ex-villagers, but for more urbanized Ukrainians.[64] Ivasiuk's music united generations. Mariia Kazimira, the resident of Kryvchytsia who remembered no rock music in their town, said both she and her children were ardent fans of Ivasiuk's music in the 1970s.[65] Ivasiuk has rightly been called the Ukrainian equivalent of Russian bard singer Vladimir Vysotsky, whose lyrics attracted both young and old throughout the Soviet Union.[66]

One ethnic Russian argued that rock music represented something that was true, not the lies on red propaganda banners common in late Soviet socialist society. Oleksandr Balaban saw rock music bringing down the Soviet Union through its message of individual freedom.[67] Such connections between rock music and individual freedom ring clear in other Soviet accounts.[68] What made Lviv different was that national and regional elements mattered. Carpathian Mountain folk scenes and jazz and rock rhythms led to music that won over more young Lvivians than perhaps Jimi Hendrix's guitar riffs. The public sphere's accommodation of rock and pop music demonstrated that the state could not ignore young people's desire for individual and collective freedom. Soccer and the movies posed similar challenges.

Soccer, Films, and Youth Identities

To be young in Lviv was about more than rock-and-roll. Under late socialism, cheering for the home soccer team and finding adventure in movies also mattered to young Lvivians. Increasing amounts of free time for white-collar and blue-collar workers made such forms of leisure more accessible.[69] In this emerging society of leisure, soccer and the movies offered young people ways of defining themselves as individuals and as part of a larger community.

Foreign movies influenced young Lvivians already in the years after World War II. In 1951 the "trophy" film *Tarzan,* captured from the Germans during the war, drew huge crowds of Lvivians. According to historian Richard Stites, its portrayal of man in the wild, free of society, intrigued a generation growing up in the last years of Stalin's rule. As one of many Lviv viewers, former student Mykola Krykun, said, the film was unusual and striking exactly in this way. Young men imitated Tarzan's call in the wild not just in Russia's big cities but also in Galician small towns, as Volodymyr Sereda recalled when he talked about his youth in the Ternopil Region.[70]

In the early 1960s, the American western *The Magnificent Seven* had a similar impact. Its image of free, individualistic American cowboys roughing it in the Wild West inspired young people to emulate them. After a tape-recorded interview about hippies, former biker Ihor Ventselovskyi (nick-named "Penzel" [Paint Brush] for his long beard) revealed the power this movie had on him as a child. As we sat in his tiny, run-down apartment in Lviv and listened to a Polish-produced Johnny Cash album from Soviet times and then a Czechoslovak country group, Penzel said that when he first saw *The Magnificent Seven* at the age of 12, in 1961, the Wild West and its cowboys utterly captivated him. He went on to watch it thirty-four times. Despite being a good Pioneer with his red tie properly donned, he increasingly turned to the life of the cowboys. He later joined motorbike adventures. After pointing out his stovepipe hat, Western leather boots, and bandanna, Penzel proudly concluded that for himself, "Westerns plus hippies plus bikers equals freedom!"[71]

Penzel thus incorporated a variety of symbols to shock the values and behavior of the wider public around him, similar to the strategies of punks mentioned by Dick Hebdige.[72] Others, too, incorporated the attributes of American cowboys to be different from everyone else, in ways that troubled local law enforcement agencies. Future concert violinist Iurii Bashmet, another early Lviv fan of *The Magnificent Seven,* said he and other children, enthralled by the knives carried around in the movie, did everything they could to get thin, long-bladed knives and show them off. These weapons, inspired by *The Magnificent Seven,* had become such a problem that the commander of the local people's militia presented a number of such knives and other weapons to Communists assembled at the city's Polytechnic Institute in 1963. He displayed this cache of weapons, including a sword stolen from the city historical museum, to make the point that such things needed to show up "only in Hollywood movies and not among us."[73]

For intellectual circles, the movies offered a perspective on art that did not fit in neatly with the simple, optimistic, and edifying message that mainstream Soviet films or Hollywood films carried. Lviv film clubs featured such films, including those by Polish director Andrzej Wajda, Italian directors Federico Fellini and Michelangelo Antonini, and Soviet director Andrei Tarkovsky. They were films connected with issues of existentialism and surrealism popular elsewhere among cinematographers in the postwar world. As in other Soviet cities like Thaw-era Riga, such clubs brought together intellectuals from a variety of backgrounds and generations, encouraging relatively more open discussions about culture and politics than what was allowed elsewhere in the public sphere.[74] In 1967–68, one such Lviv film club, located in an old theater building, attracted as many as 300 people before Party leaders and the KGB distrusted the conversations going on there. According to oral interviews and online press materials, a similar club surfaced at the end of the 1970s in the Building of Culture of Communication Workers on Khasanska Street, commonly known as "the cinema on Khasanska."[75]

Public reception of foreign films and Soviet ones posed challenges to local and republic functionaries. A republic Central Committee commission investigating ideological work in the Lviv Region in August 1965 thus noted as a shortcoming the fact that foreign films were enjoying much wider audiences in Lviv than some leading Soviet pictures.[76] Films provoked condemnation from audiences themselves, such as pensioners who wrote complaints to local authorities about films having a negative influence on young people's behavior.[77] Soviet films, too, became identified with such negative influences. In 1966, a Lviv State University instructor in Marxism-Leninism, speaking to other university Party members, blamed two Soviet films that had premiered that year, Sergei Alekseev's *Conscience* (1965) and Leon Saakov's *Three Times a Year* (1965), for helping pit younger generations against the old.[78]

While movies redefined young Lvivians as individuals, the city's soccer team, Karpaty (Carpathians), realized collective freedom for young people and older fans. The team, named for the Carpathian Mountains, was composed almost completely of Western Ukrainian players and coaches. It attracted a cult following in Lviv in its peak years, the late 1960s and the late 1970s. Huge, boisterous crowds greeted the team at its home games at

Friendship Stadium (today's Ukraine Stadium). Young fans blew whistles, rattled small wooden rattlers, and, braving police retaliation, even threw bottles of homemade explosives onto the field. Sector Thirteen, filled mostly with students from city trade schools who had recently come from Western Ukrainian villages, occupied center stage in such ruckuses, putting on a real show for everyone else in the late 1970s. After major victories against Moscow teams and other giants, huge, spontaneous demonstrations of between 10,000 and 20,000 people paraded from the stadium all the way to the central boulevard of Lviv, Lenin Avenue (today's Freedom Avenue). These demonstrations became unofficial alternatives to May Day and October Revolution processions. By the mid-1970s, they were replete with alternative flags, made at home, in the team's colors of green and white.[79] In the center of the city, across from a square on Lenin Avenue nicknamed the Flower Bed (site of the city's Shevchenko monument since 1992), Karpaty fans young and old got together to talk soccer, earning the site the nickname the Soccer Exchange.

As in other Soviet cities, soccer became a substitute for political discourse. Robert Edelman argues that such spectator sports helped diffuse grievances against the state that people privately shared. Like Lviv's Soccer Exchange, the Liars' Market in downtown Kharkiv, a place for conversations about soccer, almost immediately transformed itself into a forum for open-air political debates during Perestroika.[80] Karpaty soccer fans, however, engaged in their own sort of identity politics by rallying around Lviv, Western Ukraine, and to some extent Ukraine itself as they rooted for their team against opponents from Moscow and other Soviet cities. The public use of flags other than the Soviet flag, as well as demonstrating out of loyalty for the home team rather than on the orders of one's boss, teacher, or Komsomol leader (as was the case with all state demonstrations), represented daily life choices taken independent of the state if not against the state.

As with the teenagers who tried to float blue-and-yellow Ukrainian nationalist flags on balloons for May Day, young people took advantage of major soccer victories to flirt with nationalist themes. Around 1969, when Karpaty won the USSR national title in Moscow without even being an upper-division team, young fans in these victory processions through downtown Lviv yelled "Freedom to Ukraine!" and other political slogans on behalf of Ukrainians.[81] The team's 1969 all-Union victory sent passions soaring so high in Lviv that a crowd of fans supposedly picked up a police car (which they nicknamed the "lunar probe" in honor of America's recent moon landing) and hauled it to the Flower Bed, next to fans' traditional gathering spot, the Soccer Exchange. In Moscow itself, young fans called on the leaders of the 2,000 or so parading along the Moscow River to take their gigantic three-by-four-meter poster and head right through Red Square for an experience they would remember the rest of their lives. As Ilya Lemko, one of the young fans there, recalls, "more mature" heads intervened: "Guys! The *moskali*'ll surely lock us up!" With "common sense" prevailing, the joyful crowd instead went along the left side of the Kremlin wall, chanting slogans and continuing along the river.[82]

Provocative calls for Ukraine to be free, suggestions to show off Lviv's victory to Red Square, references to Soviet leaders as the *moskali*, the daring theft of a police vehicle in Lviv, and the very nicknaming of this vehicle in honor of a feat accomplished by the Soviet Union's archrival (man's landing on the moon) suggest that soccer demonstrations by Lvivians became acts of resistance, "weapons of the weak," where people momentarily subverted symbols of authority and proclaimed the unmentionable without punishment.[83] Such acts of resistance asserted a local identity, be it Lvivian, Galician, or Western Ukrainian. In the late 1970s, when Karpaty again scored victories over major Soviet rivals, one such demonstration in downtown Lviv included the slogan "Long live the team of Western Ukraine!" in its repertoire.[84]

An anecdote, dated from the late 1970s, suggests that rooting for Karpaty was part of a city-wide identity, one transcending ethnic and language groups. In it, a crowd of teenage, Russian-speaking soccer fanatics, armed with chains, gets ready to go to a major soccer match between Karpaty and Moscow's Lokomotiv. They gather at a major hangout in the new working-class outskirts of Lviv, a place called the Cross, the site of a former cemetery, on today's Volodymyr the Great Street (formerly Artema Street). Noticing the crowd assembling, a boy their age shouts out from a neighboring apartment window, "Where are you going?" Someone in the crowd of soccer hooligans responds, in Russian, "We're going to beat up the *moskali!*" The boy from the apartment window, changing from Ukrainian to Russian, shouts back in amazement, "But *you're* a *moskal'!*" One of the boys in the crowd then joyfully retorts in Russian, "I'm a *moskal'*, but I'm a Lviv *moskal'*, and we're going to beat up the Moscow ones!"[85] Street toughs' rallying behind the home team against the *moskali*, even if they spoke the same language as the *moskali*, points to a larger collective identity. The mass culture of soccer thus brought together ethnic Russians, Jews, Russian-speaking

Ukrainians, and Ukrainian-speaking Ukrainians. They resisted Moscow, the imperial metropole, but they also were having a very good time.

Local law enforcement frowned upon soccer demonstrations. In the late 1970s, rows of soldiers broke up one near the Mickiewicz Monument on Lenin Avenue. Komsomol patrols did the same after later games. Law enforcement organs prevented large crowds from parading outside the stadium.[86] Local functionaries also looked down on gatherings at the Soccer Exchange. One city Party secretary complained to Lviv State University Communists in 1968 about the "loafers" spending time there "from morning to evening," noting with disapproval the presence of "respectable people," "even full professors and associate professors," there.[87] Nonetheless, they tolerated the city's cult of soccer fans; at worst, they considered them a disturbance of the peace. Otherwise, the stunts pulled by fans in Section Thirteen continued in Friendship Stadium. Fans elated with victories paraded around town with their green-and-white flags and chanted slogans supporting the team. It was a great thrill, almost like a Hollywood movie.

Hippies and the Countercultures of the Streets

Rock-and-roll of the late 1960s heralded the arrival of attributes of American hippies, bikers, and later punks to Lviv. Regarding hippies, city Komsomol and Party documents indicated two waves of this American counterculture, one at the beginning of the 1970s, the other toward the decade's end. A February 1971 Lviv gorkom report referred to a "group of young people that called itself 'hippies.'"[88] These young people congregated at a number of places in the center of Lviv, including the abandoned memorial to Polish soldiers killed defending Lviv in the Polish-Ukrainian War of 1918–19, where they decorated the remaining walls with graffiti art (Figure 8.1). A decade later, in October 1982, a city Komsomol report on problems with Lviv punks retrospectively referred to another wave of hippies who gathered around the rock group the Uncles from 1976 to 1979. The beginning of this new wave was probably related to a major "session" *(seishn)* of hippies from around the Soviet Union who gathered to hear the Uncles play live music, mentioned in a letter to the Yugoslav rock magazine *Jukebox (Dzuboks)* some years later. The city Komsomol report referred to such people as "those young people who in their external appearance and views slavishly tried to imitate followers of the hippy movement in a number of western capitalist countries."[89] These hippies and their friends gathered at the garden of an abandoned

Figure 8.1. Hippies in Lychakiv Cemetery, August–September 1970. Used with permission from the collection of Volodymyr Surmach, Warsaw.

Order of Barefoot Carmelites monastery—nicknamed the Holy Garden—less than a block away from the Lviv obkom.

While Party and Komsomol officials claimed to know who was a hippie, such a category escaped facile definition. Most likely, it was a derisive term originally imposed by others on young people for their appearance, as happened with late socialist Polish hippies.[90] The classic look of hippies was a 1980 photo of some who used to visit the Holy Garden (Figure 8.2). Men and women are wearing long hair in headbands, long necklaces, and bell-bottom jeans, jean jackets, beat-up shoes and tennis shoes, and stylish hats suggesting images from the late 1960s in San Francisco. On the other hand, one of those in the picture, wearing a jean jacket, said in an interview that he did not consider himself a hippie. He simply went to the Holy Garden to listen to rock music and share his interests in it with others. One of his Holy Garden friends said that he merely "acted like a hippie" (*hipii-uvav* in Ukrainian) for a while. Even Ilya Lemko, leader of the Uncles, the heart of this new hippie movement, said that he and other members of the Uncles were not hippies and that some of them were far from being hippies at all. By the end of the 1970s, neighborhood toughs with criminal records ("hooligans") took on hippies' long hair, further blurring the boundaries of who was a hippie.[91]

Figure 8.2. Lviv hippies from the Holy Garden, 1980 (Oleh Olisevych far left; Ihor Zborovskyi seated lower right). Photo provided by Oleh (Alik) Olisevych, Lviv, from the author's collection.

Besides this amorphous definition of who was a hippie, those called hippies underwent an evolution over the 1970s. Party and Komsomol reports indicated that the hippies who gathered at the Lychakiv Cemetery took on the ideals of peace and nonviolence, helping people in need, living together without set rules, and respecting the views of one another. Such teachings surfaced in their Lychakiv Cemetery graffiti, such as the slogans "Make love, not war!" "Free love!" and the Peace sign. An oral interview with one such hippie revealed that they kept a notebook of sayings attributed to hippies in the capitalist West.[92] As in other Soviet cities in the early 1970s, like Moscow in July 1971, these hippie gatherings quickly came to an end as a result of KGB provocations.[93] A young man who had organized a band of aspiring robbers and gotten into trouble with the law in 1967, Viacheslav Ieresko, met these young people and tried to set up an organization with its own dues, statute, elected officers, and anthem. A partially paralyzed invalid who acquired the unfortunate nickname "Jointy" (Sharnir), Ieresko spoke at a "congress" of hippies in the resort town of Briukhovychi outside Lviv on 7 November 1970. He shocked his audience by appearing in a "fascist" uniform. Trying to agitate hippies with a fascist uniform on the official state anniversary of the October Revolution had all the signs of a setup. Not surprisingly, after Ieresko was arrested on 26 November for illegal possession of firearms, all these hippies who gathered at the Lychakiv Cemetery—at least twenty-one in all, based on a Lviv gorkom report—faced expulsion from the university or disciplinary actions at work.[94]

The Holy Garden hippies of the late 1970s were different. The 1982 city Komsomol report describing them mentioned that some of them were known to have discussed religion (namely, Christianity and Buddhism) and opposed violence.[95] The venue's name, Holy Garden, conveyed this interest in religion. One of its frequenters added a mystical ethos to the place. Oleksandr Chaika recalled that Serhiy Mardakov, nicknamed "Holy" (Sviatyi), was known for his power to predict things.[96] However, one song by the Uncles associated with the Holy Garden, "Bashkir Rock," with its references to "wine, soccer, and rock-and-roll," suggested group attributes hardly unique to hippies.[97] While they shared an interest in blues rock guitar artists like Jimi Hendrix, even planning a gathering, a "session" in his memory in 1977, their choice of music tended to be Deep Purple, Led Zeppelin, and other hard rock groups that gained popularity after the turbulent counterculture of the late 1960s. By contrast, the hippie graffiti art at Lychakiv Cemetery featured portraits of Jimi Hendrix and John Lennon and the names of such groups as Cream, the Mothers of Invention, and the Doors, those associated with this earlier era's sounds. Holy Garden hippies moreover confronted the disco age, an age made fun of in one Uncles song.[98] It was only after this hippie scene had faded away, at the beginning of the 1980s, that issues like war and peace, namely, the Soviet invasion of Afghanistan, became relevant.

While Lviv hippies were never a mass phenomenon, it would be naïve to dismiss them as a mere fashion statement expressed by an "upper middle class" in 1970s Soviet society.[99] If the Soviet "upper middle class" in the 1970s consisted of "Communist Party and police officials, engineers, lawyers, and college professors," there is a lack of strong evidence that the hippies who hung out at Lychakiv Cemetery in late 1970 belonged to this class. A Komsomol report on twenty-one such hippies mentions only six whose parents were engineers, lawyers, or university professors or administrators. Eight more had parents whose occupations were not from this "upper middle class," while one hippie was orphaned, one hippie's father was retired, and five hippies had no information on their parents' occupations. While four hippies had one or both parents who were Party members, none of the twenty-one had parents who were Party officials.[100] Dismissing hippies as a fashion misses the point about countercultures. Hippies and later countercultures were very amorphous and constantly changing, a moving kaleidoscope of sounds, images, and gestures that defied classification into a political movement of any sort. As with the birthplace of the hippie counterculture, San Francisco's Haight-Ashbury district, such countercultures were not so much about opposition to a system as negating that system, living in the moment instead of designing a political program for the future, distancing oneself from political causes rather than joining or opposing them.[101] Hippies, bikers, and later punks created social spaces of their own that mocked and shocked the wider world around them without necessarily opposing that world. These countercultures appropriated their own "hangout," or *tusovka* in Russian, allowing them to form intimate bonds of friendship and enjoy their free time.[102] Rather than characterize these countercultures as potential opposition groups to the state, it would be more worthwhile to talk about the disruptive power of the space they inhabited.[103] The variety of people who inhabited the Holy Garden—hippies, bikers, or just ordinary teens and university students, as emphasized by Oleksandr Kritskyi—underscored its role as alternative social space rather than as a set of behaviors and values explicitly called hippie.[104]

Such spaces like Lychakiv Cemetery and the Holy Garden thus were about young people who played with and made fun of the wider world around them. The hippies at Lychakiv Cemetery created a parody of Komsomol organizations rather than a real one. Their statute was a notebook of teachings attributed to hippies in the West, their anthem was the Beatles' song "Yellow Submarine," and the so-called membership dues were money collected for ice cream.[105] The Holy Garden became the parody of a republic, the "Republic of the Holy Garden," or the "Republic of Underdeveloped Bashkirs," with an anthem of about twenty verses, whose chorus sounded thus:

Crazy, crazy nut	*Kreizi, kreizi nat*
that's our garden,	*to ie nash sad,*
shit on the red clover!	*srav pes v chervoniy koniushyni!*[106]

Such lines were shocking in their profanity, yet Lviv's local humor was rich in parodies of official life. People called the public toilets near Mickiewicz Square the "Lenin Mausoleum." They subverted atheist campaigns with jokes. Iaroslava Sereda heard one such joke from her husband. During Easter, when an orchestra played on a square to entertain students who had to clean the nearby park during the holiday, people on their way to Saint George's Cathedral said that the orchestra was playing to welcome those going to the cathedral to church services.[107] In being named for the "Underdeveloped Bashkirs," the Holy Garden made fun of Soviet nationalities policies, which helped advance the cause of this Turkic nationality in European Russia.

As part of the *tusovka,* such spaces offered great meaning to these young people's lives. Even if they knew little about hippies, the symbols connected with them, such as rock music, gave at least a more interesting lifestyle than what most people their age had. An interview with Vasyl Babiy, one of these earlier hippies from Lychakiv Cemetery gatherings, suggested such sentiments. Komsomol records reveal that these Lychakiv Cemetery hippies could express their frustrations with the Komsomol and law enforcement organs openly with each other, thus helping them cope with daily life.[108] Furthermore, these spaces gave an alternative sense of masculinity to their inhabitants. Lemko recalled the Holy Garden to be marked by "openness and honesty in relations." Unlike the world of the school, the institute, or the factory, in such places formed by the street like the Holy Garden, the privileged sons of Communist Party chiefs mattered little. Instead, he wrote, "If you have pumped biceps, can play soccer or the guitar well—you are always number one." Lemko implies here that the Holy Garden was a more just world, but a more just world for men.[109]

On the other hand, these were spaces that were both a part of the system of late socialism as well as distanced from it. This position of being within the system invisibly can be seen in the hippie art at Lychakiv Cemetery (Figure 8.1). The Russian words on the cemetery wall, "May there always be sunshine!" *(Pust' vsegda budet solntse!)*, as well as the Russian word for peace *(mir)*, came not from hippie slogans in the West, but from Soviet popular culture. "Let There Always Be Sunshine," a song advocating world peace, was composed by Arkady Ostrovsky, with lyrics by Lev Oshanin. Beginning in 1962, Soviet media promoted this song as evidence that Soviet schoolchildren, like all children and adults in the world, desired peace, and that the Soviet state aimed to promote world peace. These hippies presumably learned the song when they were in the Pioneers in elementary school.[110] The space of the Lychakiv Cemetery hippies advocated the Soviet cause of peace, the ideals of these hippies' Pioneer childhood, while it also separated them from the model youth of the Komsomol.

Nonetheless, relations between these countercultures of the street and the state were much like those with underground networks of students and young intellectuals. Just as KGB investigators were determined to find an organization among the university students spreading leaflets in 1973, so did they view the hippies gathering at Lychakiv Cemetery in 1970 as belonging to one. After Ieresko's arrest, students from the city's Polytechnic Institute involved in these gatherings were expelled from the Komsomol and from the institute. Their friends faced similar disciplinary actions at work or in school, though some cooperated with Komsomol investigators or had family connections with the KGB. [111] Local state and Party officials ironically viewed hippies as linked to the bourgeoisie's plans in the West to dampen the revolutionary aspirations of young people throughout the world, as someone from the city's Prosecutor's Office told city Komsomol members in December 1971.[112]

Similar associations with reactionary forces appeared in September 1977, when security organs prevented a "session" dedicated to Jimi Hendrix's memory. State authorities regarded the session, planned for 18 September in the Holy Garden, as a protest against official celebration of "Golden September," 17 September, the anniversary of Western Ukraine's unification with Soviet Ukraine.[113] On the other hand, these accusations sounded strange even for security organ agents. An interview with "Leonid," then a student of the Polytechnic Institute, suggests this. Leonid had planned to go to this session. During a prophylactic discussion with him, the Polytechnic Institute's KGB representative, frustrated with his responses, cursed in Russian, "I don't want to know who your fucking Jimi Hendrix is, but I want to know what's his attitude toward the Soviet state!" (*Ia ne khochu znat' khto takoi vash iobanyi Dzhimi Khendriks, no ia khochu znat' kakoe on imeet otnoshenie k sovetskoi vlasti!*)[114]

While these hippies could be viewed as an international phenomenon, local law enforcement agencies treated hippies and Ukrainian nationalists equally. Hippie Oleh (Alik) Olisevych recalled a drunken police officer and a member of the People's Volunteer Militia calling him and his friend, Stas Kokinskyi, "hippies" and "nationalists" as they tried to haul them in for questioning in 1977. One of them even suspected Kokinskyi of having a ring with the name of Metropolitan Andrei Sheptytskyi, a "bourgeois nationalist" figure from Galician politics, carved on it. Ironically, Kokinskyi was originally from Odessa and spoke no Ukrainian, and the ring had the inscription of the Russian town of Kostroma, not Sheptytskyi, on it.[115] Greater emphasis on finding bourgeois nationalism across 1970s Soviet Ukraine thus intersected with crackdowns on other "bourgeois" phenomena like hippies.

Local police organs and their volunteers consequently saw nationalists, black market speculators, and hippies as undesirables that needed to be taken off the street. While Leonid was being interviewed at Lviv's Buddhist Center, another Buddhist, a former Komsomol law enforcement patrol member, spoke up. He said that he sincerely believed he was making the city a better place by conducting these raids against hippies. He changed his views toward such people only in the early 1980s, when he came to know some of them personally.[116] Such crackdowns thus bore a sporadic, knee-jerk character, suggesting a begrudging kind of tolerance. Moreover, within the local Komsomol apparatus, attitudes toward hippies were divided, at least by the end of the 1970s. Olisevych, while passing by the former headquarters of the city Komsomol law enforcement patrol on today's Freedom Avenue, near the Mariia Zankovetska Theater, pointed out that one leader in the city Komsomol tried to play the "good cop," trying to research and understand who hippies were, while another preferred rounding them up and punishing them.[117]

Komsomol and obkom leaders acted against Lviv's punk movement only in 1982, after punks had caused problems at concerts for Magnetic Band

and the Hungarian group Pyramid.[118] Protocols of city Komsomol meetings from the early 1980s, as well as a local Party report from 1982, revealed numerous problems with such Komsomol law enforcement patrols and the People's Volunteer Militia. They failed to make sure discos played appropriate music. Brigades were poorly prepared for raids. They wound up not taking part in patrols, or their members were drunk or failed to put on armbands showing they were on patrol. Brigade members speculated on the black market. Brigade recruits themselves had broken the law, and service on patrols was their way to repay past offenses. As late as December 1984, Komsomol law enforcement patrols could not stop gang fights involving as many as fifty to a hundred people. While officials by October 1984 bragged that the punk movement had been liquidated, there were voices suggesting a pyrrhic victory. As one Komsomol member noted in December 1984, Ukrainian television, the radio, and the press still featured the infamous Magnetic Band that had drawn punk fans two years before.[119]

Unable to prevent gang fights, patrols wound up getting caught in them. Hippies and their friends at the Holy Garden fought with such Komsomol patrols and the People's Volunteer Militia. One Komsomol patrol report for the month of September 1983 talks about a street gang of approximately thirty young men that, probably wanting revenge, attacked a city patrol. After dancing had ended at the Policemen's Club, an even larger group of about sixty young men lobbed bottles and rocks at a patrol outside.[120]

As they evolved in the 1970s, hippies grew closer to the values and behavior of Western Ukrainians. Hippies at first tended to be from Russian-speaking milieus, not from families native to Galicia. In late 1970, the hippies gathering at Lychakiv Cemetery wrote graffiti in Russian and English, not Ukrainian. Only two among them spoke Ukrainian. A gorkom report on their activities indicates that a majority of these earlier hippies were ethnic Ukrainians (eight), but also a high proportion of Russians (five), Jews (three), and Belarusians (one), while others' nationality was not indicated (four). The data were incomplete, as Volodymyr Surmach in an interview noticed that some hippies were left off the report's list because of family connections with the KGB. However, it did suggest that non-Ukrainians and Russian-speaking Ukrainians from Eastern Ukrainian families dominated this milieu. Only gradually did Ukrainian-speaking Ukrainians become a part of Lviv's hippie counterculture. By the late 1970s, for instance, a Galician Ukrainian historian's daughter had become a hippie, said a friend of her brother.[121]

Hippies of the Holy Garden had taken on the humor and slang of Galician Ukrainians as they mocked the public sphere. They used to greet one another with the Galician Ukrainian expletive *"Srav pes!"* which means literally "Let the dog shit!" or figuratively "Shit on!" The other person being greeted made a sign of "V" with his fingers and responded in Ukrainian with a phrase that sometimes made explicit references to the Communist Party (as the CPSU) or more subtle references to the regime, such as "the red clover" or "the barbed wire." Some of the verses in their "anthem," which was entirely in Ukrainian, used this expletive or other Galician Ukrainian slang.[122]

Prominent citizens of this republic, members of the amateur rock band the Uncles (*Vuyky* in Ukrainian), had named their band Vuyky as a sort of taunt toward Russian speakers who referred to local Ukrainians as *"vuyky,"* slang for "hicks" as well as "uncles" in Ukrainian. This band and its Ukrainian-language songs were not involved in open political protest. One rock musician who had heard their songs on a reel-to-reel tape referred to their performances as a "student party" poking fun at daily life. Yet this humor about Galician Ukrainians, as well as biting satire toward the Communist Party in Galician Ukrainian slang, suggested that members of Holy Garden used stereotypes about Galician Ukrainians, as well as their manners of speaking, to make themselves different from the rest of society.[123]

Their strategies of resistance had become, like Lviv itself, situated within the framework of the western borderlands. While they may have been making fun of Galician Ukrainians by adopting their slang, the Holy Garden's inhabitants nonetheless had adopted the Galician Ukrainian identity as a matter of self-mockery and an affront to the wider world around them, like Dick Hebdige's punks rebelling against the wider world through a variety of conflicting symbols. In addition, Russian-speaking hippies at Lychakiv Cemetery unwittingly took part in Lviv's Ukrainianization by helping trash a former monument to Poles who had tried to take Lviv away from Ukrainians. Negative stereotypes about Polish rule in Lviv fostered in the press and in the schools might have made their actions seem less reprehensible to themselves. Though part of a Russian-speaking young international, such countercultures as the hippies had thus become regional in orientation, if not nationalist.

When Pop Went Nationalist

Mass culture and countercultures bore elements of Ukrainian nationhood because Lviv itself, in its institutions and public sphere, had become Ukrainian, even "eternally" Ukrainian. Yet mass culture and countercultures showed that the language and culture of the empire, Russians' language and culture, affected Lviv significantly. Films tended to be in Russian, and foreign films were dubbed in Russian.[124] By the end of the 1970s, Russian rock and pop hits increasingly dominated Western Ukraine's airwaves. Underground, Vladimir Vysotsky became popular for youth born after World War II, including among Western Ukrainians.[125] Lviv's rock music culture was under heavy Russian influence by the mid-1980s. In 1986, Iuriy Hryhorian and Oleh Kalytovskyi ("Kalych") started an amateur art rock band, roughly translated as Damned Pleasure *(Sobachaia radost')*, that performed in Russian. In interviews, they explained that they performed in Russian because nearly all of Lviv's rock groups were playing in Russian then. Oles Starovoit, recalling his university years in the mid-1980s, mentioned that he took frequent trips to Leningrad to see new Russian bands performing at the Leningrad Rock Club. He thought at the time that Ukrainians would never be able to perform rock music like the kind he heard there, which provoked a gentle remark from his father, a Ukrainian philologist, not to become so infatuated with Russian rock music.[126] Others, namely, those hostile to Soviet rule, could see such treatment of Ukrainians as evidence that Lviv was still far from being truly Ukrainian.

Such grievances over perceived discrimination came to the surface after one morning in May 1979, when the dead body of Lviv's most beloved pop figure, composer Volodymyr Ivasiuk, was found in the woods of nearby Briukhovychi, the site of Ieresko's hippie "congress" almost nine years earlier. Ivasiuk had been missing for nearly a month. While officially his death was ruled a suicide, many were convinced that someone else, notably the KGB, had killed him. One fellow musician described Ivasiuk having a mental breakdown at a concert in Romantyk.[127] However, a recent newspaper account interviewing Ivasiuk's close friends suggests that he had been murdered. It was a homicide by friends of Ivasiuk's girlfriend, who had gotten into an argument with him while at the restaurant Kolyba in Briukhovychi. To cover up the crime, they staged a scene where it looked as if Ivasiuk had hung himself in the woods. The culprits probably had friends in the KGB who protected them and helped turn the case into a suicide.[128] Though many questions still remain about how Ivasiuk died, the impact of his death was profound. The circumstances were hushed up, and suspicions of foul play grew. Over ten thousand people showed up for the funeral, mostly from Lviv but also from other Ukrainian cities (Figure 8.3). Local writers who had collaborated with Ivasiuk

Figure 8.3. Mourning for Ukrainian pop: the burial of Volodymyr Ivasiuk, Lychakiv Cemetery, Lviv, 22 May 1979, from Liubomyr Krysa, *Fotoal'bom "Vernys' iz spohadiv . . ."* (Lviv: Ukrpol, 2008). Used with permission of Liubomyr Krysa and Halyna Ivasiuk.

presented poems and eulogies strongly hinting that Ivasiuk had been stolen from Ukrainians.[129]

According to those present at the funeral, like Andriy and Tetiana Vorobkevych, as well as literary scholar Mykola Ilnytskyi, Ivasiuk's funeral at the Lychakiv Cemetery was a silent protest, where people had doubts about Ivasiuk's suicide. Among those present was Lviv poet Roman Kudlyk, who read a poem that equated Ivasiuk's death with a great loss for Ukraine.[130] After the burial, Ivasiuk's grave became a favorite place for laying flowers and homemade poems. Ihor Dobko, who was finishing the tenth grade in school at the time, recalls that this trend of laying flowers and writing allegedly "anti-Soviet" poems to Ivasiuk continued all the way until his second year at the Polytechnic Institute (1980–81), when the leader of his academic group advised classmates not to go to Ivasiuk's grave.[131] But at the end of May 1979, the situation was relatively calm.

The specter of nationalism arose later, throwing Party leaders in Lviv and Kyiv into a momentary state of alarm. A father and son, Petro and Vasyl Sichko, on the Greek Catholic and Orthodox holiday of Trinity Sunday, 12 June 1979, organized a public requiem at the gravesite. The father had been in the postwar national underground, setting up a conspiratorial network at Lviv State University before his arrest. The son had been expelled from Kyiv University in 1978 over alleged nationalist activities. The Sichkos put anti-Soviet writings on Ivasiuk's grave and read aloud some poems they had composed in his memory. Both Sichkos directly accused the Soviet regime of having killed Ivasiuk. The meeting ended with "Glory to Ukraine!" *(Slava Ukraini!)* a slogan of greeting and farewell used by the OUN and later the UPA. Among those present at what the local Komsomol newspaper described as a wild "nationalist orgy" *(shabash)* was the widow of the UPA's late commander, Roman Shukhevych. Shukhevych had been killed by Soviet forces in 1950.[132]

Following this scandal, in which both Sichkos were given prison sentences, local authorities, in consultation with Kyiv, cracked down on alleged nationalist activity among Ivasiuk's mourners. The local Komsomol newspaper wrote an article in July 1979 condemning the Sichkos and others who were trying to use Ivasiuk's memory for their "dirty" deeds. Rostyslav Bratun, head of the Writers' Union and one of the main orators at Ivasiuk's funeral, was denied a second term as head of the union at the end of 1979. One obkom secretary accused Bratun of "trying to add grandiosity to the funeral" and "attract as much of the public as possible" to it. Unknown persons, probably connected with the KGB or local Party officials, set on fire flowers and wreaths placed on Ivasiuk's grave. At Lviv's television studio, they destroyed the original of a film musical based on his music. For years, family members could not get permission to erect a headstone for his final resting place. At the beginning of the school year that followed Ivasiuk's death, a student was expelled from the Komsomol and the university because he had visited Ivasiuk's grave.[133]

This protest and local officials' knee-jerk response show that nationalism had taken over pop culture in Lviv. Nationhood, combined with pop, could rally the masses against the Soviet state. Mass culture, as well as the counterculture, took part in the Soviet Union's disintegration at the end of the 1980s. Hippie Alik Olisevych initiated the Lviv branch of a Moscow human rights group called Trust, with ties to both Soviet and Polish human rights groups. Another hippie, Volodymyr Surmach, designed for the semilegal journal *The Lectern (Kafedra)* that dissidents and establishment intellectuals began publishing in 1988.[134]

In the sphere of rock music, the forces of pop, rock, and nationalism made their greatest fusion at the end of the 1980s, thanks to a nascent political upheaval in Kyiv. A new republic-wide rock festival, the Red Rue

(Chervona Ruta), organized in memory of Ivasiuk in 1989, did much to articulate young people's demands for the Communist Party to step down and for Ukraine to become independent. The 1991 Red Rue festival, held on the eve of the fateful coup attempt in Moscow, symbolized these forces of rock, pop, and nationalism coalescing. Organized by the republic opposition party, Rukh, it was held in the eastern city of Zaporizhzhia to link the democratic opposition to Ukrainians' Cossack freedom-loving roots. In this 1991 festival, the Lviv rock group Snake Brothers created a sensation with the song "We're the Boys from Banderstadt." The group emerged from a circle of Russian-speaking friends (primarily ethnic Russians and Jews), some of whom used to hang out at the Armenian Street Café. According to one of the band's early leaders, it was originally a Russian-language group. It turned to making Ukrainian-language hits out of inspiration from jokes band members made about local Ukrainians with the aid of Galician Ukrainian slang. The rise of Ukrainian-language groups like Vopli Vidoplasova (V. V.) in Kyiv also inspired them to perform in Ukrainian. By the time of the first Red Rue festival in 1989, as noted by scholar Romana Bahry, the group's songwriter Serhiy Kuzminskyi ("Kuzia") had written a number of Ukrainian rock songs with deliberate themes of political protest, including a song that described recent police beatings of a peaceful demonstration in Lviv. In using the half-Ukrainian, half-German term "Banderstadt," the band's song greatly appealed to rock festival listeners. For such listeners, this word, a response to the marginalization of Western Ukrainians in Lviv as "Banderites" and "Nazi collaborators," explicitly rejected Soviet definitions of being Ukrainian. The song created a fury among the audience, with half a dozen people brandishing the red-and-black banners of the bourgeois nationalist OUN. Similar to the Uncles in the late 1970s, stereotypes about Lviv's Ukrainians were being used to rebel, this time calling for a nation free of Soviet constraints.[135] By 1991, being a Banderite was no longer feared or despised as backward. It was considered cool.

Conclusion

Banderite flags waving to a rock band's beat was an awesome sight. The year before, Lvivians had toppled their Lenin statue themselves. Now, at a nationwide rock concert in 1991, they could say to Ukrainians everywhere that it was time to leave the Soviet Union behind. In a few days, nervous Soviet leaders declared a state of emergency and removed Mikhail Gorbachev from power, fatally weakening the center. Their actions caused the western periphery, and then the rest of the Soviet Union, to break away. The "Boys from Banderstadt" had signaled the Soviet Union's coming end.

Lviv itself could not have brought the Soviet Union crashing down. Mikhail Gorbachev started the Soviet Union's collapse by allowing the end of coercion and censorship and by encouraging democratic forces from below to organize. Such actions brought about a mostly peaceful end to the Soviet experiment.[1] One journalist's life story indicated the degree to which events in Moscow, rather than those in Lviv, inspired him to help overthrow the Soviet system. Gorbachev's program of *glasnost* transformed his consciousness, shattering past beliefs in the Soviet system that had been encouraged by the "purely Communist" upbringing he had received at home from his Russian-speaking family. Revelations about the Soviet Union inspired him to organize a local chapter of the opposition movement, Rukh, at the city television station. He became friends with Viacheslav Chornovil, one of the leaders of Rukh who, elected head of the Lviv Regional Council in 1990, oversaw the dismantling of Lviv's Communist rule. The next year, this journalist campaigned for Chornovil as the latter ran for the Ukrainian presidency, coming in second place to Leonid

Kravchuk.[2] This journalist, and presumably many other Lvivians, lacked the "mental tools" needed to articulate an alternative to Soviet civilization until *glasnost* provided them.[3]

Another example of the impact of Moscow policies was one of the first mass-circulated non-Communist newspapers in Ukraine, *For a Free Ukraine* (*Za vil'nu Ukrainu*). The Lviv Regional Council under Chornovil's leadership sponsored this newspaper, which had replaced the pro-Communist newspaper, *Free Ukraine* (*Vil'na Ukraina*). Issues from its first two years of circulation (1990–91) were rife with articles exposing the evils of Communism, Soviet rule in Western Ukraine, and central government policies highly unfavorable to Ukraine. Readers from all over Ukraine, as well as Ukrainians in other Soviet republics, wrote letters or contributed pieces to the newspaper. The 23 November 1990 edition of *For a Free Ukraine* featured letters of support and news items from readers from such southern and eastern Ukrainian cities as Mariupol, Donetsk, and Kharkiv, as well as news about Ukrainians in such remote parts of the Soviet Union as Sakhalin Island. Lviv's own local government participated in radical democratic changes affecting the country. For instance, in an interview with *For a Free Ukraine*, Chornovil talked about his efforts cooperating with opposition politicians like Boris Yeltsin. In a little over a year, people like Yeltsin dismantled the Soviet Union.[4]

For a Free Ukraine demonstrated Lviv's role as a center for Ukrainian opposition to Soviet policies, not just in Western Ukraine, but in Eastern Ukraine and in other Soviet republics. In that sense, Lviv became an "island of freedom" for other Ukrainians. Yet this newspaper's revelations, often made by Lviv's establishment intellectuals, closely resembled those of Moscow counterparts. These counterparts, who had come of age in the Thaw, also drew inspiration from Gorbachev and acquired the mental tools needed to express alternatives to the Soviet system. They rapidly shed their old faith in Soviet socialism at the end of the 1980s and began attacking the Party-state directly, without much knowledge of free-market capitalist democracies.[5] Without Gorbachev's actions from above, neither Chornovil's political career nor *For a Free Ukraine* would have been possible.

The unmaking of the Soviet order in Lviv was intimately connected with events not just in Moscow but also in Kyiv. It was in Kyiv, not Lviv, that the opposition party Rukh emerged. It was in Kyiv that Lviv's non-Communist deputies joined forces that pushed for Ukraine's declaration of state sovereignty on 24 August 1991 and conducted a nationwide referendum on 1

December 1991 ratifying Ukraine's independence. By the time of Ukraine's independence, Lviv was very much a provincial city, playing only a secondary role to Kyiv in the country's political developments.

While Lviv became the scene of some of the first mass demonstrations against Communist policies in Soviet Ukraine, Lvivians played a very cautious role in political developments. Liubomyr Senyk, a literary scholar active in Lviv's cultural renaissance at the end of the 1980s, recalled a heated discussion he had with Roman Ivanychuk, the head of Lviv's Taras Shevchenko Language Society in 1989, about making Ukrainian the republic's state language. Ivanychuk said it was too early to raise the question. Another man active in Rukh, Mykhailo Kosiv, later a deputy in independent Ukraine's Supreme Council, voiced a similar opinion. While in private they may have expressed the desire to have Ukrainian become the state language, they were nervous about raising the issue in public.[6] Notwithstanding Chornovil's claim in 1990 that Lviv had become an "island of freedom" in a sea of totalitarianism, Lviv's intelligentsia had behaved very cautiously up to the very end, when multiparty elections gave Rukh activists a chance to take power in the city. Such caution by Lvivians could be characterized as highly defensive, desperately fighting for one's own space but refusing to take bolder moves in fear of incurring greater losses. One Ukrainian political analyst recently equated this political mentality to one of "those hiding out" (*skhronshchiki*), a reference to postwar underground nationalists who fought hard for their hideouts (*skhrony* in Ukrainian) yet waited for the appropriate moment to attack Soviet forces or representatives of Soviet power.[7]

Thus the analogy to Lviv as an island of freedom merits qualification. It was the cultural and political center of a postwar Soviet construction called Western Ukraine. Indeed, as Tarik Amar has illustrated, Western Ukraine as a regional identity was the outcome of Soviet policies. This region lacked the prewar elites, institutions, and practices that blunted the impact of Sovietization in the Baltics. Soviet Lviv did not have the resources of a republic capital like Riga, Tallinn, or Vilnius. However, this regional identity and the identity of Soviet Lviv were the result of a complex set of dialogues between state actors, intellectuals, and the local population, as well as between this region and other regions of the Soviet Union. The formation of a Soviet Western Ukrainian identity involved processes that differentiated the region from other parts of Ukraine. This process of differentiation involved not just accommodating local historical legacies or appreciating its more "Western" values and behavior. It involved reifying negative stereotypes of the region as more "anti-Soviet," "bourgeois," or "nationalist" than others. Ideological campaigns and Soviet media images of Banderites indirectly fostered assumptions that Lvivians were closet nationalists, unwilling to accept Soviet power. The reification of Lviv as a Banderite other thus facilitated the turn to that other as an alternative identity to that of being Soviet. For their part, Lvivians of the post-Stalin generations, especially the older ones from the Thaw era, had vivid memories of the violent imposition of Soviet rule from above. They and younger counterparts understood that Soviet power was an alien force that had to be accommodated. Despite their interest in Soviet institutions and ideals, they were aware of composer Stanislav Liudkevych's aphorism, "They liberated us, and there's nothing we can do about it."

The turn to an explicitly anti-Soviet identity, however, was a product of the Gorbachev era. Even if rock groups like the Snake Brothers were making fun of Galician Ukrainians in songs, their references to "Banderstadt" thus became very appealing ones to younger Lvivians. Deteriorating economic conditions, a failed war in Afghanistan, Glasnost-era revelations about the past, and the legalization of public demonstrations allowed Lviv's bourgeois nationalist otherness to become one of great pride. It became an important symbol rallying opposition to the Soviet state.

Recent scholarship on borderlands and frontier regions highlights interactions across such spaces as central to the formation of state policies and people's identities. Early modern conflicts between monarchs over the Pyrenees, for instance, helped articulate identities that ultimately became national ones, in this case French and Spanish national identities.[8] Borderland cities have been places where issues of national identity especially become salient, as noted by Daphne Berdahl.[9] Over the *longue durée* of history, contested frontier regions have played a crucial role in the rise and fall of empires as well as in the formation of modern nation-states. Alfred Rieber notes that in what he calls the "Pontic Steppe," the grasslands north of the Black Sea, confrontations between Eurasian land empires and such frontier peoples as the Cossacks affected the development of competing national narratives, in this case Polish, Ukrainian, and Russian. It led to certain myths about a clash of civilizations between that of a Roman Catholic West and an Orthodox East, one of many such clashes between civilizations that have marked post–Cold War international politics.[10]

While not part of the Eurasian steppe lands, Lviv became entangled in the struggle between empires and modern national movements in the lands of the Polish-Lithuanian Commonwealth, whose future was crucially shaped by what occurred in the Pontic Steppe lands. Timothy Snyder has eloquently linked the formation of modern Ukrainian, Belarusian, Lithuanian, and Polish nation-states to interactions across this former empire's space. Such interactions led to Galicia and its capital, Lemberg/Lwów/Lviv, becoming the site of confrontation, as well as cooperation, between Polish, Ukrainian, and Zionist national projects.[11] The breakup of empires in World War I and the unleashing of ethnic cleansing and genocide during World War II instilled a local sense of being Ukrainian imbued with cultural and ethnic overtones, constructed in opposition to a Polish other. Past experiences under Austrian and Polish rule produced cultural and intellectual movements geared toward the West rather than toward Russia. Interactions with the Poles—both cooperation and confrontation—created a Soviet West that was premised on both Poles' presence and absence.

Soviet postwar integration of Lviv, Galicia, and other borderland territories into a Soviet Western Ukraine enjoyed considerable success. Lviv became an "eternally Ukrainian" city in Soviet media and scholarship. Galicia's Ukrainian national movement became incorporated into a narrative where Western Ukrainians eagerly anticipated Soviet liberation in 1939. Despite being a more provincial member of the Soviet West, Lviv attracted Russians and other Soviets. It became a window to the West via Polish media and contacts with Poles. Western-inspired countercultures like Russian-speaking hippies mocked the public sphere yet imitated its use of Soviet symbols and practices and caused no direct harm to the state. This more Western Lviv attracted and influenced other Ukrainians. Former Lvivians and cultural products from Lviv brought "harmful" influences from the West and "bourgeois nationalism" beyond Western Ukraine to places like the closed city of Dnipropetrovsk.[12] For young Kyivans like writer Volodymyr Dibrova in the 1970s, Lviv was a fascinating place for hearing Ukrainian, and among friends in Kyiv, they liked to show off such Galician Ukrainian words as *filizhanka* instead of the standard Ukrainian *chashka* for a cup of coffee.[13] Lviv was interesting not just because it was anti-Soviet, more Ukrainian, or more Western, but because it was different from places like Dnipropetrovsk and Kyiv.

Admittedly some Kyivan dissidents in their interactions with Western Ukraine changed their political views. Dissident Leonid Pliushch's encounters with Lvivians and other Western Ukrainians convinced him that Ukraine's independence was the only solution to the problems Soviet rule presented.[14] While contributing to the formation of dissent in Ukraine, Lviv did not play the same role in the Soviet Union's evolution as the Baltics. In such turbulent years as 1956 and 1968, where uprisings in Poland and Hungary and reforms in Czechoslovakia were perceived as threatening Soviet socialism on the western borderlands, organized opposition to Soviet policies came from Tallinn, Tartu, and Vilnius, not Lviv.[15] For Russians, Estonia, not Western Ukraine, was the Soviet West. Tallinn thus became a refuge, a site of internal emigration, for Russian writers like Sergei Dovlatov at the end of the 1960s.[16] Later the Baltics had considerably more influence on the Soviet Union's demise. By the end of the Brezhnev era, Baltic dissent had affected Russian *samizdat* circles in places like Moscow, convincing Russian intellectuals there of the need for radical reform of the Soviet Union.[17]

Even Lviv's reputation as being virulently anti-Soviet helped neutralize Ukrainian dissent, thus benefiting republic Party and state leaders. In his 1965 *samvydav* text *Internationalism or Russification?* dissident Ivan Dziuba observed other Kyivans labeling Kyivan Sixtiers as Banderites. As he and other members of the Club of Artistic Youth in 1963, honoring poet Ivan Franko, took part in a torchlit procession to Kyiv's Franko monument, someone in the crowd of onlookers on Kyiv's main street, Khreshchatyk Avenue, called out in Russian, "Look at all those Banderites! So many of them!" Dziuba reported Russian-speaking Kyivans referring to fans of Volodymyr Denysenko's 1964 Ukrainian poetic film, *The Dream* (based on Taras Shevchenko's poem by the same name), as Banderites. One woman with alleged satisfaction told another that her son skipped classes because he could not stand Ukrainian classes taught by a teacher he called "the Banderite woman" *(banderovka).*[18] References to activists in Ukraine's cultural renaissance as Banderites, as well as calling Ukrainian speakers Banderites, served to marginalize and stigmatize Ukrainian Sixtiers in the republic's capital. The term helped reinforce barriers between Russian and Ukrainian speakers.

As the idealism of Khrushchev's Thaw faded and Soviet baby boomers became increasingly consumer oriented and cynical, young Lvivians, too, became complacent. While some of them flirted with national dissent, others turned to acts of leisure and collective fun that posed no real threat to the Soviet state. Soccer fans took great pride in beating the *moskali* at games, and they showed off the green and white colors of Karpaty, but they stood apart from political action. They became smitten with what Robert Edelman has called "serious fun."[19] Films and rock music provided an escape to an imaginary West that was an escape from political action. Hippies, bikers, and more ordinary Lvivians mocked the public sphere in ways reminiscent of James C. Scott's Malaysian peasants employing "weapons of the weak." Yet as Scott's own work argues, such acts of resistance by subalterns may mock existing power relations, but they do not fundamentally change them.[20] As Vladislav Zubok has pointed out, political jokes and irony helped deflect people from further reflection on the problems they faced in late Soviet socialism.[21]

Notwithstanding the limits to such resistance, resistance in the broad sense of the term acquired long-term significance for postwar Lviv. Stephen Kotkin has approached resistance as an act "without necessarily rejecting, by assessing, making tolerable, and, in some cases, even turning to one's advantage the situation one is confronted with."[22] Resistance in this sense involves cooperating with, making compromises with, Party and state institutions. The new Lvivians made important compromises with such institutions, not just in Stalinist times but during Khrushchev's Thaw and later during Brezhnev's "era of stagnation." Musicians, scholars, writers, and artists all made such compromises. In this sense they took part in forming a Soviet Western Ukrainian identity. However, the making of such compromises took place asymmetrically. Party and state leaders in Lviv, Kyiv, and Moscow ultimately decided which compromises were acceptable. In that way, Lviv's situation resembled a colonial situation, where outsiders primarily determined policy. The role of outsiders in local Party and state leadership positions reinforced such a colonial situation.[23]

Postwar Lviv's compromises themselves could easily be deconstructed and transformed into anti-Soviet, anticolonial narratives. Postwar representations of urban space asserted a Ukrainian identity, but also a Soviet one, where Russians played a progressive role. Preservation of the past was highly selective. Eighteenth-century Galician churches were being preserved while some Sich Riflemen's graves faced destruction. Schools were becoming Ukrainian, and speaking Ukrainian on the city's streets became the norm. However, in many positions of leadership, speaking Russian became expected. City signs were in Russian. Rock music was considered best played in Russian, if not in English. Lviv was Ukrainian, but not nearly enough, and Kyiv was far from it. As members of the republic's cultural establishment, former Lvivians like Dmytro Pavlychko thus contributed to the formation of an anti-Soviet, pro-independence discourse in Kyiv in the Gorbachev era.

The transformation of Lviv into a Soviet, yet also Banderite, Western other, epitomized the problems the newly acquired western borderlands posed for the Soviet Union. The Soviet empire's westward expansion subdued organized political resistance in places like Lviv. However, local memories, local grievances, and local strategies of accommodation and resistance made overcoming the bourgeois past impossible. On the eve of the Gorbachev era, the Banderite other, even if he or she was the figment of Party activists' imagination, was very much on people's minds. The constant persecution of alleged Banderites alienated even those who had been fanatically devoted to the Stalinist system since childhood. This could be seen with Volodymyr Osviychuk, a native of Eastern Ukraine. For this art critic, a World War II veteran who moved to Lviv shortly after the war's end, the Soviet state's collapse was neither so shocking nor so regrettable because of what he had seen the state do to Lvivians.[24]

Soviet engagement with the capitalist West further enhanced these borderlands' significance. Khrushchev's claims that the Soviet Union would soon catch up with and overtake America, claims made in the late 1950s, made the capitalist West into an explicit standard of measurement for Soviet socialism. As in other Soviet bloc states like Czechoslovakia, officials in the Soviet Union fostered cultural developments that helped deflect challenges posed by the capitalist West, as seen with the development of Soviet rock groups and discos.[25] However, Soviet citizens grew disillusioned with it over time, as Soviet socialism became increasingly unable to repeat the capitalist West's achievements.[26] For western borderland cities like Lviv, contacts with the capitalist West—letters, gifts, and visits from relatives abroad—gave people opportunities to make more direct comparisons with that other world. Lviv was not Tallinn or Vilnius when it came to contacts with Westerners. However, Ukrainians' Western diaspora provoked discussions about Ukrainians' status in the Soviet Union and what the capitalist West was really like. Greater contacts with Western mass culture—for instance, jazz and rock music via Poland—did not necessarily foster anti-Soviet moods. They stimulated an interest in an imaginary West that nourished assumptions about what Soviet socialism was not delivering. In closed cities away from the borderlands, like Dnipropetrovsk, these comparisons with a Western other fostered young people's indifference to Soviet socialism.[27] In Lviv, such indifference, combined with an unleashing of local grievances about Soviet oppression and an emergence of mental tools articulating a different political order, eliminated any support for the Soviet state by the beginning of the 1990s. The "Island of Freedom" was born.

Lviv's different understanding of nationhood has been a highly salient issue for contemporary Ukrainian politics. As Western Ukraine's cultural and political center, its residents' attitudes toward language, national identity, and the West have greatly contrasted with those of Donetsk.[28] Such divisions between West and East in Ukraine have led to regional political forces that have had great difficulty obtaining a nationwide following. Since 1991, they have produced political deadlock. Such deadlock, along with political parties' nepotism and cronyism, has alienated Ukrainian citizens. Hopes that the Orange Revolution of 2004 would end corruption and regional divisions have faded. However, such divisions could be viewed as a strength. They have created what one political scientist has called "pluralism by default," where the absence of such a national consensus has kept Ukraine from becoming as authoritarian as Russia or Belarus.[29] Lviv, along with such cities as Donetsk and Dnipropetrovsk, has thus contributed to the development of a more pluralistic, though flawed, post-Soviet political system.

Such regional differences, however, can be exaggerated. The Sovietization of Lviv and Western Ukraine produced practices and values shared by Ukrainians further east. Despite the different contexts in which Soviet power was established, a centrally planned economy, a one-party state, and coercion by the secret police created corrupt bureaucrats, abusive police organs, disaffection with politics, and hostility toward Moscow in both Lviv and Donetsk.[30] During late socialism, young Lvivians and their counterparts in Dnipropetrovsk created their own fantasies about the "golden West."[31] Despite its regional variants, Soviet civilization united the Eurasian land mass and transformed its inhabitants' values and behavior.[32]

Lvivians, no matter how much others perceived them as European or Western, could not escape this fact at the beginning of the twenty-first century. When Lviv intellectuals, frustrated with Ukrainian politics, discussed in the local press the possibility of Galicia separating from Ukraine, Lviv historian Iaroslav Hrytsak raised vehement objections. He reminded them that Galicia remained very much Soviet. Both Lviv and Donetsk had corrupt and inert local government bosses, leaders of political parties, university professors, and ordinary secretaries. Russian language and culture remained important for Lviv as well as for Donetsk. He concluded, "Galicia was and, unfortunately, remains a place on a continent that stretches from Vladivostok all the way to Brighton Beach and is called *Sovdepiia"* (a Russian term referring derisively to the world of Soviet civilization).[33] Perhaps this common heritage, along with political and cultural influences from Poland, will lead to a more united and democratic Ukraine, overcoming Soviet-made stereotypes about nationalist Lviv.[34]

The Soviet Union's collapse has not been kind to Lviv. The state and Party institutions that supported Lviv's Ukrainian intelligentsia collapsed. Despite the 2004 Orange Revolution, on the eve of Lviv's 750th anniversary in 2006, there was a lack of a coherent state policy to finance the restoration of architectural monuments, the publication of books and journals in Ukrainian, and the release of Ukrainian-language television shows, films, and records. On the eve of this anniversary, a veteran of the Lion Society active in the late 1980s independence movement wrote a passionate newspaper article entitled "The Lviv That No Longer Is." In it, he suggested that, in contrast with Soviet times, the forces of Russian and Western mass media and pop culture, as well as egoism, materialism, and careerism, threatened to annihilate this Ukrainian center of culture.[35] The battle for Ukrainian Lviv thus continues.

As with other accounts of the past, the history of Soviet Lviv was a story of lost possibilities and lost alternatives. It was one of the contingencies creating trends and lending some of those trends historical inevitability. On the other hand, as the story of Soviet Lviv demonstrates, the past is never really dead. It resurrects itself in new forms, despite the erasure of monuments or people. The simultaneous absence and presence of Poles in the city's postwar narrative is one such example. The fact that dead UPA soldiers lived on in family sing-alongs and legends is another. Such legends and songs involved not just the collective remembering of heroes, but also the collective forgetting of Polish and Ukrainian victims of UPA violence. On the other hand, there was a Ukraine to fight for. The dead soldier did not betray it like the school textbooks said. This story of heroism survived lies that the state told, while glossing over other victims of history. This story's survival, as well as its potential to be manipulated by others for political gain, reminds us of the need to prevent lies in our own time from becoming future truths.

APPENDIX

NOTES

ARCHIVES CONSULTED

ORAL INTERVIEWS

ACKNOWLEDGMENTS

INDEX

Appendix: Note on Interviews

Oral interviews involving about 140 subjects in all (most of whom have been cited) constitute a central element in this book. They were conducted in three phases: from 1998 to 2000, when I was conducting dissertation research in Lviv and Kyiv; from 2002 to 2004, when I taught at Lviv National University as a lecturer for the Civic Education Project; and in the summer of 2007, when I began research on another project on young people in the Soviet bloc. These were primarily tape-recorded interviews with writers, artists, composers, musicians, and scholars. Recommended through friends and acquaintances in Lviv and North America, these interviewees did not constitute a representative sample of Lviv's population. In the first phase of interviews, they tended to be dissidents or friends of dissidents, as I was primarily interested in understanding Lviv's emergence as a "nationalist" city early in the project. In the second and third phases of such oral interviews, I extended the range of respondents to scholars and former university students not connected at all with dissent in Lviv. There were interviews with Russians and Russian speakers with no higher education, some of whom became associated with Lviv's hippie movement.

In the third phase of interviews, I strove to include ethnic Russians, Russian speakers, and members of the post-Stalin generation born between 1950 and 1975. This partly reflected the interests of my second project, on youth subcultures in Soviet bloc cities. Interview contacts were partially generated through friends and acquaintances but also through a newspaper ad placed in the city's leading daily, *Lviv Newspaper (Lvivs'ka hazeta)*, in early June 2007. The advertisement asked Lvivians born between 1950 and

1975 for help in supplying copies of letters, manuscripts, oral testimony, or other materials that would help preserve memories of the Brezhnev "era of stagnation" (an advertisement largely modeled on the one conducted by Alexei Yurchak in the early 1990s in St. Petersburg). The advertisement was admittedly for a newspaper chiefly read by Lviv's intelligentsia, and the results were disappointing. Only three actual oral interviews materialized. Besides these interviews, one Lvivian gave responses to questions in written form, another supplied a lengthy memoir of literary life in Lviv, and yet another submitted a memoir of the period totaling less than five pages. The use of friends and acquaintances in fact proved more successful that summer. Another attempt at broadening sources of oral testimony was my visit to the Russian Cultural Center and the Jewish Cultural Center in Lviv. I designed a questionnaire for ethnic Russians and Russian speakers asking questions about their migration to Lviv after World War II and their impressions of the city, including relations with Ukrainians, their use of the Ukrainian language, and their interest in Ukrainian culture. While the Jewish Cultural Center did not submit responses to the questionnaire, three members of the Russian Cultural Center did. In addition, I conducted two interviews with activists of the Russian Cultural Center, one of them as a tape-recorded interview. At the suggestion of a friend, I managed to contact an ethnic Russian Lvivian, whose memoirs were posted on the Internet. A former employee of the Museum of Ukrainian Art, as well as a former member of the city district committee of the Communist Party, this respondent was especially valuable in providing an understanding of Galician Ukrainians from an outsider's perspective.

In addition to these oral interviews conducted in Ukraine, others took place in the United States. Some took place during initial dissertation research in 1998, while others took place during academic conferences as well as during my time as a Shklar fellow at the Harvard Ukrainian Research Institute in 2006. This book also utilizes oral interviews conducted by Lvivians, namely, Taras Budzinskyi and Viktor Susak, archived at the Institute of Historical Research at Lviv National University.

Over the three phases of oral history interviews, my interviewing techniques improved with time. While interviews between 1998 and 2000 tended to focus on a highly structured set of questions, involving dissent and nationalism in Lviv, later interviews engaged respondents' life stories more extensively, a result of insights I gained while teaching a course in oral history techniques at Lviv National University in 2003. These interviews, like other oral interviews, were known for elements of mythmaking and collective memory, as well as highly personal experiences of events that evade the written record.[1] Respondents tended to emphasize their connections to acts of political dissent or disagreement with the Soviet regime, while not admitting elements of cooperation or accommodation. These interviews were highly rich in elements of collective memory in that they relayed jokes and anecdotes circulated through Lviv. They were especially helpful in understanding those aspects of private life passed over in silence (or in ignorance) by Communist Party and Komsomol activists and leaders in former Party archive documents. Private conversations, personal impressions of political events affecting Ukraine, and the circumstances behind the generation of documents (such as denunciations to Party organs or Komsomol hearings on students' behavior) were especially valuable for this book. At times, some respondents were highly critical of their own pasts, admitting their own naïve actions or feelings in their student years and early youth, or even at early phases of their professional careers. To help further understand the context of such interviews, I have utilized, alongside Party and state archival sources, published memoirs and diaries, recently published secondary sources, and contemporary newspapers and Internet blogs.

To protect respondents' privacy, I made some of the interviews anonymous, I left out some people's last names, or I gave people pseudonyms. In one case, I had to give a respondent a pseudonym because he objected to the absence of his life story in the book. Aware of the fact that misunderstandings occur between interviewer and interviewee over what the interviewee experienced, I spent the second half of 2009 reviewing the text with nearly all the respondents cited.[2] In December 2009 and January 2010, this led to some follow-up interviews and a few new interviews with Lviv musicians and actors. In any case, recordings of their interviews, as well as copies of notes connected with these interviews, are in the process of being archived at the Harvard Ukrainian Research Institute and the Institute for Urban History of East Central Europe in Lviv. Some respondents requested that records of their interviews not be preserved in Ukraine.

In some cases, oral testimony came from informal conversations rather than oral interviews. While lecturing at Lviv National University from 2002 to 2004, I took notes of colleagues' recollections of the past made in the office or at other venues. I did the same with my tutor in Russian and Ukrainian, who sometimes reminisced about past events in her life and her family's life in Lviv, as well as what her friends and acquaintances remembered. Some informal conversations took place with relatives of oral interview respondents or with respondents themselves before or after interviews, or with my landlord and landlady, whom I became close friends with over the course of many years of research. In a few cases, I took notes from conversations with colleagues in Ukrainian studies who had interesting recollections of Soviet-era Lviv. Because such notes were taken without the person's express consent, copies of these materials are in the process of being archived solely at the Harvard Ukrainian Research Institute.

Notes

Introduction

1. "S'ohodnishniy L'viv ochyma pol's'koho turysta," *Svoboda* (Jersey City, NJ), 12 March 1976, 1, 3.

2. Yaroslav Hrytsak and Victor Susak, "Constructing a National City: The Case of Lviv," in John J. Czaplicka and Blair A. Ruble, eds., *Composing Urban History and the Constitution of Civic Identities* (Washington, DC: Woodrow Wilson Center Press, 2003), 151.

3. Padraic Kenney, *A Carnival of Revolution: Central Europe 1989* (Princeton: Princeton University Press, 2002), 294.

4. Taras Kuzio and Andrew Wilson, *Ukraine: Perestroika to Independence* (Edmonton: Canadian Institute of Ukrainian Studies Press, 1994), 127, cited in Hrytsak and Susak, "Constructing a National City," 151.

5. Kenney, *Carnival of Revolution*, 294.

6. Bohdan Krawchenko, *Social Change and National Consciousness in Twentieth-Century Ukraine* (Houndmills, UK: Macmillan, 1985), 251.

7. Kenney, *Carnival of Revolution*, 229–32, 273.

8. Roman Ivanychuk, *Blahoslovy, dushe moia, Hospoda . . . Shchodenny-kovi zapysy, spohady i rozdumy* (Lviv: Prosvita, 1993), 123; Derzhavnyi Arkhiv L'vivs'koi Oblasti (hereafter DALO), P-3/9/225/57–63, in Iuriy Slyvka et al., eds., *Kul'turne zhyttia v Ukraini: Zakhidni zemli,* vol. 2, *1953–1966* (Lviv: Instytut Ukrainoznavstva imeni Ivana Kryp'iakevycha, Natsional'na Akademiia Nauk Ukrainy, 1995), 691.

9. Viacheslav Chornovil, *The Chornovil Papers* (New York: McGraw-Hill, 1968).

10. Stephen Kotkin, "Mongol Commonwealth? Exchange and Governance across the Post-Mongol Space," *Kritika: Explorations in Russian and Eurasian History* 8 (Summer 2007): 487–531, especially 523–25, 528–31.

11. Francine Hirsch, *Empire of Nations: Ethnographic Knowledge and the Making of the Soviet Union* (Ithaca: Cornell University Press, 2005), 1–4.

12. Ibid.; Terry Martin, *The Affirmative Action Empire: Nations and Nationalism in the Soviet Union, 1923–1939* (Ithaca: Cornell University Press, 2001); Yuri Slezkine, "The USSR as a Communal Apartment, or How a Socialist State Promoted Ethnic Particularism," *Slavic Review* 53 (Summer 1994): 414–52; Ronald Grigor Suny, *The Revenge of the Past: Nationalism, Revolution and the Collapse of the Soviet Union* (Stanford: Stanford University Press, 1993).

13. Adrienne Lynn Edgar, *Tribal Nation: The Making of Soviet Turkmenistan* (Princeton: Princeton University Press, 2004).

14. Shoshana Keller, *To Moscow, Not Mecca: The Soviet Campaign against Islam in Central Asia, 1917–1941* (Westport, CT: Praeger, 2001); Paula Michaels, *Curative Powers: Medicine and Empire in Stalin's Central Asia* (Pittsburgh: University of Pittsburgh Press, 2003); Douglas Northrup, *Veiled Empire: Gender and Power in Stalinist Central Asia* (Ithaca: Cornell University Press, 2004).

15. Matthew J. Payne, *Stalin's Railroad: Turksib and the Building of Socialism* (Pittsburgh: University of Pittsburgh Press, 2001).

16. Roman Szporluk, ed., *The Influence of East Europe and the Soviet West on the USSR* (New York: Praeger, 1975).

17. Roman Szporluk, "The Soviet West—or Far Eastern Europe?" in Szporluk, *Russia, Ukraine, and the Breakup of the Soviet Union* (Stanford: Hoover Institution Press, 2000), 272–73.

18. Roman Szporluk, "The Strange Politics of Lviv: An Essay in Search of an Explanation," in Szporluk, *Russia, Ukraine, and the Breakup of the Soviet Union* (Stanford: Hoover Institution Press, 2000), 299–314.

19. Szporluk, "Soviet West," 267–68.

20. Jörg Baberowski, *Der Feind ist überall: Stalinismus im Kaukasus* (Munich: Deutsche Verlags-Anstalt, 2003).

21. Tarik Youssef Cyril Amar, "The Making of Soviet Lviv, 1939–1953" (PhD dissertation, Princeton University, 2006), 16, 497, 786.

22. Olaf Mertelsmann, ed., *The Sovietization of the Baltic States, 1940–1956* (Tartu: Kleio, 2003), 10; John Connelly, *Captive University: The Sovietization of East German, Czech, and Polish Higher Education, 1945–1956* (Chapel Hill: University of North Carolina Press, 2000), 2.

23. Amar, "Soviet Lviv," 382, 577.

24. Ibid., 2.

25. Ibid., 691.

26. Ibid., 392, 467, 689, 691, 788.

27. Pierre Bourdieu, "Habitus," in Jean Hillier and Emma Rooksby, eds., *Habitus: A Sense of Place* (Aldershot, UK: Ashgate, 2002), 27–34; Bourdieu, *Outline of a Theory of Practice*, trans. Richard Nice (Cambridge: Cambridge University Press, 1977).

28. Timur Kuran, *Private Truths, Public Lies: The Social Consequences of Preference Falsification* (Cambridge, MA: Harvard University Press, 1995).

29. James C. Scott, *Weapons of the Weak: Everyday Forms of Peasant Resistance* (New Haven: Yale University Press, 1985). On definitions for high culture and popular culture, see Richard Stites, *Russian Popular Culture: Entertainment and Society since 1900* (Cambridge: Cambridge University Press, 1992), 1–8.

30. Lynne Viola, ed., *Contending with Stalinism: Soviet Power and Popular Resistance in the 1930s* (Ithaca: Cornell University Press, 2002); Serhy Yekelchyk, "*Diktat* and Dialogue in Stalinist Culture: Staging Patriotic Historical Opera in Soviet Ukraine, 1936–1954," *Slavic Review* 59 (Fall 2000): 597–624; Yekelchyk, *Stalin's Empire of Memory: Russian-Ukrainian Relations in the Soviet Historical Imagination* (Toronto: University of Toronto Press, 2004).

31. Elena Zubkova, *Pribaltika i Kreml': 1940–1953* (Moscow: ROSSPEN, 2008), 285–86.

32. Maxim Waldstein, "Russifying Estonia? Iurii Lotman and the Politics of Language and Culture in Soviet Estonia," *Kritika: Explorations in Russian and Eurasian History* 8 (Summer 2007): 580.

33. Romuald J. Misiunas and Rein Taagepera, *The Baltic States: Years of Dependence, 1940–1990*, expanded and updated edition (Berkeley: University of California Press, 1993), 202.

34. Vytautas Landsbergis, *Lithuania Independent Again: The Autobiography of Vytautas Landsbergis,* prepared for an English-speaking audience by Anthony Packer and Eimutis Šova (Cardiff: University of Wales Press, 2000), 67–77.

35. Ann Laura Stoler and Frederick Cooper, eds., *Tensions of Empire: Colonial Cultures in a Bourgeois World* (Berkeley: University of California Press, 1997).

36. Frederick Cooper, *Colonialism in Question: Theory, Knowledge, History* (Berkeley: University of California Press, 2005).

37. Mark R. Beissinger, "Soviet Empire as 'Family Resemblance,'" *Slavic Review* 65 (Summer 2006): 294–303.

38. Theodore von Laue, *The World Revolution of Westernization* (New York: Oxford University Press, 1987), 27–34.

39. Amar, "Soviet Lviv," 9–10.

40. Edward C. Thaden, *Russia's Western Borderlands, 1710–1870,* with the collaboration of Marianna Forster Thaden (Princeton: Princeton University Press, 1984); Theodore R. Weeks, *Nation and State in Late Imperial Russia: Nationalism and Russification on the Western Frontier, 1863–1914* (DeKalb: Northern Illinois University Press, 1996).

41. Martin, *Affirmative Action Empire*, 8–9.

42. Kate Brown, *Biography of No Place: From Ethnic Borderland to Soviet Heartland* (Cambridge, MA: Harvard University Press, 2004); Timothy Snyder, *The Reconstruction of Nations: Poland, Ukraine, Lithuania, Belarus, 1569–1999* (New Haven: Yale University Press, 2003).

43. Peter Sahlins, *Boundaries: The Making of France and Spain in the Pyrenees* (Berkeley: University of California Press, 1989).

44. Amir Weiner, "The Empires Pay a Visit: Gulag Returnees, East European Rebellions, and Soviet Frontier Politics," *Journal of Modern History* 78 (June 2006): 333–76.

45. James S. Duncan, *The City as Text: The Politics of Landscape Interpretation in the Kandyan Kingdom* (Cambridge: Cambridge University Press, 1990); Neil Leach, ed., *The Hieroglyphics of Space: Reading and Experiencing the Modern Metropolis* (London: Routledge, 2002).

46. David Harvey, *Spaces of Hope* (Berkeley: University of California Press, 2000); Harvey, *The Urban Experience* (Oxford: Basil Blackwell, 1989); Henri Lefebvre, *The Production of Space,* trans. Donald Nicholson-Smith (Oxford: Blackwell, 1991).

47. Gary B. Cohen, *The Politics of Ethnic Survival: Germans in Prague, 1861–1914,* 2nd ed. (West Lafayette, IN: Purdue University Press, 2006); Robert Nemes, *The Once and Future Budapest* (DeKalb: Northern Illinois University Press, 2005); Derek Sayer, *The Coasts of Bohemia: A Czech History* (Princeton: Princeton University Press, 1998); Scott Spector, *Prague Territories: National Conflict and Cultural Innovation in Franz Kafka's Fin de Siècle* (Berkeley: University of California Press, 2000).

48. Anthony D. Smith, *Theories of Nationalism* (New York: Harper and Row, 1972).

49. Yaroslav Hrytsak, "Lviv: A Multicultural City through the Centuries," in John Czaplicka, ed., *Lviv: A City in the Crosscurrents of Culture* (Cambridge, MA: Harvard Ukrainian Research Institute/Harvard University Press, 2005), 47–73; Hugo Lane, "The Ukrainian Theater and the Polish Opera: Cultural Hegemony and National Culture," in John Czaplicka, ed.,

Lviv: A City in the Crosscurrents of Culture (Cambridge, MA: Harvard Ukrainian Research Institute/Harvard University Press, 2005), 149–70.

50. Anna Veronika Wendland, "Neighbors as Betrayers: Nationalization, Remembrance Policy, and the Urban Sphere in Lviv," in Christopher Hann and Paul Robert Magocsi, eds., *Galicia: A Multicultured Land* (Toronto: University of Toronto Press, 2005), 139–59.

51. Liah Greenfeld, *Nationalism: Five Roads to Modernity* (Cambridge, MA: Harvard University Press, 1992), 250.

52. Ernest Gellner, *Nations and Nationalism* (Ithaca: Cornell University Press, 1983).

53. Gregor Tlum, *Obce miasto: Wrocław 1945 i potem* (Wrocław: Via Nova, 2005).

54. Bert Hoppe, *Auf den Trümmern von Königsberg: Kaliningrad 1946–1970* (Munich: R. Oldenbourg Verlag, 2000).

55. Ibid., 135.

56. Edward W. Soja, *Thirdspace: Journeys to Los Angeles and Other Real-and-Imagined Places* (Malden, MA: Blackwell, 1996).

57. Rogers Brubaker, Margit Feischmidt, et al., *Nationalist Politics and Everyday Ethnicity in a Transylvanian Town* (Princeton: Princeton University Press, 2006).

58. Patrice Higonnet, *Paris: Capital of the World,* trans. Arthur Goldhammer (Cambridge, MA: Harvard University Press, 2002), 2–6.

59. Amar, "Soviet Lviv," 613–788.

60. Ivan Khymka, "Z choho skladaiet'sia rehion," *Krytyka* (Kyiv) 4 (2003), online edition, www.krytyka.kiev.ua (accessed 10 May 2006); A. I. Miller, "Tema Tsentral'noi Evropy: Istoriia, sovremennye diskursy i mesto v nikh Rossii," *Novoe literaturnoe obozreniie (NLO)* 52 (2001), online edition, magazines.russ.ru (accessed 6 February 2004).

61. Sergei Zhuk, *Rock and Roll in the Rocket City: The West, Identity, and Ideology in Soviet Dniepropetrovsk, 1960–1985* (Washington, DC: Woodrow Wilson Center Press, 2010); Vladislav Zubok, *Zhivago's Children: The Last Russian Intelligentsia* (Cambridge, MA: Belknap Press of Harvard University Press, 2009), 116–17.

62. Alexei Yurchak, *Everything Was Forever, Until It Was No More: The Last Soviet Generation* (Princeton: Princeton University Press, 2006), 160.

63. Benjamin Tromley, "An Unlikely National Revival: Soviet Higher Learning and the Ukrainian 'Sixtiers,' 1953–65," *Russian Review* 68 (October 2009): 607–22.

64. See, for instance, Sixtiers' memoirs on writer Borys Antonenko-Davydovych, who had fought on the side of the Ukrainian People's Republic against the Bolsheviks in 1918–19, in Borys Timoshenko, ed.,

Bahattia: Borys Antonenko-Davydovych ochyma suchasnykiv (Kyiv: Vydavnytstvo imeni Oleny Telihy, 1999).

65. Roman Szporluk, "Kiev as the Ukraine's Primate City," *Harvard Ukrainian Studies* 3/4, part 2 (1979–1980): 843–49.

66. Tromley, "An Unlikely National Revival," 610–13, 616.

67. Amar, "Soviet Lviv," 403.

68. Stephen V. Bittner, *The Many Lives of Khrushchev's Thaw: Experience and Memory in Moscow's Arbat* (Ithaca: Cornell University Press, 2008); Zubok, *Zhivago's Children.*

69. Douglas R. Weiner, *A Little Corner of Freedom: Russian Nature Protection from Stalin to Gorbachev* (Berkeley: University of California Press, 1999).

1. Lviv and Postwar Soviet Politics

1. Ivan Hushchak, *Pleiada zaboronena, pryzabuta* (Lviv: Kobzar, 1998), 217.

2. Amir Weiner, *Making Sense of War: The Second World War and the Fate of the Bolshevik Revolution* (Princeton: Princeton University Press, 2001), 17, 21–39, 43–126.

3. Ibid., 29, 34–35, 38, 191–235, 348–52.

4. Karel C. Berkhoff, *Harvest of Despair: Life and Death in Ukraine under Nazi Rule* (Cambridge, MA: Belknap Press of Harvard University Press, 2004).

5. Yoram Gorlizki and Oleg Khlevniuk, *Cold Peace: Stalin and the Soviet Ruling Circle, 1945–1953* (Oxford: Oxford University Press, 2004), 12, 123–42.

6. David Brandenberger, *National Bolshevism: Stalinist Mass Culture and the Formation of Modern Russian National Identity, 1931–1956* (Cambridge, MA: Harvard University Press, 2006).

7. Weiner, *Making Sense of War*, 226, 233–35 (Jews); 149–54 (other nationalities).

8. Amir Weiner, "The Empires Pay a Visit: Gulag Returnees, East European Rebellions, and Soviet Frontier Politics," *Journal of Modern History* 78 (June 2006): 344–46.

9. Alexander Statiev, *The Soviet Counterinsurgency in the Western Borderlands* (Cambridge: Cambridge University Press, 2010), 194.

10. Ibid., 276–77.

11. Werner G. Hahn, *Postwar Soviet Politics: The Fall of Zhdanov and the Defeat of Moderation, 1946–53* (Ithaca: Cornell University Press, 1982); Gorlizki and Khlevniuk, *Cold Peace*, 31–38.

12. Weiner, *Making Sense of War* (purification); Elena Zubkova, *Russia after the War: Hopes, Illusions, and Disappointments, 1945–1957,* trans. and

ed. Hugh Ragsdale (Armonk, NY: M. E. Sharpe, 1998), 117 (assertive and restless society); Gorlizki and Khlevniuk, *Cold Peace*, 38 (Stalin's inner circle).

13. G. V. Kostyrchenko, *Tainaia politika Stalina: Vlast' i antisemitizm* (Moscow: Mezhdunarodnye otnosheniia, 2001); Yakov Rapoport, *The Doctors' Plot of 1953* (Cambridge, MA: Harvard University Press, 1991); Joshua Rubenstein and Vladimir P. Naumov, eds., *Stalin's Secret Pogrom: The Postwar Inquisition of the Jewish Anti-Fascist Committee* (New Haven: Yale University Press, 2001); Kiril Tomoff, *Creative Union: The Professional Organization of Soviet Composers, 1939–1953* (Ithaca: Cornell University Press, 2006), 152–53; Serhy Yekelchyk, "The Civic Duty to Hate: Stalinist Citizenship as Political Practice and Civic Emotion (Kiev, 1943–53)," *Kritika* 7 (Summer 2006): 529–56.

14. Serhy Yekelchyk, *Stalin's Empire of Memory: Russian-Ukrainian Relations in the Soviet Historical Imagination* (Toronto: University of Toronto Press, 2004), 53–71.

15. Jeffrey Burds, "The Early Cold War in Soviet West Ukraine, 1944–1948," *Carl Beck Papers in Russian and East European Studies*, no. 1505 (2001).

16. Statiev, *Soviet Counterinsurgency*, 263–64; Weiner, *Making Sense of War*, 169n136.

17. Gorlizki and Khlevniuk, *Cold Peace*, 124–33.

18. Amy Knight, *Beria: Stalin's First Lieutenant* (Princeton: Princeton University Press, 1993), 183–91.

19. Ibid., 186–88.

20. Gerhard Simon, *Nationalism and Policy towards the Nationalities in the Soviet Union: From Totalitarianism to Post-Stalinist Society*, trans. Karen Forster and Ostwald Forster (Boulder, CO: Westview Press, 1991), 228–29.

21. Knight, *Beria*, 188–89; Simon, *Nationalism and Policy*, 229–30.

22. Knight, *Beria*, 188.

23. Ibid., 188–89.

24. Ibid., 189.

25. Weiner, "Empires," 336n4.

26. Ibid., 336–39.

27. Ibid., 345–46.

28. Stephen V. Bittner, *The Many Lives of Khrushchev's Thaw: Experience and Memory in Moscow's Arbat* (Ithaca: Cornell University Press, 2008).

29. See, for instance, Polly Jones, ed., *The Dilemmas of De-Stalinization: Negotiating Cultural and Social Change in the Khrushchev Era* (London: Routledge, 2006).

30. Zubkova, *Russia after the War*, 149–202.

31. Ibid., 146–47.

32. Carl A. Linden, *Khrushchev and the Soviet Leadership 1957–1964* (Baltimore: Johns Hopkins University Press, 1966), 117–33.

33. Ibid., 147–48.

34. Priscilla Johnson, *Khrushchev and the Arts: The Politics of Soviet Culture* (Cambridge, MA: MIT Press, 1965).

35. Oleg Kharkhordin, *The Collective and the Individual in Russia: A Study of Practices* (Berkeley: University of California Press, 1999), 279–328.

36. Emily Lygo, "The Need for New Voices: Writers' Union Policy towards Young Writers 1953–64," in Polly Jones, ed., *The Dilemmas of De-Stalinization: Negotiating Cultural and Social Change in the Khrushchev Era* (London: Routledge, 2006), 202–3.

37. Miriam Dobson, *Khrushchev's Cold Summer: Gulag Returnees, Crime, and the Fate of Reform after Stalin* (Ithaca: Cornell University Press, 2009).

38. Simon, *Nationalism and Policy*, 233–43.

39. Ibid., 245–57.

40. Serhy Yekelchyk, *Ukraine: Birth of a Modern Nation* (Oxford: Oxford University Press, 2007), 173.

41. Petr Vail and Aleksandr Genis, *60-e: Mir sovetskogo cheloveka* (Moscow: Novoe Literaturnoe Obozrenie, 2001), 12–18.

42. Zubkova, *Russia after the War*, 201.

43. Vladislav Zubok, *Zhivago's Children: The Last Russian Intelligentsia* (Cambridge, MA: Belknap Press of Harvard University Press, 2009).

44. Heorhiy Kasianov, *Nezhodni: Ukrains'ka intelihentsiia v rusi oporu 1960–80-kh rokiv* (Kyiv: Lybid', 1995), 12–17; Romuald Misiunas and Rein Taagepera, *The Baltic States: Years of Dependence, 1940–1990,* expanded and updated edition (Berkeley: University of California Press, 1993), 133–40.

45. Simon, *Nationalism and Policy*, 230–33.

46. Ibid., 232, 254; Jaroslaw Pelensky, "Shelest and His Period in Soviet Ukraine (1963–1972): A Revival of Controlled Ukrainian Autonomism," in Peter J. Potichnyi, ed., *Ukraine in the Seventies* (Oakville, Ontario: Mosaic, 1975), 283–305.

47. John Alexander Armstrong, *The Soviet Bureaucratic Elite: A Case Study of the Ukrainian Apparatus* (New York: Praeger, 1959); Yaroslav Bilinsky, *The Second Soviet Republic: The Ukraine after World War II* (New Brunswick, NJ: Rutgers University Press, 1964); Alexander J. Motyl, *Will the Non-Russians Rebel? State, Ethnicity, and Stability in the USSR* (Ithaca: Cornell University Press, 1987), 42, 50–52.

48. Benjamin Tromley, "An Unlikely National Revival: Soviet Higher Learning and the Ukrainian 'Sixties,' 1953–65," *Russian Review* 68 (October 2009): 607–22.

49. Weiner, "Empires."

50. Remarks by Oleg Gribanov, head of the Second Main Department of the KGB, to the Ideological Department of the Central Committee of the Communist Party of the Soviet Union, dated 8 May 1964, on "national manifestations in some regions of the Soviet Union," Rossiiskii Gosudarstvennyi Arkhiv Noveishei Istorii (RGANI), 5/55/71/ 34–35, in *The Departmental Records of the Central Committee of the Communist Party of the Soviet Union, 1953–66,* Ideology Department, Reel 428.

51. Levko Lukianenko, *Ne dam zahynut' Ukraini!* (Kyiv: Sofiia, 1994), 33–34; Iuriy Zaitsev and Mykola Dubas, eds., *Ukrains'kyi Natsional'nyi Front: Doslidzhennia, dokumenty, materialy* (Lviv: Instytut Ukrainoznavstva imeni Ivana Kryp'iakevycha, Natsional'na Akademiia Nauk Ukrainy, 2000), 58.

52. Donald J. Raleigh, ed., *Russia's Sputnik Generation: Soviet Baby Boomers Talk about Their Lives* (Bloomington: Indiana University Press, 2006).

53. Herbert J. Ellison, ed., *The Sino-Soviet Conflict: A Global Perspective* (Seattle: University of Washington Press, 1982); Lorenz M. Luthi, *The Sino-Soviet Split: Cold War in the Communist World* (Princeton: Princeton University Press, 2008); Amir Weiner, "Déjà Vu All Over Again: Prague Spring, Romanian Summer and Soviet Autumn on the Soviet Western Frontier," *Contemporary European History* 15 (2006): 167.

54. Christel Lane, *The Rites of Rulers: Ritual in Industrial Society—The Soviet Case* (Cambridge: Cambridge University Press, 1981), 30–31; Zubok, *Zhivago's Children,* 322–23.

55. Alexei Yurchak, *Everything Was Forever, Until It Was No More: The Last Soviet Generation* (Princeton: Princeton University Press, 2006).

56. Kenneth C. Farmer, *Ukrainian Nationalism in the Post-Stalin Era: Myth, Symbols and Ideology in the Soviet Nationalities Policy* (The Hague: Martinus Nijhoff, 1980), 58–75.

57. Christopher J. Ward, *Brezhnev's Folly: The Building of BAM and Late Soviet Socialism* (Pittsburgh: University of Pittsburgh Press, 2009); Sergei Zhuk, *Rock and Roll in the Rocket City: The West, Identity, and Ideology in Soviet Dniepropetrovsk, 1960–1985* (Washington, DC: Woodrow Wilson Center Press, 2010).

58. Petro Shelest, "Partiynyi natsionalist (1969–1972)," in Iuriy Shapoval, ed., *Petro Shelest: "Spravzhniy sud istorii shche poperedu": Spohady, shchodennyky, dokumenty, materialy* (Kyiv: Heneza, 2003), 298–372.

59. Yekelchyk, *Ukraine,* 173.

60. Vitalii Vrublevskii, *Vladimir Shcherbytskii: Pravda i vymysly* (Kyiv: Dovira, 1993), 114–24.

61. Oles Honchar, *Shchodennyky u tr'okh tomakh,* vol. 2, *1968–1983,* ed. V. B. Honchar (Kyiv: Veselka, 2003), 197, 204, 250, 363, 373, 406, 546.

62. Yurchak, *Everything Was Forever,* 291–95.

63. Bohdan Nahaylo, *The Ukrainian Resurgence* (Toronto: University of Toronto Press, 1999).

2. The Making of a Soviet Ukrainian City

1. W. Krajewski, "Jeden dzień we Lwowie," *Dziennik Polski* (Detroit), 17–18 January 1969, 8.

2. Terry Martin, *The Affirmative Action Empire: Nations and Nationalism in the Soviet Union, 1923–1939* (Ithaca: Cornell University Press, 2001), 451–60.

3. Serhy Yekelchyk, *Stalin's Empire of Memory: Russian-Ukrainian Relations in the Soviet Historical Imagination* (Toronto: University of Toronto Press, 2004).

4. Eugen Weber, *Peasants into Frenchmen: The Modernization of Rural France, 1870–1914* (Stanford: Stanford University Press, 1976).

5. Tarik Youssef Cyril Amar, "The Conquest of the Old World: Sovietization as Encounter and Intra-Modern Imperialism," in Amar, "The Making of Soviet Lviv, 1939–1963" (PhD dissertation, Princeton University, 2006), 118–262. On such notions of Soviet socialism as an advanced form of civilization, see Stephen Kotkin, *Magnetic Mountain: Stalinism as a Civilization* (Berkeley: University of California Press, 1995), and Martin Malia, "Through the Soviet-Russian Looking-Glass, and What the West Found There: 1917–1991," in Malia, *Russia under Western Eyes: From the Bronze Horseman to the Lenin Mausoleum* (Cambridge, MA: Belknap Press of Harvard University Press, 1999), 287–408.

6. Amar, "Soviet Lviv," 148.

7. John-Paul Himka, *Galician Villagers and the Ukrainian National Movement in the Nineteenth Century* (Edmonton: Canadian Institute of Ukrainian Studies, 1987); Yaroslav Hrytsak, "Historical Memory and Regional Identity among Galicia's Ukrainians," in Christopher Hann and Paul Robert Magocsi, eds., *Galicia: A Multicultured Land* (Toronto: University of Toronto Press, 2005), 185–209; Keely Stauter-Halsted, *The Nation in the Village: The Genesis of Peasant National Identity in Austrian Poland, 1848–1914* (Ithaca: Cornell University Press, 2001); Andriy Zayarnyuk, "Framing the Ukrainian Peasantry in Habsburg Galicia: 1846–1914 (With Focus on the Sambir Area)" (PhD dissertation, University of Alberta, 2003).

8. Orest Subtelny, *Ukraine: A History,* 2nd ed. (Toronto: University of Toronto Press/Canadian Institute of Ukrainian Studies, 1994), 306–35.

9. Ibid., 367–72.

10. Alexander J. Motyl, "Ukrainian Nationalist Political Violence in Inter-War Poland, 1921–1939," *East European Quarterly* 19 (March 1985): 45–55; Motyl, *The Turn to the Right: The Ideological Origins and Development of Ukrainian Nationalism, 1919–1929* (Boulder, CO: East European Monographs, 1980), 1–2.

11. Motyl, "Ukrainian Nationalist Political Violence"; Timothy Snyder, *The Reconstruction of Nations: Poland, Ukraine, Lithuania, Belarus, 1569–1999* (New Haven: Yale University Press, 2003), 150–53.

12. Joseph Rothschild, "Poland," in Peter F. Sugar and Donald W. Treadgold, eds., *A History of Central Europe*, vol. 9, *East Central Europe between the World Wars*, by Joseph Rothschild (Seattle: University of Washington Press, 1974), 43; Snyder, *Reconstruction of Nations*, 150.

13. Martin, *Affirmative Action Empire*, 352; O. S. Rublov and Iu. A. Cherchenko, *Stalinshchyna i dolia zakhidnoukrains'koi intelihentsii* (Kyiv: Naukova Dumka, 1994), 14–130; Timothy Snyder, *Sketches from a Secret War: A Polish Artist's Mission to Liberate Soviet Ukraine* (New Haven: Yale University Press, 2005), 83–114.

14. Elena Zubkova, *Pribaltika i Kreml'. 1940–1953* (Moscow: ROSSPEN, 2008), 61–63.

15. A. Figol, V. Kubijovyc, and A. Zhukovsky, "L'viv," in Danylo Husar Struk, ed., *Encyclopedia of Ukraine*, vol. 3 (Toronto: University of Toronto Press, 1993), 222–23.

16. Amar, "Soviet Lviv," 192–97 (educational institutions); Philipp Ther, "War versus Peace: Interethnic Relations in Lviv during the First Half of the Twentieth Century," in John Czaplicka, ed., *Lviv: A City in the Cross-currents of Culture* (Cambridge, MA: Harvard University Press/Harvard Ukrainian Research Institute, 2005), 265 (Ivan Franko State University); Iuriy Slyvka et al., eds., *Kul'turne zhyttia v Ukraini: Zakhidni zemli*, vol. 1, *1939–1953* (Kyiv: Naukova Dumka, 1995), 61 (museum), 79–84 (historians).

17. Milena Rudnytska, ed., *Zakhidna Ukraina pid bil'shovykamy: IX.1939–VI.1941* (New York: Naukove Tovarystvo imeni Shevchenka v Amerytsi, 1958).

18. Grzegorz Hryciuk, *Polacy we Lwowie 1939–1944: Życie codzienne* (Warsaw: Książka i Wiedza, 1995), 44–49.

19. Jan T. Gross, "Elections," in Gross, *Revolution from Abroad: The Soviet Conquest of Poland's Western Ukraine and Western Belorussia* (Princeton: Princeton University Press, 2002), 71–113.

20. Jan T. Gross, *Revolution from Abroad: The Soviet Conquest of Poland's Western Ukraine and Western Belorussia* (Princeton: Princeton University Press, 2002), 179–81; Rudnytska, *Zakhidna Ukraina*, 465–92.

21. Orest Subtelny, *Ukraine: A History*, 2nd ed. (Toronto: University of Toronto Press/Canadian Institute of Ukrainian Studies, 1994), 554–57.

22. Amar, "Soviet Lviv," 96–97, 100–105; Kost Pankivskyi, "Nashe zhyttia pid nimets'koiu okupatsiieu," in Pankivskyi, *Roky nimets'koi okupatsii, 1941–1944* (New York: Kliuchy, 1965), 291–414; Viktor Susak, "Etnichni ta sotsial'ni zminy v naselenni L'vova v 1939–1999 rokakh" (MA thesis, Lviv National University, 2000), 17–18.

23. Dieter Pohl, *Nationalsozialistische Judenverfolgung in Ostgalizien 1941–1944: Organisation und Durchführung eines staatlichen Massenverbrechens* (Munich: R. Oldenbourg Verlag, 1997), 60–65 (pogroms), 277–78 *(Hilfspolizei)*, 283, 286–87 (Ukrainians in local government), 311–12 *(Hilfspolizei)*.

24. Amar, "Soviet Lviv," 89–91, 95–96; Pohl, *Nationalsozialistische Judenverfolgung*, 312–26.

25. Ther, "War versus Peace," 267.

26. Snyder, *Reconstruction of Nations*, 183.

27. Amar, "Soviet Lviv," 270.

28. Ibid., 280–312, 362–63; Ther, "War versus Peace," 270–71.

29. Susak, "Etnichni ta sotsial'ni zminy," 20–21.

30. Amar, "Soviet Lviv," 271, 275.

31. Martin Åberg, "Paradox of Change: Soviet Modernization and Ethno-Linguistic Differentiation in Lviv, 1945–1989," in John Czaplicka, ed., *Lviv: A City in the Crosscurrents of Culture* (Cambridge, MA: Harvard University Press/Harvard Ukrainian Research Institute, 2005), 288.

32. Amar, "Soviet Lviv," 379, 383.

33. Tarik Youssef Cyril Amar, "The Party-State and the Old Local Intelligentsia," in Amar, "The Making of Soviet Lviv, 1939–1963" (PhD dissertation, Princeton University, 2006), 384–464.

34. Amar, "Soviet Lviv," 497.

35. John Alexander Armstrong, *Ukrainian Nationalism* (Englewood, CO: Ukrainian Academic Press, 1990); Timothy Snyder, "The Ethnic Cleansing of Western Ukraine," in Snyder, *The Reconstruction of Nations: Poland, Ukraine, Lithuania, Belarus, 1569–1999* (New Haven: Yale University Press, 2003), 154–78.

36. Karol Grünberg and Bolesław Sprengel, *Trudne sąsiedzstwo: Stosunki polsko-ukraińskie w X–XX wieku* (Warsaw: Książka i Wiedza, 2005), 354–55, 392–93, 402, 422, 434.

37. Snyder, *Reconstruction of Nations*, 164.

38. Ibid., 164–67.

39. Ibid., 169, 175–77.

40. Grünberg and Sprengel, *Trudne sąsiedztwo*, 646.

41. Jeffrey Burds, "The Early Cold War in Soviet West Ukraine, 1944–1948," *Carl Beck Papers in Russian and East European Studies,* no. 1505 (2001): 34–35 (internal reports); V. Bieliaiev and M. Rudnytskyi, "Nemynuchyi kinets'," in Bieliaiev and Rudnytskyi, *Pid chuzhymy praporamy* (Kyiv: Radians'kyi Pys'mennyk, 1956), 189–205 (official publications).

42. Grünberg and Sprengel, *Trudne sąsiedztwo,* 648, 658–59.

43. Jeffrey Burds, "AGENTURA: Soviet Informants' Networks and the Ukrainian Underground in Galicia, 1944–48," *East European Politics and Societies* 11 (Winter 1997): 89–130; Alexander Statiev, *The Soviet Counterinsurgency in the Western Borderlands* (Cambridge: Cambridge University Press, 2010).

44. Burds, "AGENTURA," 97, 113.

45. Statiev, *Soviet Counterinsurgency,* 125, 133.

46. Burds, "AGENTURA," 96.

47. Henrykh Bandrovskyi, interview with the author, tape recording, Uzhhorod, 9 August 2004.

48. Burds, "AGENTURA," 104–11.

49. Ibid., 109.

50. Mykhailo Kril, interview with the author, tape recording, Lviv, 17 June 2004.

51. On increased criminal activity and assassinations in Lviv, see Amar, "Soviet Lviv," 329, 357.

52. Tarik Youssef Cyril Amar, "The Crisis of Sovietization," in Amar, "The Making of Soviet Lviv, 1939–1963" (PhD dissertation, Princeton University, 2006), 465–544.

53. Ulrike von Hirschhausen, *Die Grenzen der Gemeinsamkeit: Deutsche, Letten, Russen und Juden in Riga 1860–1914* (Göttingen: Vandenhoeck & Ruprecht, 2006); Bradley D. Woodworth, "Civil Society and Nationality in the Multiethnic Russian Empire: Tallinn/Reval, 1860–1914" (PhD dissertation, Indiana University, 2003).

54. Romuald J. Misiunas and Rein Taagepera, *The Baltic States: Years of Dependence, 1940–1990,* expanded and updated edition (Berkeley: University of California Press, 1993), 16.

55. Snyder, *Reconstruction of Nations,* 15–102; Theodore R. Weeks, "Population Politics in Vilnius 1944–1947: A Case Study of Socialist-Sponsored Ethnic Cleansing," *Post-Soviet Affairs* 23 (2007): 76–95.

56. Misiunas and Taagepera, *Baltic States,* 42.

57. Ibid., 15–75, 99–107.

58. Ibid., 83–94; Burds, "AGENTURA"; Juozas Daumantas, *Fighters for Freedom: Lithuanian Partisans versus the U.S.S.R. (1944–1947),* 2nd ed. (Toronto: Lithuanian Canadian Committee for Human Rights, 1975);

Mart Laar, *War in the Woods: Estonia's Struggle for Survival, 1944–1956,* trans. Tiina Ets, with a foreword by Tönu Parming (Washington, DC: Compass Press, 1992).

59. Burds, "AGENTURA," 97.
60. Slyvka et al., *Kul'turne zhyttia,* vol. 1, 473–81.
61. Amir Weiner, "The Empires Pay a Visit: Gulag Returnees, East European Rebellions, and Soviet Frontier Politics," *Journal of Modern History* 78 (June 2006): 337n5.
62. Geoffrey Swain, "'Cleaning up Soviet Latvia': The Bureau for Latvia (Latburo), 1944–1947," in Olaf Mertelsmann, ed., *The Sovietization of the Baltic States, 1940–1956* (Tartu: Kleio, 2003), 83.
63. Weiner, "Empires," 333–76.
64. Rossiiskii Gosudarstvennyi Arkhiv Noveishei Istorii (RGANI). 5/55/71/33–47, in *The Departmental Records of the Central Committee of the Communist Party of the Soviet Union, 1953–66,* Ideology Department, Reel 428.
65. Amir Weiner, "Déjà Vu All Over Again: Prague Spring, Romanian Summer and Soviet Autumn on the Soviet Western Frontier," *Contemporary European History* 15 (2006): 174–75.
66. Amar, "Soviet Lviv," 522–23.
67. Frederick Cooper, *Colonialism in Question: Theory, Knowledge, History* (Berkeley: University of California Press, 2005), 31–33, 157.
68. Marie Alice L'Heureux, "Representing Ideology, Designing Memory," in Olaf Mertelsmann, ed., *The Sovietization of the Baltic States, 1940–1956* (Tartu: Kleio, 2003), 207–26.
69. Dmitrii Smirnov, "Sovietization, Terror and Repression in the Baltic States in the 1940s and 1950s: The Perspective of Contemporary Russian Society," in Olaf Mertelsmann, ed., *The Sovietization of the Baltic States, 1940–1956* (Tartu: Kleio, 2003), 55–57.
70. Slyvka et al., *Kul'turne zhyttia,* vol. 1, 197–98.
71. Susak, "Etnichni ta sotsial'ni zminy," 19–20.
72. Åberg, "Paradox of Change," 288–89; V. V. Sekretariuk et al., eds., *Istoriia L'vova* (Kyiv: Naukova Dumka, 1984), 269–74, 302–15.
73. Åberg, "Paradox of Change," 287–90.
74. Susak, "Etnichni ta sotsial'ni zminy," 13, 21, 24, 34–35.
75. Slyvka et al., *Kul'turne zhyttia,* vol. 1, 69 (conservatory), 150–53 (theaters).
76. Hugo Lane, "The Ukrainian Theater and the Polish Opera: Cultural Hegemony and National Culture," in John Czaplicka, ed., *Lviv: A City in the Crosscurrents of Culture* (Cambridge, MA: Harvard University Press/Harvard Ukrainian Research Institute, 2005), 149–70.

77. Slyvka et al., *Kul'turne zhyttia,* vol. 1, 671 (art museum); Iuriy Slyvka, "Akademik Ivan Petrovych Kryp'iakevych: Uchytel', vchenyi, kerivnyk naukovoho viddilu," *Ukraina: Kul'turna spadshchyna, natsional'na svidomist', derzhavnist'* (Lviv) 8 (2001): 591, 599 (Shevchenko Scientific Society).

78. Charlotte Saikowski, "Ukraine Nationalism Disturbs Soviet Leaders," *Christian Science Monitor,* 7 May 1969, 15 (Tchaikovsky); *Teatral'nyi L'viv* (Lviv) 7 (November 1975) (theaters in Ukrainian). For press articles on the Zankovetska Theater, see M. Iu. Tarnovskyi, "Homonila Ukraina," *Litera-turna Ukraina* (Kyiv), 27 March 1964, 4 (Shevchenko); "Prem'iera u L'vovi," *Literaturna Ukraina* (Kyiv), 13 November 1964, 1 (Ivanychuk); L. Viryna, "Mashtabnist' poshuku," *Literaturna Ukraina* (Kyiv), 10 June 1969, 4 (Shakespeare and Oles); Mykola Petrenko, "Z naipovnishoiu viddacheiu," *Literaturna Ukraina* (Kyiv), 30 June 1972, 4 (Lesia Ukrainka); T. Sataeva, "Trudnoe schast'e talanta," *Komsomol'skoe znamia* (Kyiv), 29 July 1975, 3 (Shakespeare); Svitlana Veselka, "I prystrast' Hamleta u n'omu ne zha-saie . . . ," *Vysokyi zamok* (Lviv), 6 August 1999, 8 (Shakespeare).

79. P. Romaniuk, "Palitra dumok," *Molod' Ukrainy* (Kyiv), 25 October 1967, 3; N. Sambelian, "Zhivaia voda," *Komsomol'skoe znamia* (Kyiv), 25 October 1967, 3; Ihor Dychenko, "Maliunok vystavy," *Molod' Ukrainy* (Kyiv), 10 December 1967, 2; A. Borysenko, "Uspikh L'vivs'koi opery," *Literaturna Ukraina* (Kyiv), 23 August 1974, 4.

80. "'To była sprawa smaku . . .': Rozmowa z Mykołą Riabczukiem," in Bogumiła Berdychowska and Ola Hnatiuk, *Bunt pokolenia: Rozmowy z intelektualistami ukraińskimi* (Lublin: Wydawnictwo Uniwersytetu Marii Curie-Skłodowskiej, 2000), 222–23, 226.

81. Anthony D. Smith, *Theories of Nationalism,* 2nd ed. (New York: Holmes and Meier, 1983), 21; Roman Szporluk, "Ukraine: From an Imperial Periphery to a Sovereign State," *Daedalus* 126 (1997): 2.

82. Liubov Kyianovska, *Syn stolittia: Mykola Kolessa v ukrains'kiy kul'turi xx viku* (Lviv: L'vivs'ka Derzhavna Muzychna Akademiia imeni M. V. Lysenka/Naukove Tovarystvo imeni Shevchenka, 2003), 149–220; Kyianovska, *Myroslav Skoryk: Tvorchyi portret kompozytora v dzerkali epokhy* (Lviv: Spolom, 1998); Volodymyr Lyha, *I proroste posiiane zerno: Ievhen Vakhniak: Liudyna, mytets', pedahoh* (Lviv: Dyvosvit, 2001); A. Tereshchenko, *Anatoliy Kos-Anatol's'kyi* (Kyiv: "Muzychna Ukraina, 1986).

83. Lewis Mumford, *The City in History* (New York: Harcourt, Brace and World, 1961).

84. Benedict Anderson, *Imagined Communities,* rev. ed. (London: Verso, 1991).

85. Slyvka et al., *Kul'turne zhyttia,* vol. 1, 61 (1939 changes), 198 (postwar changes).

86. Roman Stepanovych Bahriy et al., *L'vivs'kyi istorychnyi muzei: Putivnyk* (Lviv: Kameniar, 1976).

87. Bert Hoppe, *Auf den Trümmern von Königsberg: Kaliningrad 1946–1970* (Munich: R. Oldenbourg Verlag, 2000); Gregor Thum, *Obce miasto: Wrocław 1945 i potem* (Wrocław: Via Nova, 2005).

88. Slyvka et al., *Kul'turne zhyttia,* vol. 1, 412.

89. Andriy Rudnytskyi and Yuriy Biryulov, *L'viv: Turystychnyi putivnyk/Lviv: Sightseeing Guide* (Lviv: Tsentr Ievropy, 1999), 111 (Jan III Sobieski); Stanisław Bockenheim, "Powrót z wakacji '68," *Rocznik Lwowski 2004* (Warsaw): 276 (Fredro).

90. "S'ohodnishniy L'viv ochyma pol's'koho turysta," *Svoboda* (Jersey City, NJ), 12 March 1976, 3.

91. A. Pashuk and I. Derkach, *L'viv: Putivnyk* (Lviv: Knyzhkovo-zhurnal'ne Vydavnytstvo, 1960), 8.

92. I. Sychevskyi, ed., *Slovo pro L'viv* (Lviv: Kameniar, 1969), 2.

93. Bahriy et al., *L'vivs'kyi istorychnyi muzei,* 48–56.

94. Iuriy Slyvka et al., eds., *Kul'turne zhyttia v Ukraini: Zakhidni zemli,* vol. 2, *1953–1966* (Lviv: Instytut Ukrainoznavstva imeni Ivana Kryp'iakevycha, Natsional'na Akademiia Nauk Ukrainy, 1995), 92–95, 100–102, 309–11, 314–27, 490–93, 633–34.

95. Conversation with an employee of the Lviv National University Research Library, 14 July 2004.

96. Slyvka et al., *Kul'turne zhyttia,* vol. 1, 673–74; Slyvka et al., *Kul'turne zhyttia,* vol. 2, 236–38, 251–53, 282–85, 293–302, 503–6, 565–66, 596–97.

97. James S. Duncan, *The City as Text: The Politics of Landscape Interpretation in the Kandyan Kingdom* (Cambridge: Cambridge University Press, 1990); David Harvey, *Spaces of Hope* (Berkeley: University of California Press, 2000); Harvey, *The Urban Experience* (Oxford: Basil Blackwell, 1989); Neil Leach, ed., *The Hieroglyphics of Space: Reading and Experiencing the Modern Metropolis* (London: Routledge, 2002); Henri Lefebvre, *The Production of Space,* trans. Donald Nicholson-Smith (Oxford: Blackwell, 1991).

98. Boris Grigorevich Komskii, *Kholm slavy: Fotoocherk* (Lviv: Kameniar, 1985), 20, 34 (obelisk); Bohdan Tscherkes, "Stalinist Visions for the Urban Transformation of Lviv, 1939–1955," in John Czaplicka, ed., *Lviv: A City in the Crosscurrents of Culture* (Cambridge, MA: Harvard Ukrainian Research Institute/Harvard University Press, 2005), 213–14 (Hill of Glory); Orest Subtelny, *Ukraine: A History,* 2nd ed. (Toronto: University of

Toronto Press, 1994), 341–43 (World War I); Lowell Tillet, *The Great Friendship: Soviet Historians on the Non-Russian Nationalities* (Chapel Hill: University of North Carolina Press, 1969).

99. Karen Petrone, *The Great War in Russian Memory* (Bloomington: Indiana University Press, forthcoming).

100. Tscherkes, "Stalinist Visions," 216; James Von Geldern, "The Centre and the Periphery: Cultural and Social Geography in the Mass Culture of the 1930s," in Stephen White, ed., *New Directions in Soviet History* (Cambridge: Cambridge University Press, 1992), 62–80.

101. Yaroslav Hrytsak and Victor Susak, "Constructing a National City: The Case of L'viv," in John J. Czaplicka and Blair A. Ruble, eds., *Composing Urban History and the Constitution of Civic Identity* (Washington, DC: Woodrow Wilson Center Press, 2003), 149–51.

102. Tscherkes, "Stalinist Visions," 209–14.

103. V. Popov, "Molodiie starodavnyi L'viv," *Molod' Ukrainy* (Kyiv), 12 April 1974, 4.

104. I. Sychevskyi, ed., *Slovo pro L'viv* (Lviv: Kameniar, 1969), front cover.

105. Derzhavnyi Arkhiv L'vivs'koi Oblasti (hereafter DALO), P-3/6/40/21; DALO, P-3/8/424/60–62, 66; Slyvka et al., *Kul'turne zhyttia,* vol. 2, 572–73, 580–81; N. Sambelian, "Grom pod surdinku," *Komsomol'skoe znamia* (Kyiv), 17 July 1968, 3.

106. Valeriy Hrabovskyi, *Krvavych* (Lviv: Vil'na Ukraina, 1997), 72, 98–109.

107. Mykhailo Nechytaliuk, "Shevchenko perestupaie Zbruch," *Zhovten'* (Lviv) 3 (March 1965): 37–42; Ostap Sereda, "From Church-Based to Cultural Nationalism: Early Ukrainophiles, Ritual-Purification Movement and [the] Emerging Cult of Taras Shevchenko in Austrian Eastern Galicia in the 1860s," *Canadian-American Slavic Studies* 40 (Spring 2006): 21–47.

108. DALO, P-3/4/692/41–43; DALO, R-1657/1/158/25, 27–28.

109. Hrabovskyi, *Krvavych,* 116.

110. Hryhoriy Kasianov, *Nezhodni: Ukrains'ka intelihentsiia v rusi oporu 1960–80-kh rokiv* (Kyiv: Lybid', 1995), 139.

111. References to this decree are in Slyvka et al., *Kul'turne zhyttia,* vol. 2, 22, 24, and DALO, P-3/4/692/200–202.

112. Roman Szporluk, e-mail correspondence with the author, 4 July 2009. Professor Szporluk had made similar comments in conversations with me while I was a postdoctoral fellow at the Harvard Ukrainian Research Institute, February–May 2006.

113. "Wycieczka do Lwowa," *Na Antenie* (Munich), 25 February 1968, 1.

114. Ivan Salo, "Surzhyky po-L'vivs'ky," *Molod' Ukrainy* (Kyiv), 21 June 1988, reprinted in *Svoboda* (Jersey City, NJ), 6 July 1988, 1, 6.

115. DALO, P-53/16/2 (Kondratiuk); DALO, P-53/16/3 (Kondratiuk); DALO, P-53/16/4 (Kondratiuk); DALO, P-53/21/1 (Makarenko); DALO, P-52/22/7 (Makarenko).

116. Iu. Zaitsev and L. Plodysta, "Prynahidni rozdumy profesora Iuriia Slyvky," *Ukraina: Kul'turna spadshchyna, natsional'na svidomist', derzhavnist'* (Lviv) 7 (2000): 87.

117. Borys Kozlovskyi, interview with the author, tape recording, Lviv, 15 June 2007.

118. Iaroslav Isaievych, interview with the author, tape recording, Lviv, 4 January 2010.

119. Weeks, "Population Politics"; Weeks, "A Multi-ethnic City in Transition: Vilnius's Stormy Decade, 1939–1949," *Eurasian Geography and Economics* 47 (2006): 153–75.

120. L. S. Bogdanov, "K voprosu rekonstruktsii tsentrov gorodov pribaltiki," *Problemy sovetskogo gradostroitel'stva* (Moscow) 5 (1955): 61, 77, cited in Bert Hoppe, *Auf den Trümmern von Königsberg: Kaliningrad 1946–1970* (Munich: R. Oldenbourg Verlag, 2000), 49, 67–68; Richards Pētersons, "The Policy of the Soviet Occupation Power towards the Protection of Monuments (1944–1953)," in Andris Caune et al., eds., *Padomju okupācijas režīms Baltijā 1944.–1959. gadā: Politika un tās sekas* (Riga: Latvijas vēstures institūta apgāds, 2003), 339–40.

121. Valda Melngaile, "Variations on the Theme of Truth: Two Contemporary Latvian Poets," *Books Abroad,* 45.2 (Spring 1971): 242–47, cited in Rolfs Ekmanis, *Latvian Literature under the Soviets: 1948–1975* (Belmont, MA: Nordland Publishing Company, 1978), 326.

122. Debrer, Maria, *Riga: Reiseführer* (Moskau: Verlag Progress, 1982), 66–70 (Brethren Cemetery), 73–75 (Freedom Monument).

123. Roman Szporluk, "The Strange Politics of Lviv: An Essay in Search of an Explanation," in Zvi Gitelman, ed., *The Politics of Nationality and the Erosion of the USSR* (New York: St. Martin's Press, 1992), 219–22; Misiunas and Taagepera, *Baltic States,* 216.

124. On ethnic Russians and Russian speakers migrating to Tallinn and Riga, see Misiunas and Taagepera, *Baltic States,* 214–16.

3. The New Lvivians

1. Albert Astakhov, interview with the author, tape recording, Russian Cultural Center, Lviv, 27 June 2007.

2. Aleksandr Khokhulin, "Chast' pervaia (1946–1972)," in "My—mankurty (zapiski russkogo l'vovianina)," www.mankurty.com (accessed 3 January 2008).

3. Lidiia Artemeva, interview with the author, tape recording, Lviv, 6 August 2004.

4. Iryna Shabat, interview with the author, tape recording, Lviv, 2 August 2004.

5. The conversation took place in Lviv National University Archives, 11 August 2004.

6. Aleksandra Matyukhina, *W sowieckim Lwowie: Życie codzienne miasta w latach 1944–1990* (Cracow: Uniwersytet Jagielloński, 2000), 13–17.

7. Ibid., 16–17; Ivan Terliuk, *Rosiiany zakhidnykh oblastei Ukrainy (1944– 1996 rr.)* (Lviv: Tsentr Ievropy, 1997), 60–63, 69–70.

8. Artemeva, interview; Khokhulin, "Chast' pervaia." On the role of space as a factor influencing social relations, see Edward W. Soja, *Thirdspace: Journeys to Los Angeles and Other Real-and-Imagined Places* (Malden, MA: Blackwell, 1996).

9. "Boevoi drug voinov-prykarpatsev," *Pravda Ukrainy* (Kyiv), 21 August 1971, 3; "Iubilei gazety," *Pravda Ukrainy* (Kyiv), 22 August 1973, 3; "L'vivs'kyi Rosys'kyi Dramatychnyi Teatr Radians'koi Armii," *Ukrains'ka radians'ka entsyklopediia,* vol. 8 (Kyiv: Holovna Redaktsiia Ukrains'koi Radians'koi Entsiklopedii, Akademiia Nauk URSR, 1962), 345; "L'vovskii Russkii Dramaticheskii Teatr Sovetskoi Armii," *Teatral'nyi L'viv* (Lviv), 7 (November 1975): 21–25; Iuriy Hordiienko, interview with the author, tape recording, Lviv, 13 June 2007 (Engels Street).

10. B. Ia. Koprzhiva-Lure, *Istoriia odnoi zhizni* (Paris: Atheneum, 1987), 191–215.

11. Derzhavnyi Arkhiv L'vivs'koi Oblasti (hereafter DALO), P-3568/1/125/8, 156; DALO, P-3568/1/141/28, 97–98; DALO, P-3567/1/150/70–72, 124–26; DALO, P-3567/1/151/66–67.

12. DALO, P-92/1/353/124; DALO, P-92/1/356/106.

13. DALO, P-3/6/82/2.

14. Anonymous male respondent, born 8 August 1917, written response to author's questionnaire, Russian Cultural Center, Lviv, 23 June 2007; anonymous female respondent, born 20 July 1919, written response to author's questionnaire, Russian Cultural Center, Lviv, 23 June 2007.

15. Liubov Mesniankina, written response to author's questionnaire, Lviv, July 2007.

16. Iaroslav Isaievych, interview with the author, tape recording, Lviv, 4 January 2010.

17. Anonymous female respondent, born 20 July 1919.

18. Iuriy Slyvka et al., eds., *Kul'turne zhyttia v Ukraini: Zakhidni zemli,* vol. 2, *1953–1966* (Lviv: Instytut Ukrainoznavstva imeni Ivana Kryp'iakevycha, Natsional'na Akademiia Nauk Ukrainy, 1996), 39.

19. Anonymous female respondent, born 20 July 1919.
20. Valeriy Sultanov, interview with the author, tape recording, Lviv, 23 June 2007.
21. Matyukhina, *W sowieckim Lwowie*, 43–45, 77, 142–43.
22. Borys Kozlovskyi, interview with the author, tape recording, Lviv, 15 June 2007.
23. Ibid.
24. "Vitaliy," interview with the author, tape recording, Lviv, 22 June 2007.
25. "Alex," e-mail to the author, 21 June 2007; Grigorii Komskii, "Teni tenei," *IY: Nezalezhnyi kul'turolohichnyi chasopys* (Lviv) 29 (2003): 272.
26. "Vitaliy," interview.
27. Mykola Riabchuk, "Pol'shcha, pol's'kyi, poliaky: Sproba filolohichnoho kraieznavstva," *Suchasnist'* (Kyiv) 11 (November 1998): 142–43.
28. "Oresta," interview with the author, tape recording, Lviv, 22 June 2007.
29. "Vitaliy," interview.
30. Ihor Dobko, interview with the author, tape recording, Lviv, 31 May 2004.
31. Viktor Susak, "Etnichni ta sotsial'ni zminy v naselenni L'vova v 1939–1999 rokakh" (MA thesis, Lviv National University, 2000), 26.
32. Hordiienko, interview.
33. Teodoziy Starak, interview with the author, tape recording, Lviv, 26 February 1999.
34. Roksolana Zorivchak, interview with the author, tape recording, Lviv, 20 April 2000.
35. Slyvka et al., *Kulturne zhyttia*, vol. 2, 39–40.
36. Liubomyr Senyk, interview with the author, tape recording, Lviv, 25 June 1998; Olha Romaniv, interview with the author, tape recording, Shchyrets, Lviv Region, 7 August 2004.
37. Nataliia Chernysh, interview with the author, tape recording, Lviv, 26 July 1999.
38. Halyna Anatoliivna Bodnar, "Mihratsiia sil's'koho naselennia do L'vova v 50–80-kh rokakh XX stolittia" (Candidate of Historical Sciences dissertation, Lviv National University, 2007); Matyukhina, *W sowieckim Lwowie*, 14, 17.
39. Matyukhina, *W sowieckim Lwowie*, 150.
40. M. I. Butsko, "Kuryllo Adam Stanislavovych," in Butsko, *Vidomi vcheni Derzhavnoho Universytetu "L'vivs'ka Politekhnika" 1844–1994: Biohrafichnyi dovidnyk* (Lviv: Vydavnytstvo Derzhavnoho Universytetu "L'vivs'ka Politekhnika," 1994), 74–77. I visited Professor Kuryllo's former home, now in possession of his grandson, several times in 1998 and in 2003–4.

41. Komskii, "Teni tenei," 268–69.
42. Kosmo-Demian Vozniak, interview with the author, field notes, Lviv, 17 March 2004.
43. "Elizaveta," "Kateryna," interview with the author, tape recording, Lviv, 4 August 2004.
44. "Pol's'kyi, narodnyi," *Ukrains'kyi teatr* (Kyiv) 1 (1970): 26; "V im'ia bratn'oho iednannia," *Literaturna Ukraina* (Kyiv) 23 January 1970; Mykhailo Lesiv, "Desiat' dniv u L'vovi: Rozmova z redaktorom Markom A. Iavors'kym," *Nasha kul'tura* (Warsaw) 9.85 (1973): 2–3.
45. Mykola Riabchuk, "Pol'shcha, pol's'kyi, poliaky: Sproba filolohichnoho kraieznavstva," *Suchasnist'* (Kyiv) 11 (November 1998): 145; Oksana Kompaniets Lane, interview with the author, field notes, New York, 25 March 2006.
46. Matyukhina, *W sowieckim Lwowie*, 87.
47. Tarik Youssef Cyril Amar, "The Making of Soviet Lviv, 1939–1953" (PhD dissertation, Princeton University, 2006), 440, 464.
48. Iryna Huzar, interview with the author, tape recording, Lviv, 12 June 2004.
49. Komskii, "Teni tenei," 271–73. Information on the Komskii family's residence in the "Incubator" comes from e-mail correspondence by Iuriy Hordiienko with the author, 23 October 2009.
50. Roman Lozynskyi, *Etnichnyi sklad naselennia L'vova: U konteksti suspil'noho rozvytku Halychyny* (Lviv: Vydavnychyi Tsentr L'vivs'koho Natsional'noho Universytetu imeni Ivana Franka, 2005), 236; Ilko Lemko, *L'viv ponad use: Spohady l'vivianyna druhoi polovyny 20-ho stolittia* (Lviv: Piramida, 2003), 139.
51. Komskii, "Teni tenei," 270.
52. Stefaniia Hnatenko, interview with the author, tape recording, New York, 26 March 2006.
53. Matyukhina, *W sowieckim Lwowie*, 84; Ihor Chornovol, e-mail to the author, 28 September 2009. See also Ihor Chornovol, "Slavni l'vivs'ki batiary," *Postup* (Lviv), 17–21 January 2001, online edition, postup.brama.com (accessed 17 January 2010).
54. Hordiienko, interview.
55. Iuriy Hryhorian and Ihor Chornovol, interview with the author, field notes, Lviv, 12 June 2007; Ihor Chornovol, e-mail to the author, 28 September 2009.
56. Volodymyr Kryvdyk, interview with the author, tape recording, Lviv, 27 July 2004.
57. Isaievych, interview.
58. "Oresta," interview.

59. DALO, R-1694/1/306/28–29; DALO, R-1694/1/301/30–32; DALO, R-1694/1/314/10–13; DALO, R-1694/1/308/31, 36, 41; DALO, P-3810/1/18/15–17.

60. DALO, P-3/19/47/29–33; DALO, P-3/19/67/29–40.

61. Henrykh Bandrovskyi, interview with the author, tape recording, Uzhhorod, 9 August 2004.

62. Slyvka et al., *Kul'turne zhyttia,* vol. 2, 565–66.

63. Ibid.

64. DALO, P-3/19/67/40.

65. Hanna Sadovska, interview with the author, field notes, Lviv, 2 November 1998.

66. Viktor Haman, *Korydory TsK: Deshcho iz zapysnykiv 1968–1972 rokiv ta piznishykh dopovnen'* (Kyiv: Ukrains'kyi Pys'mennyk, 1997), 132.

67. Ihor Pidkova, interview with the author, tape recording, Lviv, 9 July 2004.

68. Oleksiy Sukhyi, interview with the author, tape recording, Lviv, 27 July 2004.

69. Bohdan Kushnir, "'Postfaktum' dezynformuie," *Molod' Ukrainy* (Kyiv), 16 December 1990, 1.

70. Bodnar, "Mihratsiia," 143–44.

71. Slyvka et al., *Kul'turne zhyttia,* vol. 2, 29.

72. Bohdan Iakymovych, interview with the author, tape recording, Lviv, 9 July 2004; Roman Solchanyk, "Ferment in Western Ukraine: An Interview with Rostyslav Bratun'," in Roman Solchanyk, ed., *Ukraine: From Chernobyl' to Sovereignty: A Collection of Interviews,* foreword by Norman Stone (Edmonton: Canadian Institute of Ukrainian Studies Press, 1992), 97.

73. Bandrovskyi, interview.

74. Kozlovskyi, interview.

75. Susak, "Etnichni ta sotsial'ni zminy," 46.

76. Terliuk, *Rosiiany,* 68.

77. Roman Ivanychuk, *Blahoslovy, dushe moia, Hospoda . . . Shchodennykovi zapysy, spohady i rozdumy* (Lviv: Prosvita, 1993), 33; Teodoziy Havryshkevych, interview with the author, tape recording, Lviv, 12 August 2004; Stepan Zlupko, interview with the author, tape recording, Lviv, 3 June 2004.

78. Romaniv, interview.

79. Ibid.

80. "S. P." and Tetiana Chursa, interview with the author, tape recording and field notes, Lviv, 8 March 2004.

81. Kryvdyk, interview.

82. Iuriy Slyvka et al., eds., *Kul'turne zhyttia v Ukraini: Zakhidni zemli,* vol. 1, *1939–1953* (Kyiv: Naukova Dumka, 1995), 471.

83. Ibid., vol. 2, 40.

84. Iuriy Zaitsev and Mykola Dubas, eds., *Ukrains'kyi natsional'nyi front: Doslidzhennia, dokumenty, materialy* (Lviv: Instytut Ukrainoznavstva imeni Ivana Kryp'iakevycha, Natsional'na Akademiia Nauk Ukrainy, 2000).

85. Alexander Statiev, *The Soviet Counterinsurgency in the Western Borderlands* (Cambridge: Cambridge University Press, 2010), 123–37.

86. Jeffrey Burds, "AGENTURA: Soviet Informants' Networks and the Ukrainian Underground in Galicia, 1944–48," *East European Politics and Societies* 11 (Winter 1997): 98.

87. Dariia Rebet, "Z turysts'koi perspektyvy ochyma avtokhtona," *Suchasnist'* (Munich) 1 (1971): 121 (*"moskali"*); DALO, P-92/1/753/30–31 ("occupier").

88. Bodnar, "Mihratsiia," 145.

89. Ievhen Nakonechnyi, interview with the author, tape recording, Lviv, 27 July 2004.

90. DALO, P-92/1/759/61.

91. Slyvka et al., *Kul'turne zhyttia,* vol. 2, 420.

92. Amar, "Soviet Lviv," 784–88.

93. Pierre Bourdieu, *Outline of a Theory of Practice* (London: Cambridge University Press, 1977); Bourdieu, "Habitus," in Jean Hillier and Emma Rooksby, eds., *Habitus: A Sense of Place* (Aldershot, UK: Ashgate, 2002), 27–34.

94. Sheila Fitzpatrick, *Tear Off the Masks! Identity and Imposture in Twentieth-Century Russia* (Princeton: Princeton University Press, 2005); Oleg Kharkhordin, *The Collective and the Individual in Russia: A Study of Practices* (Berkeley: University of California Press, 1999), 270–78.

95. Iryna Huzar, interview with the author, tape recording, Lviv, 12 June 2004; Arkhiv L'vivs'koho Natsional'noho Universytetu imeni Ivana Franka (hereafter Arkhiv LNU), 4914/93–106.

96. Amar, "Soviet Lviv," 456.

97. Huzar, interview; Iryna Huzar, conversation with the author, Lviv, 18 July 2004; Arkhiv LNU, 4914/1 (Party membership); DALO, P-92/1/398/70–71 (ideological campaigns); DALO, P-92/1/400/64 (ideological campaigns); Bohdan Zadorozhnyi, interview with the author, tape recording, Lviv, 20 March 2000 (denunciations, mental state); Arkhiv LNU, 4914/94 (denunciations); DALO, P-92/1/993/123 (denunciations, ideological campaigns); Arkhiv LNU, 4914/93–106 (dismissal).

98. Stefaniia Hnatenko, interview with the author, tape recording, New York, 26 March 2006.

99. Jochen Hellbeck, *Revolution on My Mind: Writing a Diary under Stalin* (Cambridge, MA: Harvard University Press, 2006).

100. Mykola Mushynka, "'Ukraina—tse ne vorota do Rosii, a velyka zemlia . . .': Interv'iu z Dmytrom Pavlychkom naperedodni ioho 70-richchhia," *Dzvin* (Lviv) 10–12 (October–December 1999): 130–31.

101. Roman Szporluk, e-mail to the author, 16 October 2009; Pavlo Chernov, "Zamitky pro polityku peretryvannia i vik chesnosti," *Suchasnist'* (Munich) 11 (November 1961): 34–41.

102. Vladislav Zubok, *Zhivago's Children: The Last Russian Intelligentsia* (Cambridge, MA: Belknap Press of Harvard University Press, 2009).

103. Teodoziy Havryshkevych, conversation with the author, Lviv, 1 January 2010.

104. "Oresta," interview.

105. Bohdan Zalizniak, interview with the author, tape recording, Lviv, 24 July 2004.

106. Isaievych, interview.

107. Zorivchak, interview.

108. Kosmo-Demian Vozniak, interview with the author, tape recording, Lviv, 17 March 2004.

109. Timothy Snyder, *The Reconstruction of Nations: Poland, Ukraine, Lithuania, Belarus, 1569–1999* (New Haven: Yale University Press, 2003), 96–98; Theodore R. Weeks, "A Multi-ethnic City in Transition: Vilnius's Stormy Decade, 1939–1949," *Eurasian Geography and Economics* 47 (2006): 164–70.

110. Rüdiger Ritter, "Prescribed Identity: The Role of History for the Legitimization of Soviet Rule in Lithuania," in Olaf Mertelsmann, ed., *The Sovietization of the Baltic States, 1940–1956* (Tartu: Kleio, 2003), 103.

111. Romuald J. Misiunas and Rein Taagepera, *The Baltic States: Years of Dependence, 1940–1990,* expanded and updated edition (Berkeley: University of California Press, 1993), 131–33, 140–49, 205–8, 275–81.

112. Ibid., 114–15; Vieda Skultans, *The Testimony of Lives: Narrative and Memory in Post-Soviet Latvia* (London: Routledge, 1998), 109–10; Amir Weiner, "The Empires Pay a Visit: Gulag Returnees, East European Rebellions, and Soviet Frontier Policies," *Journal of Modern History* 78 (June 2006): 345–47.

113. Tiina Kirss, ed., *Estonian Life Stories* (Budapest: Central European University Press, 2009).

114. Eižens Valtpēters et al., *Nenocenzētie: Alternatīvā kultūra Latvijā. XX gs. 60-tie un 70-tie gadi* (Riga: Latvijas Vēstnesis, 2010), 51, 54, 155, 172.

115. Albert Leong, "Riga," in Leong, *Centaur: The Life and Art of Ernst Neizvestny* (Lanham, MD: Rowman and Littlefield, 2002), 51–60; Misiunas and Taagepera, *Baltic States,* 207 ("Yestonians"); Maxim

Waldstein, "Russifying Estonia? Iurii Lotman and the Politics of Language and Culture in Soviet Estonia," *Kritika: Explorations in Russian and Eurasian History* 8 (Summer 2007): 561–96.

116. Weiner, "Empires," 356–57.

117. Amir Weiner, "Déjà Vu All Over Again: Prague Spring, Romanian Summer and Soviet Autumn on the Soviet Western Frontier," *Contemporary European History* 15 (2006): 185.

4. The Ukrainian "Soviet Abroad"

1. V. Stanley Vardys, "The Role of the Baltic Republics in Soviet Society," in Roman Szporluk, ed., *The Influence of East Europe and the Soviet West on the USSR* (New York: Praeger, 1975), 159–66; Dmitrii Smirnov, "Sovietization, Terror, and Repression in the Baltic States in the 1940s and 1950s: The Perspective of Contemporary Russian Society," in Olaf Mertelsmann, ed., *The Sovietization of the Baltic States, 1940–1956* (Tartu: Kleio, 2003), 55–57; Elena Zubkova, *Pribaltika i Kreml'. 1940–1953* (Moscow: ROSSPEN, 2008), 3–5.

2. School summer diary of Andrei Vadimov, Dnepropetrovsk, 20 May 1974, cited in Sergei I. Zhuk, "Religion, 'Westernization,' and Youth in the 'Closed City' of Soviet Ukraine, 1964–84," *Russian Review* 67 (October 2008): 2.

3. Roman Szporluk, "Ukraine: From an Imperial Periphery to a Sovereign State," *Daedalus* 126 (1997): 1–35.

4. Ivan L. Rudnytsky, "Franciszek Duchinski and His Impact on Ukrainian Political Thought," in *Essays in Modern Ukrainian History,* ed. Peter L. Rudnytsky (Edmonton: Canadian Institute of Ukrainian Studies, 1987), 194; Yaroslav Hrytsak, "Historical Memory and Regional Identity among Galicia's Ukrainians," in Christopher Hann and Paul Robert Magocsi, eds., *Galicia: A Multicultured Land* (Toronto: University of Toronto Press, 2005), 196.

5. Timothy Snyder, *The Reconstruction of Nations: Poland, Ukraine, Lithuania, Belarus, 1569–1999* (New Haven: Yale University Press, 2003), 154–201.

6. Tarik Youssef Cyril Amar, "The Making of Soviet Lviv, 1939–1963" (PhD dissertation, Princeton University, 2006), 271.

7. Timothy Snyder, *Sketches from a Secret War: A Polish Artist's Mission to Liberate Soviet Ukraine* (New Haven: Yale University Press, 2005).

8. Ibid.

9. Karol Grünberg and Bolesław Sprengel, *Trudne sąsiedztwo: Stosunki polsko-ukraińskie w X–XX wieku* (Warsaw: Książka i Wiedza, 2005).

10. Walter D. Mignolo, *Local Histories/Global Designs: Coloniality, Subaltern Knowledges, and Border Thinking* (Princeton: Princeton University Press, 2000).

11. Ilko Lemko, *L'viv ponad use: Spohady l'vivianyna druhoi polovyny 20-ho stolittia* (Lviv: Piramida, 2003), 135–36; Mykola Riabchuk, "Pol'shcha, pol's'kyi, poliaky: Sproba filolohichnoho kraieznavstva," *Suchasnist'* (Kyiv) 11 (November 1998): 143–44.

12. Excerpts from a series of articles by this journalist, A. Ziemilski, on his trip to Lviv, published in the Warsaw newspaper *Trybuna Ludu* in December 1956, in Iuriy Slyvka et al., eds., *Kul'turne zhyttia v Ukraini: Zakhidni zemli*, vol. 2, *1953–1966* (Lviv: Instytut Ukrainoznavstva imeni Ivana Kryp'iakevycha, Natsional'na Akademiia Nauk Ukrainy, 1995), 221–24.

13. Riabchuk, "Pol'shcha," 139.

14. Rossiiskii Gosudarstvennyi Arkhiv Noveishei Istorii (RGANI), 5/55/100/1–2, in *The Departmental Records of the Central Committee of the Communist Party of the Soviet Union, 1953–1966*, Ideology Department, Reel 437.

15. Riabchuk, "Pol'shcha," 139, 144.

16. Iuriy Sandurskyi and Mykola Petrenko, interview with the author, tape recording, Lviv, 24 March 1999; Bohdan Horyn, "Dvyhun rukhu shistdesiatnykiv," in Valeriy Shevchuk et al., eds., *Dobrookyi: Spohady pro Ivana Svitlychnoho* (Kyiv: Chas, 1998), 266–67.

17. Riabchuk, "Pol'shcha," 143–44.

18. Natalia Chernysh, interview with the author, tape recording, Lviv, 26 July 1999.

19. Lemko, *L'viv*, 41, 121, 136.

20. "S. P." and Tetiana Chursa, interview with the author, Lviv, tape recording, 8 March 2004.

21. Derzhavnyi Arkhiv L'vivs'koi Oblasti (hereafter DALO), R-1694/1/217/58–59.

22. Mykola Petrenko, *Lytsari pera i charky* (Lviv: Spolom, 2000), 104–13; Sandurskyi and Petrenko, interview.

23. Riabchuk, "Pol'shcha," 144–45, 147.

24. Iuriy Hordiienko, interview with the author, tape recording, Lviv, 13 June 2007.

25. Serhiy Pashchenko, interview with the author, tape recording, Lviv, 26 July 2004; Arkadiy Orekhov, interview with the author, tape recording, Lviv, 30 May 2004.

26. Aleksandra Matyukhina, *W sowieckim Lwowie: Życie codzienne miasta w latakh 1944–1990* (Cracow: Wydawnictwo Uniwersytetu Jagiellońskiego, 2000), 120–21, 156–57.

27. Orekhov, interview.

28. Oleksandr Balaban, interview with the author, tape recording and field notes, Lviv, 14 June 2004.

29. Iuriy Peretiat'ko, *L'vivs'kyi rok, 1962–2002* (Lviv: FIRA-liuks, 2002), 9.

30. Chernysh, interview.

31. Riabchuk, "Pol'shcha," 142–43.

32. "Wycieczka do Lwowa," *Na antenie* (Munich), 25 February 1968, 1.

33. DALO, P-3/5/402/221.

34. Slyvka et al., *Kul'turne zhyttia*, vol. 2, 215.

35. Chernysh, interview; Lemko, *L'viv*, 135.

36. DALO, P-3567/1/204/134–37.

37. Riabchuk, "Pol'shcha," 146; Sandurskyi and Petrenko, interview.

38. DALO, P-3/6/275/5, 46.

39. DALO, P-3/9/225/133.

40. DALO, P-3/6/275/75.

41. Tsentral'nyi Derzhavnyi Arkhiv Hromads'kykh Ob'iednan' Ukrainy (hereafter TsDAHOU), 1/25/878/17.

42. TsDAHOU, 1/25/878/16.

43. DALO, P-576/1/82/108, 117.

44. DALO, P-3/6/275/74, 82–84.

45. DALO, P-3/6/276/125–26.

46. Mykola Krykun, interview with the author, tape recording, Lviv, 27 March 2003.

47. Slyvka et al., *Kul'turne zhyttia*, vol. 2, 215.

48. Amir Weiner, "The Empires Pay a Visit: Gulag Returnees, East European Rebellions, and Soviet Frontier Politics," *Journal of Modern History* 78 (June 2006): 374–75.

49. DALO, P-3/6/275/54.

50. DALO, P-3/6/275/51 ("cattle"); DALO, P-3/6/275/54 ("lice"); DALO, P-3/6/276/156 (streets warning); DALO, P-3/6/276/157 (Lviv); DALO, P-3/6/275/224–25 (wilted flowers).

51. Roman Petruk, interview with the author, tape recording, Lviv, 21 June 1999.

52. Riabchuk, "Pol'shcha," 144–45; "'To była sprawa smaku . . .': Rozmowa z Mykołą Riabczukiem," in Bogumiła Berdychowska and Ola Hnatiuk, *Bunt pokolenia: Rozmowy z intelektualistami ukraińskimi* (Lublin: Wydawnictwo Uniwersytetu Marii Curie-Skłodowskiej, 2000), 217–18.

53. Matyukhina, *W sowieckim Lwowie*, 152.

54. Larysa Krushelnytska, *Rubaly lis . . . (spohady halychanky)* (New York: Vydavnytstvo M. P. Kots', 2001), 219–20.

55. Aleksandr Khokhulin ("Mankurt"), "Chast' vtoraia (1972–1977)" and "Chast' tret'ia (1977–1983)," in "My—mankurty (zapiski russkogo l'vovianina)," www.mankurty.com (accessed 3 January 2008);

Oleksandr Khokhulin, interview with the author, field notes, Lviv, 24 June 2007.

56. Albert Astakhov, interview with the author, tape recording, Russian Cultural Center, Lviv, 27 June 2007. Astakhov added this comment about the Soviet Union's passing when editing his quotes for the book.

57. Vladimir Shlapentokh, *Soviet Intellectuals and Political Power: The Post-Stalin Era* (Princeton: Princeton University Press, 1990), 71n2; Vladislav Zubok, *Zhivago's Children: The Last Russian Intelligentsia* (Cambridge, MA: Belknap Press of Harvard University Press, 2009), 90.

58. Ilko Lemko, "L'viv rosiys'kyi," in Diana Klochko, ed., *Leopolis multiplex* (Kyiv: Hrani-T, 2008), 217–18.

59. Eugeniusz Bodo, *"Zhdem vas vo L'vove/Czekamy Was we Lwowie,"* www .youtube.com (accessed 3 January 2011); Diana Poskuta-Włodek, "Szwajcarski paszport na Sybir: Głośne życie i cicha śmierć Eugeniusza Bodo," *Przegląd Polski* (New York), online version, 23 July 2004, www.dziennik.com (accessed 3 January 2011). I thank Ievhen Hlibovytskyi for sharing this online version of Bodo's Russian-language performance of "Only in Lwów."

60. Slyvka et al., *Kul'turne zhyttia,* vol. 2, 220, cited in William Jay Risch, "Thinking between Borders: Polish Media and Cultural Resistance in Post-1953 L'viv," *Canadian American Slavic Studies* 40 (Spring 2006): 119n67, and Weiner, "Empires," 353n58.

61. Mykola Ilnytskyi, *Drama bez katarsysu: Storinky literaturnoho zhyttia L'vova druhoi polovyny XX stolittia* (Lviv: Instytut Ukrainoznavstva imeni Ivana Kryp'iakevycha, Natsional'na Akademiia Nauk Ukrainy, 2003), 31–32.

62. Ihor Kalynets, interview with the author, tape recording, Lviv, 7 February 1999.

63. Ilnytskyi, *Drama bez katarsysu,* 31–32.

64. Jerzy Eisler, *Marzec 1968: Geneza, przebieg, konsekwencje* (Warsaw: Panstwowe Wydawnictwo Naukowe, 1991).

65. DALO, P-3/10/248/1.

66. DALO, P-3/10/248/2.

67. Ibid.

68. Iaroslav Kendzior, interview with the author, tape recording, Lviv, 29 December 1998; Padraic Kenney, *A Carnival of Revolution: Central Europe 1989* (Princeton: Princeton University Press, 2002), 165, 229–30.

69. TsDAHOU, 1/25/2048/99–100.

70. TsDAHOU, 1/25/2048/98–99.

71. Matyukhina, *W sowieckim Lwowie,* 166–67.

72. Stefaniia Hnatenko, interview with the author, tape recording, New York,

13 March 1998; Stefaniia Hnatenko, interview with the author, tape recording, New York, 26 March 2006.

73. DALO, P-3/5/397/206, quoted in Slyvka et al., *Kul'turne zhyttia,* vol. 2, 220.

74. Weiner, "Empires," 373.

75. Slyvka et al., *Kul'turne zhyttia,* vol. 2, 448–49.

76. DALO, P-3/8/420/53.

77. DALO, P-92/1/846/20.

78. DALO, P-3/25/52/21.

79. Riabchuk, "Pol'shcha," 142.

80. Ibid., 145.

81. Theodore R. Weeks, *Nation and State in Late Imperial Russia: Nationalism and Russification on the Western Frontier, 1863–1914* (DeKalb: Northern Illinois University Press, 1996).

82. Kate Brown, *A Biography of No Place: From Ethnic Borderland to Soviet Heartland* (Cambridge, MA: Harvard University Press, 2004), 126.

83. Khachig Tölölyan, "The Nation-State and Its Others: In Lieu of a Preface," in Geoff Eley and Ronald Grigor Suny, eds., *Becoming National: A Reader* (New York: Oxford University Press, 1996), 428.

84. Orest Subtelny, *Ukraine: A History,* 2nd ed. (Toronto: University of Toronto Press, 1994), 538–72; Myron B. Kuropas, *The Ukrainian-Americans: Roots and Aspirations, 1884–1954* (Toronto: University of Toronto Press, 1991).

85. "Elizaveta," "Tetiana," interview with the author, tape recording, Lviv, 23 January 2003.

86. TsDAHOU, 1/25/878/16; Weiner, "Empires," 373.

87. Jeffrey Burds, "The Early Cold War in Soviet West Ukraine, 1944–1948," *Carl Beck Papers in Russian and East European Studies,* no. 1505 (2001): 11–18.

88. DALO, R-119/6/176/8 (academic conferences); Roman Ivanychuk, *Blahoslovy, dushe moia, Hospoda . . . Shchodennykovi zapysy, spohady i rozdumy* (Lviv: Prosvita, 1993), 78–79 (Kravchuk).

89. A copy of the initiative group's appeal, dated approximately 1960, is in DALO, P-3/8/134/280–81.

90. DALO, P-3/8/273/152. This volume *(sprava)* has a number of reports on foreign tourists, most of them Americans and Canadians of Ukrainian descent, who had traveled to rural districts, towns, and other parts of the Lviv Region.

91. DALO, P-3/9/230/215.

92. TsDAHOU, 1/25/878/16.

93. TsDAHOU, 1/25/878/17.

94. Tyt Hevryk, "Ivan vidkryv nam Ukrainu," in Valeriy Shevchuk et al., eds., *Dobrookyi: Spohady pro Ivana Svitlychnoho* (Kyiv: Chas, 1998), 393–94.

95. DALO, P-3/8/437/18–33.

96. TsDAHOU, 1/6/3859/30–31.

97. TsDAHOU, 1/10/1009/162–63.

98. DALO, P-3/19/22/78–80.

99. "'Mieliśmy wielką misję przed sobą . . .': Rozmowa z Mychajłą Horyniem," in Bogumiła Berdychowska and Ola Hnatiuk, *Bunt pokolenia: Rozmowy z intelektualistami ukraińskimi* (Lublin: Wydawnictwo Uniwersytetu Marii Curie-Skłodowskiej, 2000), 179.

100. Bohdan Horyn, "Moi zustrichi ta rozmovy z Irynoiu Vil'de," in Mariia Iakubovs'ka, ed., *Spohady pro Irynu Vil'de* (Lviv: Kameniar, 2009), 50–52.

101. Petro Shkrabiuk, *Popid zoloti vorota: Shist' elehiy pro rodynu Kalyntsiv* (Lviv: Instytut Ukrainoznavstva imeni Ivana Kryp'iakevycha, Natsional'na Akademiia Nauk Ukrainy, 1997), 88; TsDAHOU, 1/25/515/1–2; TsDAHOU, 1/25/515/5.

102. DALO, P-3/19/22/109–10.

103. Iuriy Slyvka and Iuriy Zaitsev, eds., *Ukrains'ka poeziia pid sudom KGB: Kryminal'ni spravy Iryny ta Ihoria Kalyntsiv* (Lviv: Afisha, 2004), 126–28, 143–44, 177–78, 327.

104. Hryhoriy Kasianov, *Nezhodni: Ukrains'ka intelihentsiia v rusi oporu 1960–80-kh rokiv* (Kyiv: Lybid', 1995), 122–24.

105. DALO, P-53/19/16/79.

106. Mykola Ilnytskyi, interview with the author, tape recording, Lviv, 30 March 1999; Kasianov, *Nezhodni*, 25–26; Shkrabiuk, *Popid zoloti vorota*, 45, 66, 68.

107. Grey Hodnett and Peter Potichnyj, *The Ukraine and the Czechoslovak Crisis*, Occasional Paper 6 (Canberra: Australian National University, Department of Political Science, 1970), 54, 59, 62, 72, 74; Amir Weiner, "Déjà Vu All Over Again: Prague Spring, Romanian Summer and Soviet Autumn on the Soviet Western Frontier," *Contemporary European History* 15 (2006): 172–73.

108. Levko Lukianenko, *Ne dam zahynut' Ukraini!* (Kyiv: Sofiia, 1994), 42; Iryna Kalynets, interview with the author, tape recording, Lviv, 12 April 2000.

109. M. Lesiv, "Pro pol's'ko-ukrains'ki literaturni kontakty, ukrains'ku poeziiu toshcho," *Nasha kul'tura* (Warsaw) 5.169 (1972): 2–5.

110. TsDAHOU, 1/25/878/16–22.

111. Ie. Deka, "Notatky pro Ukrainu," *Svoboda* (Jersey City, NJ), 22 November 1974, 2; Deka, "Notatky pro Ukrainu," *Svoboda* (Jersey City, NJ), 23 November 1974, 2.

112. Susan E. Reid, "Who Will Beat Whom? Soviet Popular Reception of the American National Exhibition in Moscow, 1959," *Kritika: Explorations in Russian and Eurasian History* 9 (Fall 2008): 855–904.

113. Alexei Yurchak, *Everything Was Forever, Until It Was No More: The Last Soviet Generation* (Princeton: Princeton University Press, 2006), 205–6.

114. Roksolana Zorivchak, interview with the author, tape recording, Lviv, 20 April 2000.

115. Andriy Rudnytskyi and Yuriy Biryulov, *L'viv: Turystyschnyi putivnyk/ Lviv: Sightseeing Guide* (Lviv: Tsentr Ievropy, 1999).

116. V. Popov, "Molodiie starodavnyi L'viv," *Molod' Ukrainy* (Kyiv), 12 April 1974, 4; V. S. Vuytsyk, R. M. Lypa, *Zustrich zi L'vovom/Vstrecha so L'vovom/An Encounter with Lvov* (Lviv: Kameniar, 1987), 8 (architectural preserve).

117. Grigory Semyonov, *Lvov: Tourist Guide* (Moscow: Novosti Press Agency Publishing House, 1972), 4–5; M. I. Shved, *L'viv—L'vov—Lwów—Lviv: Korotkyi putivnyk—dovidnyk* (Lviv: Kameniar, 1978), 126.

118. Popov, "Molodiie starodavnyi L'viv."

119. Matyukhina, *W sowieckim Lwowie*, 18.

120. Petrenko, *Lytsari pera*, 27, 34–35, 179.

121. Halyna Huzo, "De vidbulosia vashe pershe pobachennia u L'vovi?" *Vysokyi zamok* (Lviv), 27 October 2005, online edition, www.wz.lviv.ua (accessed 8 February 2006) (rock bands); Oleh Olisevych, Iaryna Borenko, Iania Plakhotniuk, and Andriy Pavlyshyn, "'Iakshcho svitovi bude potribno, ia viddam svoie zhyttia ne zadumaiuchys'—zarady svobody': Interv'iu z Olehom Olisevychem," *IY: Nezalezhnyi kul'turolohichnyi chasopys* (Lviv) 24 (2002): 149–50; Maryna Kursanova, "Ptentsy letiat sledom . . . Putevoditel' po literaturnoi karte L'vova," *Znamia* (Moscow), 6 (2003), online edition, magazines.russ.ru (accessed 16 October 2009).

122. Conversation with Anatoliy Kruglashov, 30 May 2006 (Chocolate Bar); Halyna Domozhirova, "Oleksandr Aksinin: Trahichna myttievist' vesny," *Halyts'ka brama* (Lviv) 7 (July 2001): 6; Ihor Diurych, "Oleksandr Aksinin," www.mankurty.com (accessed 10 July 2009).

123. Yurchak, *Everything Was Forever*, 141–46.

124. Scott Lash, "Postmodernism as Humanism? Urban Space and Social Theory," in Brian S. Turner, ed., *Theories of Modernity and Postmodernity* (London: Sage, 1990), 62–74.

125. Vasyl Babiy, interview with the author, tape recording, Lviv, 23 July 2004 ("mysticism"); Lemko, *L'viv*, 161–63 (false distinctions).

126. Roman Lubkivskyi, *L'viv: Misto ochyma pys'mennyka* (Lviv: Kameniar, 1985), 58–59; Shved, *L'viv—L'vov—Lwów—Lviv*, 126.

127. DALO, P-3/8/255/20; DALO, P-3/8/424/72–73.

128. Bohdan Iakymovych, interview with the author, tape recording, Lviv, 20 April 2000; "Oleksa Hudima: 'U stolytsi til'ky pratsiuiu, a u L'vovi zhyvu . . . ,'" *Vysokyi zamok* (Lviv), 27 October 2005, online edition, www.wz.lviv.ua (accessed 8 February 2006).

129. R. M. Iatsiv, *L'vivs'ka hrafika 1945–1990: Tradytsii ta novatorstvo* (Kyiv: Naukova Dumka, 1992), 100.

130. I. Sychevskyi, ed., *Slovo pro L'viv* (Lviv: Kameniar, 1969), 2.

131. Maia Bilan, "Mystetstvo molodykh," *Zhovten'* (Lviv) 11 (November 1965): 136–38 (café interior); Andriy Rudnytskyi and Yuriy Biryulov, *L'viv: Turystychnyi putivnyk,* 32 (opening date).

132. Rostyslav Bratun, "Zacharovanyi tramvai (L'vivs'ka khymeriia)" (1965), in Bratun, *Tvory u dvokh tomakh,* vol. 2, *Poemy, balady, pisni* (Kyiv: Dnipro, 1979), 49–64.

133. Ihor Kalynets, "Smert' Pidkovy," in *Vohon Kupala* (1966), reprinted in Kalynets, *Slovo tryvaiuche: Poezii* (Kharkiv: Folio, 1997), 28; Sychevskyi, *Slovo pro L'viv,* 38–41.

134. Lubkivskyi, *L'viv,* 10–12, 17–18.

135. Kostiantyn Iegorov, "Vysokii zamok," *Lenins'ka molod'* (Lviv), 13 February 1971, 3 ("Slavic wisdom"); Ihor Kalynets, "Italiys'ke podvir'ia: Poryvannia," in Kalynets, *Slovo tryvaiuche: Poezii* (Kharkiv: Folio, 1997), 507–16 (Lviv ghettos).

136. Ola Hnatiuk, *Pożegnanie z imperium: Ukraińskie dyskusje o tożamości* (Lublin: Wydawnictwo Uniwersytetu Marii Curie-Skłodowskiej, 2003), 207, 210.

137. Grigorii Komskii, "Teni tenei," *IY: Nezalezhnyi kul'turolohichnyi chasopys* (Lviv) 29 (2003): 267–69, 271. Komskii's Komsomol hearing for participation in this journal is in DALO, P-3568/1/88/105–6.

138. Oksana Kompaniets Lane, interview with the author, tape recording, New York, 25 March 2006.

139. Yurchak, *Everything Was Forever,* 204–5.

140. Iuriy Sharifov, interview with the author, tape recording, Lviv, 13 June 2007.

141. Oleksandr Balaban, interview with the author, tape recording, Lviv, 5 June 2007.

142. Aleksei Kozlov, *Dzhaz, rok i mednye truby* (Moscow: Ieksmo, 2005), 364.

143. Sharifov, interview.

144. Serhiy Kosolapov ("Tsepelin") and Volodymyr Vyshnevskyi ("Vyshnia"), interview with the author, tape recording, Lviv, 25 May 2007.

145. John Czaplicka, "Lviv, Lemberg, Leopolis, Lwów, Lvov: A City in the Crosscurrents of European Culture," in Czaplicka, ed., *Lviv: A City in the Crosscurrents of Culture* (Cambridge, MA: Harvard Ukrainian Research Institute/Harvard University Press, 2005), 33.

146. Anna Brazhkina, "Z tsikavosti i zvychky," *Krytyka* (Kyiv) 3 (2006), online edition, www.krytyka.kiev.ua (accessed 21 April 2006).

147. Iurii Bashmet, *Vokzal mechty* (Moscow: Vagrius, 2003), 17.

148. "Yavlinsky, Grigory Alexeyevich," *Who's Who in Russia 2005* (Moscow: Who's Who Strategic Area, 2005), 873–74.

149. "L'viv—kolyska velykykh," directed by Iuriy Hnatkovskyi (Lviv: Trident, 2006).

150. Romuald Misiunas and Rein Taagepera, *The Baltic States: Years of Dependence 1940–1990,* expanded and updated edition (Berkeley: University of California Press, 1993), 176–83, 218–21, 243–45.

151. Eižens Valtpēters et al., *Nenocenzētie: Alternatīvā kultūra Latvijā. XX gs. 60-tie un 70-tie gadi* (Riga: Latvijas Vēstnesis, 2010), 22-23, 55, 59, 106, 121-22, 130, 143, 148, 155, 310.

152. Mykola Mushynka, "'Ukraina—tse ne vorota do Rosii, a velyka zemlia . . .': Interv'iu z Dmytrom Pavlychkom naperedodni ioho 70-richchia," *Dzvin* (Lviv) 10–12 (October–December 1999): 131 (Party officials); "'To była sprawa smaku . . . ,'" 226–27, 236–37 (culture).

153. Volodymyr Kit, interview with the author, tape recording, Lviv, 4 January 2010.

154. Kursanova, "Ptentsy letiat."

155. Oleh Olisevych et al., "'Iakshcho svitovi bude potribno, ia viddam svoie zhyttia ne zadumaiuchys'—zarady svobody': Interv'iu z Olehom Olisevychem," *IY: Nezalezhnyi kul'turolohichnyi chasopys* (Lviv) 24 (2002): 141; Eleonora Havryliuk, "Tusovka vmerla—khai zhyve tusovka: Identychnist' l'vivs'kykh neformaliv," *IY: Nezalezhnyi kul'turolohichnyi chasopys* (Lviv) 24 (2002): 229.

156. Khokhulin, "Chast' tret'ia."

157. Valtpēters et al., *Nenocenzētie* 88, 106.

158. Ibid., passim.

159. Misiunas and Taagepera, *Baltic States,* 179; Weiner, "Déjà Vu All Over Again," 162–64.

160. Amar, "Soviet Lviv."

161. Amir Weiner, "Empires," 356.

162. Zubkova, *Pribaltika,* 343–44.

163. Ibid., 337.

5. Language and Literary Politics

1. Volodymyr Baran, *Ukraina: 1950–1960-kh rr.: Evoliutsiia totalitarnoi systemy* (Lviv: Instytut Ukrainoznavstva imeni Ivana Kryp'iakevycha, Natsional'na Akademiia Nauk Ukrainy, 1996), 222–25, 235–38; Hryhoriy Kasianov, *Nezhodni: Ukrains'ka intelihentsiia v rusi oporu 1960–80-kh*

rokiv (Kyiv: Lybid', 1995), 12–13; Borys Lewytzkyi, *Politics and Society in Soviet Ukraine, 1953–1980* (Edmonton: Canadian Institute of Ukrainian Studies, 1984), 23–35.

2. Mykola Mushynka, "'Ukraina—tse ne vorota do Rosii, a velyka zemlia . . .': Interv'iu z Dmytrom Pavlychkom naperedodni ioho 70-richchia," *Dzvin* (Lviv) 10–12 (October–December 1999): 130.

3. Tsentral'nyi Derzhavnyi Arkhiv Hromads'kykh Ob'iednan' Ukrainy (hereafter TsDAHOU), 1/25/217/2.

4. Ivan Hushchak, "Rostyslav Bratun," in Hushchak, *Pleiada zaboronena, pryzabuta* (Lviv: Kobzar, 1998), 262–63; Mykola Ilnytskyi, *Drama bez katarsysu: Storinky literaturnoho zhyttia L'vova pershoi polovyny XX stolittia* (Lviv: Misioner, 1999), 176–77; Mykola Petrenko, "Chy i my buly bohemoiu: Na charku z Bratunem," *Postup* (Lviv), 6 February 1999, 6.

5. Derzhavnyi Arkhiv L'vivs'koi Oblasti (hereafter DALO), P-3808/1/3/1–13. I did not gain official access to Bratun's personal Party file, but in February 1999 someone from DALO on condition of anonymity read me Bratun's petition to Stalin, ingratiating him as "my sun" *(solntse moe)* in Russian.

6. Rostyslav Bratun, *Krapka bez i: Pamflety* (Kyiv: Radians'kyi Pys'mennyk, 1959).

7. Roman Szporluk, e-mail to the author, 16 October 2009.

8. Iuriy Slyvka et al., eds., *Kul'turne zhyttia v Ukraini: Zakhidni zemli,* vol. 1, *1939–1953* (Kyiv: Naukova Dumka, 1995), 364–65, 593, 623, 644–46; Viktor Kostiuchenko, "Zapytannia Iryny Vil'de 'Vozhdevi' Stalinu i s'ohodnishn'omu dniu," *Dzvin* (Lviv) 2 (February 2000): 113–14.

9. Iuriy Slyvka et al., eds., *Kul'turne zhyttia v Ukraini: Zakhidni zemli,* vol. 2, *1953–1966* (Lviv: Instytut Ukrainoznavstva imeni Ivana Kryp'iakevycha, Natsional'na Akademiia Nauk Ukrainy, 1995), 39–40.

10. Kasianov, *Nezhodni,* 15–16; Baran, *Ukraina,* 224, 235–37.

11. DALO, P-3808/1/24/33–46 (open Party meeting, 5 June); DALO, P-3808/1/24/52–58 (closed Party meeting, 3 August 1956); DALO, P-3808/1/24/77–159 (annual Party election meeting, 7 December 1956).

12. Slyvka et al., *Kul'turne zhyttia,* vol. 2, 206–7 (Pavlychko speech); DALO, P-3808/1/24/53–54.

13. Gerhard Simon, *Nationalism and Policy towards the Nationalities in the Soviet Union: From Totalitarianism to Post-Stalinist Society,* trans. Karen Forster and Ostwald Forster (Boulder, CO: Westview Press, 1991), 246–47.

14. Slyvka et al., *Kul'turne zhyttia,* vol. 2, 362; Dmytro Pavlychko, "Kontsert u tsaria" (1958), in *Pravda klyche: Poezii* (Kyiv: Veselka, 1995), 78–80; Pavlychko, "Koly pomer kryvavyi Torkvemada . . ." (1955), in *Pravda klyche: Poezii* (Kyiv: Veselka, 1995), 140.

15. Slyvka et al., *Kul'turne zhyttia,* vol. 2, 359–64 (Melnychuk and obkom bureau); DALO, P-3808/1/32/8–14 (Writers' Union).

16. Slyvka et al., *Kul'turne zhyttia,* vol. 2, 362.

17. Ibid., 361.

18. Iaroslav Dashkevych, "Borot'ba z Hrushevs'kym ta ioho shkoloiu u L'vivs'komu universyteti za radians'kykh chasiv," in L. Vynar et al., eds., *Mykhajlo Hrushevs'kyi i L'vivs'ka istorychna shkola: Materialy konferen-tsii, L'viv, 24–25 zhovtnia 1994 r.* (New York: Ukrains'ke Istorychne Tovarystvo, 1995), 44n21.

19. Tarik Youssef Cyril Amar, "The Making of Soviet Lviv, 1939–1963" (PhD dissertation, Princeton University, 2006), 325.

20. DALO, P-3808/1/24/109–111 (signs); DALO, P-3808/1/32/12 (Pavlychko).

21. DALO, P-3808/1/24/121; "Tymish Odud'ko," *Literaturna Ukraina* (Kyiv) 5 August 1982.

22. Amir Weiner, *Making Sense of War: The Second World War and the Fate of the Bolshevik Revolution* (Princeton: Princeton University Press, 2001), 331–32.

23. DALO, P-3808/1/32/9, 13.

24. Mykola Ilnytskyi, *Drama bez katarsysu: Storinky literaturnoho zhyttia L'vova druhoi polovyny XX stolittia* (L'viv: Instytut Ukrainoznavstva imeni Ivana Kryp'iakevycha, Natsional'na Akademiia Nauk Ukrainy, 2003), 86 (Vilde); DALO, P-3/10/1932/65–67 (Petrenko); DALO, P-3808/1/47/17 (Petrenko).

25. "Zustrich z avtozavodtsiamy," *Literaturna Ukraina* (Kyiv), 15 March 1966.

26. Personal Papers of Roman Szporluk, Professor Emeritus, Harvard University.

27. Ibid.

28. Population figures for 1970 are in Viktor Susak, "Etnichni ta sotsial'ni zminy v naselenni L'vova v 1939–1999 rokakh" (MA thesis, Lviv National University, 2000), 38.

29. I thank Halyna Bodnar for conducting research of these archives for me in April 2010.

30. Iuriy Zaitsev, "Rosiyshchennia," in Iaroslav Isaievych et al., eds., *Istoriia L'vova,* vol. 3, *Lystopad 1918–poch. XXI st.* (Lviv: Tsentr Ievropy, 2007), 317.

31. Population statistics for 1979 are in Susak, "Etnichni ta sotsial'ni zminy," 38.

32. "Keruiuchys' chuttiam iedynoi rodyny," *Literaturna Ukraina* (Kyiv), 9 April 1987, 6 (Kyiv); Anatoliy Rusnachenko, *Natsional'no-vyzvol'nyi rukh v Ukraini: Seredyna 1950-kh—pochatok 1990-kh rokiv* (Kyiv: Vydavnyt-stvo imeni Oleny Telihy, 1998), 357 (Donetsk).

33. DALO, P-3808/1/24/131–32.

34. DALO, P-3/5/97/27.

35. Charlotte Saikowski, "Ukraine Nationalism Disturbs Soviet Leaders," *Christian Science Monitor,* 7 May 1969, 15.

36. Bohdan Iakymovych, interview with the author, tape recording, Lviv, 9 July 2004 (Russian and Ukrainian at Polytechnic); Oleksiy Sukhyi, interview with the author, tape recording, Lviv, 27 July 2004 (Lviv State University).

37. Yaroslav Bilinsky, "Assimilation and Ethnic Assertiveness among Ukrainians of the Soviet Union," in Erich Goldhagen, ed., *Ethnic Minorities in the Soviet Union* (New York: Frederick A. Praeger, 1968), 164–66; Iakymovych, interview; Serhy Yekelchyk, *Ukraine: Birth of a Modern Nation* (Oxford: Oxford University Press, 2007), 173.

38. Susak, "Etnichni ta sotsial'ni zminy," 40.

39. Martin Åberg, "Paradox of Change: Soviet Modernization and Ethno-Linguistic Differentiation in Lviv, 1945–1989," in John Czaplicka, ed., *Lviv: A City in the Crosscurrents of Culture* (Cambridge, MA: Harvard University Press/Harvard Ukrainian Research Institute, 2005), 291.

40. Susak, "Etnichni ta sotsial'ni zminy," 38–40.

41. Leonid Zashkilniak, interview with the author, tape recording, Lviv, 31 July 2004 ("hick language"); "Elizaveta," interview with the author, tape recording, Lviv, 4 August 2004 (Shevchenko).

42. Oleksandr Zelinskyi, interview with the author, tape recording, Lviv, 22 June 1999.

43. DALO, P-3808/1/24/38.

44. DALO, P-3808/1/24/35–37.

45. Liubomyr Senyk, interview with the author, tape recording, Lviv, 5 November 1998.

46. DALO, R-2009/1/119/3.

47. Iuriy Zaitsev, "Antyrezhymnyi rukh (1956–1991)," in Volodymyr Aleksandrovych et al., eds., *L'viv: Istorychni narysy* (Lviv: Instytut Ukrainoznavstva imeni Ivana Kryp'iakevycha, Natsional'na Akademiia Nauk Ukrainy, 1996), 564 (Sunday poetry readings); Emily Lygo, "The Need for New Voices: Writers' Union Policy Towards Young Writers 1953–64," in Polly Jones, ed., *The Dilemmas of De-Stalinization: Negotiating Cultural and Social Change in the Khrushchev Era* (London: Routledge, 2006), 193–208; Volodymyr Kvitnevyi, "Na shliakhu borot'by za ukrains'ke vidrodzhennia (iz spohadiv pro 'shistdesiatnykiv')," *Zhyvotoky* (Lviv) 1.6 (January–March 1994): 12 (Club of Artistic Youth).

48. Mykola Ilnytskyi, "Na pul'si epokhy," *Zhovten'* (Lviv) 1 (January 1964): 123–30; Ilnytskyi, "Monumental'nist' i chas," *Zhovten'* (Lviv) 8 (August

1964): 128–36; Ihor Motorniuk and Liubomyr Senyk, "Pereroblene i dopovnene," *Zhovten'* (Lviv) 4 (April 1965): 134–37.

49. Mykhailo Kosiv, "Perehuk heniiv—chy perekruchennia faktiv?" *Zhovten'* (Lviv) 3 (March 1965): 154–57.

50. This untitled review is in *Zhovten'* (Lviv) 4 (April 1965): 138–40.

51. For analysis of Antonych's poetry, see Maryna Novykova, "Mifosvit Antonycha," in Bohdan-Ihor Antonych, *Tvory,* ed. M. N. Moskalenko (Kyiv: Dnipro, 1998), 5–18.

52. Bohdan-Ihor Antonych, "Slovo pro Al'kazar," in Antonych, *Tvory,* ed. M. N. Moskalenko (Kyiv: Dnipro, 1998), 155–56.

53. DALO, P-3/9/34/16–17 (region); TsDAHOU, 1/25/217/3–4 (republic).

54. "Poet vesnianoho pokhmillia: Poeziia Bohdana Ihora Antonycha," *Zhovten'* (Lviv) 2 (October 1964): 100–109 (Antonych's poems); Stepan Trofymuk, "Poet vesnianoho pokhmillia: Slovo pro Bohdana Ihora Antonycha," *Zhovten'* (Lviv) 2 (February 1964): 134–45; Bohdan Ihor Antonych, "Dovbush," *Zhovten'* (Lviv) 9 (September 1965): 56–102.

55. Bohdan-Ihor Antonych, *Pisnia pro neznyshchennist' materii: Poezii* (Kyiv: Radians'kyi Pys'mennyk, 1967); DALO, R-2009/1/74/26–27 (Pavlychko remarks).

56. Dmytro Pavlychko, "Pisnia pro neznyshchennist' materii," in Bohdan-Ihor Antonych, *Pisnia pro neznyshchennist' materii: Poezii* (Kyiv: Radians'kyi Pys'mennyk, 1967), 7–46; Trofymuk, "Poet vesniannoho pokhmillia"; TsDAHOU, 1/24/6001/78–79 (Bratun).

57. Petro Shkrabiuk, *Popid zoloti vorota: Shist' elehiy pro rodynu Kalyntsiv* (Lviv: Instytut Ukrainoznavstva imeni Ivana Kryp'iakevycha, Natsional'na Akademiia Nauk Ukrainy, 1997), 40–41, 420 (Ihor Kalynets); Hrytsko Chubai, *Plach Ieremii: Poeziia, pereklady, spohady* (Lviv: Kal'variia, 1998), 286; "'To była sprawa smaku . . .': Rozmowa z Mykołą Riabczukiem," in Bogumiła Berdychowska and Ola Hnatiuk, *Bunt pokolenia: Rozmowy z intelekualistami ukraińskimi* (Lublin: Wydawnictwo Uniwersytetu Marii Curie-Skłodowskiej, 2000), 239 (Andrukhovych).

58. TsDAHOU, 1/24/6001/64, 80.

59. DALO, P-2941/1/159/38.

60. Ivan Dziuba, *Internatsionalizm chy rusyfikatsiia* (Kyiv: KM Academia, 1998), 140.

61. DALO, P-3/9/45/16–18; DALO, P-3/9/51/144–53.

62. Tsentral'nyi Derzhavnyi Arkhiv-Muzei Literatury ta Mystetstva Ukrainy (hereafter TsDAMLMU), 590/1/601/6–12.

63. TsDAHOU, 1/8/3258/30.

64. DALO, P-2941/1/159/37. These poems were not published in its March 1964 issue.

65. DALO, P-3/9/34/17 (literary critics); TsDAHOU, 1/24/6001/68 (writers of the past).

66. DALO, P-3/9/34/16–17.

67. Ilnytskyi, *Drama bez katarsysu* (2003), 68 (Inhulskyi); Roman Ivanychuk, *Blahoslovy, dushe moia, Hospoda . . . Shchodennykovi zapysy, spohady i rozdumy* (Lviv: Prosvita, 1993), 118–19 (Inhulskyi); TsDAHOU, 1/24/6001/68 (censors).

68. DALO, P-3808/1/24/137, 153 (drinking bout); DALO, P-3808/1/25/1–4 (drinking bout); TsDAHOU, 1/8/3290/171 (criticism of journal).

69. Petrenko, "Chy i my buly bohemoiu," 6.

70. Vitalii Vrublevskii, *Vladimir Shcherbytskii: Pravda i vymysly* (Kyiv: Dovira, 1993), 114–24.

71. TsDAHOU, 1/24/6001/75 (Ukrainian words); TsDAHOU, 1/24/6001/81–83 ("abstractionist," "formalist"); DALO, P-3/9/51/151 (Skaba).

72. Ilnytskyi, *Drama bez katarsysu* (2003), 76.

73. Ivanychuk, *Blahoslovy,* 123–24.

74. Vladimir Lakshin, *Solzhenitsyn, Tvardovsky, and Novy Mir,* trans. and ed. Michael Glenny (Cambridge, MA: MIT Press, 1980).

75. DALO, P-3/10/209/24.

76. TsDAHOU, 1/25/515/5.

77. Ivanychuk, *Blahoslovy,* 126.

78. Ilnytskyi, *Drama bez katarsysu* (2003), 88 (Podolchak and threats), 192–94 (Podolchak's removal).

79. Ibid., 87.

80. Oleksandr Irvanets, interview with the author, tape recording, Harvard Ukrainian Research Institute, Cambridge, MA, 9 March 2006.

81. Personal Papers of Roman Szporluk, Professor Emeritus, Harvard University.

82. "Disregard for People's Opinion Is Not to Be Forgiven, Says Roman Fedoriv," *News from Ukraine* (Kyiv), 19 (1989), 4.

83. DALO, P-3/10/1932/22 (Chornovil); DALO, P-3/10/1934/56–57 (Prague Spring, Yugoslav revisionism).

84. DALO, P-3/31/93/53–65 (New York); Iuriy Slyvka and Iuriy Zaitsev, eds., *Ukrains'ka poeziia pid sudom KGB: Kryminal'ni spravy Iryny ta Ihoria Kalyntsiv* (Lviv: Afisha, 2004), 253–54 (Iryna Kalynets).

85. Iuriy Sandurskyi and Mykola Petrenko, interview with the author, tape recording, Lviv, 24 March 1999.

86. Ievhen Beznisko, interview with the author, tape recording, Lviv, 28 December 2009. On the circumstances surrounding Svitlychnyi's 1965 arrest and 1966 investigation for spreading political *samvydav,* see Leonida Svitlychna, "Poruch z Ivanom," in Valeriy Shevchuk et al., eds.,

Dobrookyi: Spohady pro Ivana Svitlychnoho (Kyiv: Vydavnytstvo Chas, 1998), 26–32.

87. Ilnytskyi, *Drama bez katarsysu* (2003), 83–84; DALO, P-3808/1/44/16–18.

88. Miriam Dobson, *Khrushchev's Cold Summer: Gulag Returnees, Crime, and the Fate of Reform after Stalin* (Ithaca: Cornell University Press, 2009), 143.

89. Ivanychuk, *Blahoslovy,* 123–24; DALO, P-3808/1/44/7–10; DALO, P-3808/1/45/14–31.

90. DALO, P-3808/1/52/97–101.

91. DALO, P-3808/1/52/107–9.

92. Roman Solchanyk, "Lvov Authorities Harass Dissidents' Families," *Radio Liberty (RL)* 132/78 (14 June 1978).

93. Mariia Valio, *Bibliohrafichnyi pokazhchyk: Moi uchyteli (spohady)* (Lviv: Natsional'na Akademiia Nauk Ukrainy, Lvivs'ka Biblioteka imeni Vasylia Stefanyka, 2001), 135–36; Heorhiy Kasianov, *Nezhodni: Ukrains'ka intelihentsiia v rusi oporu 1960–80-x rokiv* (Kyiv: Lybid', 1995), 51.

94. Slyvka et al., *Kul'turne zhyttia,* vol. 2, 718.

95. Hryhoriy Demian, interview with the author, tape recording, Lviv, 9 July 1998 (school lessons); Zinoviy Krasivs'kyi, "Prohramna kontseptsiia UNF, ukladena Zinoviiem Krasivs'kym," in Mykola Dubas and Iuriy Zaitsev, eds., *Ukrains'kyi national'nyi front: Doslidzhennia, dokumenty, materialy* (Lviv: Instytut Ukrainoznavstva imeni Ivana Kryp'iakevycha, Natsional'na Akademiia Nauk Ukrainy, 2000), 56 (Ukrainian National Front).

96. Slyvka et al., *Kul'turne zhyttia,* vol. 2, 683–85.

97. Rossiiskii Gosudarstvennyi Arkhiv Noveishei Istorii (RGANI), 5/55/71/34–35, in *The Departmental Records of the Central Committee of the Communist Party of the Soviet Union, 1953–66,* Ideology Department, Reel 428.

98. DALO, P-3/9/75/94–97 (Serokvasha), DALO, P-3/9/75/99 (collective letter).

99. DALO, P-3/19/206/39.

100. Rostyslav Bratun, "Spraha pravdy," *Suchasnist'* (Munich) 11 (November 1988), 122.

101. Padraic Kenney, *A Carnival of Revolution: Central Europe 1989* (Princeton: Princeton University Press, 2002), 123–30, 270.

102. "Disregard for People's Opinion," 4.

103. Ivanychuk, *Blahoslovy,* 230–39 (language society), 239–41 (Rukh), 246–53 (Supreme Council).

104. DALO, P-3/37/4/107.

105. Ilnytskyi, *Drama bez katarsysu* (2003), 85–87.

106. Oles Honchar, *Shchodennyky u tr'okh tomakh*, vol. 2, *1968–1983*, ed. V. B. Honchar (Kyiv: Veselka, 2003), 197, 204, 250, 363, 373, 406, 546.

107. Bohdan Nahaylo, "Gorbachev, Chornobyl and the Writers' Challenge," in Nahaylo, *The Ukrainian Resurgence* (Toronto: University of Toronto Press, 1999), 53–83.

108. TsDAMLMU, 199/1/29/1.

109. TsDAHOU, 1/25/5295/27 (KGB documents), 32 (article); Benjamin Tromley, "An Unlikely National Revival: Soviet Higher Learning and the Ukrainian 'Sixtiers,' 1953–65," *Russian Review* 68 (October 2009): 607–22.

110. Dmytro Pavlychko, "Petro Shelest," *Literaturna Ukraina* (Kyiv), 24 August 2005, 2; 1 September 2005, 7; 8 September 2005, 7; 15 September 2005, 7; 22 September 2005, 7; 29 September 2005, 7; 6 October 2005, 7; 13 October 2005, 7.

111. TsDAHOU, 1/25/217/12–17.

112. TsDAMLMU, 590/1/952/43 (*The Godfather*); TsDAMLMU, 590/1/952/46–47 ("The Box Man").

113. Bohdan Iakymovych, interview with the author, tape recording, Lviv, 21 April 2000; Mykola Riabchuk, "Kinets' odniiei epokhy," in *Plach Ieremii: Poeziia, pereklady, spohady*, by Hrytsko Chubai (Lviv: Kal'variia, 1998), 277.

114. Dmytro Pavlychko, "Petro Shelest," *Literaturna Ukraina* (Kyiv) 29 September 2005, 7 (dissidents); 6 October 2005, 7 (dissidents); TsDAHOU, 1/25/217/19 (UPA involvement).

115. George Grabowicz, interview with the author, tape recording, Harvard Ukrainian Research Institute, Cambridge, MA, 24 May 2006.

116. O. V. Haran, *Ubyty drakona: Z istorii Rukhu ta novykh partiy Ukrainy* (Kyiv: Lybid', 1993), 26–27.

117. Dmytro Pavlychko, "Petro Shelest," *Literaturna Ukraina* (Kyiv), 8 September 2005, 7; Liubov Kyianovska, *Syn stolittia: Mykola Kolessa v ukrains'kiy kul'turi XX viku: Sim novel z zhyttia artysta* (Lviv: L'vivs'ka Derzhavna Muzychna Akademiia imeni M. V. Lysenka, 2003), 201–3, 214.

118. Dmytro Pavlychko, "Petro Shelest," *Literaturna Ukraina* (Kyiv), 13 October 2005, 7; "'To była sprawa smaku . . . ,'" 233–34.

119. Oles Honchar, *Shchodennyky u tr'okh tomakh*, vol. 2, *1968–1983*, ed. V. B. Honchar (Kyiv: Veselka, 2003), 123 (admirers), 184 (Iatskiv), 331 (admirers), 501 (art museum); Mykola Petrenko, *Lytsari pera i charky* (Lviv: Spolom, 2000), 26.

120. Kyiv linguist Lesya Stavytska, for instance, has pointed out to me the influence of Galician Ukrainian slang on Ukrainians in Kyiv. L. O. Stavytska, *Ukrains'kyi zhargon: Slovnyk* (Kyiv: Krytyka, 2005).

6. Lviv and the Ukrainian Past

1. P. Vail and A. Genis, *60-e: Mir sovetskogo cheloveka* (Moscow: Novoe Literaturnoe Obozrenie, 2001), 12 (Third Program); Amir Weiner, "Robust Revolution to Retiring Revolution: The Life Cycle of the Soviet Revolution, 1945–1968" (Washington, DC: Kennan Institute, 1 November 2007); Vladislav Zubok, *Zhivago's Children: The Last Russian Intelligentsia* (Cambridge, MA: Belknap Press of Harvard University Press, 2009).

2. Vytautas Landsbergis, "Čiurlionis," in *Lithuania Independent Again: The Autobiography of Vytautas Landsbergis* (Cardiff: University of Wales Press, 2000), 67–77; Rüdiger Ritter, "Prescribed Identity: The Role of History for the Legitimization of Soviet Rule in Lithuania," in Olaf Mertelsmann, ed., *The Sovietization of the Baltic States, 1940–1956* (Tartu: Kleio, 2003), 104.

3. Tarik Youssef Cyril Amar, "The Limits of Local Revolution: The Failure of the KPZU as Memory and Narrative," in "The Making of Soviet Lviv, 1939–1963" (PhD dissertation, Princeton University, 2006), 691–788.

4. Ibid.

5. Iuriy Slyvka et al., eds., *Kul'turne zhyttia v Ukraini: Zakhidni zemli,* vol. 2, *1953–1966* (Lviv: Instytut Ukrainoznavstva imeni Ivana Kryp'iakevycha, Natsional'na Akademiia Nauk Ukrainy, 1995), 818–19. This 1946 document appears as an addendum.

6. Derzhavnyi Arkhiv L'vivs'koi Oblasti (hereafter DALO), P-92/1/405/58–59.

7. Iaroslav Dashkevych, "Borot'ba z Hrushevs'kym ta ioho shkoloiu u L'vivs'komu universyteti za radians'kykh chasiv," in L. Vynar et al., eds., *Mykhailo Hrushevs'kyi i L'vivs'ka istorychna shkola: Materialy konferentsii, L'viv, 24–25 zhovtnia 1994 r.* (New York: Ukrains'ke Istorychne Tovarystvo, 1995), 32–94; Iuriy Slyvka et al., eds., *Kul'turne zhyttia v Ukraini: Zakhidni zemli,* vol. 1, *1939–1953* (Kyiv: Naukova Dumka, 1995), 351–52, 357 (Academy of Sciences).

8. Ia. Isaievych, ed., *Instytut Ukrainoznavstva imeni Ivana Kryp'iakevycha NAN Ukrainy: Naukova diial'nist', struktura, pratsivnyky* (Lviv: Instytut Ukrainoznavstva imeni Ivana Kryp'iakevycha, Natsional'na Akademiia Nauk Ukrainy, 2001), 7–17; Iuriy Slyvka, "Akademik Ivan Petrovych Kryp'iakevych: Uchytel', vchenyi, kerivnyk naukovoho kolektyvu," *Ukraina: Kul'turna spadshchyna, natsional'na svidomist', derzhavnist'* (Lviv) 8 (2001): 598–99.

9. Slyvka, "Akademik Ivan Petrovych Kryp'iakevych," 592.

10. Alter L. Litvin, *Writing History on Twentieth-Century Russia: A View from Within,* trans. and ed. John L. H. Keep (Houndmills, UK: Palgrave,

2001), 18–30; Iu. Iu. Slyvka, "Ivan Petrovych Kryp'iakevych: Vchytel', Vchenyi, kerirvnyk naukovoho kolektyvu," March 2000, 32–33, from the personal archives of the author.

11. DALO, P-171/1/6/71.

12. Mykhailo Nechytaliuk, *"Chest' pratsi!" Akademyk Mykhailo Vozniak u spohadakh ta publikatsiiakh* (Lviv: Vydavnychnyi Tsentr L'vivs'koho Natsional'noho Universytetu imeni Ivana Franka, 2000), 118–26; Tamara Halaichak and Oleksandr Lutskyi, "Instytut suspil'nykh nauk: Storinky istorii," *Ukraina: Kul'turna spadshchyna, natsional'na svidomist', derzhavnist'* (Lviv) 7 (2000): 38–39.

13. Iuriy Slyvka, "Etapy ta holovni napriamy doslidzhennia ZUNR v ukrains'kiy istoriohrafii," *Ukraina: Kul'turna spadshchyna, natsional'na svidomist', derzhavnist'* (Lviv) 6 (2000): 6.

14. O. Iu. Karpenko, "Do pytannia pro kharakter revoliutsiynoho rukhu v Skhidniy Halychyni v 1918 r.," in I. P. Krypiakevych et al., eds., *Z istorii zakhidnoukrains'kykh zemel'*, vol. 1 (Kyiv: Vydavnytstvo Akademii Nauk Ukrains'koi RSR, 1957), 59–90.

15. Iuriy Slyvka, "L'vivs'kyi period naukovo-pedahohichnoi diial'nosti Oleksandra Karpenka (1949–1978 rr.)," *Halychyna* (Ivano-Frankivsk) 5–6 (2001): 11; Stepan Kobuta and Kateryna Mytsan, "Zhyttia, prysviachene sluzhinniu nautsi: Do 80-littia Profesora O. Iu. Karpenka," *Halychyna* (Ivano-Frankivsk) 5–6 (2001): 24–25.

16. M. M. Oleksiuk et al., *Torzhestvo istorychnoi spravedlyvosti: Zakonomirnist' vozz'iednannia zakhidnoukrains'kykh zemel' v iedyniy ukrains'kiy radians'kiy derzhavi* (Lviv: Vydavnytstvo L'vivs'koho Universytetu, 1968); Halaichak and Lutskyi, "Instytut suspil'nykh nauk," 44.

17. Oleksiuk et al., *Torzhestvo*, 5–6, 233 (organic ties); 262 ("German-Austrian intrigue"); 300–301 (Russian war aims); 320–21 ("bourgeois nationalist" historians); 393 (organic ties); 453 (interwar organizations); 507–9 (Shevchenko Scientific Society).

18. Ibid., 223, 448–49, 454 ("progressive" Poles); 165, 262, 422–23, 434 (Polish émigré scholars).

19. V. Malanchuk, *Molodost' zakalennaia v boiakh* (Moscow: Molodaia gvardiia, 1960).

20. Tsentral'nyi Derzhavnyi Arkhiv Hromads'kykh Ob'iednan' Ukrainy (hereafter TsDAHOU), 1/10/1309/16.

21. Mykola Volianiuk, "Na svitanku viku: Do 95-richchia z dnia narodzhennia V. I. Lenina," *Zhovten'* (Lviv) 4 (April 1965): 6–7.

22. Ernst Renan, "What Is a Nation?" in Geoff Eley and Ronald Grigor Suny, eds., *Becoming National: A Reader* (New York: Oxford University Press, 1996), 42–59.

23. Slyvka et al., *Kul'turne zhyttia*, vol. 2, 367–68.

24. Anonymous respondent, interview with the author, tape recording, Lviv, 2 August 2004; Slyvka et al., *Kul'turne zhyttia*, vol. 2, 364–70.

25. DALO, P-575/1/52/79–93, 134; Arkhiv Instytutu Ukrainoznavstva, 2/1/302/68–76.

26. "Levynsky, Volodymyr," in Danylo Husar Struk, ed., *Encyclopedia of Ukraine*, vol. 3 (Toronto: University of Toronto Press, 1993), 96; Myroslav Oleksiuk, "Levyns'kyi bez masky," *Zhovten'* (Lviv) 4 (April 1972): 110–11 (Lenin and Bolsheviks); DALO, P-3/22/139/175–76, 193 (Soviet policies, German-occupied Lviv).

27. TsDAHOU, 1/10/1309/15 (signals); DALO, P-92/1/963/30 (Zlupko).

28. Vitalii Vrublevskii, *Vladimir Shcherbitskii: Pravda i vymysly* (Kyiv: Dovira, 1993), 115–16.

29. Oleksandr Irvanets, *Rivne—Rovno: Stina: Nibyto roman* (Lviv: Kal'variia, 2002).

30. DALO, P-3/10/61/200.

31. Halaichak and Lutskyi, "Instytut suspil'nykh nauk," 43.

32. Arkhiv Instytutu Ukrainoznavstva, 2/1/764/3–5.

33. DALO, P-171/1/6/225–28.

34. Vrublevskii, *Vladimir Shcherbitskii*, 116; Bohdan Nahaylo, *The Ukrainian Resurgence* (Toronto: University of Toronto Press, 1999), 37 (Ielchenko); "O politicheskoi rabote sredi naseleniia l'vovskoi oblasti: Postanovlenie Tsentral'nogo Komiteta KPSS 7 oktiabria 1971 g.," in *KPSS o formirovanii novogo cheloveka: Sbornik dokumentov i materialov (1965–1976)* (Moscow: Politizdat, 1976), 129–35.

35. DALO, P-3/19/22/18–19.

36. DALO, P-92/1/960/88–89.

37. Hryhoriy Kasianov, *Nezhodni: Ukrains'ka intelihentsiia v rusi oporu 1960–80-kh rokiv* (Kyiv: Lybid', 1995), 136–37.

38. Halaichak and Lutskyi, "Instytut suspil'nykh nauk," 36–37.

39. DALO, P-92/1/844/160–79.

40. DALO, P-92/1/844/164–65. On the incident at the Academy of Sciences library, see Kobuta and Mytsan, "Zhyttia, prysviachene sluzhinniu nautsi," 23–24.

41. DALO, P-92/1/1005/65.

42. DALO, P-92/1/993/56 (Slyvka); Arhkiv L'vivs'koho Natsional'noho Universytetu imeni Ivana Franka (hereafter Arkhiv LNU) 5245/35–47 (Karpenko firing); DALO, P-92/1/906/127 (Slyvka); DALO, P-92/1/1005/67 (Slyvka).

43. DALO, P-92/1/993/56.

44. DALO, P-92/1/962/7–11 (Levynskyi); DALO, P-92/1/960/55 (Levynskyi); DALO, P-92/1/960/18, 88 (Franko).

45. DALO, P-92/1/993/132–33 (students); DALO, P-92/1/994/131–32 (letter to Chernivtsi); Mykola Kravets, interview with the author, tape recording, Vinnytsia, 29 July 2004 (Vinnytsia).

46. DALO, P-92/1/908/41, 61–62, 64, 76–78, 92–93 (publications); DALO, P-92/1/906/31 (publications); S. Golubka and I. Golubka, *Viddanist' nautsi i natsii* (Lviv: n.p., 1996), 23 (graduate school); DALO, P-92/1/908/64, 66, 92 (department); DALO, P-92/1/960/17 (department).

47. DALO, P-3/19/22/141 (teaching duties); DALO, P-92/1/962/12–29 (expulsion).

48. Mykola Ilnytskyi, *Drama bez katarsysu: Storinky literaturnoho zhyttia L'vova druhoi polovyny xx stolittia* (Lviv: Instytut Ukrainoznavstva imeni Ivana Kryp'iakevycha, Natsional'na Akademiia Nauk Ukrainy, 2003), 104; Mykhailo Nechytaliuk, "Interv'iu z Mariieiu Val'o," in *"Chest' pratsi!" Akademik Mykhailo Vozniak u spohadakh ta publikatsiiakh* (Lviv: Vydavnychnyi Tsentr L'vivs'koho Natsional'noho Universytetu imeni Ivana Franka, 2000), 414–15.

49. TsDAHOU, 1/25/368/62–67 (report); DALO, P-171/1/6/26 ("nationalists").

50. DALO, P-171/1/6/54–55 (reprimand); TsDAHOU, 1/25/368/65 (firing); DALO, P-171/1/6/53 (firing).

51. DALO, P-171/1/6/75, 120–21 (commissions); Nechytaliuk, "Interv'iu z Mariieiu Val'o," 417–18 (firings).

52. DALO, P-3/16/28/39–41 (Hurladi); DALO, P-3/22/137/164–73 (Levynskyi); DALO, P-3/25/28/150–51 (students).

53. DALO, P-92/1/993/33–36 (Karpenko); DALO, P-92/1/993/52–53, 56–58 (Karpenko, Kravets, Slyvka); DALO, P-92/1/1005/65–70 (History Faculty).

54. Volodymyr Chorniy, "Avtobiohrafichni notatky," in Chorniy, *Slov'ianoznavchi studii: Statti, vystupy ta iuvileini materialy* (Lviv: L'vivs'kyi Natsional'nyi Universytet, 2002), 300.

55. DALO, P-3/25/17/4 (reprimands, demotions); DALO, P-3/25/28/115–16 (KGB materials); DALO, P-92/1/1029/9–10 (firings, early retirements).

56. DALO, P-3/31/146/22.

57. Volodymyr Chorniy, remarks on the author's presentation, *"Iak rozpravylys' z LDU u 1973 r.: Sproba dokumental'noho analizu,"* given at *Ukraina Moderna* Seminar, Lviv National University, tape recording, 18 June 2004.

58. Arkhiv LNU, 8015/4–7 (Trubitsyn); Chorniy, remarks (Trubitsyn); DALO, P-92/1/844/161 (Menshov).

59. DALO, P-171/1/6/40–53, 171–201.

60. DALO, P-171/1/6/227.

61. Iuriy Slyvka, interview with the author, tape recording, Lviv, 6 August 2004; Feodosiy Stebliy, interview with the author, tape recording, Lviv, 19 July 2004; Kravets, interview.

62. DALO, P-92/1/960/88.
63. Oleksiy Sukhyi, interview with the author, tape recording, Lviv, 27 July 2004 (Hrosman and Herbilskyi); anonymous respondent, interview, 2 August 2004 (Herbilskyi nationality).
64. Anonymous respondent, interview, 2 August 2004; Arkhiv LNU, 14148/98.
65. Anonymous respondent, interview, 2 August 2004 (Osechynskyi); Stepan Zlupko, interview with the author, tape recording, Lviv, 3 June 2004 (Menshov and Bilchenko).
66. Anonymous respondent, interview, 2 August 2004 (compromising document); Kobuta and Mytsan, "Zhyttia, prysviachene sluzhinniu nautsi," 29 (dissertation defense).
67. DALO, P-92/1/759/55.
68. Anonymous respondent, interview, 2 August 2004 (chancellor, Party committee secretary); DALO, P-92/1/1005/65–70 ("Trojan horses").
69. DALO, P-3/19/206/219–31; DALO, P-3/22/139/178–99; DALO, P-3/22/139/174–77; DALO, P-3/2/137/164–73; DALO, P-171/1/6/226; DALO, P-3/31/145/52–54.
70. Arkhiv LNU, 8015/4, 14; Arkhiv LNU, 505/4; Arkhiv LNU, 6156/3, 11.
71. DALO, P-171/1/6/226 (Bilchenko); DALO, P-3/19/206/219–31 (Bilchenko, Nazarenko); DALO, P-3/22/139/178–99 (Nazarenko); DALO, P-3/22/139/174–77 (Nazarenko); DALO, P-3/2/137/164–73 (Nazarenko).
72. DALO, P-3/31/145/52.
73. DALO, P-92/1/993/34; DALO, P-3/19/22/142; DALO, P-3/19/206/229–30; Arkhiv LNU, 8015/32.
74. DALO, P-3/19/49/47–49.
75. "O politicheskoi rabote," 131.
76. DALO, P-171/1/6/226.
77. Iuriy Slyvka, letter to the author, 3 November 2009; Slyvka, interview.
78. Slyvka, interview.
79. DALO, P-92/1/963/28–38 (Tomenchuk); Arkhiv LNU, 8015/34, 51, 55 (Trubitsyn).
80. Anonymous respondent, interview (Biliakevych, Brodskyi); DALO, P-92/1/993/59, 104–6, 118–20 (archives).
81. Anonymous respondent, interview, 2 August 2004 (Karpenko undiplomatic); Leonid Zashkilniak, interview with the author, field notes, Lviv, 27 July 2004 ("special bird").
82. DALO, P-92/1/725/243–45 (1964 incident); Golubka and Golubka, *Viddanist' nautsi,* 25–27 (publishing); DALO, P-92/1/960/14, 17 (discrepancies).
83. O. Vinnychenko and O. Tseluyko, *Istorychnyi fakul'tet L'vivs'koho natsional'noho universytetu imeni Ivana Franka (1940–2000): Iuvileina*

knyha (Lviv: L'vivs'kyi Natsional'nyi Universytet imeni Ivana Franka, 2000), 81.

84. Tamara Marusyk, *Zakhidnoukrains'ka humanitarna intelihentsiia: Realii zhyttia ta dial'nosti (40-50-ti XX st.)* (Chernivtsi: Ruta, 2002), 194, cited in Tarik Youssef Cyril Amar, "The Making of Soviet Lviv, 1939–1963" (PhD dissertation, Princeton University, 2006), 430.

85. Arkhiv LNU, 13496/1 (Brodskyi); Arkhiv LNU, 8015/4, 6–7 (Trubitsyn).

86. Arkhiv LNU, 8015/6–7.

87. In this joke, Brodskyi enters a room, pitch black, where another colleague of his, Oleksandr Beilis, is seated. Brodskyi asks him, "Why are you sitting here like in a black guy's ass?" *(Shto vy sidite v temnote, kak u negra v zhope?)* "Yes, Roman Mykhailovych," Beilis replies matter-of-factly, "you've been everywhere, so you should know." *(Da, Roman Mykhailovich, vy vsiudu byvali, vam vidnee.)*

88. Mykola Krykun, interview with the author, tape recording, Lviv, 27 March 2003.

89. Iuriy Slyvka, "Neakademichni rozmovy na Akademichniy: Spohady," *Ukraina: Kul'turna spadshchyna, natsional'na svidomist', derzhavnist'* (Lviv) 7 (2000): 91–93.

90. Kobuta and Mytsan, "Zhyttia, prysviachene sluzhinniu nautsi," 32 (Karpenko); Kravets, interview.

91. DALO, P-3/31/145/52–54.

92. DALO, P-92/1/963/98.

93. Arkhiv LNU, 14148/71.

94. Arkhiv LNU, 14148/171.

95. Chorniy, remarks.

96. Slyvka, interview; Stebliy, interview, Lviv, 19 July 2004.

97. Iuriy Slyvka, "L'vivs'kyi period naukovo-pedahohichnoi diial'nosti Oleksandra Karpenka," 19–20.

98. DALO, P-171/1/6/226 (Ivanenko and *Triumph of Historic Justice*); Kravets, interview (Ivanenko, Inkin); Arkhiv LNU, 10694/2 (Ivanenko); Mykola Krykun, "Peredmova," in Vasyl Inkin, *Sil's'ke suspil'stvo Halyts'koho Prykarpattia u XVI–XVIII stolittiakh: Istorychni narysy* (Lviv: L'vivs'kyi Natsional'nyi Universytet imeni Ivana Franka, Instytut Istorychnykh Doslidzhen', 2004), ix (Inkin).

99. Golubka and Golubka, *Viddanist' nautsi*, 7 (Zlupko); Isaievych, *Instytut Ukrainoznavstva imeni Ivana Kryp'iakevycha*, 265 (Oleksiuk).

100. Kravets, interview; Kobuta and Mytsan, "Zhyttia, prysviachene sluzhinniu nautsi," 22–24 (Karpenko); Slyvka, "Akademik Ivan Petrovych Kryp'iakevych," 589–90, 607.

101. Karpenko, "Do pytannia pro kharakter revoliutsiynoho rukhu"; Amar, "Soviet Lviv."

102. DALO, P-171/1/6/187–88.

103. Homi K. Bhabha, "Introduction: Narrating the Nation," and "Dissemi-Nation: Time, Narrative, and the Margins of the Modern Nation," in Bhabha, ed., *Nation and Narration* (London: Routledge, 1990), 1–7, 291–322.

104. Myroslav Irchan, "Halyts'ki typy (Malyi feileton)," *Zhovten'* (Lviv) 12 (December 1965): 96–97.

105. Alexander Statiev, *The Soviet Counterinsurgency in the Western Border-lands* (Cambridge: Cambridge University Press, 2010), 133.

106. DALO, P-92/1/758/21-22. Secondary sources make reference to a collection of confessions by former OUN and UPA activists published in Lviv: *Ti, shcho kanuly v pit'mu* (Lviv: Kameniar, 1964).

107. Mykola Riabchuk, interview with the author, tape recording, Kyiv, 4 November 1999.

108. Wolfgang Schivelbusch, "The American South," in *The Culture of Defeat: On National Trauma, Mourning, and Recovery,* trans. Jefferson Chase (London: Granta Books, 2004), 37–101.

109. Elena Zubkova, *Pribaltika i Kreml'. 1940–1953* (Moscow: ROSSPEN, 2008), 191–93.

110. Marina Loskutova, "S chego nachinaetsia rodina? Prepodavanie geografii v dorevoliutsionnoi shkole i regional'noe samosoznanie (XIX—nachalo XX v.)," *Ab Imperio* 3 (2003): 159–96.

111. N. Bruskova, "O rektore," *Komsomolskaia pravda* (Moscow), 25 May 1968, 2 (UPA stories); TsDAHOU, 1/25/1044/128 (caroling).

112. Hryhoriy Demian, *Ukrains'ki povstans'ki pisni 1940–2000 rokiv* (Lviv: Halyts'ka Vydavnycha Spilka, 2003), 243–44 (UPA carols); Iaroslava Sereda, interview with the author, tape recording, Lviv, 25 July 2004 (singing songs); Iryna Shabat, interview with the author, tape recording, Lviv, 2 August 2004 (singing songs); Ievhen Shabat, interview with the author, tape recording, Lviv, 2 August 2004 (singing songs).

113. DALO, P-3/4/800/247–49.

114. Ievhen Shabat, interview.

115. Aleksandra Matyukhina, *W sowieckim Lwowie: Życie codzienne miasta w latakh 1944–1990* (Cracow: Wydawnictwo Uniwersytetu Jagielloń-skiego, 2000), 87 (All Saints' Day); Andriy and Tetiana Vorobkevych, interview with the author, Lviv, tape recording, 26 July 1999 (Ianiv Cemetery visits); DALO, P-53/16/4/40 (graduate student expulsion); "Virni u L'vovi zapovniaiut' tserkvy, pam'iataiut' pro strilets'ki mohyly," *Svoboda* (Jersey City, NJ), 11 September 1975, 1 (continued visits).

116. Bohdan Popovych, interview with the author, tape recording, Lviv, 9 May 1999.

117. Petro Kulyk, interview with the author, tape recording, Lviv, 23 April 2000.

118. Dmytro Karpiak, "Nikhto heroia vid sela ne zabyraie," *Chas* (Kyiv), online edition, www.chas.cv.ua (accessed 2 February 2010).

119. This was noted on the reverse side of a photo of the statue, donated by Kulyk to the author.

120. TsDAHOU, 1/25/20/180–81.

121. Larysa Kadyrova, interview with the author, tape recording, Kyiv, 10 November 1999.

122. Iulian Turchyn, interview with the author, tape recording, Lviv, 29 December 2009.

123. Roman Ivanychuk, interview with the author, tape recording, Lviv, 7 June 2004.

124. Fedir Stryhun, interview with the author, tape recording, Lviv, 29 December 2009.

125. "Ikhav kozak na viynon'ku," in B. Liatoshyns'kyi, ed., *Pisni chervonoi armii* (Kyiv: Ukrains'ke Derzhavne Vydavnytstvo, 1946), 52; "Ikhav strilets' na viynon'ku," in I. V. Shcherbakov, ed., *Strilets'ki pisni: Pisennyk* (Kyiv: Muzychna Ukraina, 1992), 14–15.

126. M. I. Shved, *L'viv—L'vov—Lwów—Lviv: Korotkyi putivnyk-dovidnyk* (Lviv: Kameniar, 1978), 95; I. Sychevs'kyi, ed., *Slovo pro L'viv* (Lviv: Kameniar, 1969), 135–40; Mariana Dolynska, interview with Taras Budzinskyi, tape recording, Lviv, 13, 22, 29 July 1993, Institute of Historical Research, Lviv National University.

127. Ivan Dmytrovych Krasivskyi, *Muzei narodnoi arkhitektury i pobutu u L'vovi/Muzei narodnoi arkhitektury i byta vo L'vove/Museum of Folk Architecture and Life in Lvov* (Lviv: Kameniar, 1975); Slyvka et al., *Kul'turne zhyttia,* vol. 1, 248, 342 (earlier plans); DALO, R-1694/1/295/1–9 (petition); Shved, *L'viv—L'vov—Lwów—Lviv,* 69 (opening).

128. Katerina Clark, *The Soviet Novel: History as Ritual,* 3rd ed. (Bloomington: Indiana University Press, 2000), 241–46 ("village prose"); Geoffrey Hosking, *Rulers and Victims: The Russians in the Soviet Union* (Cambridge, MA: Belknap Press of Harvard University Press, 2006), 338–59 (historical preservation); Zubok, *Zhivago's Children,* 306–8, 330–31 (conservatism and regime support).

129. Oles Honchar, *The Cathedral: A Novel,* trans. Yuri Tkach and Leonid Rudnytzky (Washington, DC: St. Sophia Religious Association of Ukrainian Catholics, 1989); Chingiz Aitmatov, *The Day Lasts More Than a Hundred Years,* trans. John French, foreword by Katerina Clark (Bloomington: Indiana University Press, 1983).

130. Roman Fedoriv, *Otchyi svityl'nyk: Roman,* vol. 1 of *Tvory v tr'okh tomakh* (Kyiv: Dnipro, 1990); Roman Ivanychuk, *Mal'vy: Istorychnyi roman* (Kyiv: Dnipro, 1968).

131. Roman Fedoriv, interview with the author, tape recording, Lviv, 15 December 1998.

132. Roman Ivanychuk, *Blahoslovy, dushe moia, Hospoda . . . Shchodennykovi zapysy, spohady i rozdumy* (Lviv: Prosvita, 1993), 115–17 (library fire), 41–43 (confiscation); Anatoliy Rusnachenko, *Natsional'no-vyzvol'nyi rukh v Ukraini: Seredyna 1950-kh—pochatok 1990-kh rokiv* (Kyiv: Vydavnytstvo imeni Oleny Telihy, 1998), 342–50 (confiscation).

133. Iuriy Slyvka and Iuriy Zaitsev, eds., *Ukrains'ka poeziia pid sudom KGB: Kryminal'ni spravy Iryny ta Ihoria Kalyntsiv* (Lviv: Afisha, 2004), 238–39.

134. TsDAHOU, 1/25/20/179–80.

135. Iulian Turchyn located the date of its final performance for me in the theater's archives.

136. Volodymyr Osviychuk, interview with the author, tape recording, Lviv, 27 December 2009.

137. Iryna Vilde and Bohdan Antkiv, "Sestry Richyns'ki," 47–48. Iulian Turchyn kindly allowed the author to look at this copy of the script, preserved in the Mariia Zankovetska Theater archives. For the version in the novel, see Iryna Vilde, *Tvory v p'iaty tomakh*, vol. 2, *Sestry Richyns'ki* (Kyiv: Dnipro, 1987), 371.

138. Roman Korohodskyi, interview with the author, tape recording, Kyiv, 4 November 1999.

139. Liudmyla Puliaieva, "Oleksandr Hryn'ko: 'U sorok rokiv ia pochav zhyttia spochatku,'" *Vysokyi zamok* (Lviv) 10 September 2009, online edition, www.wz.lviv.ua (accessed 27 December 2009). On Hrynko's gulag experiences, see Oleksandr Hrynko, *Bili nochi, chorni dni: Avtobiohrafichna povist' kolyshn'oho politv'iaznia Komi-HULAHu* (Lviv: Dzerelo, 1997).

140. "Virni u L'vovi zapovniaiut' tserkvy," 1.

7. Youth and the Nation

1. Vladislav Zubok, *Zhivago's Children: The Last Russian Intelligentsia* (Cambridge, MA: Belknap Press of Harvard University Press, 2009).

2. Roman Ivanychuk, *Blahoslovy, dushe moia, Hospoda . . . Shchodennykovi zapysy, spohady i rozdumy* (Lviv: Prosvita, 1993), 99–100.

3. Derzhavnyi Arkhiv L'vivs'koi Oblasti (hereafter DALO), P-3808/1/45/22–23.

4. Zubok, *Zhivago's Children*, 47–51; Svetlana Boym, *Common Places: Mythologies of Everyday Life in Russia* (Cambridge, MA: Harvard University Press, 1994), 93–95.

5. On this notion of space transforming social relations, see Edward W. Soja, *Thirdspace: Journeys to Los Angeles and Other Real-and-Imagined Places* (Malden, MA: Blackwell, 1996).

6. Heorhiy Kasianov, *Nezhodni: Ukrains'ka intelihentsiia v rusi oporu 1960–80-x rokiv* (Kyiv: Lybid', 1995); Anatoliy Rusnachenko, *Natsional'no-vyzvol'nyi rukh v Ukraini: Seredyna 1950-kh—pochatok 1990-kh rokiv* (Kyiv: Vydavnytstvo imeni Oleny Telihy, 1998).

7. Kendall Bailes, *Technology and Society under Lenin and Stalin: Origins of the Soviet Technical Intelligentsia, 1917–1941* (Princeton: Princeton University Press, 1978); Yitzhak M. Brudny, *Reinventing Russia: Russian Nationalism and the Soviet State, 1953–1991* (Cambridge, MA: Harvard University Press, 1998), 15–16, 31–33; Sheila Fitzpatrick, "Stalin and the Making of a New Elite," in Fitzpatrick, *The Cultural Front: Power and Culture in Revolutionary Russia* (Ithaca: Cornell University Press, 1992), 149–82; Leopold Labedz, "The Structure of the Soviet Intelligentsia," in Richard Pipes, ed., *The Russian Intelligentsia* (New York: Columbia University Press, 1961), 63–79; Martin Malia, "What Is the Intelligentsia?" in Pipes, *The Russian Intelligentsia*, 1–18; Marc Raeff, *Origins of the Russian Intelligentsia: The Eighteenth-Century Nobility* (New York: Harcourt, Brace and World, 1966); Vladimir Shlapentokh, *Soviet Intellectuals and Political Power: The Post-Stalin Era* (Princeton: Princeton University Press, 1990), 9.

8. Zubok, *Zhivago's Children*, 161–63.

9. Michael D. Kennedy and Ronald Grigor Suny, "Introduction," in Ronald Grigor Suny and Michael D. Kennedy, eds., *Intellectuals and the Articulation of the Nation* (Ann Arbor: University of Michigan Press, 1999), 1–51.

10. Sheila Fitzpatrick, "The Party Is Always Right," in Fitzpatrick, *Everyday Stalinism: Ordinary Life in Extraordinary Times: Soviet Russia in the 1930s* (New York: Oxford University Press, 1999), 14–39.

11. Iuriy Slyvka et al., eds., *Kul'turne zhyttia v Ukraini: Zakhidni zemli*, vol. 2, *1953–1966* (Lviv: Instytut Ukrainoznavstva imeni Ivana Kryp'iakevycha, Natsional'na Akademiia Nauk Ukrainy, 1995), 525–26.

12. Bohdan Zadorozhnyi, interview with the author, tape recording, Lviv, 20 March 2000.

13. Ivanychuk, *Blahoslovy*, 83.

14. Ibid., 79; Mykhailo Kosiv, interview with the author, tape recording, Lviv, 2 January 1999.

15. Ivan Svarnyk, interview with Viktor Susak and Taras Budzinskyi, tape recording, Lviv, 27 March 1993, Institute of Historical Research, Lviv National University (research groups, *Cheremosh*); Iaroslav Isaievych,

interview with the author, tape recording, Lviv, 18 May 1998 (research groups).

16. Svarnyk, interview.

17. Leonid Zashkilniak, interview with the author, tape recording and field notes, Lviv, 27 July 2004.

18. "Elizaveta" and "Kateryna," interview with the author, tape recording and field notes, Lviv, 4 August 2004.

19. Ihor Pidkova, interview with the author, tape recording, Lviv, 9 July 2004.

20. Oles Starovoit, interview with the author, tape recording, Lviv, 7 June 2004.

21. Ivan Ostafiychuk, interview with the author, tape recording, Lviv, 17 April 2000 (Komsomol organizations); Petro Shkrabiuk, *Popid zoloti vorota: Shist' elehii pro rodynu Kalyntsiv* (Lviv: Instytut Ukrainoznavstva imeni Ivana Kryp'iakevycha, Natsional'na Akademiia Nauk Ukrainy, 1997), 48 (student conferences).

22. Kasianov, *Nezhodni,* 19.

23. Volodymyr Kvitnevyi, ed., *U vyri shistdesiatnyts'koho rukhu* (Lviv: Kameniar, 2003).

24. Oleksandr Zelinskyi, telephone interview with the author, field notes, 10 August 2004. A former student of the conservatory, Semen Shkurhan, stated similar aims in a chance meeting with the author in Cracow, Poland, 28 April 2004.

25. Gleb Tsipursky, "Re-Imagining the Model Communist in the Thaw: Grassroots Activism and Youth Initiative Clubs," paper presented at the American Association for the Advancement of Slavic Studies (AAASS) National Convention, Boston, 12 November 2009.

26. Kosiv, interview.

27. Liubomyr Senyk, interview with the author, tape recording, Lviv, 25 June 1998.

28. Padraic Kenney, *A Carnival of Revolution: Central Europe 1989* (Princeton: Princeton University Press, 2002), 125–26.

29. Zubok, *Zhivago's Children,* 322–23.

30. Larysa Kadyrova, interview with the author, tape recording, Kyiv, 10 November 1999; Bohdan Kozak, interview with the author, tape recording, Lviv, 30 December 2009. On Borys Mirus's 1949 arrest, gulag imprisonment, and later career at the theater from 1957 on, see Borys Mirus, "Spohady," in Khrystyna and Bohdan Melnychuk, eds., *Borys Mirus: Spohadi artysta, druzi pro n'oho* (Ternopil: Ekonomichna Dumka, 2000), 92–169.

31. Feodosiy Stebliy, interview with the author, tape recording, Lviv, 13 April 2000.

32. DALO, P-3567/1/56/19.
33. See this discussion of walking in the city in Michel de Certeau, *L'invention du quotidien,* 2 vols. (Paris: Inédit, 1980), vol. 2 (1980), 171–74.
34. Iaroslava Sereda, interview with the author, tape recording, Lviv, 25 July 2004.
35. Isaievych, interview.
36. Iaroslava Sereda, interview.
37. Volodymyr Sereda, interview with the author, tape recording, Lviv, 4 August 2004; DALO, P-92/1/407/81.
38. DALO, P-92/1/403/87.
39. DALO, P-92/1/405/19.
40. Iaroslava Sereda, interview.
41. Kozak, interview. The translation of "Moses" comes from Vera Rich (www .utoronto.ca, accessed 22 January 2010).
42. Kozak, interview.
43. DALO, P-3567/1/149/97 ("nationalism"); DALO, P-92/1/1005/56 (Ukrainian poetry).
44. Benjamin Tromley, "An Unlikely National Revival: Soviet Higher Learning and the Ukrainian 'Sixtiers,' 1953–65," *Russian Review* 68 (October 2009): 616–17; Zubok, *Zhivago's Children,* 130–31.
45. Anonymous respondent, interview with the author, tape recording, Lviv, 2 August 2004 (early 1950s); "Elizaveta" and "Tetiana," interview with the author, tape recording and field notes, 23 January 2003 (late 1960s).
46. Volodymyr Kryvdyk, interview with the author, tape recording and field notes, Lviv, 27 July 2004.
47. Iaroslava Sereda, interview.
48. DALO, P-3/6/7/137–39.
49. DALO, P-3/6/7/56.
50. DALO, P-3/6/7/98 (dormitory figures); DALO, P-92/1/403/72 (railroad station).
51. DALO, P-92/1/629/134.
52. Ie. Deka, "Notatky pro Ukrainu," *Svoboda* (Jersey City, NJ), 21 November 1974, 2.
53. M. I. Shved, *L'viv—L'vov—Lwów—Lviv: Korotkyi putivnyk-dovidnyk* (Lviv: Kameniar, 1978), 26.
54. DALO, P-3/6/7/135–36, 144–45; DALO, P-92/1/661/37.
55. Tsentral'nyi Derzhavnyi Arkhiv Hromads'kykh Ob'iednan' Ukrainy (hereafter TsDAHOU), 1/25/515/1-5.
56. Andriy and Tetiana Vorobkevych, interview with the author, tape recording, Lviv, 26 July 1999.
57. Ilia Erenburg, *Ottepel': Povest'* (Moscow: Sovetskii Pisatel', 1956).

58. Roman Krypiakevych, interview with the author, tape recording, Lviv, 24 November 1998.

59. Teodoziy Havryshkevych, interview with the author, tape recording, Lviv, 30 November 2002.

60. DALO, P-92/1/392/39–45, 47.

61. DALO, P-92/1/392/43.

62. DALO, P-92/1/392/47.

63. DALO, P-3/6/116/72–73 (question-and-answer session); DALO, P-3/6/7/137–39 (philology students); DALO, P-3/6/7/13 (physics student); DALO, P-3/6/116/72–74 (physics student); DALO, P-3/6/7/137–39 (Russian, Ukrainian philology).

64. DALO, P-3/5/402/220.

65. Amir Weiner, "The Empires Pay a Visit: Gulag Returnees, East European Rebellions, and Soviet Frontier Politics," *Journal of Modern History* 78 (June 2006): 333–76.

66. Shkrabiuk, *Popid zoloti vorota*, 39; Teodoziy Starak, interview with the author, tape recording, Lviv, 26 February 1999.

67. Zubok, *Zhivago's Children*, 47–51.

68. Ivanychuk, *Blahoslovy*, 98 (art shops); Roman Ivanychuk, interview with the author, tape recording, Lviv, 11 April 2000 (writers' apartments); Iuriy Slyvka, "Neakademichni rozmovy na Akademichniy: Spohady," *Ukraina: Kul'turna spadshchyna, natsional'na svidomist', derzhavnist'* (Lviv) 7 (2000): 90–103 (graduate student dormitory).

69. DALO, P-92/1/412/73–79; P-92/1/412/53–54.

70. Iuriy Slyvka, "Neakademichni rozmovy," 97–98.

71. Liudmila Alekseeva and Paul Goldberg, *The Thaw Generation: Coming of Age in the Post-Stalin Era* (Boston: Little, Brown, 1990); Elena Zubkova, *Russia after the War: Hopes, Illusions, and Disappointments, 1945–1957*, trans. and ed. Hugh Ragsdale (Armonk, NY: M. E. Sharpe, 1998), 191–201; Zubok, *Zhivago's Children*, 51.

72. Volodymyr Bieliaiev, letter to Petro Kozlaniuk, 26 June 1954, Tsentral'nyi Derzhavnyi Arkhiv-Muzei Literatury i Mystetstva Ukrainy (hereafter TsDAMLMU), 86/1/156/1–2 (Ehrenburg); DALO, P-3808/1/32/11 (Dudintsev); Anatoliy Dimarov, "Perezhyty i rozpovisty: Povist' pro simdesiat lit," *Berezil'* (Kharkiv) 3–4 (1998): 58–59 (Pomarantsev).

73. Ievhen Beznisko, interview with the author, tape recording, Lviv, 20 April 2000.

74. Bohdan Horyn, conversation with the author, Kyiv, 23 December 2009.

75. Stefaniia Hnatenko, interview with the author, tape recording, New York, 13 March 1998.

76. Oleksiy Sukhyi, interview with the author, tape recording, Lviv, 5 July 2004.

77. Mykola Ilnytskyi, *Drama bez katarsysu: Storinky literaturnoho zhyttia L'vova druhoi polovyny XX stolittia* (Lviv: Instytut Ukrainoznavstva imeni Ivana Kryp'iakevycha, Natsional'na Akademiia Nauk Ukrainy, 2003), 48–53; Ihor Kalynets, interview with the author, tape recording, Lviv, 7 February 1999; Iaroslav Kendzior, interview with the author, tape recording, Lviv, 29 December 1998; Shkrabiuk, *Popid zoloti vorota,* 41–42.

78. Tarik Youssef Cyril Amar, "The Making of Soviet Lviv, 1939–1963" (PhD dissertation, Princeton University, 2006), 467.

79. Stefaniia Pavlyshyn, "Borets' v zhytti i tvorchosti," undated manuscript from the personal archive of Stefaniia Pavlyshyn.

80. "Virnist' pisni," *Molod' Ukrainy* (Kyiv), 27 September 1972, 3.

81. Roman Petruk, interview with the author, tape recording, Lviv, 21 June 1999; Roman Iatsiv, "Mystets'kyi L'viv do i pislia 1956 roku: Imunitet Contra Kanon," *Narodoznavchi zoshyty* (Lviv) 4.22 (July–August 1998): 442–43.

82. Ivanychuk, *Blahoslovy,* 92–93; Kadyrova, interview ("godmother"); Kosiv, interview ("godmother").

83. Pavlyshyn, "Borets'."

84. Lev Poliuha, "Ivan Kryp'iakevych—liudyna i vchenyi—iak symvol dlia molodi," *Ukraina: Kul'turna spadshchyna, natsional'na svidomist', derzhavnist'* (Lviv) 8 (2001): 628 (Soviet functionaries); Lidiia Kots-Hryhorchuk, "Buly z namy," *Ukraina: Kul'turna spadshchyna, natsional'na svidomist', derzhavnist'* (Lviv) 8 (2001): 636 ("careerists, charlatans, and carpetbaggers").

85. Zubok, *Zhivago's Children,* 163–68.

86. O. S. Rublov and Iu. A. Cherchenko, *Stalinshchyna i dolia zakhidnoukrains'koi intelihentsii* (Kyiv: Naukova Dumka, 1994).

87. Pavlyshyn, "Borets'."

88. L. Iarosevych, "Vydatnyi mytets'-hromadianyn: Do 100-richchia vid dnia narodzhennia kompozytora Stanislava Pylypovycha Liudkevycha," *Lenins'ka molod'* (Lviv), 23 January 1979, 2.

89. Taras Shevchenko, "Kavkaz," in *Kobzar* (Kyiv: Naukova Dumka, 1997), 217–22.

90. Zelinskyi, interview. For the 27 December 1974 Party committee bureau meeting dealing with the case, see DALO, P-576/1/89/ 247–48.

91. Ivanychuk, *Blahoslovy,* 81.

92. Bohdan Horyn, "Moi zustrichi ta rozmovy z Irynoiu Vil'de," in Mariia Iakubovska, *Spohady pro Irynu Vil'de* (Lviv: Kameniar, 2009), 50–52.

93. For instance, see Bohdan Horyn, *Ne til'ky pro sebe: Knyha persha (1955–1965)* (Kyiv: Pul'sary, 2006), 62–64.

94. DALO, P-92/1/629/41–42, 159–60.

95. Liubomyr Senyk, interview with the author, tape recording, Lviv, 7 July 1998.

96. Zubok, *Zhivago's Children,* 8.

97. Ibid., 90.

98. Roman Petruk, interview with the author, tape recording, Lviv, 21 June 1999.

99. Kalynets, interview; Ivan Hubka, *U tsarstvi svavolia* (Lviv: Ukrains'ki Tekhnolohii, 2001), 291–93.

100. Hnatenko, interview.

101. Kosiv, interview (university); Bohdan Popovych, interview with the author, tape recording, Lviv, 9 May 1999 (art institute).

102. DALO, P-3567/1/36/133.

103. M. Byelinsky, "The Face of God's Army—Bankruptcy," *Molod' Ukrainy* (Kyiv), 11 September 1964, 2, in "Members of Uniate Church Sentenced in Lviv," *Digest of the Soviet Ukrainian Press* 8.10 (1964): 23–25.

104. DALO, P-3/25/52/149–52, 160–62.

105. Oksana Kuzyk, interview with the author, tape recording, Shchyrets, Lviv Region, 7 August 2004.

106. Bohdan Iakymovych, interview with the author, tape recording, Lviv, 20–21 April 2000.

107. Iuriy Slyvka et al., eds., *Kul'turne zhyttia v Ukraini: Zakhidni zemli,* vol. 2, *1953–1966* (Lviv: Instytut Ukrainoznavstva imeni Ivana Kryp'iakevycha, Natsional'na Akademiia Nauk Ukrainy, 1995), 230–32.

108. Hnatenko, interview.

109. Kosiv, interview; Zelinskyi, interview.

110. DALO, P-3/6/41/44.

111. Shkrabiuk, *Popid zoloti vorota,* 164–65 (mid-1960s); Aleksandra Matyukhina, *W sowieckim Lwowie: Życie codzienne miasta w latakh 1944–1990* (Cracow: Wydawnictwo Uniwersytetu Jagiellońskiego, 2000), 73–74 (law enforcement); Andriy and Tetiana Vorobkevych, interview with the author, tape recording, Lviv, 15 July 2004 (disguising carols).

112. DALO, P-3568/1/62/103–4 (reprimands); Hubka, *U tsarstvi svavolia,* 380 (tree removal).

113. Hryhoriy Demian, *Ukrains'ki povstans'ki pisni 1940–2000 rokiv* (Lviv: Halyts'ka Vydavnycha Spilka, 2003), 243–44, 401.

114. Ie. Deka, "Notatky pro Ukrainu," *Svoboda* (Jersey City, NJ), 22 November 1974, 2.

115. Ivanychuk, *Blahoslovy,* 98.

116. Kendzior, interview.
117. Stephen F. Cohen, ed., *An End to Silence: Uncensored Opinion in the Soviet Union from Roy Medvedev's Political Diary,* trans. George Saunders (New York: Norton, 1982). On the emergence of dissident circles in Moscow, see Zubok, *Zhivago's Children,* 261–69.
118. Mykola Dubas and Iuriy Zaitsev, eds., *Ukrains'kyi natsional'nyi front: Doslidzhennia, dokumenty, materialy* (Lviv: Instytut Ukrainoznavstva imeni Ivana Kryp'iakevycha, Natsional'na Akademiia Nauk Ukrainy, 2000), 71–323.
119. Ludmilla Alekseyeva, *Soviet Dissent: Contemporary Movements for National, Religious, and Human Rights,* trans. Carol Pearce and John Glad (Middletown, CT: Wesleyan University Press, 1985), 267–398; Kasianov, *Nezhodni,* 88–120.
120. Shkrabiuk, *Popid zoloti vorota,* 57–58.
121. Vakhtanh Kipiani, "Horinnia Mykhaila Horynia," *Ukrains'ka pravda* (Kyiv) 17 June 2005, www.pravda.com.ua (accessed 17 June 2005).
122. "'Mieliśmy wielką misję przed sobą . . .': Rozmowa z Mychajłą Horyniem," in Bogumiła Berdychowska and Ola Hnatiuk, *Bunt pokolenia: Rozmowy z intelektualistami ukraińskimi* (Lublin: Wydawnictwo Uniwersytetu Marii Curie-Skłodowskiej, 2000), 177–85.
123. "'Ta książka zmieniła cale moje życie . . .': Rozmowa z Iwanem Dziubą," in Bogumiła Berdychowska and Ola Hnatiuk, *Bunt pokolenia: Rozmowy z intelektualistami ukraińskimi* (Lublin: Wydawnictwo Uniwersytetu Marii Curie-Skłodowskiej, 2000), 95–96.
124. Taras Batenko, *Opozytsiyna osobystist': Druha polovyna XX st. Politychnyi portret Bohdana Horynia* (Lviv: Kal'variia, 1997), 48–49.
125. For Kyivans, see Tromley, "Unlikely National Revival," 620–22.
126. Slyvka, "Neakademichni rozmovy," 92. Roman Ivanychuk characterized such sentiments as typical of most of Lviv's intelligentsia during the 1960s. Ivanychuk, interview, 19 April 2000.
127. Mykhailo Horyn, "Arkhitekt shistdesiatnyts'koho rukhu," in Valeriy Shevchuk et al., eds., *Dobrookyi: Spohady pro Ivana Svitlychnoho* (Kyiv: Vydavnytstvo Chas, 1998), 269–70.
128. Mykhailo Horyn, interview with the author, tape recording, Lviv, 26 February 1999; Mykhailo Horyn, "Arkhitekt," 273. For the text of "Contemporary Imperialism," see "Suchasnyi Imperializm," in Anatoliy Rusnachenko, *Natsional'no-vyzvol'nyi rukh v Ukraini: Seredyna 1950-kh—pochatok 1990-kh rokiv* (Kyiv: Vydavnytstvo imeni Oleny Telihy, 1998), 448–56.
129. Mykhailo Horyn, interview. See also his recently published memoirs: Mykhailo Horyn, *Zapalyty svichu* (Kharkiv: Prava Liudyny, 2009).

130. Mykhailo Horyn, interview (childhood, school); Batenko, *Opozytsiyna osobystist'*, 26 (father).
131. Bohdan Krawchenko, *Social Change and National Consciousness in Twentieth-Century Ukraine* (Houndmills, UK: Macmillan, 1985), 251.
132. TsDAMLMU, 590/1/601/30–31, 33.
133. Kasianov, *Nezhodni*, 48–49.
134. Kenney, *Carnival of Revolution*, 231–32, 272, 294; Bohdan Nahaylo, *The Ukrainian Resurgence* (Toronto: University of Toronto Press, 1999), 266, 274, 336.
135. Svarnyk, interview.
136. Rusnachenko, *Natsional'no-vyzvol'nyi rukh*, 205–6.
137. DALO, P-3/25/28/115–16 (compromising materials); DALO, P-92/1/1029/9–10 (firings and early retirements).
138. Mariana Dolynska, interview with Taras Budzinskyi, tape recording, Lviv, 13, 22, 29 July 1993, Institute of Historical Research, Lviv National University.
139. Alexei Yurchak, "Living 'Vne': Deterritorialized Milieus," in *Everything Was Forever, Until It Was No More: The Last Soviet Generation* (Princeton: Oxford University Press, 2006), 126–57.
140. Dolynska, interview.
141. Ibid. (Dolynska); Ilnytskyi, *Drama bez katarsysu*, 107 (Sluka).
142. Dolynska, interview.
143. Ibid.
144. Nataliia Mysak, "Kadebitsts'kyi pohrom u L'vivs'komu universyteti na pochatku 1970-kh rr.," *Moloda natsiia* (Kyiv) 1.17 (2000): 144–60 (Lviv); Rusnachenko, *Natsional'no-vyzvol'nyi rukh*, 196–209 (small towns and villages).
145. Stepan Pavliuk, interview with the author, tape recording, Lviv, 4 August 1999.
146. Oleksandr Tsiovkh, interview with the author, tape recording, Lviv, 22 June 2004.
147. DALO, P-3/25/52/13–15.
148. DALO, P-3/25/52/13.
149. Roman Stepanovych Bahriy et al., *L'vivs'kyi istorychnyi muzei: Putivnyk* (Lviv: Kameniar, 1976), 185.
150. DALO, P-3/19/22/17.
151. Pidkova, interview.
152. Ibid.
153. Iatsiv, "Mystets'kyi L'viv," 443; Petruk, interview.
154. Sylvestr Kordun, "Karlo Zviryns'kyi—mystets' i vchytel'," *Dzvin* (Lviv) 1 (January 1996): 156 (radio broadcasts); Petruk, interview; Oleh Minko,

interview with the author, tape recording, Lviv, 17 February 2000; Andriy Bokotei, interview with the author, tape recording, Lviv, 17 February 2000.

155. Petruk, interview; Valeriy Hrabovskyi, *Krvavych* (Lviv: Vil'na Ukraina, 1997), 59–60.

156. Zubok, *Zhivago's Children,* 94–96, 105–6.

157. Ihor Kalynets, *Slovo tryvaiuche: Poezii* (Kharkiv: Folio, 1997); Shkrabiuk, *Popid zoloti vorota,* 69–70 (Zvirynskyi pupils).

158. Mykola Riabchuk, interview with the author, tape recording, Kyiv, 4 November 1999; Hrytsko Chubai, *Plach Ieremii: Poeziia, pereklady, spohady* (Lviv: Kal'variia, 1998).

159. Halyna Chubai graciously allowed me to copy the original edition of *The Chest.*

160. Slavenka Drakulic, "Introduction: The Trivial Is Political," in Drakulic, *How We Survived Communism and Even Laughed* (New York: Harper-Perennial, 1993), xi–xvii.

161. Iuriy Slyvka and Iu. D. Zaitsev, eds., *Ukrains'ka poeziia pid sudom KGB: Kryminal'ni spravy Iryny ta Ihoria Kalyntsiv* (Lviv: Afisha, 2004), 71–84, 98–108 (poems as evidence), 365–77, 385–87, 454–65 (poems as evidence), 531 (removal of evidence).

162. Ibid., 99.

163. "'To była sprawa smaku . . .': Rozmowa z Mykołą Riabczukiem," in Bogumiła Berdychowska and Ola Hnatiuk, *Bunt pokolenia: Rozmowy z intelekualistami ukraińskimi* (Lublin: Wydawnictwo Uniwersytetu Marii Curie-Skłodowskiej, 2000), 238 (meeting Viktor Neborak), 239–40 (meeting Iuriy Andrukhovych).

164. George G. Grabowicz, "Mythologizing Lviv/Lwów: Echoes of Presence and Absence," in John Czaplicka, ed., *Lviv: A City in the Crosscurrents of Culture* (Cambridge, MA: Harvard Ukrainian Research Institute/Harvard University Press, 2005), 333–36; Viktor Neborak, *Vvedennia u Bu-Ba-Bu: Khronopys kintsia tysiacholittia,* 2nd ed. (Lviv: Piramid, 2003).

165. Certeau, *L'invention du quotidien,* vols. 1–2.

166. Serhiy Pashchenko, interview with the author, tape recording, Lviv, 26 July 2004. For the 18 December 1970 hearing of this incident by the Polytechnic Institute Komsomol committee, see DALO P-3568/1/88/105–18.

167. Iuriy Hordiienko, interview with the author, tape recording, Lviv, 13 June 2007.

168. "Oleksandr Aksinin—khudozhnyk-myslytel'," special edition of *Halyts'ka Brama* (Lviv) 7 (July 2001); Ihor Vvedenskyi, "Aks Libris, abo Knyha v hrafichnomu sviti Oleksandra Aksinina," *Fine Art* (Lviv) 7–8 (2009): 50–57.

169. Hordiienko, interview; Pashchenko, interview.

170. Halyna Domozhyrova, "Oleksandr Aksinin: Trahichna myttievist' vesny," *Halyts'ka brama* (Lviv) 7 (July 2001): 6; Ihor Diurych, "Oleksandr Aksinin," www.mankurty.com (accessed 10 July 2009).

171. L. Iliukhina, *Engelina Buriakovskaia: Tvorchestvo v kontekste lichnosti i lichnost' v kontekste tvorchestva* (Lviv: Initsiativa, 2006), 120 (Ostafiychuk); "Oleksandr Aksinin: Chas i mistse dii," *Halyts'ka brama* (Lviv) 7 (July 2001): 2 (Pikulytskyi).

172. Serhiy Symonenko, "Oleksandr Aksinin: Ideini ta dukhovni dzherela tvorchosti," *Halyts'ka brama* (Lviv) 7 (July 2001): 7; "Oleksandr Aksinin: Chas i mistse dii," 3.

173. DALO, P-3568/1/88/107 (Chekhov), 113 (Mayakovsky).

174. Iliukhina, *Engelina Buriakovskaia,* 204–6; Vvedenskyi, "Aks Libris," 50.

175. Petro Mavko, "Rosiys'kyi L'viv iak mif," in Diana Klochko, ed., *Leopolis multiplex* (Kyiv: Hrani-T, 2008), 224–26.

176. Ihor Chornovol, "Krutyi marshrut: Ievheniia Ginzburg," *L'vivs'ka hazeta* (Lviv), online edition, www.gazeta.lviv.ua (accessed 8 December 2006); conversation with Bohdan and Mykhailo Horyn, Kyiv, 23 December 2009. On Ginzburg's memoirs, see Eugenia Ginzburg, *Journey into the Whirlwind* (New York: Harcourt Brace Jovanovich, 1967).

177. Soja, *Thirdspace.*

178. Hilary Pilkington, *Russia's Youth and Its Culture: A Nation's Constructors and Constructed* (London: Routledge, 1994), 21.

179. Mariana Dolynska, conversation with the author, Lviv, 22 December 2009.

8. Mass Culture and Counterculture

1. Ilko Lemko, *L'viv ponad use: Spohady l'vivianyna druhoi polovyny 20-ho stolittia* (Lviv: Piramid, 2003), 40–41, 114–23.

2. Letter by Rostyslav Bratun to Iuriy Barabash, 10 January 1970, Tsentral'nyi Derzhavnyi Arkhiv-Muzei Literatury i Mystetstva Ukrainy (hereafter TsDAMLMU), 842/1/12/1.

3. Carl Boggs, *Intellectuals and the Crisis of Modernity* (Albany: State University of New York Press, 1993), 73–74. For the Soviet bloc, see Paulina Bren, *The Greengrocer and His TV: The Culture of Communism after the 1968 Prague Spring* (Ithaca: Cornell University Press, 2010); Kristin Joy Roth-Ey, "Mass Media and the Remaking of Soviet Culture, 1950s–1960s" (PhD dissertation, Princeton University, 2003).

4. Derzhavnyi Arkhiv L'vivs'koi Oblasti (hereafter DALO), P-3/1/82/60–61; DALO, P-3/6/7/19, 32, 134; DALO, P-92/1/412/119–20.

5. Mark Edele, "Strange Young Men in Stalin's Moscow: The Birth and Life of the Stiliagi, 1945–1953," *Jahrbücher für die Geschichte Osteuropas* 50 (2002): 37–61; Juliane Fürst, "The Importance of Being Stylish: Youth, Culture, and Identity in Late Stalinism," in Fürst, ed., *Late Stalinist Russia: Society between Reconstruction and Reinvention* (London: Routledge, 2006), 209–30; S. Frederick Starr, *Red and Hot: The Fate of Jazz in the Soviet Union, 1917–1980* (New York: Oxford University Press, 1983), 248.

6. DALO, P-3/6/7/164–65.

7. Mariia Krykh, interview with the author, tape recording, Lviv, 11 April 2000.

8. Ihor Kalynets, "Usmishka pryiatelia zamolody," in Liubov Horbenko, ed., *Litaiuchyi ambasador: Teodoziy Starak: Osobystist'* (Lviv: Prostir-M, 2001), 163–64.

9. Krykh, interview; Mykhailo Kosiv, interview with the author, tape recording, Lviv, 2 January 1999; Petro Shkrabiuk, *Popid zoloti vorota: Shist' elehiy pro rodynu Kalyntsiv* (Lviv: Instytut Ukrainoznavstva imeni Ivana Kryp'iakevycha, Natsional'na Akademiia Nauk Ukrainy, 1997), 204.

10. DALO, P-92/1/412/119–20.

11. Mykola Krykun, interview with the author, tape recording, Lviv, 27 March 2003 (watch); Volodymyr Sereda, interview with the author, tape recording, Lviv, 4 August 2004 (villagers).

12. Aleksandra Matyukhina, *W sowieckim Lwowie: Życie codzienne miasta w latakh 1944–1990* (Cracow: Wydawnictwo Uniwersytetu Jagiellońskiego, 2000), 16–17.

13. Volodymyr Kit, interview with the author, tape recording, Lviv, 4 January 2010.

14. Roksolana Zorivchak, conversation with the author, Lviv, 12 December 2009. Zorivchak made these comments while reviewing where she had been quoted in this book.

15. Iaroslav Isaievych, interview with the author, tape recording, Lviv, 4 January 2010.

16. Iryna Shabat, interview with the author, tape recording, Lviv, 2 August 2004 (late 1950s); Andriy Sodomora, *Liniamy doli* (Lviv: Litopys, 2003), 27 (first half of the 1950s).

17. Isaievych, interview.

18. Mykola Petrenko, interview with the author, tape recording, Lviv, 12 February 1999.

19. Krykun, interview.

20. Iaroslava Sereda, interview with the author, tape recording, Lviv, 25 July 2004; Volodymyr Polonskyi and Leonid Shemeta, "To khto zh avtor 'Hutsulky Kseni'?" *Dzerkalo tyzhnia* (Kyiv), 17–23 March 2001, online edition, www.dt.ua (accessed 28 July 2009).

21. Krykun, interview ("The Embroidered Towel").

22. Timothy W. Ryback, *Rock around the Bloc: A History of Rock Music in Eastern Europe and the Soviet Union* (New York: Oxford University Press, 1990), 16–17, 51–55; Richard Stites, *Russian Popular Culture: Entertainment and Society since 1900* (Cambridge: Cambridge University Press, 1992), 132–34.

23. Ihor Pidkova, interview with the author, tape recording, Lviv, 9 July 2004; Mariia Kazimira, interview with the author, tape recording, Lviv, 27 July 2004.

24. Oleksiy Sukhyi, interview with the author, tape recording, Lviv, 5 July 2004 (Ternopil Region); "Elizaveta" and "Tetiana," interview with the author, tape recording and field notes, Lviv, 23 January 2003 ("lagging behind").

25. Oleksandr Zelinskyi, interview with the author, tape recording, Lviv, 22 June 1999.

26. Kit, interview.

27. Ryback, *Rock around the Bloc,* 150–52; Artemy Troitsky, *Back in the USSR: The True Story of Rock in Russia* (London: Omnibus Press, 1987), 18–19; Oleksandr Balaban, interview with the author, tape recording and field notes, Lviv, 14 June 2004; Oleksandr Balaban, interview with the author, tape recording, Lviv, 5 June 2007.

28. DALO, P-3/8/255/158; DALO, P-3/8/424/46–47 (Kos-Anatolskyi), 72–73 (Pavlychko).

29. Kit, interview; Daryna Horova, "Na tantsiakh mozhna, a ofitsiyno—ni," *Ukraina moloda* (Kyiv) 25 December 2009, online edition, www.umoloda. kiev.ua (accessed 2 January 2010).

30. Kit, interview.

31. DALO, P-3/8/446/3; DALO, P-3/8/422/126.

32. Kit, interview.

33. K. Stetsenko, "Ukraina: Rok-muzyka," in Artemii Kirovich Troitskii, ed., *Rok-muzyka v SSSR: Opyt populiarnoi entsiklopedii* (Moscow: Kniga, 1990), 344; Starr, *Red and Hot,* 279–80.

34. P. Romaniuk, "Mazhorni rytmy estrady," *Lenins'ka molod'* (Lviv), 18 April 1970, 3; "Mazhor i minor estrady," *Lenins'ka molod'* (Lviv), 1 May 1971, 3.

35. Lemko, *L'viv,* 115–25, 131–32, 144–46; Iuriy Peretiatko, *L'vivs'kyi rok 1962–2002* (Lviv: FIRA-liuks, 2002), 4–8.

36. Thomas Cushman, *Notes from Underground: Rock Music Counterculture in Russia* (Albany: State University of New York Press, 1995); David Gurevich, *From Lenin to Lennon: A Memoir of Russia and the Sixties* (San Diego: Harcourt Brace Jovanovich, 1991); Sabrina Petra Ramet, Sergei Zamascikov, and Robert Bird, "The Soviet Rock Scene," in Sabrina

Petra Ramet, ed., *Rocking the State: Rock Music and Politics in Eastern Europe and Russia* (Boulder, CO: Westview Press, 1994), 181–218; Yury Pelyushonok, *Strings for a Beatles Bass: The Beatles Generation in the USSR* (Toronto: n.p., 2004); Ryback, *Rock around the Bloc;* Troitsky, *Back in the USSR;* Sergei I. Zhuk, *Rock and Roll in the Rocket City: The West, Identity, and Ideology in Soviet Dniepropetrovsk, 1960–1985* (Washington, DC: Woodrow Wilson Center Press, 2010).

37. Balaban, interview, 14 June 2004 (East German students); Volodymyr Surmach, interview with the author, tape recording and field notes, Warsaw, 7 July 2004 (African students); Lemko, *L'viv,* 118 (Arab students).

38. DALO, P-53/22/10/7.

39. Romana Bahry, "Rock Culture and Rock Music in Ukraine," in Sabrina Petra Ramet, ed., *Rocking the State: Rock Music and Politics in Eastern Europe and Russia* (Boulder, CO: Westview Press, 1994), 253.

40. Besides Bahry, see also Lemko, *L'viv,* 40–42, 120, 136; Peretiatko, *L'vivs'kyi rok,* 41–44.

41. Stites, *Russian Popular Culture,* 32.

42. DALO, P-53/22/7/38.

43. Peretiatko, *L'vivs'kyi rok,* 11–12.

44. Lemko, *L'viv,* 106 ("guitarists"); "S. P." and Tetiana Chursa, interview with the author, tape recording, Lviv, 8 March 2004 (noise); Vasyl Savchak, "Vin rozdratuvav smikh, a sl'ozy tamuvav u sobi (Zamist' peredmovy)," in Iryna Manastyrska and Leonila Stefurak, eds., *Oleh Myhal': Portret u real'nostiakh chasu* (Lviv: Kameniar, 2003), 10–11 (Taras Myhal).

45. Lemko, *L'viv,* 121.

46. Ibid., 155–58.

47. Oleh Vorobiov and Ihor Chornovol, interview with the author, tape recording, Lviv, 9 January 2003.

48. Balaban, interview, 14 June 2004; Balaban, interview, 5 June 2007.

49. Kit, interview.

50. Ibid.; Viktor Morozov, interview with the author, tape recording, Lviv, 12 June 2004.

51. Kit, interview; Morozov, interview.

52. Morozov, interview; Balaban, interview, 14 June 2004; Balaban, interview, 5 June 2007.

53. D. Dumytrash, "Liubov'iu na liubov," *Lenins'ka molod'* (Lviv), 27 June 1970, 3.

54. Ryback, *Rock around the Bloc,* 159–61.

55. I. Lepsha, "Dyskoteka na shliakhakh stanovlennia," *Molod' Ukrainy* (Kyiv), 27 January 1980, 3 (numbers of discos); Lemko, *L'viv,* 164 ("rotten" disco); Vorobiov and Chornovol, interview (Romantyk).

56. Liubomyr Krysa, *Fotoal'bom "Vernys' iz spohadiv . . ."* (Lviv: Ukrpol, 2008); Paraskoviia Nechaieva, ed., *Volodymyr Ivasiuk. Zhyttia—iak pisnia. Spohady ta ese* (Chernivtsi: Bukrek, 2003), 208–10.

57. Rostyslav Bratun, "Ne zovsim lirychna elehiia," in Paraskoviia Nechaieva, ed., *Volodymyr Ivasiuk. Zhyttia—iak pysnia. Spohady ta ese* (Chernivtsi: Bukrek, 2003), 32 (rock, country); Iuriy Semyvolov, "Virnist' pisni," *Molod' Ukrainy* (Kyiv), 27 September 1972, 3 (Beatles); Taras Unhurian, *Monoloh pered oblychchiam brata* (Kyiv: Prosvita, 2003), cover jacket; "S. P." and Chursa, interview (Crosby, Stills, and Nash).

58. DALO, P-53/22/7/38 (Komsomol); I. Egorova, "Oni zazhgli 'Vatru,'" *L'vovskaia pravda* (Lviv), 17 January 1982; A. Iaremchuk, "Kryla molodykh talantiv," *Molod' Ukrainy* (Kyiv), 20 June 1981, 1–2; V. Lozovyi, "Spivucha duma Karpat," *Molod' Ukrainy* (Kyiv), 10 March 1981, 3.

59. Matyukhina, *W sowieckim Lwowie*, 46.

60. Ilya Semenov (Ilya Lemko), interview with the author, tape recording, Lviv, 11 December 2002.

61. Myroslav Trofymuk, interview with the author, tape recording, Lviv, 11 April 2003.

62. T. Nikolaienko, "Liudyna z intelihentnym khvostom," *Lenins'ka molod'* (Lviv), 17 April 1971, 4.

63. Ihor Melnyk, "Pisnia bude pomizh nas," *Postup* (Lviv), 30 June 2005, online edition, www.postup.brama.com (accessed 29 June 2005).

64. Matyukhina, *W sowieckim Lwowie*, 58.

65. Kazimira, interview.

66. Catherine Wanner, *Burden of Dreams: History and Identity in Post-Soviet Ukraine* (University Park: Pennsylvania State University Press, 1998), 122.

67. "S. P." and Chursa, interview (truth); Balaban, interview, 5 June 2007 (freedom).

68. Gurevich, *From Lenin to Lennon*, 136.

69. Anne White, *De-Stalinization and the House of Culture: Declining State Control over Leisure in the USSR, Poland and Hungary, 1953–1989* (London: Routledge, 1990), 21–22, 39.

70. Krykun, interview (Tarzan in Lviv); Volodymyr Sereda, interview (small towns); Stites, *Russian Popular Culture*, 125–26 (Soviet audiences).

71. Ihor Ventselovskyi ("Penzel"), interview with the author, field notes, Lviv, 28 February 2004.

72. Dick Hebdige, *Subculture: The Meaning of Style* (London: Methuen & Co., 1979), 121–22.

73. Iurii Bashmet, *Vokzal mechty* (Moscow: Vagrius, 2003), 18; DALO, P-380/1/270/94.

74. Leonija Mundeciema and Andrejs Ģērmanis, "Rīgas Kinodiskusiju Klubs," in Eižens Valpēters et al., eds., *Nenocenzētie: Alternatīvā kultūra Latvijā. XX gs. 60-tie un 70-tie gadi* (Riga: Latvijas Vēstnesis, 2010), 194–95.

75. Stefaniia Hnatenko, interview with the author, New York, 13 March 1998 (1967–68 club); Halyna Huzio, "De vidbulosia vashe pershe pobachennia u L'vovi?" *Vysokyi zamok* (Lviv), online edition, www.wz. lviv.ua (accessed 8 February 2006) (late 1970s); Myroslav and Lesia Trofymuk, interview with the author, field notes, Lviv, 8 June 2004 (late 1970s).

76. Tsentral'nyi Derzhavnyi Arkhiv Hromads'kykh Ob'iednan' Ukrainy (hereafter TsDAHOU), 1/6/3859/35.

77. Sofiya Dyak, "Cinemas between Cultural Enlightenment and Entertainment: Case Study of L'viv during the Brezhnev Era" (MA thesis, Central European University, 2002).

78. DALO, P-92/1/760/94.

79. Lemko, *L'viv,* 109 (Friendship Stadium); Oleksiy Sukhyi, interview with the author, tape recording, Lviv, 31 July 2004 (Section Thirteen); Ihor Pidkova, interview with the author, tape recording, Lviv, 9 July 2004 (flags).

80. Robert Edelman, *Serious Fun: A History of Spectator Sports in the USSR* (New York: Oxford University Press, 1993); Gurevich, *From Lenin to Lennon,* 282.

81. Lemko, *L'viv,* 108; Ie. Dek, "Notatky pro Ukrainu," *Svoboda* (Jersey City, NJ), 22 November 1974, 2.

82. Lemko, *L'viv,* 108–10.

83. James C. Scott, *Weapons of the Weak: Everyday Forms of Peasant Resistance* (New Haven: Yale University Press, 1985).

84. Pidkova, interview.

85. Oleksiy Sukhyi, interview with the author, tape recording, Lviv, 31 July 2004. Emphasis is in the original anecdote.

86. Pidkova, interview.

87. DALO, P-92/1/879/32.

88. DALO, P-3/19/115/2.

89. DALO, P-3/47/27/29; Oleh Olisevych, letter to editor, *Dzuboks* (Belgrade), 13 August 1982, 62.

90. Kamil Sipowicz, *Hipisi w PRL-u* (Warsaw: Baobab, 2008), 161, 209.

91. Ihor Zborovskyi, interview with the author, tape recording, Lviv, 24 February 2004 (rock music); Oleksandr Chaika, interview with the author, tape recording, Lviv, 21 February 2004 ("hipiiuvav"); Lemko, *L'viv,* 159; Oleh Komarchuk, "Zi sviatoho sadu," *Arhument-hazeta* (Lviv), 22 May 2003, 27 ("hooligans").

92. DALO, P-3/19/115/2; Vasyl Babiy, interview with the author, tape recording, Lviv, 23 July 2004.

93. Andrei Makarevich, *Sam ovtsa: Avtobiograficheskaia proza* (Moscow: Zakharov, 2001), 122–24.

94. DALO, P-53/15/29/136–38 (Ieresko 1967); DALO, P-3/19/115/2–9 ("organization" and arrest).

95. DALO, P-3/47/27/29.

96. Chaika, interview.

97. Peretiatko, *L'vivs'kyi rok*, 9.

98. Oleh Olisevych et al., "'Iakshcho svitovi bude potribno, ia viddam svoie zhyttia ne zadumaiuchys'—zarady svobody': Interv'iu z Olehom Olisevychem," *IY: Nezalezhnyi kul'turolohichnyi chasopys* (Lviv) 24 (2002): 141 (Deep Purple, Led Zeppelin), 151–52 (Hendrix); Lemko, *L'viv*, 146 (Deep Purple, Led Zeppelin), 164 (disco).

99. Sergei Zhuk claims that an earlier work of mine argues that Lviv's hippies were a mass phenomenon, that they were not very different from Western hippies, and that I took post-Soviet interview respondents' words at face value. My article argues that Lviv hippies were marginalized by both state and society and that while they resembled Western hippies, their behavior was very much Soviet. It moreover utilizes not just oral interviews but also archival sources and published memoirs. William Jay Risch, "Soviet 'Flower Children': Hippies and the Youth Counter-culture in 1970s L'viv," *Journal of Contemporary History* 40 (July 2005): 565–84; Zhuk, *Rock and Roll*, 170n3.

100. Zhuk, *Rock and Roll*, 170; DALO, P-3/19/115/3-9.

101. Nadya Zimmerman, *Counterculture Kaleidoscope: Musical and Cultural Perspectives on Late Sixties San Francisco* (Ann Arbor: University of Michigan Press, 2008), 14.

102. Hilary Pilkington, *Russia's Youth and Its Culture: A Nation's Constructors and Constructed* (London: Routledge, 1994), 239–40.

103. On this notion of space, see Edward J. Soja, *Thirdspace: Journeys to Los Angeles and Other Real-and-Imagined Places* (Malden, MA: Blackwell, 1996).

104. Oleksandr Kritskyi, interview with the author, tape recording, Buddhist Center, Lviv, 26 February 2004.

105. Babiy, interview (real anthem, statute, dues); Surmach, interview (Komsomol).

106. Babiy, interview (hippies at Lychakiv Cemetery); Chaika, interview, 21 February 2004; Chaika, telephone interview, 20 November 2004 (Holy Garden).

107. Lemko, *L'viv*, 117; Iaroslava Sereda, interview.

108. Babiy, interview (more interesting lifestyle); DALO, P-3/19/115/2, 7, 16 (Komsomol, law enforcement); DALO, P-3568/1/88/85 (Komsomol, law enforcement).

109. Lemko, *L'viv,* 162.

110. Catriona Kelly, "Defending Children's Rights, 'In Defense of Peace': Children and Soviet Cultural Diplomacy," *Kritika: Explorations in Russian and Soviet History* 9 (Fall 2008): 731–33.

111. DALO, P-3568/1/88/82–104 (Komsomol hearings); DALO, P-3568/1/104/6–8 (Komsomol hearings); DALO, P-3568/1/88/83, 86, 88, 90, 93, 97–99, 102, 104 ("organization"); DALO, P-3568/1/104/6, 8 ("organization"); DALO, P-3/19/115/6 (punishment mitigated); Surmach, interview (KGB connections).

112. DALO, P-53/16/4/53–54.

113. Olisevych et al., "Interv'iu z Olehom Olisevychem," 151–52.

114. "Leonid" ("Leon"), interview with the author, tape recording, Buddhist Center, Lviv, 23 February 2004.

115. Oleh (Alik) Olisevych, interview with the author, tape recording, Lviv, 6 December 2002.

116. "Leonid" ("Leon"), interview.

117. Oleh (Alik) Olisevych, conversation with the author, Lviv, 2 July 2007.

118. DALO, P-53/22/10/7.

119. DALO, P-3/19/110/59 (poor preparation); DALO, P-53/21/1/30, 168 (poor preparation); DALO, P-53/23/1/65 (poor preparation); DALO, P-53/21/1/30 (speculating); DALO, P-53/21/1/30, 108 (discos); DALO, P-53/23/7/42 (past offenses); DALO, P-53/23/1/65–66 (gang fights); DALO, P-53/23/7/42, 100 (punks liquidated); DALO, P-53/23/1/100–101 (Magnetic Band).

120. Lemko, *L'viv,* 159–60 (hippies); DALO, P-53/22/10/46 (Policemen's Club).

121. Babiy, interview (Ukrainian speakers); DALO, P-3/19/115/3–9 (Lychakiv Cemetery); Surmach, interview; Oleksiy Sukhyi, interview with the author, tape recording, Lviv, 5 July 2004 (historian's daughter).

122. Oleksandr Chaika, interview with the author, tape recording, Lviv, 21 February 2004; Oleksandr Chaika, telephone interview with the author, field notes, 20 November 2004; Lemko, *L'viv,* 154.

123. Balaban, interview, 14 June 2004; Balaban, interview, 5 June 2007 ("student party"); Lemko, *L'viv,* 154 (Vuyky).

124. Dyak, "Cinemas," 68–69.

125. Pidkova, interview (Russian pop and rock); Trofymuk, interview (Vysotsky); "S. P." and Chursa, interview (Vysotsky).

126. Iuriy Hryhorian and Ihor Chornovol, interview with the author, tape recording, Lviv, 12 June 2007; Oleh Kalytovskyi ("Kalych"), interview with

the author, tape recording, Lviv, 1 July 2007; Oles Starovoit, interview with the author, tape recording, Lviv, 7 June 2004.

127. Balaban, interview, 5 June 2007.

128. Ihor Hurhula, "Vsykhaie derevo, na iakomu rozip'ialy Volodymyra Ivasiuka . . . ," *Vysokyi zamok* (Lviv), 22 May 2002, online edition, www .wz.lviv.ua (accessed 18 February 2006).

129. Mykola Ilnytskyi, *Drama bez katarsysu: Storinky literaturnoho zhyttia L'vova druhoi polovyny xx stolittia* (Lviv: Instytut Ukrainoznavstva imeni Ivana Kryp'iakevycha, Natsional'na Akademiia Nauk Ukrainy, 2003), 216–17 (poems, eulogies); Wanner, *Burden of Dreams,* 122 (numbers of mourners).

130. Andriy and Tetiana Vorobkevych, interview with the author, tape recording, Lviv, 17 July 2004; Ilnytskyi, *Drama bez katarsysu,* 216–17.

131. Ihor Dobko, interview with the author, tape recording, Lviv, 31 May 2004.

132. Heorhiy Kasianov, *Nezhodni: Ukrains'ka intelihentsiia v rusi oporu 1960–80-x rokiv* (Kyiv: Lybid', 1995), 169 (Sichkos); Mykola Toropovskyi, "Brudnym diiam naklepnykiv—ni!" *Lenins'ka molod'* (Lviv), 19 July 1979 (Shukhevych widow). A copy of this 1979 article, in the personal archive of Roman Szporluk, Professor Emeritus, Harvard University, failed to indicate the page number.

133. DALO, P-3808/1/57/70 (Bratun); Ilnytskyi, *Drama bez katarsysu,* 217 (Writers' Union term); Unhurian, *Monoloh,* 16–17 (grave, film); DALO, P-3567/1/218/5–15 (student expulsion).

134. Padraic Kenney, *A Carnival of Revolution: Central Europe 1989* (Princeton: Princeton University Press, 2002), 164–66 (Olisevych and Trust); Surmach, interview.

135. Bahry, "Rock Culture and Rock Music in Ukraine," 254, 267; Halyna Huzio, "De vidbulosia vashe pershe pobachennia u L'vovi?" *Vysokyi zamok* (Lviv), 27 October 2005, online edition, www.wz.lviv.ua (accessed 8 February 2006) (Armenian café); "Sasha" ("Shulia"), interview with the author, tape recording, Lviv, 28 June 2007 (Galician-Ukrainian slang); Catherine Wanner, "Festivals," in Wanner, *Burden of Dreams: History and Identity in Post-Soviet Ukraine* (University Park: Pennsylvania State University Press, 1998), 121–40 (Red Rue, "Banderstadt").

Conclusion

1. Stephen Kotkin, *Armageddon Averted: The Soviet Collapse 1970–2000* (Oxford: Oxford University Press, 2001).

2. Borys Kozlovskyi, interview with the author, tape recording, Lviv, 15 June 2007.

3. On "mental tools" needed to articulate alternative worldviews, see Lucien Febvre, *The Problem of Unbelief in the Sixteenth Century: The Religion of Rabelais,* trans. Beatrice Gottlieb (Cambridge, MA: Harvard University Press, 1985).

4. Volodymyr Sakvuk, "Viacheslav Chornovil: 'Iel'tsyn vnis duzhe konstruktyvnyi moment u politychnu real'nist' v Ukraini'," *Za vil'nu Ukrainu* (Lviv), 23 November 1990, 1.

5. Vladislav Zubok, *Zhivago's Children: The Last Russian Intelligentsia* (Cambridge, MA: Belknap Press of Harvard University Press, 2009), 344–46.

6. Liubomyr Senyk, interview with the author, tape recording, Lviv, 25 June 1998.

7. Dmytro Vydrin, "Tigipko—privet iz proshlogo ili gost' iz budushchego?" *Ukrains'ka pravda* (Kyiv), 11 December 2009, www.pravda.com.ua (accessed 23 January 2010).

8. Peter Sahlins, *Boundaries: The Making of France and Spain in the Pyrenees* (Berkeley: University of California Press, 1989).

9. Daphne Berdahl, *Where the World Ended: Re-Unification and Identity in the German Borderland* (Berkeley: University of California Press, 1999).

10. Alfred J. Rieber, "The Comparative Ecology of Complex Frontiers," in Alexei Miller and Alfred J. Rieber, eds., *Imperial Rule* (Budapest: Central European University Press, 2004), 184–87; Samuel P. Huntington, *The Clash of Civilizations and the Remaking of World Order* (New York: Simon and Schuster, 1998).

11. Timothy Snyder, *The Reconstruction of Nations: Poland, Ukraine, Lithuania, Belarus, 1569–1999* (New Haven: Yale University Press, 2003).

12. Sergei Zhuk, *Rock and Roll in the Rocket City: The West, Identity, and Ideology in Soviet Dniepropetrovsk, 1960–1985* (Washington, DC: Woodrow Wilson Center Press, 2010), 31, 48–52, 67–68, 83, 95, 100, 233–37.

13. Volodymyr Dibrova, interview with the author, tape recording, Harvard Ukrainian Research Institute, 15 May 2006.

14. Leonid Pliushch, *History's Carnival: A Dissident's Autobiography* (New York: Harcourt Brace Jovanovich, 1979), 190.

15. Amir Weiner, "The Empires Pay a Visit: Gulag Returnees, East European Rebellions, and Soviet Frontier Politics," *Journal of Modern History* 78 (June 2006): 356–57; Weiner, "Déjà Vu All Over Again: Prague Spring, Romanian Summer and Soviet Autumn on the Soviet Western Frontier," *Contemporary European History,* 15 (2006): 185–86.

16. Sergei Isakov, "Problemy izucheniia istorii russkogo natsional'nogo men'shinstva v Estonii (itogi issledovanii)," in Viktor Boikov and Navtolii

Bassel, eds., *Russkie v Estonii na poroge XXI veka: Proshloe, nastoiash-chee, budushchee* (Tallinn: Russkii Issledovatel'skii Tsentr v Estonii, 2000), 16; Naftolii Bassel, "Evoliutsiia Estonskoi temy v tvorchestve russkikh pisatelei v Estonii," in Viktor Boikov and Navtolii Bassel, eds., *Russkie v Estonii na poroge XXI veka: Proshloe, nastoiashchee, budushchee* (Tallinn: Russkii Issledovatel'skii Tsentr v Estonii, 2000), 46, 54.

17. Aleksandr Andiiel, "Baltiiskoe dvizhenie soprotivleniia v periodicheskikh pravozashchitnykh izdaniiakh rossiiskogo *Samizdata* 1960–1980 godov," in Andris Caune et al., eds., *Padomju okupācijas režims Baltijā 1944.– 1959. gadā: Politika un tās sekas* (Riga: Latvijas vēstures institūta apgāds, 2003), 391–98.

18. Ivan Dziuba, *Internatsionalizm chy rusyfikatsiia?* (Kyiv: KM Academia, 1998), 104.

19. Robert Edelman, *Serious Fun: A History of Spectator Sports in the USSR* (New York: Oxford University Press, 1993).

20. James C. Scott, *Weapons of the Weak: Everyday Forms of Peasant Resistance* (New Haven: Yale University Press, 1985), 330.

21. Zubok, *Zhivago's Children,* 319–20.

22. Stephen Kotkin, *Magnetic Mountain: Stalinism as Civilization* (Berkeley: University of California Press, 1995), 22.

23. Frederick Cooper, *Colonialism in Question: Theory, Knowledge, History* (Berkeley: University of California Press, 2005).

24. Volodymyr Osviychuk, interview with the author, tape recording, Lviv, 27 December 2009.

25. Paulina Bren, "Mirror, Mirror on the Wall . . . Is the West the Fairest of them All? Czechoslovak Normalization and Its (Dis)Contents," *Kritika: Explorations in Russian and Eurasian History* 9 (Fall 2008): 831–54.

26. Zubok, *Zhivago's Children,* 116.

27. Zhuk, *Rock and Roll.*

28. Yaroslav Hrysak, "National Identities in Post-Soviet Ukraine: The Case of L'viv and Donets'k," *Harvard Ukrainian Studies* 22 (1998): 263–81.

29. Lucan Way, "Authoritarian State Building and the Sources of Regime Competitiveness in the Fourth Wave: The Cases of Belarus, Moldova, Russia, and Ukraine," *World Politics* 57 (January 2005): 231–61.

30. Hiroaki Kuromiya, *Freedom and Terror in the Donbas: A Ukrainian-Russian Borderland, 1870s–1990s* (Cambridge: Cambridge University Press, 1998).

31. Zhuk, *Rock and Roll.*

32. Stephen Kotkin, "Mongol Commonwealth? Exchange and Governance across the Post-Mongol Space," *Kritika: Explorations in Russian and Eurasian History* 8 (Summer 2007): 487–531.

33. Iaroslav Hrytsak, "Natsiia pohanykh tantsiurystiv," *Postup* (Lviv), 13–19 June 2002, online edition, postup.brama.com (accessed 22 December 2010).

34. The potential for Poland and Lithuania to influence lands further east is considered in Timothy Snyder, *Reconstruction of Nations*, 290–93.

35. Iuriy Voloshchak, "L'viv, iakoho vzhe nemaie," *L'vivska hazeta* (Lviv), 13 April 2006, online edition, gazeta.lviv.ua (accessed 13 April 2006).

Appendix

1. Alessandro Portelli, "What Makes Oral History Different," in Robert Perks and Alistar Thomson, eds., *The Oral History Reader* (New York: Routledge, 1998), 63–74; Portelli, *The Battle of Valle Giulia: Oral History and the Art of Dialogue* (Madison: University of Wisconsin Press, 1997).

2. Katherine Borland, "'That's Not What I Said': Interpretive Conflict in Oral Narrative Research," in Robert Perks and Alistar Thomson, eds., *The Oral History Reader* (New York: Routledge, 1998), 320–32.

Archives Consulted

Public Archival Sources

Arkhiv Instytutu Ukrainoznavstva imeni Ivana Kryp'iakevycha
(Arkhiv Instytutu Ukrainoznavstva)

Fond 2. Academic Council, Institute of Social Sciences, Lviv.

Arkhiv L'vivs'koho Natsional'noho Universytetu imeni Ivana Franka
(Arkhiv LNU)

Sprava 505 (Personal File of Mykhailo Dmytrovych Menshov).
Sprava 1335 (Personal File of Halyna Serhiivna [Davydova] Smyrnova).
Sprava 4941 (Personal File of Iryna Iulianivna Huzar).
Sprava 5245 (Personal File of Oleksandr Iukhymovych Karpenko).
Sprava 6156 (Personal File of Iosyp Mykhailovych Tomenchuk).
Sprava 7081A (Personal File of Mariia Hryhorivna Bilchenko).
Sprava 8015 (Personal File of Fedir Petrovych Trubitsyn).
Sprava 10694 (Personal File of Liubov Andriivna Ivanenko).
Sprava 13496 (Personal File of Roman Mykhailovych Brodskyi).
Sprava 14148 (Personal File of Petro Petrovych Chelak).

The Departmental Records of the Central Committee
of the Communist Party of the Soviet Union, 1953–66, Microfilm,
Widener Library, Harvard University

Derzhavnyi Arkhiv L'vivs'koi Oblasti (DALO)

Fond P-3. Regional Party Committee, Lviv Region.
Fond P-4. Lviv City Party Committee.
Fond P-53. Komsomol City Committee, Lviv.
Fond P-66. Komsomol Regional Committee, Lviv Region.
Fond P-92. Party Committee, Lviv State University.
Fond P-171. Party Committee, Institute of Social Sciences, Lviv.
Fond P-380. Party Committee, Lviv State Polytechnic Institute.
Fond P-575. Party Committee, Institute of Social Sciences, Lviv.
Fond P-576. Party Committee, Lviv State Conservatory.
Fond P-2941. Industrial Regional Party Committee, Lviv Region.
Fond P-3567. Komsomol Committee, Lviv State University.
Fond P-3568. Komsomol Committee, Lviv State Polytechnic Institute.
Fond P-3808. Party Committee, Lviv Organization, Writers' Union of Ukraine.
Fond P-3810. Party Committee, Lviv Organization, Artists' Union of Ukraine.
Fond R-119. Lviv State University.
Fond R-402. Lviv City Department of People's Education.
Fond R-1657. Lviv Organization, Architects' Union of Ukraine.
Fond R-1694. Lviv Organization, Artists' Union of Ukraine.
Fond R-2009. Lviv Organization, Writers' Union of Ukraine.

Teatr imeni Marii Zan'kovets'koia u L'vovi

Iryna Vilde and Bohdan Antkiv, "Sestry Richyns'ki."

Tsentral'nyi Derzhavnyi Arkhiv Hromads'kykh Ob'iednan' Ukrainy
(TsDAHOU)

Fond 1. Central Committee, Communist Party of Ukraine.

Tsentral'nyi Derzhavnyi Arkhiv-Muzei Literatury i Mystetstva Ukrainy
(TsDAMLMU)

Fond 86. Petro Kozlaniuk, writer.
Fond 199, Opys 1, Sprava 29. Letter from Anatoliy Kos-Anatolskyi (composer, Lviv) to Petro D. Haidamak (composer, Kharkiv).
Fond 590. Writers' Union of Ukraine.
Fond 842, Opys 1, Sprava 12. Letters from Rostyslav Bratun (writer, Lviv) to Iuriy Barabash (writer, Moscow).

Private Archival Sources

Chubai, Hryhoriy, et al. *Skrynia*. Lviv, 1971. Typed manuscript from the personal papers of Halyna Chubai.

Pavlyshyn, Stefaniia. "Borets' v zhytti i tvorchosti." Undated manuscript from the personal papers of Stefaniia Pavlyshyn.

Slyvka, Iu. Iu. "Akademik Ivan Petrovych Kryp'iakevych: Vchytel', Vchenyi, kerivnyk naukovoho kolektyvu," March 2000. Typed computer manuscript from the personal papers of Iu. Iu. Slyvka.

Szporluk, Roman, Professor Emeritus, Harvard University. Research project on the history of the Soviet Ukrainian press.

Oral Interviews

Interviews Conducted by the Author

Anonymous respondent, Lviv, tape recording, 2 August 2004.

Artemeva, Lidiia, born 1926, Lviv, tape recording, 6 August 2004.

Astakhov, Albert, born 1935, Russian Cultural Center, Lviv, tape recording, 27 June 2007.

Babiy, Vasyl, born 1953, Lviv, tape recording, 23 July 2004.

Balaban, Oleksandr, born 1952, Lviv, tape recording and field notes, 14 June 2004; tape recording, 5 June 2007.

Bandrovskyi, Henrykh, born 1929, Uzhhorod, tape recording, 9 August 2004.

Beznisko, Ievhen, born 1937, Lviv, tape recording, 20 April 2000, 29 December 2009.

Bokotei, Andriy, born 1938, Lviv, tape recording, 17 February 2000.

Chaika, Oleksandr, born 1958, Lviv, tape recording and field notes, 21 February 2004; telephone interview, field notes, 20 November 2004.

Chernysh, Natalia, born 1948, Lviv, tape recording, 26 July 1999.

Demian, Hryhoriy, born 1929, Lviv, tape recording, 9 July 1998.

Dibrova, Volodymyr, born 1951, tape recording, Harvard Ukrainian Research Institute, 15 May 2006.

"Elizaveta," born 1948, and "Kateryna," born 1918, Lviv, tape recording, 4 August 2004.

"Elizaveta," born 1948, and "Tetiana," born 1948, Lviv, tape recording, 23 January 2003.

Fedoriv, Roman, born 1930, Lviv, tape recording, 15 and 17 December 1998.

Havryshkevych, Teodoziy, born 1930, Lviv, tape recording and field notes, 30 November 2002, 12 August 2004.

Hnatenko, Stefaniia, born 1946, New York, tape recording, 13 March 1998, 26 March 2006.

Hordiienko, Iuriy, born 1952, Lviv, tape recording, 13 June 2007.

Horyn, Mykhailo, born 1930, Lviv, tape recording, 26 February 1999.

Hryhorian, Iuriy, born 1963, and Ihor Chornovol, born 1966, Lviv, tape recording and field notes, 12 June 2007.

Huzar, Iryna, born 1905, Lviv, tape recording, 12 June 2004.

Iakymovych, Bohdan, born 1952, Lviv, tape recording, 20–21 April 2000; tape recording, 9 July 2004.

Ilnytskyi, Mykola, born 1934, Lviv, tape recording, 30 March 1999.

Irvanets, Oleksandr, born 1961, Harvard Ukrainian Research Institute, tape recording, 9 March 2006.

Isaievych, Iaroslav, born 1936, Lviv, tape recording, 18 May 1998, 4 January 2010.

Ivanychuk, Roman, born 1929, Lviv, tape recording, 19 April 2000, 7 June 2004.

Kadyrova, Larysa, born 1943, Kyiv, tape recording, 10 November 1999.

Kalynets, Ihor, born 1939, Lviv, tape recording, 7 February 1999.

Kalynets, Iryna, born 1941, Lviv, tape recording, 12 April 2000.

Kazimira, Mariia, born 1929, Lviv, tape recording, 27 July 2004.

Kendzior, Iaroslav, born 1941, Lviv, tape recording, 29 December 1999.

Kosiv, Mykhailo, born 1934, Lviv, tape recording, 2 January 1999.

Kosolapov, Serhiy ("Tsepelin"), born 1963, and Volodymyr Vyshnevskyi ("Vyshnia"), born 1952, Lviv, tape recording, 25 May 2007.

Kozak, Bohdan, born 1940, Lviv, tape recording, 30 December 2009.

Kozlovskyi, Borys, born 1940, Lviv, tape recording, 15 June 2007.

Kravets, Mykola, born 1928, Vinnytsia, tape recording, 29 July 2004.

Kril, Mykhailo, born 1954, Lviv, tape recording, 17 June 2004.

Kritskyi, Oleksandr, born 1965, Buddhist Center, Lviv, tape recording, 26 February 2004.

Krykh, Mariia, born 1934, Lviv, tape recording, 11 April 2000.

Krykun, Mykola, born 1932, Lviv, tape recording, 27 March 2003.

Krypiakevych, Roman, born 1925, Lviv, tape recording, 24 November 1998.

Kryvdyk, Volodymyr, born 1957, Lviv, tape recording, 27 July 2004.

Kuzyk, Oksana, born 1949, Shchyrets, Lviv Region, tape recording, 7 August 2004.

Lane, Oksana Kompaniets, born 1962, New York, tape recording and field notes, 25 March 2006.

"Leonid" ("Leon"), born 1958, Buddhist Center, Lviv, tape recording, 23 February 2004.

Morozov, Viktor, born 1950, Lviv, tape recording, 11 June 2004.

Olisevych, Oleh (Alik), born 1958, Lviv, tape recording, 6 December 2002.

Orekhov, Arkadiy, born 1949, Lviv, tape recording and field notes, 30 May 2004.

"Oresta," born 1957, Lviv, tape recording, 22 June 2007.

Ostafiychuk, Ivan, born 1940, Lviv, tape recording, 17 April 2000.

Osviychuk, Volodymyr, born 1924, Lviv, tape recording, 27 December 2009.

Pashchenko, Sergei, born 1948, Lviv, tape recording and field notes, 26 July 2004.

Pavliuk, Stepan, born 1948, Lviv, tape recording, 4 August 1999.

Petruk, Roman, born 1940, Lviv, tape recording, 21 June 1999.

Pidkova, Ihor, born 1960, Lviv, tape recording, 9 July 2004.

Popovych, Bohdan, born 1930, Lviv, tape recording, 9 May 1999.

Riabchuk, Mykola, born 1953, Kyiv, tape recording, 4 November 1999.

Romaniv, Olha, born 1930, Shchyrets, Lviv Region, tape recording, 7 August 2004.

"S.P.," born 1958, and Tetiana Chursa, born 1959, Lviv, tape recording and field notes, 8 March 2004.

Sadovska, Hana, born 1929, Lviv, field notes, 2 November 1998.

Sandurskyi, Iuriy, born 1938, and Mykola Petrenko, born 1925, Lviv, tape recording, 24 March 1999.

"Sasha" ("Shulia"), born 1967, Lviv, tape recording, 28 June 2007.

Semenov, Ilya (Ilya Lemko), born 1951, Lviv, tape recording, 11 December 2002.

Senyk, Liubomyr, born 1930, Lviv, tape recording, 25 June 1998, 7 July 1998, 5 November 1998.

Sereda, Iaroslava, born 1942, Lviv, tape recording, 25 July 2004.

Sereda, Volodymyr, born 1934, Lviv, tape recording, 4 August 2004.

Shabat, Ievhen, born 1940, Lviv, tape recording, 2 August 2004.

Shabat, Iryna, born 1944, Lviv, tape recording, 2 August 2004.

Sharifov, Iuriy, born 1946, Lviv, tape recording, 13 June 2007.

Slyvka, Iuriy, born 1930, Lviv, tape recording, 6 August 2004.

Starak, Teodoziy, born 1931, Lviv, tape recording, 26 February 1999.

Starovoit, Oles, born 1965, Lviv, tape recording, 7 June 2004.

Stebliy, Feodosiy, born 1931, Lviv, tape recording, 13 April 2000, 19 July 2004.

Stryhun, Fedir, born 1939, Lviv, tape recording, 29 December 2009.

Sukhyi, Oleksiy, born 1957, Lviv, tape recording, 5, 27, and 31 July 2004.

Sultanov, Valeriy, born 1958, Lviv, tape recording, 23 June 2007.

Surmach, Volodymyr, born 1951, Warsaw, tape recording and field notes, 7 July 2004.

Trofymuk, Myroslav, born 1960, Lviv, tape recording, 11 April 2003; field notes, 8 June 2004.

Tsiovkh, Oleksandr, born 1951, Lviv, tape recording, 22 June 2004.

Turchyn, Iulian, born 1930, Lviv, tape recording, 29 December 2009.

Ventselovskyi, Ihor ("Penzel"), born 1949, Lviv, tape recording and field notes, 28 February 2004.

"Vitaliy," born 1952, Lviv, tape recording, 22 June 2007.

Vorobiov, Oleh, born 1966, and Ihor Chornovol, born 1966, Lviv, tape recording, 9 January 2003.

Vorobkevych, Andriy, born 1942, and Tetiana, born 1943, Lviv, tape recording, 26 July 1999; tape recording, 15 and 17 July 2004.

Vozniak, Kosmo-Demian, born 1956, Lviv, tape recording and field notes, 17 March 2004.

Zadorozhnyi, Bohdan, born 1914, Lviv, tape recording, 20 March 2000.

Zalizniak, Bohdan, born 1946, Lviv, tape recording, 24 July 2004.

Zashkilniak, Leonid, born 1949, Lviv, tape recording and field notes, 27 July 2004.

Zborovskyi, Ihor, born 1958, Lviv, tape recording, 24 February 2004.

Zelinskyi, Oleksandr, born 1934, Lviv, tape recording, 22 June 1999; telephone interview, field notes, 10 August 2004.

Zlupko, Stepan, born 1931, Lviv, tape recording, 3 June 2004.

Zorivchak, Roksolana, born 1934, Lviv, tape recording, 20 April 2000; field notes, 19 July 2004.

Interviews Conducted by Others

Dolynska, Mariana, born 1952, interview with Taras Budzinskyi, Lviv, tape recording, 13, 22, 29 July 1993. Institute of Historical Research, Lviv National University.

Svarnyk, Ivan, born 1952, interview with Viktor Susak and Taras Budzinskyi, Lviv, tape recording, 27 March 1993. Institute of Historical Research, Lviv National University.

Written Responses to Author's Questionnaires

"Alex," born 1972 in Lviv, received by e-mail from Israel 21 June 2007.

Anonymous female respondent, born 20 July 1919 in Bashkiriia, written response to author's questionnaire, Russian Cultural Center, Lviv, received 23 June 2007.

Anonymous male respondent, born 8 August 1917 in Volgograd, Russian Cultural Center, Lviv, received 23 June 2007.

Mesniankina, Liubov, born 1955 in Lviv, received 2 August 2007.

Acknowledgments

This book is the result of over ten years of work. Like history itself, very fortunate accidents along the way kept it alive. It has been a long, amazing, and sometimes exhaustive journey, and I am glad that so many kind people have helped me see it through to the end.

Writing a book like this would not have been possible without generous financial support from several institutions, namely, the International Research and Exchanges Board, the Foreign Language and Area Studies program, the Kennan Institute, the Harvard Ukrainian Research Institute, the Civic Education Project, and Georgia College and State University.

This book could not have been written without the generosity of so many eyewitnesses to the past. In the course of ten years, I interviewed about 140 people for this project, nearly all of them in taped interviews. Their stories were inspiring and in need of being told, and I had to make the very difficult decision of relaying only a few of them. Many of those whom I had spoken with are no longer living, and I hope that this book and the subsequent archiving of their interviews will honor their memory. When the writing and rewriting of this book became overwhelming, I thought of them and carried on. Some of them generously shared photos and manuscripts with me. Many of them offered valuable comments and criticisms as I reviewed the manuscript with them. Their views do not necessarily reflect those in this book.

I could not have carried out this research without the advice and assistance of many librarians and archivists, whose work is never appreciated enough. In Lviv, Lesia Kravets and Larysa Poliakova not only provided advice and assistance but also provided some of the best celebrations over *horilka*, coffee, and food I had in Ukraine. The pine tree that grows near their building is a testament to our ten years of friendship. At the last minute, Oksana Yurkova in Kyiv took the time to find me documents in Kyiv that I had neglected to copy. Halyna Bodnar did the same in Lviv. Ksenya Kiebuzinski at the Harvard Ukrainian Research Institute Library was the very first to help my project, originally a research paper for the 1997 Harvard Ukrainian Summer School. Years later, when my parents' neighborhood dogs chewed up newspaper articles I had sent home, she replaced them.

Scholars of impeccable quality inspired this book. David Hoffmann encouraged me to explore the post-Stalin period and readily offered his support, be it getting a research grant or a job in academia. Allan K. Wildman taught me how to research, how to write and rewrite, how to take the harshest criticism ("This paper is terrible," with "terrible" underlined three times), and how to share my interests with others. He did not live to see this book, but his moments of praise gave me strength. Dying of cancer, he spent his last days on Earth writing about Russian history, showing that humans can do anything. Roman Szporluk at Harvard inspired this book first from afar, then as a Harvard Ukrainian Summer School professor, then as an office colleague during my postdoctoral fellowship. He introduced me to the topic of cities like Lviv as units of historical analysis, and he generously shared with me materials from his own research.

Many others steered this project along. I benefited enormously from the criticisms, nurturing, and encouragement of Eve Levin, first when she was at Ohio State, then when she was at the University of Kansas. Fellow graduate students at Ohio State became loyal critics and lifelong friends, most notably Sean Martin, Basia Nowak, Aaron Retish, Matt Romaniello, and Tricia Starks. Tricia saved the project from oblivion by reminding me, when I was teaching in Russia and Ukraine, that the job was not done.

During and after graduate school, other North American scholars encouraged the project along and provided invaluable advice, namely, Tarik Amar, Vera Andriushkiv, John Czaplicka, Patrice Dabrowska, Alex Dillon, Barbara Falk, Michael Flier, John-Paul Himka, Jeffrey Jones, Padraic Kenney, Nathanial Knight, Hugo Lane, George Liber, David McDonald, Paula Michaels, Kelly O'Neill, Blair Ruble, Roman Senkus, Yuri Shevchuk, Halyna Sydorenko, Frank Sysyn, Ben Tromley, Alex Tsiovkh, Gleb Tsipursky, Mark Von Hagen, Catherine Wanner, Zenon Wasyliv, Ted Weeks, Amir Weiner, Serhy Yekelchyk, and Sergei Zhuk. The book would have ground to a halt sometime in 2005 had it not been for a postdoctoral fellowship at the Harvard Ukrainian Research Institute. I benefited enormously not just from the resources of the Widener Library and the institute library but also from the advice and friendship of all its faculty, staff, and fellows. I would not want to pick favorites, but Anatoliy Kruglashov was a live reference tool for late Soviet Ukrainian society, and Liubomyr Hajda was the spirit of the institute, in the best sense of the word.

In Ukraine, the late Solomea Pavlychko shared her excitement about my project when I began it in August 1997, and Iaroslav Hrytsak and Heorhiy Kasianov offered valuable comments on my early manuscript. I acquired four academic homes in Lviv, Lviv National University's History Faculty, its Institute of Historical Research, the Ivan Krypiakevych Institute of Ukrainian Studies, and the Center for Urban History of East Central Europe. These institutions provided invaluable help with arranging oral interviews and archival research. Iaroslav Hrytsak, the late Iaroslav Isaievych, and Iuriy Slyvka became some of my best teachers and friends. Teaching at Lviv National University from 2002 to 2004 was a historian's dream. Not only was my chair, Leonid Zashkilniak, very supportive of the project, but he offered very valuable comments on the manuscript, and his collective at the Department of the History of Slavic Countries were eyewitnesses to history. Halyna Bodnar, Sofiia Diak, Oleksiy Lutskyi, Liudmyla Pavliuk, Oleh Pavlyshyn, Ihor Pidkova, Vasyl Rasevych, Viktoriia and Ostap Sereda, Viktor Susak, Zynoviy Timenyk, Andriy Zayarniuk, and Iuriy Zazuliak gave useful advice and contacts for interviews. Some of them provided manuscripts from their own research. Taras Budzinskyi graciously let me reproduce and cite his oral interviews. Oksana Dmyterko made the Institute of Historical Research an oasis of calm in a very hectic, overworked institution. Lviv was my home for four years. Teodoziy Havryshkevych and Mariia Smeshko became not just landlords, but a second set of parents. While I made many friends in Lviv, Mykola Petrenko and Oleh Olisevych became far more than interview subjects. Bolek Malinovskyi and Tetiana Polishchuk reminded me that there was a Russian-speaking Lviv deserving a place in this story. Friends from Andriy Tereshchak's gym in Sykhiv, and countless other Lvivians, made their city my home.

In the United States, the University of Toledo miraculously offered me a one-year appointment just as my Lviv appointment ended. At Georgia College and State University, Lee Ann Caldwell arranged a leave of absence so that I could be at Harvard, and faculty research grants helped me refine the manuscript further. Colleagues at the Department of History, Geography, and Philosophy encouraged me to stick to the task.

At Harvard University Press, I am very grateful to Professor Patrice Higonnet for taking an interest in this manuscript. Its anonymous readers fundamentally improved the structure and prose, as well as the thematic scope. Kathleen McDermott and Heather Hughes patiently guided the book through numerous editing and revisions. Ellen Lohman and John Donohue made it a more reader-friendly book. I also want to thank the press's staff for their help with illustrations, tables, and other design work. Any errors or shortcomings are mine.

Last, but not least, I owe my family everything. My brothers, George and Randy, lifted my spirits. My nephews, Dennis and Henry, and my nieces, Olivia and Gwynyth, did not exist at this project's beginning. Their growth inspired me to finish it. My grandmother, Gertrude Risch, who did not live to see this book, taught me lifetime lessons in positive thinking and generosity. Her parents' stories about their small town of Rocky Ridge, Ohio, inspired me to publish a local history of it years later, a project that introduced me to oral history. My parents, William and Georgeanna Risch, helped me out when there was no graduate funding in the early years, but their gifts were more than financial. My mother's searching for her grandmother's grave and her deciphering the family Bible first drew me to history. My father's life, which took him from Riga, Latvia, to Poland and then Germany and the United States, did the same. My first foreign research trip was finding his "aunt" in England while studying abroad. That "aunt" turned out to be his biological mother, Erna (Lindenberg) Zielinski, whose stories about Petrograd and Riga made the western borderlands my passion. Erna did more than inspire me to pursue the history of Eastern Europe. She gave me money during my research. Her apartment outside Manchester became a calm refuge from research and teaching abroad, where I would sink into her thick, plush couch and tell her what it was like in Ukraine. I would like to think she is very proud of me now, though she did not live to see the final product.

Index